MENTAL IMAGERY IN
THE CHILD

Mental Imagery in the Child

A study of the development of imaginal representation

JEAN PIAGET

AND

BÄRBEL INHELDER

in collaboration with

M. BOVET, A. ÉTIENNE, F. FRANK, E. SCHMID,
S. TAPONIER AND T. VINH-BANG

Translated from the French by

P. A. CHILTON

LONDON
ROUTLEDGE & KEGAN PAUL

Translated from the French
L'Image Mentale chez l'Enfant
Presses Universitaires de France 1966
First published in Great Britain in 1971
by Routledge and Kegan Paul Ltd
Broadway House, 68–74 Carter Lane,
London, E.C.4
Printed in Great Britain
by The Camelot Press Ltd.
London & Southampton
English translation
© Routledge and Kegan Paul 1971

ISBN 0 7100 6921 9

List of Collaborators

Aboudaram, Maurice, Ancien assistant à l'Institut des Sciences de l'Éducation.

Anthonioz, Monique, Ancienne assistante I.S.E.

Antonini, Paulette, Psychologue au Service médico-pédagogique.

Bliss, Joan, Assistante I.S.E.

Boehme, Marianne, Psychologue à la Clinique psychiatrique universitaire de Genève.

Bovet, Magali, Chargée de recherche I.S.E.

Droz, Rémy, Assistant au Laboratoire de Psychologie de la Faculté des Sciences, Université de Genève.

Émery-Menthonnex, Claire, Ancienne assistante I.S.E.

Étienne, Ariane, Chargée de recherche au Laboratoire de Psychologie de la Faculté des Sciences, Université de Genève.

Fot, Catherine, Assistante I.S.E.

Frank-Pfaelzer, Françoise, Ancienne assistante I.S.E.

Levret, Monique, Assistante I.S.E.

Matalon, Benjamin, Ancien assistant I.S.E.

Mounoud, Pierre, Assistant I.S.E.

Nicollier, Daniel, Ancien assistant I.S.E.

Niedorf, Hanna, Ancienne assistante I.S.E.

Papert-Christofides, Androula, Ancienne assistante I.S.E.

Pascual-Leone, Juan, Ancien assistant I.S.E.

Paternotte-Agoston, Françoise, Ancienne assistante I.S.E.

Pecsi, Laszlo, Assistant I.S.E.

Poirier, Louis-Paul, Assistant I.S.E.

Politi, Albert, Ancien assistant I.S.E.

Schmid-Kitsikis, Elsa, Assistante I.S.E.

Sella, Adina, Ancienne assistante I.S.E.

v

Contents

CONTENTS

CONTENTS

CHAPTER SEVEN
STATIC REPRODUCTIVE IMAGES AND ACTION

CHAPTER EIGHT
MENTAL IMAGES AND OPERATIONS

CHAPTER NINE
THE SPATIAL IMAGE AND 'GEOMETRICAL INTUITION'

CHAPTER TEN
GENERAL CONCLUSION

Preface

It might, we thought, be helpful if we were to point out the two main defects of this book. Not only will this enable us to clear them up, but it will enable the reader to pick out the points which interest him.

In the first place, there is a considerable omission from this work as it does not deal with the mental images involved in symbolic play, in spontaneous drawing or, in short, in any behaviour which is only on the fringe of understanding in the strict sense, i.e. the solution of problems. Our objective was not the child's 'creative imagination' – a splendid subject which still remains to be investigated, but only representation by images in its relations with the functioning of thought. Even more precisely, we have primarily asked if the images are the source of intellectual operations or not, and, if not, what kind of assistance or obstacle they give rise to in the formation of these operations. The present work is thus essentially an extension of one of our earlier programmes of research into perceptual mechanisms, which bears in a general way on the relations between the figurative and operational aspects of the cognitive functions on the visual and, at times, on the tactile-kinaesthetic level.

This leads on to the second defect. The reader will no doubt find that the book contains far too many facts, and that shorter demonstrations might have sufficed. But, since we have had the honour and the pleasure to have our statements checked by psychologists in many different countries, we have felt obliged more and more to protract our own proofs. Hence our increasingly meticulous approach and the proliferation of the counterproofs. Certainly it is right that this should be so, but in the present work it must unfortunately be at the price of a weightier volume. In particular it might seem that the statistical tables are excessively numerous. We would ask the reader to bear with us in this, and to accept that the numerical data are due to these reasons, and not to some congenital or compulsive tendency.

It should perhaps also be pointed out that we do not accept these frequency tables absolutely. We would not expect other observers to find exactly the same averages. In fields like that of the mental image where there are no stages in the full sense of the term, individual variations are even more marked than in the case of operations. The purpose of our tables, therefore, is simply to acquaint the reader with our findings and to suggest the general trend of the evolution observed. The important thing is the order of succession, not the average for different age groups, which may be subject to considerable fluctuations.

Finally, we should say something about the book's title. Several colleagues have advised us to change it, on the grounds that it might come under suspicion of 'mentalism', and because many writers no longer believe in the existence of images, or at least believe that nothing of import can be said about them. But it must be said that we care little about fashions in psychology, and even less about positivist prohibitions. If we may no longer speak of images, then it may still be possible, as Penfield has shown, to speak of imaginal memories, or imaginal representation, and to speak of them in a verifiable manner, as we have endeavoured to do here. As it is our intention next to make a study of memory in the child, we naturally had to begin by examining 'images' – even if it is fashionable to pass over the problem in silence.

J. P. and B. I.

Introduction

Having studied all aspects of the development of intellectual operations, and having attempted to analyse some of the characteristics of perceptual development, it was necessary to go on to tackle the question of the evolution of mental images.

Our central problem has always been the psychological nature of cognition. The classic option is between knowledge as a copy, and knowledge as an assimilation of reality. It follows that, depending on the choice made, the image will be seen either as fulfilling an essential function in acts of cognition, or as playing a primarily symbolic role. Now the advantage of the knowledge-as-copy hypothesis is that the emphasis is directly on the properties of the object, whereas if we posit that reality is assimilated to the subject's structures, there is a danger of leaving the object out. But the object is merely an instant cut out from the continuous flux of causal relations. Sooner or later reality comes to be seen as consisting of a system of transformations beneath the appearance of things. These transformations cannot be copied unless they are actively reproduced by being prolonged. This means that there cannot be a copy at all in any strict sense. In order to know objects it is necessary to act on them, to break them down and to reconstruct them. In other words, knowledge, in virtue of such a process, becomes assimilation, but not in the sense that the object is distorted by being integrated in the subject. Assimilating an object means participating in the systems of transformation that go to produce it, entering into a relationship of interaction with the world by acting upon it. Hence the important part played by the operations, which are the sole means of apprehending transformations. The operations have a dual function. From the logico-mathematical standpoint, they work out the possible transformations by a process of deduction, and from the physical standpoint, they achieve objectivity by going back to actual or experimentally verifiable transformations.

This being the perspective which our inquiries have led to, how are we to interpret the nature and the role of the image? The general problem from which we started out has epistemological as well as psychological significance. There are two sides also to the more specific problem of the image. In the first place, it can only be solved by means of psychological experimentation. And in the second place, it long occupied a central position in the psychology of intelligence, until it was discovered that it was both less central and more complex. It is true that these days the image seems to many writers to be either an outmoded concept or completely inaccessible by the usual experimental methods. But a brief review of the history of this problem will convince the reader of the renewed importance of the problem, once we modify the context and perspective in which it is usually regarded. And we shall see that, though the problem may indeed be unapproachable by experiment on the adult alone, an analysis of the evolution of images in the child is capable of throwing considerable light on their role in the cognitive processes.

In the early years of experimental psychology, when associationism had reached its apogee, the image was viewed in three principal ways. (1) It was viewed as a direct product not only of thought but of sensation, and it was held to be the residual trace of the latter. (2) It was one of the two fundamental elements of thought, the other being association. Thought itself was conceived of as a system of association of images. (3) It was an accurate copy of objects or events, and not a symbol subordinate to some operational activity. In his famous book *On Intelligence*, H. Taine characterized intelligence as a 'polypary of images'. On the primacy of the image he based an unqualified vindication of the knowledge-as-copy hypothesis. In 1897 Alfred Binet was able to write a whole work on the *Psychology of Reasoning*, in which he presented reasoning processes as a series of associations between images.

During the second period, starting about 1903, Binet in his *Étude expérimentale de l'intelligence* and Marb, Külpe and the *Denkpsychologie* of the Wurzburg school discovered the existence of 'imageless thought' (affirmation and negations, formation of relations, etc.). They concluded that the image could not be considered an element of thought, but, at the most, an auxiliary. The emphasis thus came to be removed from analysis of the image itself, and this line of investigation passed into the background without leading to any further strictly experimental work,[1] with the single exception of the field of memory and memory-images.[2] The distinction between

---

[1] An exception must be made for the work of Jaensch on 'eidetic' images. Even so, the effect of his work was to contribute to psychologists' indifference towards the general problems of the image, for Jaensch's results were not always corroborated. Moreover, on this slender basis he developed a complete and rather overbold typology.

[2] We mention in particular Bartlett's analyses in his celebrated work *Remembering*.

memory characterized by recognition and memory characterized by evocation (the first being earlier and independent of images, the second being later and the only one of the two necessarily involving images) was a step towards understanding the non-primitive character of the image. But while psychology was beginning to dissociate the image from the intelligence, and to glimpse the latter's active role, the philosophers failed to see the consequences. The whole of Bergson's critique of intelligence (cinematographic process reconstituting the continuous by means of the discontinuous, inability to grasp change and movement, etc.) is in fact an excellent description of the inadequacies of imaginal representation, and in no way tells against the operations. Bergson forgot the motor winding the film – the operational dynamism.

In the third period coming up to the present day, there was progress in three main directions in our understanding of the image. The first is theoretical, but fundamental. The image is no longer interpreted as an extension of perception, and tends (as Dilthey had already seen) to acquire the status of a symbol.[3] This kind of thesis fits in with Head's ideas on the symbolic function, and with his work on aphasia, where he demonstrates the links between language disturbances and disturbances in spatial representation (which obviously involves some degree of imaginal representation).

Second, research in child psychology has led to two results relevant to the psychology of images. In the first place, it has shown that images are not utilized, and probably, therefore, not acquired, until a relatively late stage. The process of their acquisition appears to be bound up with the symbolic function, as in the hypothesis just mentioned. In the second place, it has defined the conditions of the formation of the symbolic function as based on imitation, which consequently might also be the source of the images.

It is relevant to the first of these points to recall one of our earlier works,[4] in which we described the functioning of sensori-motor intelligence, the foundation of permanent object schemes,[5] sensorimotor space, causality, and so on. We found that the image was not needed in any of the activities observed before the stage during the second year when language, symbolic play and deferred imitation are acquired. The permanence of objects, for example, would have been far more quickly discerned if the baby had been able to use images in order to evoke localizations, etc.

[3] See I. Meyerson's excellent chapter on 'Les images' in Dumas' *Nouveau Traité de Psychologie*, 1932.
[4] Piaget, J., *The Origin of Intelligence in the Child.*
[5] In this work the French *schème* has been translated *scheme* rather than *schema* in view of the distinction made by Piaget between *schème* and *schema* in Chapter Ten, section 4 [Translator's Note].

Now if the emergence of images seems to be bound up with the formation of the symbolic function, as a differentiated system of signifiers and signifieds enabling the subject to evoke objects and events not actually perceived, it is no doubt because imitation ensures the transition between the sensori-motor and the representational, and because the image itself is internalized imitation. On the one hand, there is sensori-motor imitation consisting of an actual representation and action acquired in the first instance in the presence of the object. At a later stage it is able to assume a 'deferred' form (in other words a new imitative act is carried out without the object); it then becomes an evocation proper, though still in terms of action. If it is then internalized (as it is in the case of the co-ordinations characteristic of intelligence from the middle of the second year on), it is prolonged as an image. On the other hand, at the level where deferred imitation comes into being, play becomes symbolic, as a result of the same process of imitative evocation, and the faculty of language is acquired, also within a context of imitation.[6]

It is therefore the development of imitation which ensures the differentiation of signifiers and signifieds, and which consequently ensures, simultaneously, formation of the symbolic function and the emergence of the image considered as deferred and internalized imitation.

This hypothesis concerning the role of imitation as a transitional factor between the sensori-motor and the representational was taken up again in 1942 by H. Wallon,[7] who introduced some new arguments. In his view imitation would be regulated by the postural system and would, through the correspondence of attitudes, lead to interpersonal communication favouring both affective symbiosis and representation. The *simulacrum* and the symbol would proceed from imitation. This formative role of the imitation process could be seen in the earliest figurative theories of knowledge, such as the Platonic theory of Ideas.

But while genetic investigations stressed the importance of imitation and motor or postural factors in the formation of the image, a third step was being made in the same direction under the influence of psychophysiological and psychopathological lines of inquiry. The psychophysiology of the image was confronted with two problems: the question of the *sensible* or *simili-sensible* nature of the images – in other words, the problem of their visual, auditory, etc., content, which associationist psychology would have claimed to be a prolongation of perception; and the problem of its motor

[6] If language were transmitted only by conditioning, it would be acquired at a much earlier age (second or third month).
[7] *De l'acte à la pensée*, Flammarion, 1942.

nature – in other words, the active reproductive element which is precisely the feature distinguishing it from perception.

The neurosurgical techniques of electronic stimulation of the brain introduced by Foerster and developed in a remarkable way by Penfield and his associates have produced conclusive insights into the first problem. Stimulation in the cortical regions of the optic and auditory tracts gives rise only to sensorial states, which, according to Penfield, have nothing in common with hallucinations, even less with images, and constitute sensations proper. However, temporal stimulation produces mnemic states which present images varying in kind and vividness. In some the content seems to be present and immediate, as in dreams where the subject is both actor and spectator; in others the content is vivid but recalled as past; others are simple memories, with no vividness, and no aesthesia. The *simili-sensible* character of the image, therefore, is to be interpreted in terms of the combined activity, at the level of the temporal lobes, of mnemic and sensorial mechanisms which come into play with varying degrees of reactivation.[8]

But this sensorial reactivation does not mean that the image is no more than a residual perception. If there *is* reactivation, it takes place in connection with motor patterns, and it is these we have most information about. For instance, it has been possible to show (Allers, Scheminsky)[9] that the representation of arm movements does not consist of a representational image unconnected with the movements themselves, but rather of a sketch in a literal sense. Electromyograms have revealed the presence of slight peripheral muscular activity during the preliminary outlining that supports representation. This activity resembles that involved in the physical execution of the act represented. Similarly, Gastaut,[10] using electro-encephalograms, has observed the same waves in the mental representation of flexing the hand as when the flexion is actually performed. Facts of this kind show clearly enough that the motor image is much more than a faded perception, and that it consists rather of an internalized imitation.

Now the same is true of visual images. The similarity of motor and visual images already comes out clearly in A. Rey's work.[11] Rey shows that it is impossible to imagine the movement of one's forefinger tracing a given figure if the finger is simultaneously

[8] See Ajuriaguerra and Hécaen, *Le Cortex cérébral*, 2e éd., 436.
[9] Allers, R., Scheminsky, F., 'Ueber Aktionsstörme der Muskeln bei motorischen Vorstellungen und verwandten Vorgängen', *Arch. f. de. ges. Physial.*, 1926, 169–82.
[10] Gastaut, H., Bert, I., 'EEG changes during cinematographic presentation', *EEG Clin. Neurophysial.*, vi (1954), 433–44.
[11] Rey, A., 'L'évolution du comportement interne dans la représentation du mouvement (image motrice)', *Arch. Psychol.*, xxxii (1948), 209–34.

occupied with a simple rhythmic flexion. This is due to the motor image. But, in instances where there is also a visual representation of such a movement, the precision of the image is increased by complex oculo-manual co-ordinations. In 1947 F. Morel,[12] using a patient whose prominent eyes facilitated observation, studied the way in which visual representation of a square table, a round bowl, etc., was accompanied by eye movements imitating the shape imagined. By analysing recordings of the eye movements accompanying visual images, Schifferli[13] obtained similar results.

The most remarkable technique, however, that has so far been developed is the electronic recording of eye movements during sleep. In 1955 Aserinsky and Kleitman[14] distinguished two types, one of which was a rapid movement which the authors related to dream imagery. In 1958 W. Dement and E. Wolpert[15] believed they had confirmed this hypothesis in an experiment involving sixteen adult subjects who were awakened and asked to recount their dreams whenever eye-movement was registered.

In short, the imitative character of the image seems confirmed by all observations. The image appears to have a motor as well as a *simili-sensible* aspect. These motor functions may seem in some respects similar to those found in perceptual exploration. But perceptual exploration does in any case involve imitative movements in following the contours of the perceived object.[16] Similarly the

[12] Morel, F., *Introduction à la psychiatrie neurologique*, Paris, Masson, 1947.

[13] Schifferli, P., 'Etude par enregistrement photographique de la motricité oculaire dans l'exploration, dans la connaissance et dans la représentation visuelles', *Rev. mensuelle psychiatr. neurol.*, cxxii (1953), 53–118.

[14] Aserinsky, E., Kleitman, N., 'Two types of ocular motility occurring in sleep', *J. appl. Physiol.*, viii (1955), 1–10.

[15] Dement, W., Wolpert, E. A., 'The relations of eye movements, body motility and external stimuli to dream content', *J. exp. Psychol.*, lv (1958), 543–53.

[16] On the other hand, it might well be asked whether the studies of Aserinsky, Kleitman, Dement, *et al.*, on eye movements in sleep and their part in producing dream imagery do not also tend to suggest that the image appears much earlier than the symbolic function. The psychoanalysts (Freud, M. Klein, *et al.*), of course, are led to regard the image, which they view as a wish-hallucination, as appearing at a very early age, if not existing right from birth. When we were discussing this thesis at the Menninger Foundation, Topeka, we suggested that the debate could be settled once and for all by applying Aserinsky's technique to the child soon after birth or during the first few weeks. The experiment has since been carried out by Dement and others on newly-born children and on certain animals. The results were quite unexpected. Rapid eye movements (*REM*) during sleep are more abundant in the newly-born child than later, and in that living fossil the opossum, than in cats or in man! The *REM*, then, before the level where they can acquire some degree of direction and produce images, are present merely as undirected and unorganized motor excitation (which the authors are at present inclined to attribute to nervous detoxication). This does not exclude dreaming in a global motor or sensori-motor form, but it does not

sensible nature of the image does not result from a residual prolongation of the sensorial aspects of perception, but from an
imitation of perception – which is not the same thing, even if it is a
matter of outlines in reactivation. For this reason we shall use the
term *simili-sensible*, not just *sensible*, or *quasi-sensible*.

Finally, it is extremely difficult to define the image in a general
way, since any definition naturally depends on the overall system of
interpretation. According to the knowledge-as-copy hypothesis the
image is a copy of the object, which is presumed to be given in a
completely organized state with all its properties. The image in this
view is isolable and definable together with its quasi-perceptual
characteristics, and it is consequently considered as an essential
instrument of cognition. According to the hypothesis which we have
adopted – that knowledge is an assimilative process – the object can
be known only by being conceptualized to varying degrees. The
image is indeed still the product of an attempt to produce a concrete
and even *simili-sensible* copy of the object. But this copy is fundamentally symbolic, since the effective signification is to be found in
the concept. We are thus faced with the same kind of difficulty as
is met in attempting to understand the 'words' of language. It is
possible to isolate their phonemic and syntactic aspects, but the
semantic aspect is infinitely bound up with the whole process of
conceptualization. In the case of the image the obstacles are even
greater. The image being internal and not communicated as such,
its semantic aspect is easy to grasp because it is connected with the
whole process of conceptual representation. But its morphological
and syntactical aspect – which is precisely what goes to make up
the image – remains difficult of access and difficult to define. We
shall therefore use the term 'image' constantly in its broad sense,
including its semantic aspect – in a sense, that is, which is equivalent
to 'imaginal representation'. This is all part of our problem – the
relation between image and thought. If we had studied the images
of semi-sleeping or -waking states (the hypnagogic and hypnopompic
'hallucinations' of earlier writers), dream images, or the images of
children's symbolic games, we might have arrived at a more stringent
definition and dissociated the syntax of images from their semantics.
But in fact their 'semantics' will concern us just as much as their
'morphology'.

---

permit us to assert that clearly defined, quasi-perceptual images are produced.
Thus Dement concludes a recent account (*Psychiatric Spectator*, Feb. 1964,
page 13) by saying: 'It is suggested that these findings may not be compatible
with the psychoanalytic theories of dreaming.'

CHAPTER ONE

Classification of Images and Statement of the Problems

In fields where a particularly clear evolution related to age exists – for instance, in the operations of the intelligence – and where such a development expresses itself as a gradual formation whose workings are relatively accessible, there is, of course, no need for preliminary classification. The description of stages and sub-stages will in itself provide the basis of a natural classification in the form of a hierarchical table. The problem of images, however, is much less straightforward, and their stages of development, if there are any, much less obvious. So in order that we may present our results, an initial classifying of the different types of image is indispensable, even if this serves only to define our terms. But such a classification will yield more than a mere system of definitions. In sorting out different categories, its main purpose will be to clarify the problems with which we are faced – in particular, the problems of filiation.

1. *Outline for a classification*

Images may be classified in terms of their content (i.e. they are visual, auditory, etc.), or according to their structure. This second viewpoint is the only all-inclusive one, and the only one which will concern us here. The normal adult is able to imagine static objects (a hexagon, a table, etc.), movement (e.g. the swinging of a pendulum, the accelerated downward motion of a moving body on an inclined plane), and known transformations (e.g. the dividing of a square into two rectangles). He is able, too, to anticipate in images transformations which are new to him – to anticipate, for instance, that when a square sheet of paper is twice folded into two equal parts and the point of intersection of the folds cut off, a single hole will be seen, whereas if it is folded *three* times into two, *two* holes will be seen.[1] But it is clear that these imaginal representations are not formed with the same facility in each case, and that there is therefore a hierarchy of image levels, which may correspond to

[1] Cf. one of Terman's intelligence tests.

stages of development, but which certainly corresponds to degrees of increasing complexity. It is these degrees of complexity which we shall attempt to sort out into a structural classification, in order to make easier the task of genetic analysis.

A basic division into two large groups emerges if images are distinguished as *reproductive images* (*R*), which evoke objects or events already known, and *anticipatory images* (*A*), which, by figural imagination, represent events – be they movements, transformations or their culmination or results – that have previously not been perceived. Simple as this basic distinction is in theory, it is not, however, so easy to apply in practice. First, one can never be certain what the subject has already perceived, and second – and most important – it may be the case that any reproduction of a transformation, of a movement, and even perhaps of a static configuration involves a certain amount of anticipation, at least when it is executed. We shall, for example, be led to conclude that even a drawing reproducing a single line presupposes the coming-into-play of some kind of anticipatory scheme.[2] This complicates our classification at the outset. However, this complication in itself is instructive. The purpose of our classification is, of course, to enable us to state the genetic problems properly, and the problem that comes up here is precisely that of establishing whether the image is merely the direct prolongation of perception, or whether it is a process of active internal imitation. If it is the latter, execution schemes would naturally be necessary at the start of each new image.

We shall distinguish, therefore, between two types of anticipation: 'executional anticipation' – when, in order to reproduce an object *X* that is already known or even at that moment being perceived, it is necessary to anticipate the gesture *X* (external or internalized), by means of which the object will be reproduced; and 'evocational anticipation' – when *X* is not already known and has itself to be anticipated. Thus we shall use the term *anticipatory image* (*A*) exclusively for those images which involve 'evocational anticipation', without questioning the possibility of 'executional anticipation' being brought into play in the case of *reproductive images* (*R*).

Having said this, we may now classify reproductive images (*R*) according to two aspects: their content, and their degree of internalization. As far as their content is concerned, we shall distinguish three types: *static* reproductive images (*RS*), where such images refer to a motionless object or configuration (e.g. the image of a straight line); *kinetic* reproductive images (*RK*), where they evoke a movement figurally (e.g. the reproduction of two motions of the same constant speed crossing one another); and finally reproductive

[2] See Introduction, Note 5 [Translator's Note].

2

images of *transformations* (*RT*), where they represent in a figural manner transformations already known to the subject (e.g. the transformation of an arc into a straight line, when the subject has already verified this in his own perceptual experience with a piece of wire whose form is modified gradually). Between the types *RK* and *RT*, there are, of course, all the intermediary types, but here we shall speak of *transformation* only if the moving body is changing its *form*, and not if it merely changes its position.

As for the types of the reproductive image varying from the point of view of internalization, we are faced with a double problem – one both of method and of theoretical interpretation. As far as method is concerned, the difficulty of getting at the mental image being what it is, there seemed to us to be only four possible procedures: a verbal description by the subject based on introspection; a drawing by the subject; a choice made by the subject from several drawings prepared by the experimenter of the one best corresponding to his mental image; and reproduction by gesture. As the verbal method cannot be used with children unless it is combined with the others, we shall rely mainly on the last three methods. Now all three raise a problem of practical interpretation, since they get at the mental image only indirectly. But they also raise a problem of theoretical interpretation, since they themselves relate directly to other forms of image (graphic, gestural, and thus non-mental or not exclusively mental images). The relationship of such images to the mental image proper needs to be established.

If the mental image is interpreted as a mere product of perception, the drawing or the gesture demanded of the subject has no relationship to that image as such, and constitutes only an approximately equivalent symbolic translation. But in the view that we shall adopt, according to which the mental image is an active and internalized imitation, there is a more or less close relationship between the mental image, the imitative gesture, and the graphic image. The mental image is the only internalized one. The imitative gesture is also an act of reproduction and thus an image, though not an internalized one. The graphic image is likewise a non-internalized image, but differs from straightforward imitation in that it is separate from the subject's body by virtue of a process of concretization involving a particular technique (the motor factors in the pencil-stroke), though it is still in character an imitative image. It follows from this, that when we ask subjects to translate their mental image *R* into terms of a gesture or drawing (*G* or *D*) we are in fact asking them to express an image *R* in terms of other images (*RG* or *RD*). These latter are related to the first, and include certain motor factors (*m*) which were present already in *R*, but which, when they become specific, as in *RG* or *RD*, may be reflected in *R* or refine it, by prolonging the formative mechanism which was already in play in *R*. While the drawing *RD* is more complex than the mental image *R* and may therefore remain on an inferior level, the gesture *RG* is without doubt simpler than the mental image *R* itself and constitutes a kind of return to its origins.

3

It is easy to see, therefore, why it is necessary to classify the reproductive images R not only according to their content (static, kinetic, or transformation), but also according to their degree of internalization. The degree of internalization itself depends on two things: firstly on the more or less immediate (I), or deferred (II) character of the reproductive behaviour (R, RG or RD), and secondly on the internalization of the movements which this presupposes. That is, on the internalization which is apparent in the case of the mental image itself (R), on the possibly zero internalization in the imitative gesture (RG), although here a mental image might also be present, and on the internalization which necessarily occurs in drawing, since drawing consists in externalizing a previously internalized mental image. Even in the immediate (I) graphic copy of an external model, there occurs in varying degrees what Luquet has called an 'internal model'.

In each of these cases it is possible to distinguish what we shall call immediate reproductive images (R I) and deferred reproductive images (R II, RG II, RD II). These last may be said to be 'consecutional' (i.e. occurring immediately on the disappearance of the object), or deferred for greater intervals of time. This takes us back to the problem we raised earlier concerning the distinction between reproductive images R, and anticipatory images A. It takes us back also to the allied problem of the existence of an 'executional anticipation' that is quite distinct from 'evocational anticipation'. It is easy to understand what is meant by immediate gestural copies or reproductions (RG I or RD I), since they consist of the reproduction of a model which remains before the subject, and which thus makes demands of perception and not of evocation. On the other hand, is it not misleading to speak of an immediate mental image R I, since the mental image is defined as the evocation of a model without direct perception of it? But if, in a gestural or drawn copy (RG I and RD I), or merely in a drawn copy, some element of 'executional anticipation' is involved, and if, furthermore, the image is in fact the result of the internalization of imitative gestures, then this anticipatory execution scheme is just that – an immediate mental image R I. We shall therefore keep this term in our classification, but we must make two essential specifications regarding it. Firstly, it never exists in a pure state, but only as an integral part of a gestural reproduction (RG I or II), or of a graphic reproduction (RD I or II). Secondly, we are not dealing with an image proper, but with what we shall call a 'fore-image', because for one thing it cannot be isolated, and for another it precedes internalization. It will be none the less indispensable to study it (see Chapter Two), for it is the existence of this the 'fore-image' which seems to us best to justify the hypothesis according to which the mental image is not just a prolongation of perception, but involves an external element of active imitation which is also capable of being internalized.

Let us now turn to the *anticipatory images A*. We shall not distinguish static anticipatory images, but only *kinetic* (AK) and *transformation images* (AT). The reason for this is that in order to anticipate by means of an image a static position unknown to him, the child will have to take into account the movements or the transformation that lead to this position. This would be so, for example, for the final static position of a length of tube turned round in mid-air through 180° so that the position of its red and blue ends is reversed – in other words, so that the red end, say, would be on the child's right before the rotation, and on his left after it. But we shall distinguish – and this is an essential distinction too from the genetic point of view – two types of transformation image. First, the transformation image – whether anticipatory AT or reproductive RT – that bears only on the result or product P of the transformation, giving either ATP or RTP; and second, the transformation image that bears on the process of modification itself M, and not merely on its result, giving RTM or ATM.[3] Although the child must take this modification (M) into account in order to anticipate its result (ATP), this does not imply his being able to imagine it in detail. The image ATP may therefore be superior to the image ATM. We cannot strictly speak of the former as an anticipation of static position – though the child does of course have a tendency to impart static characteristics to his first images concerning transformation and even movement (AK), by omitting for instance the factor of continuity, etc.

There is, however, no point in trying to distinguish immediate (I) or deferred (II) varieties amongst anticipatory images, since they are all deferred. We must not forget, though, that the distinction between kinetic and transformation images is based on the fact that the former are concerned with changes of *position* only, the latter with changes of *form* only. Such a distinction is not always easy to make. It is as hard to make in fact as the distinction between reproductive transformation images (RT) and anticipatory images (AT), because any RT image probably presupposes an anticipatory execution scheme which is difficult to dissociate in this case from evocational anticipation.

Taking all this into account we arrive at the following outline for a classification:

[3] In the same way it is possible to distinguish between the types AKP or RKP and AKM or RKM, according to whether it is the result of a movement or the movement itself which is in question.

Images	Immediate (I=fore-images) or deferred (II)	Bearing on product (P) or on modification (M)
A. reproductive (R):		
static[4] (RS)	RS I or RS II	
kinetic (RK)	RK I or RK II	RKP or RKM
transformation (RT)	RT I or RT II	RTP or RTM
B. anticipation (A):		
kinetic (AK)		AKP or AKM
transformation (AT)		ATP or ATM

Each of the images thus classified may be in itself either gestural (imitation), mental or graphic.

2. *Statement of the problems*

The main purpose of the classification we have suggested is to provide a guide in our analysis of the facts, and to help us to present the problems which we shall have to discuss in relation to such an analysis. Let us be more specific, therefore, concerning the general questions which we shall meet in relation to virtually every set of facts.

(1) The first problem, which will naturally come up again and again, is that of the order in which mental images follow one another. For each particular test it will be easy to establish stages of reaction. These stages will be seen to be relatively well differentiated – more so, it goes without saying, than in the case of primary perceptual effects where no distinct stages are to be observed at all, and even more so than in the case of the various perceptual activities themselves. But is it possible, by a process of gradual comparison, to infer from these particular stages the existence of

[4] Static images, as we have said, are those bearing on motionless configurations. But in the pages that follow we shall have occasion to speak of the static character of images at the preoperational stage (before 7 to 8 years) in situations where the child is asked to reproduce or to form kinetic or transformation images, and where he fails since he is unable to go beyond the static stage. In this second sense the term 'static' refers therefore to a developmental stage or to a general characteristic, and not to a particular category of image. Apart from the fact that the context will always dispel any possible ambiguity, it seemed to us that this double sense does not cause any inconvenience, for at the preoperational stage the child is generally only able to form static reproductive images, and fails in categories RK, RT, AK and AT, unless he gets by with some kind of static symbolization.

6

more general stages of the mental image, fulfilling all the stage criteria as verifiable in the sphere of operational development?[5] This will be the problem. For instance, does the formation of anticipatory images A always come later than that of simple reproductive images R? And if so, will we find a constant lag between transformation images AT and the kinetic anticipatory images AK? Further, is this lag present already at the level of reproductive images (between RK and RT)? Can we even expect to meet a more or less regular order of succession for static images (RS) and kinetic images (RK)? These are the questions we will need to examine carefully within each set of facts, and above all as we pass from one set to another.

(2) A central problem whose solution may well furnish a guideline in studying almost all the remaining ones – including those concerning the nature of the image and its symbolic role – will be that of whether the development of images is autonomous or not. As a point of reference we have a case of an evolution which we know to be autonomous – that of the operational structures. Although their content may be influenced by perception, etc., it is in fact from one another that the operational structures develop, by means of progressive differentiations and combinations, the preceding structures becoming integrated in the next, these in turn opening up into new structures, and so on. As an example of non-autonomous evolution we have the evolution of perceptual structures whose progress is marked by external contributions coming from activity as a whole, and by influence exerted in turn by the intelligence, etc.

One of the main problems concerning mental images will be to decide whether the anticipatory images derive from an increasing extension and articulation of reproductive images – assuming that they are formed successively and that their order is constant – or whether they depend on the coming into play of factors external to the image, such as the operational mechanisms. This question will frequently arise with regard to the kinetic images (RK), for we shall come across many circumstances where it is evidently not enough to perceive a movement in order to be able to reproduce it.

Thus one can see the significance of the question of the autonomous or non-autonomous evolution of images in relation to the problem of their genesis. If the image is merely a prolongation of perception, it should be possible for any new perception (quite independently of the factors involved in its own acquisition) to be translated into an image. If, on the other hand, the image is an internalized imitation, the subject will generally only imitate what

[5] See Piaget and Inhelder, 'Les opérations intellectuelles et leur développement' in Fraisse and Piaget, *Experimental Psychology*, VII, Chapter XXIV.

he can comprehend or what he is near to comprehending – which implies the subordination of imitation to the functioning of the intelligence. This being so, the evolution of the imitative faculty would appear to be an instance of non-autonomous evolution. Not only does it depend on the intelligence as a whole, constituting as it does its accommodatory pole, but also any new behaviour may give rise to new types of imitation which do not derive directly from previous types, even though the behaviours imitated may be filiated. The problem can be stated in similar terms for the case of mental images.

(3) The third problem which we have to examine is that of the relationship between the *sensible* or *simili-sensible* aspect of the image (the inner picture, as it were, analogous to but less 'real' than a perceptual picture with its sensorial characteristics) and its motor or postural aspect *qua* outlined motor reproduction. Our field of investigation does not extend beyond the 3–4 to 11–12 age group, and we shall not therefore deal with the transition stage between the sensori-motor period and the beginnings of representation. Our problem thus amounts to establishing for each group of images we study the relationship between its laws and those governing the corresponding perceptions, and, if there is any discrepancy, looking for the possible imitative characteristics of the image. This, however, is not at all a simple matter. Primary perception, considered as field effects, remains, when viewed synchronologically at a given stage of development, quite independent of motor functions – though, of course, this is not to say that the latter has played no genetic role at the formative levels. On the other hand, there are perceptual activities, in particular acts of 'exploration', which involve eye movements. Such movements are found also in the visual images (cf. Morel, and Schifferli, Dement and Aserinsky, *et al.*). But even so it is clear that an imitative attitude is involved already in the movements of the eyes as they more or less faithfully trace the contours of a figure – if by imitation we mean the prolongation of the processes of accommodation to the object, which occurs in any adaptation activity. Further, in so far as the image seeks to copy (or imitate) the perception, it is obvious that its evocative movements will reproduce and thus rejoin the exploratory movements of perception not at the primary level of field effects, but at the secondary level of the sensori-motor activity which directs it. It should of course be pointed out that to say that the image copies or imitates perception is not the same as saying, as classical associationism did, that the image derives directly from perception in a single continuous process. The problem of the relationship between image, perception and imitation is then far more complex than it would seem at first sight.

8

And it is in these more specific terms that it will need to be couched again and again as we deal with each set of data.

(4) As far as the question of the symbolic or realistic nature of images is concerned, it must be said that this problem is not, any more than the last, capable of being determined by drawing solely and simply on the considerations discussed in our Introduction. For the situation is different at the operational and preoperational levels. When the operational functions are sufficiently developed to be able to master a system of transformations, it is understandable that the image is inadequate (hence only symbolic) when it attempts to evoke such transformations. It is unable to apprehend either the continuity or the dynamism of transformations and could well be compared with the 'cinematographic process' that Bergson held to be a component of intelligence itself, in that it is limited to symbolizing the continuous by means of a succession of discontinuous frames and the dynamism of transformations by evoking a few selected states. It would be to the point, therefore, if we were to look more closely at the nature of reproductive 'transformation images' *RT*, and also and especially at the anticipatory 'transformation images' *AT*, in order to verify, or invalidate, any such interpretation, however plausible it may seem to be. Further, if it is more or less apparent that the image of a number or category can only be symbolic, we shall have to ask ourselves whether spatial images do not have particular advantages compared with geometrical operations (see 7, *infra*), and in what sense they may still be considered symbolic. This sense may differ from case to case.

But if we go from the operational to the preoperational level, we find that the situation changes appreciably both from the subject's and from the observer's viewpoint. As the subject has as yet no operational functions at his disposal, he thinks in terms either of configurations, or states, as opposed to transformations, or in terms of assimilations to his own actions. In both cases the part played by imaginal representation is considerable, and, so to speak, out of place, in the sense that it is not yet subordinate to the operational functions (hence non-conservations, etc.). But what accounts for the illusions that are peculiar to the images at this level? Are they due to the incompleteness of the images (arising, for instance, from lack of *simili-sensible* reafference)? Or to the fact that they are aberrant (because of lack of sufficient support of an operational or simply motor kind)? Furthermore, if the subject's thought at this level is not yet operational, will the observer be bound to conclude that the image is not yet symbolic because it expresses a thought whose content (i.e. what is signified or symbolized) is itself imagined? Or ought he to see in these preoperational structures simply a thought ill-differentiated from what is symbolizing it in images (the symbolizing agent being all the more important as language is partially inadequate at this level)?

(5) This leads us to the problem of the relationships between image and thought in general. Thought, as representation or evocation, i.e. as a system of significations that can be handled independently of actual perception, requires 'signifiers'. It is language that plays the main part in this. But is language altogether adequate? As it is collective and hence relatively conventional and abstract, it only expresses what is communicable. In spite of the fact that language is particularized in style and usage and differs from one person to the next, an individual's thought may still be in need of a symbolism to take account of personal interpretations which are not directly expressible, but which are indispensable for concretization and investigation. Between primary perception with its undefined differentiations relating to actual objects and the verbally expressed concepts, there is a system of intermediary agents made up of perceptual schemes (cf. E. Brunswik's 'empirical *Gestalten*', J. Bruner's 'temporal schemes', and so on). In the same way, is it not perhaps necessary for a system of personal intermediary agents to come into play between the representation as experienced and perceived by each individual and the general concepts? And is it not precisely the mental images which constitute such a system, so that it is possible for perceptual situations which are not actual to be evoked symbolically, at least in a schematic way?

Such is the general problem. It can be seen that between the old outworn thesis that the image is an element of thought and the thesis that images serve as an auxiliary and occasional symbolism, there is room for an interpretation which restores a more important role to this symbolism, without, however, confusing image and thought. Now this third thesis is interesting from the genetic point of view. For it establishes a link between that aspect of adult thought which remains individual, imaginal and partly incommunicable, and the preoperational thought of the child which we have earlier characterized in terms of egocentrism. Vygotsky has seen in the child's egocentric language, which we have described elsewhere, the start of an internal language. In the same way, would it not be possible to view imaginal and intuitive representation, which stands in the place of operations at the levels where these are not yet formed, as the starting point of the personal and imaginal symbolism required by all adults in order to concretize the abstract thought related to verbal signs and mathematical language? This personal symbolism is particularly alive in mathematicians themselves. Like all creative people they have continual recourse to their imagination, whether they think as analysts or as geometers. The minds which are best able to control abstractions are those which succeed in embodying them in concrete examples or schemes which then serve as symbolic spring-boards without introducing any limitations. Of course, this does not mean to say that preoperational, imaginal thought is not still bound, as in the early language of the child, to its own dimensions. The problem is thus to know whether a systematic slackening of centration of activity at the image level, as well as at the level of other manifestations of thought, is not necessary in order that imaginal symbolism may perform its auxiliary function in abstraction and concretization, and in order that it may rid itself of initial illusions due to centration of activity at the representational level.

(6) This question of the relationship between image and thought-processes is, however, only a particular case of a more general problem whose structural aspects we shall now deal with. The symbolic adjuvant which the image constitutes is not only a matter of a preference for the representation of concrete instances, whereby each concept, which would otherwise remain abstract, is coupled with a figuration that gives it 'exemplarity'. In comparing the working of images with the working of the operations, as we shall do continually, we might ask ourselves whether the role of the images is not even greater, whether for the representation of 'states' they are not essential, and whether the operations, on the other hand, do not relate rather to transformations.

Here we come to a dichotomy of great significance within the cognitive functions. These latter can be divided into two large categories. They do not constitute two types of 'faculty', but two more or less differentiated or polarized aspects of cognition: the figurative aspect and the operative aspect. The first tends to include the figural character of reality, i.e. configurations as such. With it can be grouped: (a) perception, which functions only when an object is present and through the intermediary of a sensorial field; (b) imitation in the broad sense of the term (gestural, phonic, graphic, etc.) which functions either with or without the presence of the object, but in any case through overt or covert motor reproduction; (c) the mental image, which functions only when there is no object present. The operative aspect on the other hand takes in those forms of cognitive experience or of deduction whose function consists in modifying the object in such a way as to apprehend transformation as such. This includes: (a) sensori-motor actions (with the exception of imitation), the sole instruments of sensori-motor intelligence to be organized before language; (b) internalized actions that prolong previous ones right from a preoperational level; (c) the operations proper of the representational intelligence, or reversible internalized

11

actions which organize themselves as a set of structures or as transformation systems.

Now the figurative aspects of cognition bear more particularly
on the 'states' of reality, though transformations may be perceived,
imitated or imagined, in which case, however, they are given a
character which is either figural, direct (movement, *Gestalt*, etc.), or
symbolic (transformation images). The operative aspects, for their
part, relate in particular to transformations, although a state may
be taken operationally in so far as it is a result of anterior transformations, a starting point of subsequent transformations, or a nullified
or compensated transformation.

The problems, then, are first to establish whether the transformation images (RT or AT) are equivalent – and this question stands even
in the cases where these images would never be autonomous but are
oriented by the operational functions – and secondly, to establish
whether operational concepts of states can be formed independently
of a symbolic figuration. In other words, the central problem here is
this. Does thought, beginning from the preoperational level where
there is no awareness of transformation, and where as we shall see
imagery is too limited and too static to be able to represent even the
most common movements and changes, evolve towards an increasingly
close collaboration between the figurative and operative aspects,
centred on the co-ordination of states and transformations? Or, on the
other hand, does the development of the operative aspect, after the initial phase where configurations and imaginal representations are dominant, indicate a gradual movement away from the figurative aspects?

(7) It is particularly instructive to study the problem of the progressive collaboration or discrepancy between image and thought,
figurative and operative aspects, in connection with spatial images.
This is the domain known to mathematicians as 'geometrical intuition'. In this connection it should be noted that it can be extremely
useful to examine the problems of development, whenever possible,
in spheres where we can draw on two complementary kinds of
information – that drawn from genetic psychology, and that drawn
from the history of the sciences and historico-critical analysis. In
this way the study of initial genetic stages is illuminated by the higher
levels of thought, even if they are in no way final; reciprocally, useful
data for the interpretation of these levels themselves may be provided by an examination of their genesis. The psychological analysis
of recent developments in the sciences yields two rather different
sorts of result as far as the relationship between imaginal representation and operational systems of transformation are concerned.

One of these results, which is not however final as yet, emerges from the
evolution of microphysics. It is well known that in the realm of atomic

physics the most fundamental intuitions concerning space, time, causality, permanence of the object, etc., have had to be abandoned at the lower end of the scale of our approach to reality. The outcome of all this was a crisis of imaginal representation. In 1933 G. Juvet wrote that it was impossible 'to carry on physics with the imagination'.[6] In other words, the complexity of the new transformation systems made it impossible for them to be represented in images. Since then the thinking of physicists at the intra-atomic level has oscillated continually between rejection of imaginal representation and return to figurative description. L. de Broglie, in the chapter he kindly wrote on the role of representation in microphysics for a collection of essays on epistemology edited by us,[7] finally came round to the latter course. This did not of course mean that there was no need for considerable diversification of the representational schemata compared with those which are current in macrophysics.

The other instructive example is provided by the evolution of geometry. At first sight geometry, as the science of spatial figures, might appear to be the very model of a purely figurative science. It would be tempting to see in it an instance decisively contradicting what we have suggested concerning the progressive dominance of transformation systems in the development of thought. This is how it was still viewed in the nineteenth century, when it was considered as a branch of 'applied' mathematics (as opposed to the theory of numbers, algebra and analysis, which were then seen as 'pure' mathematics) in so far as it was based on 'intuition' and not on mere deduction – on an intuition which was held to issue directly from percep-tion. But since then 'the geometries' have multiplied, and transformation groups have been applied to diverse kinds of space. Thus F. Klein in his 'Erlangen programme' was able to conceive of each geometry as referable to a 'fundamental group' of transformations and of the different geometries as deriving one from another, each constituting a 'sub-group' of the pre-ceding one in a genealogical tree springing from topology. This being so, geometry becomes, like other exact sciences, a science of transformations, and, however important the figurative aspect may be, it is nevertheless subordinate to operational considerations. Now as far as the part played by images is concerned, geometrical intuition, though deprived of its conclusive character, retains notwithstanding a heuristic function. More-over, – and this is of great importance for the psychology of imaginal representation – it has differentiated itself in a remarkable way, without direct experience, to the point of allowing, by a kind of training in general-ization, the intuition of the non-Euclidian structures, of the torsions, the 'spins', the structures with n dimensions, etc., as well as of the spatial structures corresponding to physical objects on our scale.

An essential problem, then, will be to examine the role of images at the origins of spatial intuitions, and, in particular, to examine the precise nature of such images. Do they remain tracings, made faith-fully from perception, or do they differ from perception even in their

---

[6] *Les structures des nouvelles théories physiques*, Alcan, 1933.
[7] *Logique et connaissance scientifique*, Encyclopédie de la Pléiade.

most elementary forms? Above all, do they evolve autonomously, or do they become increasingly controlled by the operations? In general terms, why does the co-operation of image and operation appear to be both tighter and more fruitful in the spatial sphere than in any other sphere? We have here a series of questions all specially related to geometrical intuition, and yet very illuminating for the whole question of mental images.

CHAPTER TWO

Experiments on Elementary Static and Kinetic Reproductive Images

('*Fore-images*' *and the beginnings of reproduction*)

In classifying the images, we have seen that it is possible that at the moment of the gestural and more especially of the graphic copy some sort of anticipatory execution schemes are involved, coming between the perception and the reproduction of the model. If this is indeed the case, such executional anticipations would have considerable theoretical importance for the solving of the first of the problems under examination – namely, that of the relationship between mental images and perception.

In this chapter we shall only consider static reproductive images (*RS I*), and kinetic reproductive images (*RK I*) – though these are immediate in the sense that the copies in question occur actually in the presence of the object, which may be displaced without making comprehension any the more difficult. The problem then is to compare the image of the object with its perception. It is in such a comparison that the anticipatory execution scheme can yield useful information, though naturally only in so far as it can be made to vary according to particular situations. If the result of the anticipation were the same in all situations one could only see an indication of motor inhibition, etc., peculiar to the activity of drawing. (In fact the result is, as we shall see, a tendency of the younger subjects to underestimate lengths.) But if we succeed in making it vary for the subjective conditions of the imagination, other things being objectively equal, we should then be able to look in the anticipatory scheme for a kind of fore-image which might be imitative, but which would not have any quasi-sensible elements. This would mean that the image can be fairly clearly opposed to perception.

Further, in some of the situations we take we shall try to include certain standard perceptual conditions (such as vertical and horizontal lines, divided spaces, etc.), in order to see what they correspond to from the point of view of mental or graphic images (and even of imitations given by pointing).

1. *Reproduction of a horizontal line in objectively identical positions but after varying imagined preliminary displacements*

The following experiment conducted with B. Matalon was carried out on 110 children of 5, 7 and 11 years of age, and on sixty adults.

The subject was presented with a black-coloured, rigid wire rod *A*, 20 cm long, and 1·8 mm in diameter. It was placed on the left half of a large sheet of paper perpendicularly to the sagittal axis (the position we shall call 'horizontal'). Then the subject was asked three times to draw the rod in the same position (*A*) – that is as a direct extension of the rod in position *A*, on the right half of the paper and without a break between positions *A* and *A'*. The three copies were made in the following three ways: (1) after imagination of a rotation, (2) after imagination of a translation, (3) without imagination of a displacement. Questions were put as follows:

(1) The subject was told that the rod would be rotated. The rod was then rotated through 180° to position *A'*. It was returned to position *A*. The subject was asked to draw the rod *A* with the right length, as it would be in position *A'*. The rod itself remains at *A*.

(2) The subject was asked to draw the rod with its right length as it would be in *A'*, but this time after simple translation movement to *A'* and back to *A*.

(3) Finally, the subject was asked to copy the rod in position *A'*, without its having been moved from *A*, and without the experimenter's having said anything about moving it.

To avoid the learning effect, the subjects were split up into six groups, and their drawings done in the six possible orders (1, 2, 3; 1, 3, 2; etc.). In order to determine whether any part is played by non-conservation of the lengths when displaced, the (operational) reaction to conservation was examined in children of 5 years after the copying experiments. This was done first for questions 1 and 2, and then for two rods aligned and then staggered in the usual way.[1]

The results on the one hand showed a general reduction in the size of the drawings in the case of the young children, with the gradual disappearance of this 'underestimation', as we shall call it, according to age. On the other hand they showed variation in the underestimations corresponding to questions 1, 2, 3, as we had hoped, which also tended to disappear with age (see Table 1).

---

[1] The usual experiment on the conservation of lengths consists in first presenting the child with 2 rods 15 cm in length. The child is asked to observe that they are equal in length. One of the rods is then moved 7–8 cm sideways, and 2–3 cm upwards. They remain parallel. The child is then asked if the rods are still the same length, or if one is longer than the other.

TABLE 1 *Systematic errors in drawings representing the length of a 20 cm rod after imagination of a rotation, of a translation, or by simple copy*
(Averages given as % of 20 cm; average lengths of the drawings given in brackets)

	1. Rotation	2. Translation	3. Copy
5 years ($N=30$):			
%	− 20·5 (15·9 cm)	− 19·0 (16·2 cm)	− 13·5 (17·3 cm)
σ	2·8	2·2	1·7
7 years ($N=20$):			
%	− 20·5 (15·9 cm)	− 17·0 (16·6 cm)	− 10·5 (17·9 cm)
σ	2·9	2·2	1·8
11 years ($N=60$):			
%	− 5·0 (19·0 cm)	− 4·5 (19·1 cm)	− 8·5 (18·3 cm)
σ	1·7	1·2	1·0
Adults ($N=60$):			
%	+ 3·5 (20·7 cm)	− 2·5 (19·5 cm)	+ 2·0 (20·4 cm)
σ	1·5	1·2	1·1

The following facts emerge:

(*a*) The younger subjects show an underestimation in the case of all three drawings, including the simple copy without displacements (3).

(*b*) This underestimation disappears progressively with age.

(*c*) The 5-year-old subjects give drawings which are shorter after the imagination of a displacement (1 and 2) (there is no significant difference between rotation and translation: Student's $t=$ a non-significant 1·29). The drawings are not so short in a simple copy (3) (here the difference is very significant: $t=3·65$ or $3·14$, between drawings 3 and 1 or 3 and 2, taking into consideration the fact that the measurements are taken from the same subjects).

(*d*) This difference between 1 or 2 and 3 decreases above 7 years, and has disappeared in the child of 11 years and in the adult.

In order to interpret these facts it will be necessary first of all to see whether the underestimations that occur after imagination of a displacement might not be due to preoperational non-conservation of lengths. We therefore tested conservation in thirty-two children aged 5 years for displacements I (realization of what is imagined in 1), II (realization of 2) and III (translation and staggering in the usual way). See Table 2.

Conservation is affirmed in 77 per cent of cases for questions I and II, whereas it is negated in 74 per cent of cases for question III. It is therefore not this factor which is responsible for the underestimations of Table 1 for questions 1 and 2.

TABLE 2 *Conservation of lengths (in terms of $+$ and $-$) for rotation (I), translation as extension (II) and staggering (III), as % of 32 subjects aged 5[2]*

$$(I+) (II+) (III+) \qquad (I+) (II+) (III-)$$

$$\overline{}$$

$$21 \qquad\qquad 56$$

$$(I-) (II-) (III+) \qquad (I-) (II-) (III-)$$

$$\overline{}$$

$$5 \qquad\qquad 18$$

We are thus left with two problems. Why do general underestimations of lengths occur in the drawings? And what is the reason for the differences in the reactions to questions 1 and 2 and in the reactions to question 3?

We will take up the first of these problems again in section 2 of this chapter along with some more general facts. Let us limit ourselves for the moment to the supposition that the underestimation of length in the simple copy of a line implies the existence of an anticipatory execution scheme, since the distribution of errors (in terms of $+$ and $-$) is not just random. It would appear that the younger children, when they attempt to estimate in advance the extent of the pencil stroke needed to reproduce the model, concentrate above all on not going beyond the boundary of its end point (we shall see numerous examples of this kind of 'boundary taboo': Chapter Three, etc.). One might ask, however, whether this execution scheme does not in that case arise in the drawing only – in the graphic image therefore, and not in the mental image. But apart from the fact that a concern with the boundary relates to the representation in general and not just to the drawing, the results in Table 1 are sufficient to show that this anticipatory scheme is linked with the image itself, since it is modified as soon as imagination of a preliminary displacement takes place – even though in all three situations (questions 1, 2 and 3) the subject has to do no more than to copy in position A' the rod as it remains in position A. In short, the anticipatory execution scheme has already some of the characteristics of the image, in so far as it is a motor sketch of an imitative nature (copy). But, since it is not accompanied by *simili-sensible* elements, and since the object is present as perception and not evoked as representation, we shall in this case speak of a 'fore-image', and not speak of a mental image in the strict sense.

For the time being we shall thus be concerned with the problem (problem 2) of explaining the reasons why this 'fore-image' or executional anticipation should give rise to greater underestimation when imagination of preliminary displacements is involved than when it is only a simple copy that is being executed. The shortening of the length of the line that occurs in this underestimation cannot

[2] The symbols $I + II + III +$ signify affirmation of conservation in questions I, II and III. The symbols $I + II + III -$ signify rejection of conservation in III and its affirmation in I and II; etc.

be due to a belief in non-conservation, as we have seen from the results of Table 2. But in the case of rotation or translation nearly all the subjects refuse to accept conservation until they have carefully inspected the rods (one remaining as it is, the other actually being displaced in the case of Table 2). Even the subjects who finally conclude that they are of equal length appear to start off with a bias against conservation, and often look for indications of non-conservation before accepting that there has been no change. According to our hypothesis the general shortening of lines in drawings is due to some inhibition relative to boundary points. Such an inhibition would be reinforced by any hesitation occurring when a movement is imagined. It would thus be a kind of precautionary reaction guarding against error. This would be analogous to the precautions against error to be observed in adults in depth perception, where it is important to compensate apparent diminution in size. But would it not be possible to think of a simpler explanation?

First of all it should be noted that the shortening shown by the graphic images in questions 1 and 2 could not be due to perceptual factors, since in visual transfers on a frontal-parallel plane, distance produces over-estimation, and not underestimation.[3] At the time of these observations we undertook an investigation with Lambercier on five adults and five children of between 5 to 7 years of age.[4] We asked them to reproduce in a drawing the height of a rod of 10 cm tall as seen at the distances of 3·25, 100, 200 and 300 cm. Now these drawings indicated that there was over-estimation (10·3 to 11 mm in the adult and 10·4 to 11·1 mm in the child) at a distance of 25 cm and over, consonant with the results yielded by direct perceptual comparison of two rods at the same distances. This is the contrary of what we have observed in the present case. Shall we simply say then that in questions 1 and 2 the imitative motor anticipation of lengths is impeded by the fact of imagining a preliminary displacement, independently of the question of boundaries? But, if it is simply a matter of an arresting of graphic gestures, why should it be reinforced by this preliminary act of imagination? In all cases the child has the model before him all the time; moreover one would expect the displacement of the rod to suggest extension rather than arrest (if the paper is too small and the drawing stops near the edge, the child is strongly inclined to go on till he comes to it). Nor is it that the subject is distracted by the effort of imagining the detail of the rotation, for as we shall see (Chapter Three, sections 3–4), he is not always able, at the age of five or six, to visualize the intermediary stages between extreme positions.

All things considered, the most plausible explanation seems to be the following. The perception of the length of a horizontal line is a

[3] Piaget, J., and Lambercier, M., 'La comparaison des hauteurs dans le plan fronto-parallèle', *Arch. Psychol.*, xxxix (1942), Rech. II.
[4] *Ibid.*, 209.

simultaneous, integral, unfragmented apprehension of the data in question – the two extremities and the distance between them. Contrary to this, the graphic image, or reproduction by drawing, is an imitation of the object aiming at reproducing its essential characteristics, and starting with and having a fore-image, or executional anticipation. In this case, if a length is to be imagined in terms of kinetic reproduction (i.e. a pencil drawing, or as in section 2 a straightforward digital or motor tracing), the important thing is the end point. This would necessitate one of two precautions. Either one must be careful not to go beyond it, or one must be careful not to stay this side of it. But as the image is bound up with imitative movement, and as such movement will tend to be carried on, the main concern is to avoid going beyond the terminal point. This attitude is evident even in the case of the simple copy (question 3). It is further reinforced when preliminary imagination of a displacement is introduced (questions 1 and 2). The reason is simply that the object is then mobile (displacement of original terminal boundary) and further care seems necessary in order not to overstep the end point. Hence a shortening of the line drawn which is significantly greater than when a movement is not imagined. This effect diminishes with age, in spite of the fact that the older children, who are no longer satisfied with a single continuous stroke, show more concern for exactness. The reason is that the older children pay increasingly more attention to the line's starting point, to the intervening space therefore, and no longer concentrate exclusively on the finishing point.

A point to which we will return later might be mentioned in this connection. The characteristics of the image which we have so far observed may be compared to the laws of preoperational representation. In all fields (lengths, speeds, duration, etc.) preoperational representation begins with ordinal rather than metric consideration (whence an identification such as 'longer' = 'farther away', etc.)[5] and tends to overestimate the importance of the end-point compared with the actual lengths. The fact that notions of order precede metric notions has nothing to do with the image but results from factors relating to the elementary nature of operations or notions. However, the fact that the line's end-point receives more attention than the starting point can be attributed to factors relating to the image – for the reasons we have already discussed above. Thus one can see already from these few experiments that there is probably some interaction between image and notion, although one does not necessarily derive from the other.

[5] Or, in the French, *plus long* = *plus loin* [Translator's Note].

2. *The underestimation of lengths in simple copies*

The reactions we observed earlier in the case of the simple copy (question 3 in Table 1) call for further information. To control the suggested interpretations it is necessary first to find out whether the underestimations we have observed arise generally in all simple copies, second, to check whether underestimation occurs also in gestural reproduction (motor outline independent of an actual drawing), and, third, to discover whether underestimation would be eliminated if the subject were merely to point to the line's extremities with his finger. This last point is important, since if the length is indicated between the index fingers, the emphasis is laid on the actual distance between the two extremities and not on the finishing-point (in the case of the drawing the main problem is precisely where to stop the pencil stroke). Moreover, the gestural image is thereby freed from the imitative process taking place in time as a movement in space.

In experiment 1 the subject was presented with a rod 15 cm long and 1·8 mm in diameter, placed horizontally on a sheet of white paper 33 cm square. The child had a sheet of the same sort and size to draw on. This point is important as the results are affected by the nearness of the edges, if the paper is too small – as they are of course also if there are any reference markings, squares, etc., on the paper. The rod was shifted upwards and to the left (or right); the subject was placed at the mid-point between the two sheets. The results were the same whether the rod was moved to the left or to the right, but when the rod was placed at the level of the drawing and in the middle of its sheet (here the margin between the ends of the rod and the edge of the paper may help the subject) the underestimation is slightly less marked. The conditions are thus not the same as those in question 3 for Table 1 – which explains why the underestimations in Table 3 are slightly greater. It should also be pointed out that the results of Table 3 are those taken from the first drawing done by the child, without any further corrections, whereas the facts given in Table 1 take into account any corrections spontaneously introduced by the subject.

II. It seemed useful to complement these results in the following way. The subjects were shown previously prepared drawings of lines 13, 14, 15, 16 and 17 cm long, and were asked to select the one which matched. If the younger subjects pick several it is a good idea to get them to estimate which drawings are 'too big', 'the same', or 'too small'. The rod was removed and replaced each time in order to avoid any error concerning the standard length against which the drawings were being compared.

III. The same subjects were asked to reproduce the length of the rod by placing the index fingers on the sheet of white paper (33 cm square as before). The distance between was measured.

Table 3 gives the results obtained from sixty subjects in collaboration with Tuât Vinh-Bang.

TABLE 3   *Copies of the length of a 15 cm rod*
(Errors as % of 15 cm)[6]

	I. Drawing	II. Choice	III. Pointing
6– 6 years (22)	– 22 (= 11·7 cm)	– 4·9 (= 14·2 cm)	+ 9·3 (= 16·4 cm)
7– 8 years (18)	– 14 (= 12·9 cm)	– 4·6 (= 14·3 cm)	+10·2 (= 16·5 cm)
9–10 years (20)	– 14 (= 12·9 cm)	– 3·0 (= 14·6 cm)	+ 3·7 (= 15·6 cm)

What emerges first of all is the fact that underestimation of length in drawings is general. On average the underestimation is greater here than in question 3, Table 1. This result is due to factors in the procedure which we have already mentioned. Above 7 to 8 years it would be less marked if the subject's spontaneous corrections were taken into account.

Next it emerges that there is still some degree of underestimation when the subject is asked to choose the matching length from the prepared drawings. If it were merely a matter of ordinary perceptual comparison, the distortions in terms of + and − would, in the absence of systematic errors, more or less cancel out. Clearly therefore the subject's choice is influenced by the drawing done immediately before.

Most noteworthy, however, is the complete contrast between the drawing and the digital estimation. The latter shows a tendency to overestimate that decreases with age. The reason for this may be of a perceptual order. An empty space will appear shorter than a full space of the same dimensions. Thus before a space is perceptually equivalent to a rod 15 cm long it will actually have to be longer than this. But the important thing is that underestimation now no longer occurs. There are probably two interrelated reasons for this. The first of these could be that the length of the rod is not being imitated by means of a movement (the pencil stroke) retracing it as a distance to be covered. This means that the problem of where to stop the pencil stroke, the problem of the boundary, would be eliminated. The second could be that the emphasis is on both the boundaries − the initial and the terminal points − and thus on the distance between them as such, and not just on the line's finishing point. To the extent that underestimation in the drawings can be said to be due to a precautionary reaction guarding against going beyond the finishing-point of the line, these two differences between graphic imitation and

[6] The figures in brackets represent the averages of the lengths drawn, selected or indicated (in cm).

digital estimation would be enough to explain why underestimation tends to disappear in the second mode of reproduction.

To check this interpretation and to show that it is not simply a matter of the difference between predominantly visual imitation and gestural imitation, one only needs to ask the subject to reproduce the length of the rod by means of a gesture of the forefinger in a single continuous movement. This is equivalent to making a pencil-stroke, except that no mark is made on the paper. We carried out this control experiment in association with Mme Tuât Vinh-Bang in the way described below.

(*a*) First, the child was presented with a rod 15 cm long, which he was asked to copy directly (the intention being to compare motor reproduction and graphic reproduction in the same subject). The rod was placed to the left of the subject as in Table 1, question 3, and not to his right as in Table 3.

(*b*) Instead of going on to the selection of a matching drawing as before, in order to vary the sources of our information, we asked the child to reproduce the length of the rod by means of small segments 1·5 cm long. Obviously these are too large (one tenth of the total length of the rod) to allow us to compare the average error with that arising in the drawings (where the margin of error is much finer). But even so there is considerable interest in seeing whether there will be any underestimation or not.

(*c*) We went on to visual perception of the object. We asked the child to reproduce it by tracing it on the table with his forefinger. The child was allowed to see the model during this procedure, but not his own gesture. We used a curtain (rather than a rigid screen, which would have impeded the action), under which the child passed his hand before executing the gesture.

(*d*) Then we asked the child to move his finger along the model rod itself out of sight behind the curtain, and, still behind the curtain, to trace out a straight line of equivalent length.

(*e*) He was asked to move his finger again along the rod without seeing it, and to reproduce it by means of a visible drawing.

(*f*) Finally, we asked him to give the length of the rod, which he was this time allowed to see, by indicating its extremities with his forefingers (as for Table 3).

Table 4 (overleaf) shows the results obtained from twenty subjects aged 5, ten aged 6, ten aged 7, eleven aged 8, eleven aged 9 and ten adults, using a horizontal rod of 15 cm.

It can be seen from this that while the length of the rod is overestimated when indicated between the fingers (column *f*), when the finger actually traces out the length (columns *c* and *d*) there is underestimation which on average is up to twice as great as the underestimation in the drawing (column *d*: average of − 25 per cent from 5 to 9 years, as against − 12·4 per cent for column *a* and − 11·8 per cent for column *e*). This is the evidence we were looking for in

TABLE 4 *Graphic reproduction (a); construction (b); motor tracing (c–e); static pointing (f) – to indicate the length of a 15 cm rod* (As % of 15 cm)

	(a) Drawn copy	(b) Construction	(c) Visual perception motor representation
5 years	− 13·3 (= 13·0)	− 9·3 (= 13·6)	− 19·0 (= 12·15)
6 years	− 14·6 (= 12·8)	− 6·6 (= 13·9)	− 30·6 (= 10·4)
7 years	− 11·7 (= 13·25)	− 8·0 (= 13·8)	− 7·3 (= 13·9)
8 years	− 4·6 (= 14·4)	− 10·7 (= 13·5)	− 24·0 (= 11·3)
9 years	− 8·0 (= 13·8)	− 4·7 (= 14·2)	− 18·7 (= 12·2)
Adults	− 1·3 (= 14·8)	− 0·3 (= 14·9)	− 5·3 (= 14·2)

	(d) Tactile perception motor representation	(e) Tactile perception graphic representation	(f) Pointing (static)
5 years	− 29·3 (= 10·6)	− 13·3 (= 12·9)	+ 13·3 (= 17·0)
6 years	− 27·3 (= 10·9)	− 20·0 (= 12·0)	+ 6·0 (= 15·9)
7 years	− 22·7 (= 11·6)	− 10·0 (= 13·5)	+ 10·0 (= 16·5)
8 years	− 18·7 (= 12·2)	− 8·0 (= 13·8)	+ 6·0 (= 16·0)
9 years	− 27·3 (= 10·9)	− 8·0 (= 13·8)	+ 4·8 (= 15·7)
Adults	− 18·2 (= 12·3)	− 3·2 (= 14·7)	+ 4·0 (= 15·6)

order to show that overestimation in the case of static indication between index fingers is due to the absence of movement and not simply to the gestural factor.

It is interesting to see, on the other hand, that when the rod is reproduced by means of the segments (column *b*) there is general underestimation, just as there is in the drawings (although no significance can be attached to the quantitative aspect of this, for the reasons already mentioned). The fact is that reproduction by construction also proceeds by reference to finishing points.

We are left with the question whether these phenomena remain qualitatively the same when the size or form of the objects involved in the experiments is altered. Table 5 gives the results obtained using a rod of 22 cm instead of 15 cm for reproduction by drawing, reproduction by construction (by means of rigid segments), and static indication between forefingers.

This shows that both underestimation in the drawing and overestimation in pointing get less when the rod is longer. But if the size of the rod is reduced and squares are added, we find, presenting

TABLE 5 *Graphic reproduction, construction and pointing, to indicate the length of a 22 cm rod*

Ages and number of subjects	Drawing	Construction	Pointing
5 years (10)	− 17·2 (=18·1)	− 12·2 (=19·3)	+16·3 (=25·7)
6 years (10)	− 10·4 (=19·7)	− 11·3 (=19·5)	0 (=22·0)
7 years (10)	− 2·2 (=21·5)	− 14·0 (=18·9)	− 2·2 (=21·5)
8 years (11)	− 7·9 (=20·2)	− 9·5 (=19·8)	+ 6·8 (=23·5)
9 years (11)	− 2·2 (=21·4)	− 11·3 (=19·5)	− 1·0 (=21·8)
Adults (10)	+ 0·9 (=22·2)	0 (=22·0)	+ 0·2 (=22·05)

them in concentric order, that they yield results as set forth in Table 6.[7]

In this connection we also carried out tests on fifteen subjects aged 5 years – again in collaboration with Mme Vinh-Bang. The child was shown rods from 1 cm to 15 cm in length (five distinct lengths), and squares from 1 to 7·5 cm square; he was asked to copy them in ascending, descending and concentric order.[8] See Table 7.

TABLE 6 *Copies of rods and squares of variable dimensions*
(As % of the lengths)

	Rods				
	1 cm	2·5 cm	5 cm	7·5 cm	15 cm
5 years (15 s.)	+10	+ 4	− 7·2	− 20·8	− 16·5
6 years (20 s.)	− 12	− 28	− 17·7	− 16·1	− 12·0
7 years (15 s.)	− 8	− 16	− 13·4	− 24·2	− 20·1
8 years (15 s.)	− 5	− 11·2	− 6	− 11·7	− 1·3
9 years (15 s.)	− 3	− 1·6	− 6·8	− 5	− 3·8

	Squares			
	1 cm²	2·5 cm²	5 cm²	7·5 cm²
5 years (15 s.)	+34	− 5·6	− 28·6	− 34·4
6 years (20 s.)	− 8	− 26·8	− 22·6	− 32·5
7 years (15 s.)	+ 3	− 15·6	− 21·6	− 22·4
8 years (15 s.)	− 2	− 21·6	− 22·4	− 17·46
9 years (15 s.)	+10	− 22	− 16·4	− 19·73

[7] For the squares, which are very distorted in the younger children (so much so that it was necessary to exclude the 15 cm squares), we measured each side separately and took the average of all four.
[8] These precautions, which are generally unnecessary when dealing with problems relating to images – though they are when problems of perception are concerned – were necessary here because of the lengths of 1–2·5 cm.

TABLE 7 *Copies of rods and squares of variable dimensions*
(As % of the lengths)

	Rods				
Order	1 cm	2·5 cm	5 cm	7·5 cm	15 cm
Ascending	− 8	− 14·8	− 19·8	− 20·3	− 16·8
Descending	+10	− 9	− 19·4	− 20·6	− 17·3
Concentric	+10	+ 4	− 7·2	− 20·8	− 16·5

	Squares			
Order	1 cm²	2·5 cm²	5 cm²	7·5 cm²
Ascending	+ 9	− 12	− 38	− 20
Descending	+10	− 9·6	− 24·2	− 22·2
Concentric	+34	− 5·6	− 28	− 34

Firstly, it can be seen that all the lengths occasion some under-estimation, except for the smallest lengths (five overestimations for the 1 cm and one for the 2·5 cm lengths). But it is illuminating to find that overestimation in the case of these very small lengths only occurs as an effect of a particular order of presentation. In the ascending order the 1 cm rod is still underestimated by 8 per cent, because the series begins with this length. But in the descending or concentric order, the 1 cm rod, and even in one instance the 2·5 cm rod, is overestimated in the drawings under the influence of the longer elements (drawings or models) already perceived. This is simply an effect of perseveration. (It is a known fact that in temporal series of this type, perseverations prevail over contrast effects at about 5 years.) This is also true for the 1 cm squares, since they are drawn immediately after the rods.

Secondly, it seems that a *maximum* underestimation occurs around the 7·5 cm (or 5 to 7·5 cm) length, as if the risk of going beyond the boundary point decreased in proportion as the lengths involved increase.

3. *The underestimation of lengths of oblique, vertical and horizontal lines after an imagined rotation of 90°*

We have established the existence of fore-images in the anticipatory execution schemes in dealing with simple copies (section 1), and have confirmed that this phenomenon is general (section 2). We now need to go on to ask what would happen if the subject were required to imagine a familiar elementary displacement whose final position is not, as it was in section 1, simply a repetition of the initial position.

At the same time this will enable us to establish what part is played by the control tests or practice in the underestimations which, we have suggested, may be attributable to the inhibiting effects of boundary points. So, in association with B. Matalon, we examined drawings of rods remaining visible and static while the subject imagined the results of various rotations.

The child was shown a sheet of white paper 45 cm × 45 cm (this size was used so that the edges would not appear too close to the rod), and a black metal rod 15 cm in length and about 2 mm in diameter. The rod was placed horizontally, to the left of the centre of the paper. The child was shown the general movement of the rod (180° rotation starting from the right). It was then replaced in its initial position, and with his finger the experimenter indicated a particular direction of about 30°. The child was asked to draw the rod 'as you would see it when it has turned round and got as far as this'. When the first drawing had been executed the experimenter covered it, indicated a movement of 60° and asked the subject to do as before. This was repeated every 30° up to 180°. A control group had previously worked with drawings which were not covered.

Table 8 contains the results obtained from tests on forty-five subjects aged 4,5 to 8,11 years.

TABLE 8   *Drawings in oblique positions (from 30° to 180°) of a horizontal rod of 15 cm serving as a visible model*

	Initial drawings covered (N = 30)		Initial drawings visible (N = 15)	
	Length + St. var. *(as mm)*	*Error* *(%)*	*Length + St. var.* *(as mm)*	*Error* *(%)*
30°	136·7 ± 14·0	− 8·9	140·8 ± 8·0	−6·1
60°	134·0 ± 23·1	− 10·7	148·4 ± 16·2	−1·7
90°	130·6 ± 15·7	− 12·9	142·2 ± 18·3	−5·2
120°	136·4 ± 16·6	− 9·1	146·3 ± 20·0	−2·5
150°	126·1 ± 10·0	− 15·9	151·9 ± 24·3	+1·3
180°	139·3 ± 12·0	− 7·0	155·4 ± 30·3	+3·6

From this emerges, firstly, the difference between the errors made when previous drawings are covered and those made when they are not. In the latter case the negative error decreases markedly and tends to become positive. Most probably this is due to learning – not simply by practice and repetition, but by perceptual checking and comparison with preceding drawings, with the drawings in hand and with the model. This is of interest in relation to the question of the boundary effect.

Secondly, the drawings of the oblique lines give a general average of −11·5 per cent (excluding the 180° rotations; including them the general average is −10·7 per cent), which is comparable to the error of −11·2 per cent which we shall find occurring at 5 years in the case of images of rods rotated through 90° (see Table 9a).

4. The image of the final position of 90° rotations

To complement the preceding tests, we carried out a further investigation. We presented the subjects with rods 215 mm long in vertical or horizontal position, and asked them to draw the rods as they would be when turned through 90° to a horizontal or vertical position.[9] We did not ask the subject to represent any intermediate positions this time – we will return to this in Chapter Three – but only the final positions. The images we studied here thus belong to the category of reproductive images which bear on the result of known movements *RKP*. We will of course again find the kind of underestimations that we have observed already. But we shall also be able to show that there are some learning effects arising from the eight possible combinations presented in a constant order (*A–H*: see Figure 1).[10]

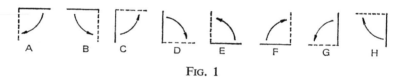

FIG. 1

Classifying the results according to whether the rotation is from left to right (*lr*) or the reverse (*rl*), from top to bottom (*tb*) or the reverse (*bt*), and from vertical to horizontal (*vh*) or the reverse (*hv*), we arrived at Table 9.

To make results easier to read off in the order of presentation, Table 9a gives the same results in terms of the series *A–H* (see Figure 1 and Table 9a).

The results obtained were as follows:

(1) The average underestimation of the rods by the graphic image before the subject has had practice is slightly higher than it was for the simple copies in Table 1 (−16·4 per cent for *A–C* at 5 to 6

[9] The experimenter says: 'Draw the stick as you will see it when it has turned.' He shows the child the complete movement, and then returns the rod to its initial position.

[10] Our thanks are due to M. Vinh-Bang and L. Piaget, who kindly drew the diagrams for this book.

years, as against -13.5 per cent in Table 1). But it is a little lower than it was in those cases in Table 1 in which the child drew the rod after imagining a rotation or translation.

(2) This underestimation decreases with age, as in Table 1.

(3) It decreases also with repetition and practice, particularly at 5 to 6 years (from -16.5 per cent for $A-B$ to -6.3 per cent for $G-H$), and again at 8 to 10 years (-12.1 to -2.8 for AB to GH), though this is no longer the case in the adult.

(4) The drawings of movement from horizontal to vertical (hv) show greater underestimation than the reverse movement (vh) for all three age-groups and for all pairs of movement. There is one exception to this at 5 to 6 years for the pair FC and one instance of equivalence in the adult group (for AG).

TABLE 9   Drawings of rods of 215 mm after imagination of a rotation of 90°
(As % of 215 mm)

	lr		rl	
	tb	bt	tb	bt
5–6 years ($N=22$):				
hv	(B) -18.6	(F) -7.4	(A) -14.4	(E) -8.4
vh	(D) -10.2	(C) -16.3	(G) -9.3	(H) -3.3
8–10 years ($N=17$):				
hv	(B) -11.6	(F) -9.8	(A) -12.6	(E) -9.3
vh	(D) -6.5	(C) -4.2	(G) -4.2	(H) -1.4
Adults ($N=20$):				
hv	(B) -3.7	(F) -3.7	(A) -3.7	(E) -2.3
vh	(D) $+0.5$	(C) $+0.5$	(G) -3.7	(H) -0.5

TABLE 9a   Drawings of rods presented in the order A–H

	A	B	C	D	E	F	G	H	General Average
5– 6 years	-14.4	-18.6	-16.3	-10.2	-8.4	-7.4	-9.3	-3.3	-11.2
8–10 years	-12.6	-11.6	-4.2	-6.5	-9.3	-9.8	-4.2	-1.4	-7.9
Adults	-3.7	-3.7	$+0.5$	$+0.5$	-2.3	-3.7	-3.7	-0.5	-2.1

In connection with the higher degree of underestimation found here we might mention the phenomenon of perceptual overestimation of verticals. Once drawn, a vertical line would be overestimated perceptually, and would therefore seem subjectively the same length as the horizontal model, though actually shorter. Reciprocally, the vertical model (*C*, *D*, *G* and *H*) would be perceptually overestimated, so that the drawing of the corresponding horizontal would be longer than in the reverse case, though still too short. But it is impossible to decide whether we are dealing here with exclusively perceptual phenomena relating only to the perception of the model or of the completed drawing, or whether the mental image of a vertical includes a relatively overestimated length in the same way as perception. Perception overestimates verticals and underestimates horizontals, while the graphic image underestimates both – but the graphic image still underestimates less in the case of verticals than horizontals.

To take this comparison with the perception a little further, we carried out the same experiment on twenty subjects aged 6 years, and twenty aged 9 years. This time we used only forms *A* and *D*, and rods 200 mm long divided by thin black lines into five segments – $a = 50$ mm, $b = 20$ mm, $c = 40$ mm, $d = 60$ mm, and $e = 30$ mm. The aim was to find out whether there would be a general effect of increased length comparable to the Oppel–Kundt illusion. The subjects were asked to do two things: (1) to draw each segment in turn, and (2) to draw the whole length without taking any notice of the segments. In each group of twenty subjects, ten were asked question 1 first (order *A* 1, *A* 2, *D* 1, *D* 2), and ten were asked question 2 first (order *A* 2, *A* 1, *D* 2, *D* 1). The results are set out in Table 10.

TABLE 10 *Length of drawings (in mm) and errors (as %) for the segments (a–e) and their sum (S) – also for the whole rod (T) – after an imagined rotation of 90° (forms A and D)*

	a (50)	*b* (20)	*c* (40)	*d* (60)	*e* (30)	*S* (200)	*T* (200)	*Err. S*	*Err. T*
6 years:									
A 1–2	44	22	30	44	28	168	178	− 16·0	− 11·0
2–1	45	16	31	48	21	161	160	− 19·5	− 20·0
D 1–2	44	18	29	44	24	159	179	− 20·5	− 10·5
2–1	45	16	33	46	20	160	161	− 20·0	− 19·5
9 years:									
A 1–2	42	17	31	46	25	161	158	− 19·5	− 21·0
2–1	48	19	37	56	24	184	172	− 8·0	− 14·0
D 1–2	51	22	36	57	23	189	172	− 5·5	− 14·0
2–1	53	24	39	57	28	201	185	+ 0·5	− 7·5

The following facts emerge:
(1) The errors for the total length (*T*) are at least equally as great for the segmented rod as for the unsegmented rod in Table 9*a*; on

the whole in fact they are slightly greater, whether one compares them with the general averages of Table 9a (which takes into account the effects of practice), or whether one compares them with the particular averages for forms A and D.

(2) The segments themselves nearly always lead to underestimation: thirty-five cases of underestimation as against five overestimations (three of these were for the 2 cm segments, and two at 9 years for the 5 cm segments).

(3) The average underestimations of the segments do not seem to depend on their objective length, except that the 2 cm segment is on average the least underestimated: -4 per cent error (for an average length of 19·6 mm of the eight measurements), as against -17 to $-19·6$ per cent for the 30 to 60 mm lengths. Segment a (50 cm), however, yields -7 per cent, and for segments a and b it is necessary to take into account influence of the effect mentioned below in 4, which no doubt adds to the size factor in the case of the small segment b.

(4) On the other hand underestimation does appear to rise in accordance with the order of the drawings (a, b, c, d, e): -7 per cent, -4 per cent, -17 per cent, $-17·1$ per cent and $19·6$ per cent! This is a paradoxical fact in so far as it occurs in spite of repetition and practice. But it can be easily explained within the hypothesis that underestimation is due to an arresting before the terminal boundary point: the nearer the subject comes to this point the more inclined he is to underestimate the segments.

(5) As for the influence of the order of the questions (1–2 or 2–1: thus ST or TS), out of eight pairs there are four errors which are greater in the drawing executed first, three values which are almost equal, and one clearly exceptional case for D 1–2 at 9 years. This influence would thus be consistent with a learning effect.

(6) Finally, if S errors are greater than T errors at 6 years, the reverse is true at 9 years, and there is hardly any difference between the general averages: $-13·5$ and $-14·7$ taking the eight values of S and T, and $-15·3$ and $-15·2$ if one confines oneself to the drawings done first (S in order 1–2 and T in order 2–1).

The main point arising from this experiment is that a segmented rod does not give rise to lower underestimation of a non-segmented rod. It is rather the contrary that is the case. Now from the perceptual point of view the divided spaces are *over*estimated. It is true that if the divisions are not equal this perceptual effect is reduced because of internal over- and underestimation of the unequal segments, but if there are no very small segments (1–2 mm) it is not negative. The fact that dividing the length increases rather than decreases underestimation of the graphic image, taken in conjunction with what we have already seen, leads to the supposition that these underestimations constitute specific phenomena peculiar to the image, and that they are not merely transpositions of perceptual laws.

5. Gestural reproduction of paths of luminous points parallel to a straight line

In the foregoing experiments we have only been concerned with the reproduction of motionless lines by means of drawings – by means, that is, of a moving pencil stroke. This being so one might ask whether the boundary effect that we have observed is not primarily due to the contrast between the static model and the necessarily kinetic character of the pencil stroke. We have already seen (Tables 3 to 5) that if the rod's length is indicated statically by pointing, so that the emphasis is on the extremities and the distance separating them rather than on a drawing motion linking them, then the result is overestimation, not underestimation. It was important, therefore, to transpose the whole problem into kinetic terms in the case of the model to be copied, and into both kinetic and static terms for the copy itself.[11] The model used for this investigation was a luminous point moving at a distance of 2–3 cm above a motionless horizontal line 15 cm in length placed in the centre of the apparatus. The path of the luminous point either followed the fixed line (Figure 2, *A*), or started 5 cm before or after one of its ends in a variety of ways (see Figure 2, *B* to *F*, and *D2*, *D3*). The luminous point was moved from

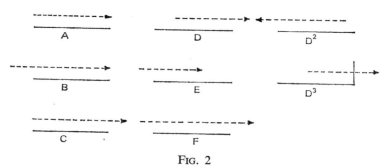

FIG. 2

left to right except in *D2*. In *D3* it crossed a vertical line 4 cm in length. The fixed lines were marked on frosted glass, behind which the point was moved. The luminous point and the reference line were the only things actually visible on the screen.

The child was asked to do the following three things as soon as

[11] The investigation was carried out in collaboration with Dr Juan Pascual-Leone, neurologist and Assistant Professor of Psychology.

the luminous point had completed its course (which was repeated for each question): (1) to show the extremities of the path traversed by the light with both forefingers simultaneously; (2) to show separately the starting point and then the finishing point; (3) to reproduce the path with the finger on the glass. The tests A to F were carried out in a systematically variable order after a preliminary random run-through. Tests $D2$ and $D3$ were studied separately as a control.

After examining about a hundred subjects aged between 5 and 9 years, we were able to select the following facts as being particularly instructive. First, we found no difference between the responses to the three separate questions. This shows that if the model is kinematic (length traversed) and not static (length of line), then static indication of the path's length between the forefingers does not differ from tracing it out in motion. The boundary effect will then occur independently of the subject's movements, in situations where he is required to compare a path to a fixed point of reference.

The second important point is that these boundary effects are the same in the purely gestural images involved here as in the type of situation examined earlier. Here are the reactions to tests $A–E$ and $D2–D3$ tabulated in terms of the initial point (I) and the terminal point (T):

TABLE 11 *Percentage of successes based on reactions to initial and terminal boundaries*
(As % of the responses)

	Tests														
	A		B		C		D		E		F		D2		D3
	I	T	I	T	I	T	I	T	I	T	I	T	I	T	I	T
5 years	87	89	27	89	51	40	9	49	49	25	51	40	26	48	17	20
6–7 years	93	99	31	84	72	50	49	54	46	32	63	55	26	64	67	42
8–9 years	97	96	59	89	88	73	35	90	62	29	79	88	26	84	22	66

First of all the terminal points T. The striking thing is that in all the tests where the luminous point does not stop at the end of the fixed line, but goes beyond it (C, D, F, $D2$ and $D3$), or stops before it (E), the subject fails (less than 75 per cent success) up to the age of 8 or 9 years, and in the case of E there is failure at all ages. As the successes are assessed on a broad basis (anything above 1 cm beyond the end of the line is counted, although the actual amount is 5 cm), this is a clear confirmation that the boundary effect is general.

Further, it is noteworthy that in $D3$, where the vertical line reinforces the effect of the boundary, the number of successes is reduced at all ages: 20 per cent as against 49 per cent in D at 5 years, 42 per cent as against 58 per cent at 6 to 7 years, and 66 per cent as against 90 per cent in D at 8 to 9 years!

The reactions to the initial points I. Successes are lower here than for T reactions in the case of B, where the stopping point of the light coincides with the end of the fixed line. They are still appreciably lower in the cases of D, $D2$ and $D3$ (except for the 6 to 7-year-olds in $D3$), where the point begins its course 5 cm along the fixed line. On the other hand, however, the successes for I are greater than those for T in the case of C, E and F (except for the 8- to 9-year-olds in F) and equivalent in A.

6. *The gestural reproduction of compound rectilinear movements*

We have seen that errors occur regularly in reproductive images of a fixed line, and even in gestural reproductions of the path of a luminous point. One should expect, therefore, to come across further difficulties when the subject is asked to reproduce movements, which, although rectilinear and very straightforward, involve two separate moving bodies. We shall see that this is indeed the case as we examine the image copies of various kinds of dual motion. We examined these in the form of gestural imitations executed first in the presence of the model, and second, immediately after the motion has stopped. In the first case we shall speak of 'simultaneous reproduction'. In the second we shall use the term 'consecutional images', to avoid using the word 'consecutive'. 'Consecutive images' have no connection with what we are concerned with here, and they are not in any case images in the sense of mental images.

Some time ago one of us took up Michotte's experiments on perceptual causality with Marc Lambercier, and observed during the course of these experiments how difficult it is for young children to succeed in reproducing the kinetic combinations used by Michotte, and which he termed *entraining, launching,* and *triggering.* We therefore undertook with A. Étienne a re-examination of this question, independently of any problems of the perception of causality. We asked the subject to imitate certain kinetic sequences by manipulating small blocks of wood. The movements to be imitated were likewise presented by means of small wooden cubes.

Two 1 cm cubes placed on the top edge of a screen are manipulated from behind by a system of wires along a path of 75 cm. The child watches these movements from a position facing the mid-point of the objects' path, seated at a large table. He is given two cubes similar to those used in the model. His task is to retrace as precisely as possible the 'road' followed by the 'motor cars', etc.

Some preliminary practice is indispensable (especially for the 3 to 4-year-olds!) to make sure the child really tries to copy the 'roads' he sees.

In the first procedure we tried the subject could see both the finishing and the starting point. This we corrected by covering the whole with a large sheet of paper as soon as the moving cubes had been stopped. This did not, however, prevent the younger children from concentrating almost exclusively on the finishing point. On the other hand, it did prevent them from making comparisons between simultaneous and consecutive copies, which we will mention later. Our final procedure, therefore, was to present a track fitted with a cover at each end. This ensures that start and finish will not be visible to the subject (in the cases where the cube starts in the middle of the track we sometimes used an extra cover). As some of the reproductions seemed too erratic, the experimenter did, however, indicate starting points for the subjects' cubes.[12] In most cases the child could correct his errors and when a copy failed he tried again. The child was asked to describe what he saw and did. If he made a wrong copy his copy was reproduced immediately after the presentation so that he could indicate whether the copy corresponded or not (in these instances the precaution was taken of bringing in a third person, so that the subject would not answer 'right' or 'wrong', thinking that the whole thing had been reproduced as usual by the experimenter).

The models to be reproduced were as follows:

(1) *Launching:* the red cube appears on the left and moves up to the blue cube in the centre; the red cube stops, and the blue cube moves to the right. (This is carried out with a cover in the centre, as the experiment is not concerned with causality or impact but with the reproduction of movements.

(2) *Entraining:* the red cube moves off from the left side, meets the blue cube in the centre and continues its movement pushing the blue cube before it (cover in centre).

(3) *Symmetry:* the red cube moves off from the left, the blue from the right; they meet in the centre and then return the way they came to their initial positions (cover in centre).

(4) *Overtaking:* both cubes move off from the right, the red one behind the blue one; under the cover in the centre the red cube overtakes and moves on ahead to the left.

(5) *Crossing:* the red cube moves off from the left, the blue from the right; they cross behind the cover in the centre and continue their respective paths.

(6) *Launching without central cover:* as for 1, except that only the end points are covered.

(7) *Launching with reversing of red cube:* the red cube moves off from the left, meets the blue in the centre; the blue cube moves to the right while the red returns to the left (no central cover).

---

[12] Later controls showed that those who made successful copies could manage without this aid, and that those who failed when there was no fixed starting point failed also when they were given a fixed point. The precaution was therefore unnecessary. But the difficulties met when it was used are thus all the more remarkable.

(8) *Entraining* as for 2 but without cover in centre.
(9) *Overtaking* as for 4 but without cover in centre.
(10) *Crossing* as for 5 but without cover in centre.
(11) *Launching with reversing of red cube* as for 7, with the difference that the red cube does not reverse until the blue cube has completed its motion.
(12) *Double crossing*, without central cover and with each cube returning in the direction from which it came when it reaches the end point.

Finally, we made use of some extra procedures – mainly to compare a motor model (the child's hands holding the cubes guided by the experimenter) with a purely motor imitation (a curtain excluding visual regulation), and to compare the simultaneous copies with the copies done immediately after the model has been shown (as in questions 1 – 12).

I. Let us begin by examining the initial degree of difficulty presented by the twelve different models studied in relation to fifteen subjects aged 4 years. Table 12 gives the average successes established for the first trial and for the total number of subsequent trials for each test. The ranking of the tests is on the basis of success in the first trial.

TABLE 12   *Successes for reproduction of models at 4 years old*

(As % of the responses)

Tests	1	2	3	4	5	6
1st Trial	13	50	77	27	50	7
Total	33	58	85	36	58	43
Ranking	XI	V(=VI)	I	VIII	VI(=V)	XII

Tests	7	8	9	10	11	12
1st Trial	15	62	36	73	22	67
Total	30	70	63	82	55	84
Ranking	X	IV	VII	II	IX	III

Certain clear results emerge from this table.

(1) Apart from the crossing test, which comes V–VI in rank with central cover and II without it, one sees firstly that tests executed with and without the central cover yield results occurring together on the success scale. Thus the launching test comes at XI with and at XII without the cover; the entraining test comes at V–VI and IV, and the overtaking test at VIII and VII. This enables us to establish a general order for the tests as a whole.

(2) The most easily reproduced images are clearly those entailing symmetry, whether simple as in 3, or as in the crossing 5, or the double crossing 12. These rate I, II and III (except for the crossing with cover, which rates V and VI).

(3) Next the two cases of entraining (2 and 8), which rate V–VI and IV.

(4) Then the overtaking (4 and 9), rating VIII and VII.

(5) Finally, the most difficult models to reproduce – launching (1, 6, 7 and 11), at IX to XII. It is interesting, however, to see that the launching with reversing of the red cube (7 and 11) comes higher on the scale (X and IX), this model having a partial symmetry.

The central problem, then, raised by these facts is this. Is the hierarchical order due simply and solely to the actual complexity of the models (just as it is harder to copy a pentagon than a square)? Or is it due to the intervention between model and copy of some kind of fore-image resulting from the assimilation of the external model to some internal model and acting as an anticipatory scheme for the required gestures? Now we can doubtless explain why more difficulty is encountered in the overtaking than in the entraining by pointing to the complexity of the change of order in the former. And the ease with which symmetries are reproduced, even in the complex case of double crossing (III), naturally calls to mind the most pregnant sensori-motor schemes, the 'good motor forms' (such as crossing the arms, synkinesis, etc.).

But in this case a preliminary problem arises which had claimed our attention earlier when we took up Michotte's experiments on the very small children along with Lambercier. What are the reasons for the difficulties encountered in reproducing asymmetric dual movements such as launching, and for the significance of symmetrical movements? Are the reasons perceptual or motor? From our present point of view, however – that of the mental image considered as an internalized imitation prolonging actual imitation – the question is less urgent. For, if the causes are perceptual they could relate only to difficulties of exploration and not to field effects. Now the exploration of a complex form by means of eye movements following contours constitutes a particular case of imitation in the broad sense of the term. Our problem is therefore, to find out whether any fore-images involved in the facts observed are due: (1) to a correct visual imitation (i.e. exploration) of the models inadequately translated in the gestural imitation; (2) to inadequate visual imitation, or exploration, expressed as it stands in gestural imitation; or (3) to visual imitation and gestural imitation both inadequate to the external model because co-ordinated according to the same laws.[13]

To try to resolve these two problems we shall now go on to four different kinds of analysis: analysis of errors, analysis of develop-

[13] Cf. A. Rey's experiments on the representation of the movement of the fore-finger marking out a figure (mentioned in our Introduction), in which he observed oculo-manual co-ordinations of varying complexity.

ment according to age, comparative analysis of successes with visual perception and with tactile-kinaesthetic perception, and finally a comparative analysis of simultaneous and consecutive imitations.

II. The first thing to note is the striking fact that 60 per cent of the subjects made errors which introduced symmetrical movement into the reproduction of one or more models when none was in fact involved. Now the test in which the subjects most often succeeded was test 3, which presents two phases of symmetrical motion, and which is perceptually fairly complex. (Several adults pointed out that the movements in this test could be confused with a crossing motion if the subject did not pay attention to the colours of the two cubes as they go behind and come out from the central cover. This means some difficulty for the child.) There are two possibilities here. Does the subject perceive the dual symmetry of test 3 inaccurately, but react with a good motor form that is equivalent to an accurate copy, without being aware of the correspondence? Or does he perceive the symmetries accurately as a result of the convergence of the symmetry in eye movements with the good motor forms in the gesture? It is instructive to compare the following three facts in this connection: (a) only one child actually confused the dual symmetry of test 3 with the crossing movement with cover 5, whereas the adults pointed out that such a confusion was possible; (b) the distinction between the dual symmetry of test 3, the crossing without cover, and dual crossing motion is on average good, since these three tests rank at positions I, II and III (which are very close together as percentages); (c) on the other hand, 42 per cent of the subjects in test 5 (crossing with cover) confused this movement with dual symmetrical movement (test 3). This explains the lower position, V – VI, for success in test 5. Thus, until more extensive information is available, it appears that the symmetry in test 3 is relatively correctly perceived, and that it is in fact the crossing motion with cover (test 5) which is less well structured perceptually, since the crossing motion without cover (test 10) rates at II.

Turning now to the next best success score – the two cases of entraining (tests 2 and 8, at V–VI and IV) – we see that the sequences in question are easy to structure perceptually, since the direction is single, since the red cube is in fixed relationship to the blue, and since there is no change in order. Even so, entraining shows only 62–70 per cent of successes without cover and 50–58 per cent with it. In the latter case the errors arise predominantly from the substitution of traction for the entraining (17 per cent), which is no doubt derived from an interpretative analogy encouraged by the cover (although the same sometimes occurs when the cover is not used). Other errors raise the question of symmetry again. Symmetry is in fact the predominant cause of failure in the case of entraining without cover (15 per cent). Our problem thus comes up again. Is this fore-image which distorts reproduction due to perceptual factors, or motor factors, or to both at once? Some subjects at first produce a symmetry and then spontaneously correct themselves in the next attempt. Here it is possible to argue that a perception that can be rectified so quickly could be correct all the time, and that the error was due to a faulty motor connection (to an assimilation, that is, to the motor scheme easiest to execute), possibly favoured by lack of attention. But in other cases the subject persists and still cannot properly distinguish his own movement, reproduced for him by the experimenter, from that of the model. It can therefore be said that the error is due to the difficulty of translating what has been correctly perceived into an equivalent image, and that the absence of such an image accounts for the failure of motor reproduction. But this provides us with no new solution. This inadequately elaborated image is in fact merely a fore-image, considered as a successful or unsuccessful imitative outline. Now this imitation deficiency may exist at the level of visual exploration, it may result from the gestural copy only, or it may be related to both at once.

In so far as the subject is unable properly to distinguish his copy from the model, it would seem reasonable to consider the third possibility. This does not, of course, exclude the possibility that the same kinetic model might be much easier for the subject to structure if it were presented on a track 15–20 cm rather than 75 cm long.

In the overtaking tests (9 and 4, at VII and VIII) the majority of errors occur as a result of oversimplification, the change in order being suppressed and replaced by a constant or even in some cases zero gap between the two cubes.

As for the four launching tests (1, 6, 7 and 11, at IX and X with reversing of red cube, and XI and XII for simple launching), it goes without saying that the launchings with reversing of the red cube produce errors tending towards total symmetry. This was so for 54 per cent of the subjects in test 7 in which the second phase is in fact symmetrical, and for 22 per cent in test 11, where the red cube does not return to starting point until after the blue one has stopped. The other errors were either over-simplifications with one phase of the movement being suppressed, or else arbitrary distortions (successive displacements in any direction). Analysis of each of these errors makes it possible to distinguish different levels. The two extremes are: (a) inadequacy of perceptual structuring, so that the subject is unable to distinguish the model from his own copies as reproduced for him by the experimenter (this is especially true for the errors consisting of arbitrary distortions, though also for some cases of complete symmetry); and (b) correct perception but failure of motor co-ordination (this is especially the case for errors of symmetry or over-simplification; the child may go on to correct himself, he may persist in his error although able to distinguish the model from his copy, or he may be able to make the distinction to begin with but not subsequently). In the case of launchings without reversing of the red cube (1 and 6), one cannot account for why there are so few successes in the first (rates at XI), either by reference to the presence of the central cover or by the fact that it was the first of the twelve tests to be performed, since the success score in test 6 is even lower (at XII). The most frequent errors are alteration of the temporal sequence (20 per cent and 22 per cent), introduction of two symmetrical phases or of crossing motions (22 per cent), change of direction of one of the moving bodies, which may bring in semi-symmetry (73 per cent and 17 per cent), and various arbitrary complications. When the models were compared to the copies reproduced by the experimenter, there was as before a range of reactions varying from insufficiency in perceptual structuring (inability to distinguish model from inaccurate copy) to lack of co-ordination between accurate perception and motor functions.

III. Before going on to the question of development with age, we should like to mention an experiment carried out with ten subjects between the ages of 3,2 and 5,4 years of age in which a comparison was made between reproduction after tactile-kinaesthetic perception and reproduction after visual perception.

In the first part of the experiment, the child passes his hands under a screen, and takes hold of a cube between his thumb and forefinger. The experimenter executes the movements, guiding the subject's hands. The child is asked to reproduce the movements which he has just perceived by tactile-kinaesthetic means. This is also done behind the screen, and thus without any visual control. In the second part of the experiment he is allowed to see the movements and reproduces them in the way described earlier in this section.[14] In the third part, which varies from subject to subject, the experimenter guides the child's hands over any error he has made. Then this erroneous copy and the correct corresponding model are presented visually by means of the usual apparatus. The subject is asked which of the two visual sequences is the same as the tactile-kinaesthetic sequence.

The following sequences were used:

(1) The cube starts off on the left and moves as far as the centre, where it meets the blue cube, which it entrains to the right.

(2) The red cube starts off on the left; in the centre it meets the blue cube which then moves off to the right (launching).

[14] A fortnight's interval separates the first and second parts of the experiment

(3) Simple crossing motion (along the whole length).

(4) The blue cube moves from left to centre, and the red cube from centre to right.

(5) Overtaking.

(6) Launching with reversing of the red cube to starting-point, the blue cube moving from centre to right.

(7) Symmetry (as 3 in the preceding series of tests, but this time without the central cover).

There is no purpose in giving here in detail results with which we shall be dealing again in IV. Our immediate concern is to show the relationships between the tactile-kinaesthetic and the visual results. These correlations are calculated on the basis of the total number of trials, except in those cases where there is immediate success in one of the series and only gradual success in the other. In this way, using the average of the total number of tests, we find the following:

50 per cent success in both series;

12 per cent failure in both series, with the same errors in both;

2 per cent failure in both series, but with different errors;

24 per cent superior reproductions in the tactile-kinaesthetic series;

12 per cent superior reproductions in the visual series.

In all there is a clear 62 per cent correspondence between the two series, and 36 per cent difference in one direction or another. Symmetrical and crossing movements have the more favourable responses in both cases and the entraining movement elicits a better response in the tactile-kinaesthetic series than in the visual series. Launching occasions the same errors in both cases. Generally speaking, it may be said that the tactile-kinaesthetic series scores slightly higher than the visual series, if we take into account *inter alia* the fact that the visual tests necessarily come second, and the fact that they may in consequence draw not on memories but, in spite of the fortnight's interval, on practice.

IV. To examine the development of the kinetic reproductions according to age, we used six out of the seven tests described above. We omitted the overtaking movement, as change of order may constitute a special factor. In the visual series we removed the aid – not in any case very helpful – which served to determine the starting-points. This made the two series more homogeneous. Ten subjects from each of three age-groups (4, 5 and 6 years) were tested, with a fortnight's interval between the tactile-kinaesthetic and the visual series. Table 13 shows for each test (*a*) the immediate successes, and (*b*) the successes with spontaneous correction after repetition, no other assistance being given. (In the table immediate and subsequent successes are indicated by 'imm.' and 'subsq.')

41

TABLE 13 *Successes (as % of subjects) for tactile-kinaesthetic (I) and visual (II) tests*

	4 years (N = 10)				5 years (N = 10)				6 years (N = 10)			
	I		II		I		II		I		II	
	Imm.	Subsq.	Imm.	Subsq.	Imm.	Subsq.	Imm.	Subsq.	Imm.	Subsq.	Imm.	Subsq.
1′	0	30	10	30	20	30	40	60	20	80	40	60
2′	10	10	10	20	10	40	20	60	40	70	80	80
3′	70	80	40	50	100	100	90	100	40	70	80	80
4′	60	70	20	30	50	70	50	80	100	100	100	100
6′	0	10	10	10	10	30	70	90	40	60	80	90
7′	80	100	60	60	70	80	80	80	50	70	90	100
Average	36·6	50·0	25·0	33·3	43·3	58·3	58·3	78·3	56·6	78·3	80·8	88·3

These results are a further demonstration of what we have already seen in III (we did not use the same subjects for the 4 to 5 year stage) – namely, that at 4 years the tactile-kinaesthetic series scores higher than the visual series by 3 to 1, that at 5 years the reverse is true in the same ratio, and that at 6 years the success scores tend to equalize.

This reversal throws light on the question of the part played by perceptual factors (visual exploration where the outline of the kinetic figure in question is traced out in a sort of oculo-motor imitation) and by motor factors (motor reproduction imitating the perceived kinetic figure) in the fore-image's failure adequately to anticipate a copy, or in its success in the case of symmetrical forms. The fact that tactile-kinaesthetic perception produces better motor reproduction at the age of four than visual perception goes to prove either that visual structuring is inadequate at this age, or that there is some lack of co-ordination between vision and gestural motor functions. But, since at 5 years the ratio is reversed, instead of being equalled out, there must have been some development in visual structuring as well as in the vision-gesture co-ordination – otherwise we would find equal progress in the tactile-kinaesthetic series which depends directly on the gestural motor functions. These facts then would seem to favour the conclusion that there is some inadequacy in visual structuring at 4 years – though this does not of course exclude the other factors.

More generally speaking, however, these facts seem to support the thesis maintained by one of us concerning Michotte's perceptual causality. According to this thesis visual perception of causality derives, by means of assimilation, from the tactile-kinaesthetic perception of causality.[15] It is in fact probable that a large number of perceptual structurations in the child are elaborated within a context of progressive co-ordination of the tactile-kinaesthetic and visual ranges (based no doubt on the constancy of shapes and sizes), and that it is only later that vision becomes completely

[15] In the reply which he kindly addressed to us ('Théorie de la causalité phénoménale, Nouvelles perspectives' in *Causalité, permanence et réalité phénoménales*, Louvain, 1962), Michotte declares that the question remains open in the absence of direct proof, and appeals to and calls for indirect indications. We think we have one here!

independent, after a whole legacy of tactile-kinaesthetic experience has been acquired. The present facts seem to show that this process also includes the formation of fore-images. This would explain once again why the tests for crossing and symmetrical movements (3' and 7') are peculiarly successful (see Table 13).

V. It remains to make a comparison between what we shall call 'simultaneous' reproductions obtained step by step as the model is in action, and 'consecutional' reproductions carried out (as up till now) immediately after the model has been presented. Table 14 gives the overall results for the six tests used for Table 13 (visual presentation):

TABLE 14 *Comparing successes for simultaneous and consecutional reproductions*
(As % of the responses)[16]

	Simultaneous reproduction		Consecutional reproduction	
	Immediate	*Subsequent*	*Immediate*	*Subsequent*
3 years ($N=$ 7)	38	64	0	0
4 years ($N=21$)	64	81	15	35
5 years ($N=12$)	77	97	58	93
6 years ($N=10$)	100	100	80	100

The great difference between the two types of reproduction is that the consecutional type has to reconstitute the form of the movements as a whole after they have stopped, whereas simultaneous reproduction proceeds step by step before completion of the presentation (and thus requires no overall perceptual structuring). The decrease in the divergence between success scores for the two types of reproduction is thus a measure of the progress made in the formation of the image from the fore-image. It can be seen that there is still a considerable difference at 3 and 4 years, that it diminishes noticeably at 5 years, and disappears almost completely at 6 years. There is striking correspondence here with the inversion of the relations between the tactile-kinaesthetic and the visual as seen in Table 13.

7. *The gestural reproduction of curvilinear movements*

In the last investigation we were concerned with rectilinear motions. Clearly it was required to go on to consider the reproduction of

---

[16] The 'immediate' columns, it will be remembered, correspond to the reactions considered before any correction made by the subject, the 'subsequent' columns to the final result considered after repetitions and spontaneous corrections.

curvilinear movements in a similar way. We did not in fact do so till later. However, when we were studying the way children at 4 to 8 years imagine the path of three beads threaded on a rod rotated through 180° and 360°, we found that there was considerable difficulty (only 6–22 per cent successes at 7 years, depending on the procedure: Tables 61 to 63), and that the 4 to 6-year-old subjects produced some very curious figures (rectilinear strokes, near squares, random curves), although 62 per cent from 4½ years understood well enough the change in the beads' orders. This led us to wonder whether there was not some systematic difficulty in imagining curvilinear paths. Hence the present inquiry, which, as well as settling the question, brought up certain other worthwhile facts.[17]

The apparatus consists of a wooden frame with a horizontal axis and four metal wires each with a different curvature (see Figure 3). Threaded along these wires are three movable objects, each with a different shape and colour (red oval, blue triangle and yellow circle). They are manipulated by rods. All this is set up behind a pane of frosted glass, so that the child can see the axis and the moving objects but not the fixed wires. The subject is given three similar coloured shapes attached to rods. His task is simply to reproduce on the screen the movements he has just perceived. As two or even three shapes are moved at the same time, two methods of reproduction are used: (a) which we shall call *successive*, when the child moves one shape after another, and (b) which we will term *synchronized*, when the experimenter, after showing the paths of two or three of the shapes moving together, reproduces (behind the screen) the movement of one of the two (or of two of the three), while the child simultaneously reproduces the movement of the second (or third) shape. We shall make an essential distinction between the reproductions with a visible finishing point where the model remains in place after completing its path, and the reproductions with an 'invisible' finishing point, where the moving shape disappears after the movement. Finally, we shall distinguish between reproductions with a 'free' starting-point – where the starting-point is not corrected for any error, and reproductions with corrected starting points in which the child is taken back to the correct point if he makes an error.

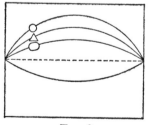

Fig. 3

[17] The investigation was carried out in collaboration with E. Schmid-Kitsikis.

As a control the experimenter may run through a test again in slow-motion, or stop at certain points along the path before going on.

The trajectories we used are shown in Figure 4, P being the basic one:

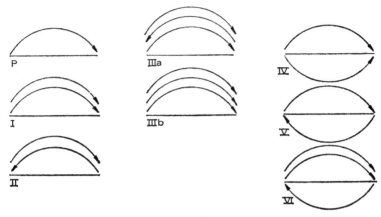

FIG. 4

The main interest of the results of this investigation lies in the qualitative nature of the errors, but in order to make things clear, we give the percentage of successes for fourteen subjects aged 3,2 to 4,11 years, twenty subjects aged 5,0 to 5,10 years, and ten subjects aged 6,0 to 6,10 years.

TABLE 15 *Percentage of successes for synchronized reproduction with invisible finishing point*
(Figures in brackets – with *visible* finishing-point)

	P	*I*	*II*	*III*	*IV*	*V*
3–4 years	50 (66)	18 (100)	40 (66)	20 (80)	43 (50)	33 (100)
5 years	100	68	75	50	53	67
6 years	100	100	100	40	80	80

Column III shows the average number of successes in tests III*a* and III*b*.

It can be seen that, except where the relation 'between' is involved (in III), these tests are successful at 6 years, as in Table 13. In particular, the crossing motions (II and V) are correctly reproduced from 5 years upwards (75 per cent and 67 per cent), as is the crossing motion 3′ in Table 13. It thus seems that it is hardly any more difficult to reproduce curvilinear than rectilinear paths. As far as the relation 'between' is concerned its relative difficulty is worth noting. The subjects did not maintain the middle position of the second path between the first and third, and even in successive reproductions 80 per cent of the children failed in this test (III). We shall meet this problem in a different form when we come to deal with the rotation of the beads (Chapter Four, section 8, Table 65).

Let us turn to the errors arising in these tests. While we are on the subject of rotation of beads, which in fact led us on to the present investigation, it is worth mentioning the *individual* errors – those errors, that is, which are not systematic considered in isolation, but which are none the less numerous taken together. We found that these simple reproductions of a perceived moving body show the curious aberrant forms which we shall describe more fully in Chapter Four, section 8, in connection with kinetic anticipation (where there is no preliminary perception since the wire and the beads are put in a tube, so that the tube alone remains visible during the rotation). These forms include straight lines, near squares following the frame of the apparatus,[18] sinusoidal curves, spirals of various sizes, figures of eight, hyperbolic and parabolic curves, and so on. Thus it seems that it is at the copy stage, in the reproductive not the anticipatory images, and even in the gestural fore-images, that these strange shapes appear.

We turn now to the systematic errors. First, one which concerns the starting point of the movements. For boundary effects, which are characterized by a concern not to go beyond the end point (for examples, see sections 1–5 of this chapter), are generally also associated with fairly constant neglect of the starting point. It is remarkable, for instance, that in the present tests none of the 3 to 4-year-olds took any notice of the actual starting points. If the end points were hidden they chose odd and arbitrary starting points. If the objects remained visible at the finishing point, all the subjects at this age began by reproducing them, and then went on to make inferences from this about the starting point. At 5 years the errors are fewer. They consist mainly in placing the starting point either at the wrong side, or on the right side but too far above or too far below the horizontal axis, or else actually on the axis but not at the end of it; sometimes it is placed at random above or below it. Finally, the 4-year-old's reproduction of the paths is not modified if his starting point is corrected; but at 5 years the child is able to make use of help of this kind.

Considering now the finishing points, there is a striking difference at 3 to 4 years between the results obtained when the objects dis-

[18] One of the younger subjects even climbed on to a chair in order to reach the top of the glass and point along three of its sides as if this was the way the shape had moved!

appear at the finishing point and those obtained when the objects remain where they are (18 per cent and 33 per cent as against 100 per cent in tests I and V, 20 per cent as against 80 per cent in test III, and so on). This contrast, which is less marked, however, at 5 years and disappears almost entirely at 6 years, is somewhat like the difference at 3 to 4 years between simultaneous and consecutional reproduction (see section 6, Table 14). In the present case all the reproductions are carried out immediately after the model has been seen. But in those tests where the objects remain visible at the finishing point, the perception has the same part to play as in the simultaneous copy (Table 14). This also shows the extent to which imaginal representation or gestural imitation of the trajectories is organized in terms of the final positions.

The important point concerning the paths of the moving objects themselves is the contrast, similar in some respects to the one just mentioned, between successive reproductions (one shape moved after another) and synchronized reproductions (the experimenter moves one of the shapes while the child reproduces the course of the other). In the first case the striking fact is the total absence at 3 to 4 years, and partial absence at 5 years, of any attempt at relating the movements, particularly where the relation between the path of an object and the one preceding it is concerned. For example, in test I, one of the shapes is thought to describe a semi-circle, and the other a straight line which does not coincide with the extremities of the first path. At 5 years, however, 40 per cent of the subjects do take account of these relative positions. The most difficult test in this respect was found to be number III – 80 per cent failed in the successive reproduction of the object. Instead of keeping the middle shape in position 'between' the other two, the subjects at this level still allow the second path to overlap the first and third.

As one would expect, the results are better for synchronized reproduction (see Table 15). But there are still errors of orientation, of making the paths cut across one another (which of course they do not either in II or in V), of position in relation to the axis, and of substituting straight lines for curves (with all the variations mentioned above – near square, etc.).

Finally, however early these gestural reproductions may be (most children acquiring them between 5 and 6 years), imitation, as we have shown in section 6, is not immediate. On the contrary, like the internalized image itself, it rests on the formation of relations on the one hand between starting and finishing points (the latter being the more significant and even governing the whole trajectory) and on the other hand between the forms themselves (both internally amongst themselves and externally with the frame). The problem in fact is this. The trajectories are events taking place in time and in order to reproduce them it is necessary to co-ordinate successive perceptions with the corresponding movements. When it is a question, as here, of consecutional imitation (and not simultaneous imitation), the former are as it were already 'extinguished' when the latter are executed. The problem for the fore-image is to arrive at an executional anticipation early enough, so that the perceptions will not have been forgotten at the moment when they are required to be imitated (either by gesture or imaginal representation).

8. *Conclusion*

The most striking fact arising from the various observations set forth in this chapter is the existence of 'fore-images', or anticipatory schemes of the imitative element. These come into play both in the tentative graphic or gestural motion made by the child before he puts pencil to paper or traces a line with his finger, and in the reproduction of external movements presented to him as models. These fore-images are manifested in the underestimations observed in the former and in the confusion of types of movement observed in the latter. They constitute the transitional terms between physical or external imitation and internalized imitation or image. In Table 14 we saw how the transition from one to the other is consolidated between 3 and 6 years.

Now the fore-images are involved even at the level of the direct copy, and they raise two problems which will confront us again and again in connection with the image proper. That is to say, in connection not just with images which are copies of simultaneously perceived objects, but with those images that constitute an evocation of not actually perceived objects. It is a question of whether the mental image is symbolic or objective in character, and of the nature of its relations with concepts. We may distinguish perceived objects, images of the objects, and the concepts by means of which the objects can be characterized (described or interpreted). The fundamental problem then that a genetic study of the image might be expected to resolve (and it is a problem that also needs to be raised in connection with the fore-image and image-copies or direct copies) may be formulated in the following way. Either percepts, images and concepts are generated in linear succession, i.e. the image derives from the percept and the concept from the percept and the image, so that the latter has the status of objective knowledge and is as valid in this respect as the other terms of the series. Or there is some relation of interaction between perception and concept, the latter taking certain data from the former, but in turn enriching it with elements external to it (structurations forming as soon as sensori-motor schemes or action-concepts come into play). In this case the image would not be merely a direct derivative from perception, but an active imitation of it, sharing some of the forms of organization of the concept. It would not be related by a necessary causal link to the properties of the perceived object, but would act as a symbol. However, the symbol is a 'motivated' signifier rather than an 'arbitrary' sign – that is, it is based on some resemblance to the thing symbolized. This being so, the process of active imitation, which is what constitutes the symbol, could, if it played a useful role in conceptual representation, come near, asymptotically as it were, to being an exact copy. But the difference would be that it would not be an automatic copy in an inevitable process – as it would by the first interpretation according to which everything derives direct from the object. Rather it would be a deliberate copy, an imitation which is both conscious and conscientious.

Naturally we will need more than the fore-images analysed in this chapter to enable us to decide which of these two possible solutions is correct. But they do provide us with some indications to start with. For instance, it is a remarkable fact that in the copies of a straight line (section 2), where one would not expect anything to come between perception of the line and its mental image ('internal model') or its graphic image, the errors do not show a symmetrical distribution of + and − as they would if they depended merely on the size as perceived. They are in fact determined by the desire to avoid going beyond the end boundary point of the line. This concern is not far removed from those lying behind the preoperational concepts found in ordinal estimation of lengths. This partial link between concept and image means that the image can be said to be symbolic, since even in a graphic copy the mental image constitutes not so much an attempt to produce a totally adequate representation of the thing 'seen', as an idea used by the subject to express the characteristics of what he 'sees'. Luquet demonstrated this some time ago. This symbolization may be seen quite clearly in the extreme cases in which the subject is content to represent lines of 10–15 cm by lines only a few centimetres long. It is even clearer when the child is imitating movements. At 4 to 5 years the child will frequently translate the model into a form which in all probability he does not perceive as identical, but which he conceives as being similar in virtue of various analogies. From this approximate symbolism there is a whole range of intermediate types right up to a totally adequate symbolism; but a congruous and exact copy still has its symbolic function.

CHAPTER THREE

Kinetic Reproductive Images

In the previous chapter we examined some examples of immediate reproductive images, or copy images, without going beyond mental fore-images. We now need to go on to look at mental images proper, and we shall do so from three different points of view: from the point of view of the level at which they are formed, the way they are elaborated, and their degree of fidelity.

It would seem right to start with reproductive images of static configurations, since we know that these have an early role in symbolic play and memory, and that the emergence of both these activities coincides with that of the symbolic function. The relationship between these images and the mnemic structure is in itself a considerable problem far exceeding our present field of study. In any case the static reproduction images are of interest only in their inceptive forms, or in their general relation to perception and action. The former are dealt with in the discussion of examples of copy images contained in sections 1 and 2, Chapter Two. To the latter we shall devote a special chapter later (Chapter Seven). It will be best to postpone analysing this question until we are in a position to utilize the information to be gathered in the meantime concerning the part played by actions and operations in the evolution of kinetic or transformation images.

We shall therefore begin by examining the kinetic reproductive images from the three points of view mentioned above. We have two kinds of data for this. Chapter Two, section 4, was concerned with the graphic image of a rod moving from a vertical to a horizontal position, or vice versa. This image was the image of the result of a movement (thus *RKP*). Two questions arise from this. First, does this image imply or involve images of the movement itself in its kinetic stages (thus *RKM*)? In this connection we investigated the imagination of the intermediate positions between the initial vertical position and terminal horizontal position of a rod. Second, in the tests described in Chapter Two, sections 1 and 4, the terminal position presented no difficulty, because it was shown to the subject in advance. The question is: given very elementary and well-known movements (e.g. a translation), would the image of the result of a displacement (*RKP*) still be as easy to form, if the result were *not* shown in advance? To answer this we shall now study the simple displacement of one square in relation to another with various starting positions.

1. *Translation of a square relative to another*

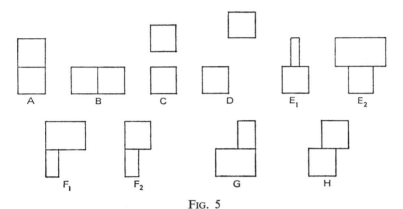

FIG. 5

One square was placed above a second in the horizontal plane (A in Figure 5).[1] The child was asked to imagine a slight shift from left to right of the upper square to give the staggered position shown in H. It would be hard to find a more elementary example, drawing on less learnt knowledge. Day-to-day experience furnishes situations of this kind right from the sensori-motor level preceding language. It is of some interest, therefore, to establish whether this kind of image can be obtained at any age, or whether its formation is late and complex. With F. Frank and T. Vinh-Bang we discovered that in fact it is not until 7 years that there is a successful response in 75 per cent of subjects.

The fact that it is formed late raises a preliminary question concerning classification. Is the image under consideration a reproductive image or an anticipatory image of movement? In fact our analysis will show that the demarcation between the two categories is arbitrary, and that even when the imagined movement is known for certain, the evocation of its result presupposes a complex reconstitution which not only involves anticipation of the execution but also what might be called a *reanticipation* of the content. The differ-

[1] We shall speak of 'superposition' for this Figure A, as opposed to 'superimposition' in Figure 7.

51

ence between what we shall call kinetic reproductive images (Chapter Three) and what we shall call kinetic anticipatory images (Chapter Four), is simply the difference between image content more frequently observed in everyday perception and the content less frequently observed. It is necessary, however, methodologically, to draw a formal distinction between a simple reproduction of something known and an anticipation of new combinations, even though experiment later shows that in fact the simplest kinetic reproductions are analogous to anticipations.

I. *The basic experiment* The following method was used. The child was presented with two pieces of cardboard 5 cm square, superposed and contiguous (A in Figure 5). First of all we made sure that he was able to draw this kind of configuration. Then he was asked to draw the figure resulting when the upper square is moved slightly from left to right, while the bottom one stops as it is (H). Finally, he was asked to choose the right figure from a number of prepared drawings, including the correct representation and some examples of habitual errors. Two precautions needed to be taken. Firstly, only a few drawings at a time should be presented, even if this means a subsequent comparison of drawings chosen from the sub-groups. Secondly, if several figures are chosen as correct, it is necessary to ask for 'the best one'. As the choices made seemed to imply a perseveration from the subject's preliminary drawing we preceded to a systematic control and examined the choices in separate groups. (As it turned out our fears were groundless – that is to say, the choices remained the same.) After the questions, the subject was asked to copy the correct figure H to make sure that he was capable of producing such a drawing.

Let us take a look first at the results yielded by this direct copy of the correct figure H. Although it comes at the end of the experiment this question conditions our interpretation of the spontaneous drawings done previously. If the child fails here it would of course be impossible to take his spontaneous drawing as an adequate indication of his mental image. Further, examination of this copy provides us with another example of an immediate reproductive image or copy-image, and thus enables us to check its relation with the image proper which is the object of the present test. Below, then, are the results for the copy of figure H yielded by eighty-four subjects aged between 4 years and 5,11 years.

TABLE 16   *Direct copy of figure H*
(As % of the subjects)[2]

Ages	4 years ($N=19$)	5,0 to 5,5 ($N=46$)	5,6 to 5,11 ($N=19$)
Successes	21% (42)	55% (68)	79%

[2] The percentage for 4 years and for 5,0 to 5,5 years are for the completely correct drawings – i.e. those in which the lower side of the top square and the

These results are interesting from two points of view. (1) To start with, they confirm a fact which is very well known, but which is worth recalling in any study of the mental image. It is not enough simply to perceive a structure to be able to copy it, that is, to imitate it in a drawing – even though it may be no more complicated than the two partially superposed squares. The copy presupposes, therefore, an anticipatory fore-image which decomposes and recomposes the model, and guides its realization in the drawing. (We have already seen in Chapter Two that this is necessarily the case even for a single straight line.) (2) Concerning the fore-image of the partially superposed squares, three important facts may be noted: (*a*) the fore-image is elaborated only very gradually; (*b*) it precedes by approximately two years the formation of the mental image proper, that is, the evocational image (since the copy is successful in 75 per cent of cases from $5\frac{1}{2}$ years, the image at $7\frac{1}{2}$ years on average – see Table 17); (*c*) moreover, before success is achieved, it gives rise to errors which are of exactly the same type as those which affect the mental image itself, persisting, in this last case, till 7 years and above. Indeed, if we attempt to classify the drawings obtained for Table 16 into the different categories of Figure 5, we find only four subjects aged 4 years and two aged 5 to 5,5 years who do not fit into these categories. These subjects substitute for the squares various kinds of triangle, closed figures, completely dissociated figures (cf. C), or dissociated figures joined by lines. The classifiable errors all came under the types A–D (15·8 per cent at 4 years and 8·6 per cent at 5 years), E1–E2 (0 at 4 years and 4·4 per cent at 5 years) and F–G (21·2 per cent at 4 years and 14·8 per cent at 5 years). This convergence of copy-images and later evocational images is of some theoretical interest, since it would confirm that the 'fore-images' (referred to already in Chapter Two) obey laws analogous to those of the mental images themselves.

The results obtained for imaginal representation itself as it appears in the evocational drawings of the child and in his choice of prepared drawings are given in Table 17 overleaf.

First of all there is remarkable agreement between correct drawings (H) and correct choice from prepared drawings, where one would have expected the choice to have a distinct lead over the drawings. This fact shows that the infrequency of adequate responses before 7 years is not – at least within the limits outlined in Table 16 – due to the difficulty of drawing figure H, but

upper side of the bottom square have a common segment. The percentages in brackets are for the drawings in which this common segment is reduced to a point (i.e. those in which the apex of the bottom left-hand corner of the top square coincides with that of the top right-hand corner of the bottom square).

rather to the inadequacy of visualization by means of mental images.

Now this inadequacy derives from certain quite obvious causes. When the child is asked to reproduce gesturally the displacement of the upper square, he can manage this perfectly well. But this action is merely a global symbol, and as soon as it is a question of visualizing its details the difficulties start. The simplest solution for the

TABLE 17 *Graphic representations of displaced squares and choice from prepared drawings, classified according to forms A–H of Figure 5* (As % of the responses)

	A–D		E1–E2		F1–F2–G		H (correct)	
	Drawing	Choice	Drawing	Choice	Drawing	Choice	Drawing	Choice
4 years	55·5	41·4	11·1	6·9	5·6	24·2	27·8	27·5
5 years	29·0	33·3	4·0	9·8	33·0	23·5	34·0	33·3
6 years	7·0	12·6	7·0	6·3	40·0	28·2	53·0	53·0
7 years	0	0	7·0	7·0	15·5	15·5	77·5	77·5

child is to separate the two squares from one another (55 per cent at 5 years) – though they may be left in place as in A or put together in some other way as in B. The reason for these reactions A–D is provided in the drawings E–G. The difficulty lies in using an adapted image to imagine how the terminal boundary Y of the moving square will be situated in relation to corresponding boundary Y' of the fixed square, if initial boundary X is displaced in relation to the corresponding X'. Consequently, when the child attempts to imagine the glide, he does one of two things. Either he imagines the two staggered steps as symmetrical (E1 and E2), by expansion (E2) or contraction (E1) of the top square, or he succeeds in one of the shifts (F1, F2, G) – whether of X in relation to X' (F1, F2) or Y in relation to Y' (G) – but leaves the other two boundaries unchanged, with no staggering. In a word, this type of imagery represents schemata which have no relation with any perception, but which are structured in accordance with the notions usual at this level of development which are ordinal rather than metric. In each of the figures E1 to G, the length of the horizontal sides of one of the squares is neglected as distance, and the whole problem (unsolved) for the child appears to centre on the order of these extremities or boundaries (X in relation to X' or Y in relation to Y').

Now it is essential to realize that these difficulties concern the visual image only. We asked the subjects to do two things: (a) to indicate with their finger the displacement of the upper square 'when it is pushed along a bit'; and (b) to complement this gesture verbally by saying whether the lower square remains motionless. From twenty subjects aged 4 to 6 years we obtained the following results (Table 18).

TABLE 18 *Gestural and verbal indications of the correct displacement* (As % of subjects)

4–5 years	6 years
87%	100%

The two sole exceptions were vertical displacement of the top square (found also in the drawing) and movement of the bottom square. It is not, therefore, the imagining of the displacement as such that causes difficulty, but solely and simply the imagining of the positions or the boundaries.

II. *Controls* To verify the part played by the boundaries we carried out an investigation in collaboration with Mme T. Vinh-Bang to see whether the image of the displacement would be aided by using a red and a blue square, in other words, by increasing the perceptual dissociation of the squares. Using ten subjects aged from 4,10 to 5,4 years we found no difference at all in the image and none even in the copy.

Then we returned to the usual type of square, adding a short red line in the middle of the base of the top square and extending vertically into the bottom square (Figure 6). When the top square is displaced the two marks no longer coincide and a space is introduced between them. On the other squares we drew these lines some distance apart, so that when the top square is displaced the gap between the lines is closed and the two meet in a continual straight line from one square to the other (Figure 6).

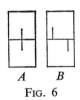

A   B

FIG. 6

In the first case all the subjects, including the 4-year-olds, accepted the possibility that the displacement of the top square would break the extension of the vertical lines. On the other hand, however, when they were asked to imagine the new position of the marks as a function of the displacement of the squares, it was found that up to 7 years the presence of the lines, rather than acting as a guide and aid to imagination, constituted an additional problem complicating the habitual difficulties. Out of fifteen subjects from 4 to 6 years, eight produced drawings of a type (as far as the squares themselves are concerned) inferior to the drawings done without markings, four produced superior drawings, and three drawings of the same type (H). The marks themselves were positioned regardless of the position of the squares (except for the three drawings type H), and occasionally kept the lines in continuous extension.

In the second case where there is a gap between the marks to start off with (Figure 6*B*), half the subjects aged 4 to 5 years thought it impossible to place them in continuous extension by displacing the top square.

For instance Sil (5,7) said that '*one line is near one edge and the other near the other edge, so they can't ever come opposite one another*'.

The other half of the subjects accept the possibility of extending the line by displacing the top square. Even so, out of fifteen subjects between 5 and 6 years we obtained only two correct drawings. Curiously enough, however, these did not seem right to either of the children who did them (5,9 and 6,6). The other drawings were, on the other hand, on a level equal or inferior to that of the drawings without the lines.

Finally, we replaced the lines by points. This test proved to be of genuine interest, and in fact originated a further piece of research which we shall return to and treat more systematically in Chapter Four, section 3. We confine ourselves for the present to noting two types of reaction to this test. First, the drawings which keep the points in the right positions relative to the squares. Second, the far more curious graphic images in which the points may be moved about anywhere at all within the squares and even pass from one square to the other according to the displacements of the top square! It should be noted that the drawings of the first category do not necessarily represent correct displacements of the square. Conversely, a correct drawing of the squares (type H) may not correspond to a correct displacement or conservation of the position of the points. In short, in the case of the points, as in the case of the lines, the subject has to deal with a new problem not necessarily related to the problem of the movements of the square.

III. *The spaced squares.* Further possible confirmation of the role which we have hypothetically attributed to the lateral limits of the squares – those limits, that is, which are involved when the upper square is displaced from left to right – is provided if we introduce a gap of approximately 1 cm between the two 5 cm squares. The two lateral sides of the top square thus do not appear as a direct extension of the sides of the bottom square. It is interesting to see that the solving of the problem then becomes a little easier, though it is none the less impeded by the usual general difficulties associated with kinetic imagery.

The procedure followed was identical with that described in I, except that in addition to imagining the results of the displacement of the top square, we brought in representation of the effects of two simultaneous displacements. The bottom square was to be imagined displaced to the left, the top square to the right. The child was asked to choose as before from a number of prepared drawings and to make a copy of the correct configuration H'. (We shall use the letters A′–H′ to refer to the Figure 5 configurations modified by the 1 cm space.) The results obtained are set out in Table 19. (Nine subjects aged 4 years, nineteen aged 5 years, and twelve aged 6 years were used.)

TABLE 19 *Drawings of displaced squares spaced 1 cm apart, choice from models and copies of six correct figures*
(In brackets: simultaneous displacements)
(As % of the responses)

	A–D		E′1–E′2		F′1–F′2–G		H′ (correct)		
	Drawing	Choice	Drawing	Choice	Drawing	Choice	Drawing	Choice	Copy
4 years	66	21	17	3	17	10	0	55	41
5 years	53	24	0 (47)	0	5	12	42	64	56
6 years	9 (42)	10	9	0	17	8	65	82	88

The most frequent drawings are of type D′ (33 per cent at 4 years and 32 per cent at 5 years) which correct themselves gradually to give H′. As for the progress expected in view of the detachment of the boundaries, it is most obvious in the column for the choice of H′, which shows a clear advance over the corresponding column of Table 17. On the other hand, progress in the drawings is less clear, and does not begin till 5 years, the subject first attempting a solution with type D′. This solution shows a need to cross the boundary lines, but apart from that it remains a victim of the difficulties found in the situation examined in I, where the boundaries were not so far apart as here (Figure 5).

2. *The displacement of superimposed figures*

FIG. 7

To complete the analysis of the difficulties experienced by the young subject in section 1 we undertook in collaboration with F. Frank and J. Bliss a study of the images relating to the displacement of figures (squares or circles), whose initial arrangement is a *super-imposition* in the third dimension, rather than in a single plane as before.[3] For example, we used two transparent squares with a red border, equal in size and 'covering' one another exactly (two equal

[3] We shall use the term 'superimposition' for Figures 1–6 as opposed to the 'superpositions' of section 1.

57

square frames) as in I (Figure 7), or a small square placed under a larger transparent (II) or opaque (III) square, etc. Now the problem facing the subject's imagery is quite different from the problem we studied in section 1. There the figure as a whole constituted what might be called a *union* of juxtaposed spatial elements, and, as we have seen, the child's difficulty lay in imagining the displacements while at the same time trying to stay within the figure's external limits. In the present case, however, the initial figure is a structure with spatial *intersection* in the sense that two of its elements occupy tne same part of the total space. Suppose the subject once again comes up against the boundary problem. There are two distinct possibilities. Either the child will want to conserve the external perimeter – in which case he will be unable to get the lower square from under the upper one. (We shall find this kind of difficulty for II, Figure 7.) Or else he will want to keep the initial *internal* perimeter, since he is unable to imagine any intersections other than those given, and he will fail to imagine any boundary of the fixed square in I intersecting the space occupied by the mobile square. (We shall find this for form I.) Now this problem has two interesting aspects. On the one hand, one might wonder whether the images in question evolve in accordance with the operations, adequate images only being formed at the level of the operational structures of *union* and *intersection*. On the other hand, for an understanding of the nature of images, it is useful to try to compare pseudo-conservations which the initial images appear to obey (conservation of certain external boundaries but not the total surface in section 1) with operational conservations by which they are subsequently more or less governed.

Configuration I. The child was presented with the two equal, superimposed 5 cm squares with the red border. He was required to anticipate a translation of 2·5 cm of the mobile square. Five types of response were found (Figure 8):

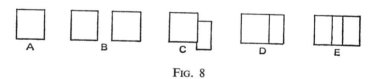

FIG. 8

A: no anticipation of the displacement; *B*: separation without intermediate positions; *C*: the movable square is made to overlap, but the dimensions of the square are distorted and the left side is not represented; *D*: correct overlapping but the left side not represented; *E*: successful drawing. Before going on to examine the distribution of results in Table 20, here are some examples of individual reactions.

Chri (5,4) produces a type *B* drawing: 'Can you move it a shorter distance than that? – *No*. – But is the square outside all the time? – *No*. – Well, do me a drawing of when it is not completely out. (He draws a type *B* drawing again, but reduces the gap.) *There, it's almost touching*. – But if you hardly move it at all, does it still go out? – *No*. – Well, draw what it would be like, then.' (He produces the same drawing *B*.)

Mart (6,0) produces a type *C* drawing: 'Will you only be able to see the part that overlaps? – *There is still some behind* (the large transparent fixed square). – One can't see it, then? – *No*. – When can one see it? – *When it comes out*. – But why can't one see it there? (The transparent square is indicated.) – *Because it's hidden behind*. – But one can see it there (the model is shown). – *Yes*. – Then one can see it? – *No, one can't see it there* (shows his drawing). – But why not? – *You won't be able to see it in the square*.'

The following is the distribution we obtained:

TABLE 20 *Frequencies (as %) of the types of reaction to Configuration I*

	A	B	C	D	E
4,5–5,5 years	31	15	15	31	8
5,6–6,5 years	5	25	15	40	15
6,6–7,5 years	0	3	11	33	53

The reactions to these problems of displacements from super-impositions are quite different from the reactions in section 1 (superpositions). In the latter the dominant concern of the young subjects was to avoid overlapping the figure's external boundary. This type of reaction is not found in the present case. The only exceptions perhaps are the drawings of type *A* and *B* where overlapping is not imagined, and those of type *C* where the overlap that is imagined involves reduction of the mobile square – as if it were necessary to mark its abnormal situation and distinguish it from the fixed square. But the striking new reaction is type *D*, which occurs at all ages. Here the child has no difficulty in indicating the overlap, and thus crosses the external boundary. But he refuses to draw in the left-hand side of the square which would cross the internal boundary! Let us note at once how paradoxical this result is compared with the drawings usually found at this level, when the child frequently points out by 'transparency' (Luquet) objects that cannot be seen because hidden by some opaque screen (potatoes in the ground, or inside a man's stomach). But in the present case the squares are actually transparent and the red side of the internal square is perfectly visible! If the child does not indicate it, it is not therefore due to his drawing technique.[4]

The hypothesis we shall seek to verify is as follows. The image, which tends to represent the essential characteristics of the objects, by this very fact accords these characteristics a sort of pre- or pseudo-conservation. (We shall see many more examples of this in Chapter Eight.) When the elements of a configuration are presented in a disjoined and additive form as they are in the superpositions in section 1, one of the characteristics calling for conservation will be the general external perimeter of the configuration. Hence the difficulty experienced in going beyond it. In the case of *superimposed* elements occupying a common volume of space by *intersection*, one of the characteristics to be conserved will be the surface area within the limits of the superimposed square. Consequently, when the square underneath is displaced, it is a question of preventing it crossing the boundary line of the upper square – the *internal* boundary, that is, not the *external* limits, for these present scarcely any problem. If it were to cross it the form of the fixed square would be spoiled and the space within the two boundaries divided into two. Hence the child's reluctance to mark in the left side of the bottom square after it had been displaced. In other words, the difficulty concerns the intersection (or an imaginal representation of what would from the operational standpoint be equivalent to an intersection with one part common and two parts not common) resulting from pseudo-conservation of the internal boundaries of the fixed square. In the *superpositions* in section 1 the problem was one not of *intersection* but of *addition* (or of imaginal representation of what from the operational standpoint would be equivalent to a lateral extension of the overall figure after displacement of the top square) resulting from pseudo-conservation of external limits.

Evidence favouring this interpretation is provided by the children's reactions to the tests in which they are asked to choose from prepared drawings (types *A*, *B*, *D* and *E*). There is no point in giving statistics for this, as the subjects almost always chose the drawing corresponding to their own. But the explanation given for rejecting the correct drawing (*E*) is interesting: '*It's wrong because there are three squares!* – '*there are three there* (i.e. in the correct drawing) *and there* (i.e. the apparatus) *there are only two*' – and '*the squares are too small*'. In other words, the left hand side of the partially displaced square divides the surface within the limits of the fixed square into two quadrilaterals. It seems that it is precisely this that constitutes the main obstacle.

[4] Out of nine subjects aged 5 years, seven (i.e. 77 per cent) copied the squares correctly when presented in position *E*, and the other two who failed to do so were on the other hand able to copy the corresponding drawings immediately.

A control test was carried out using two square frames of equal size, one red, the other black. In this test the type C reaction is not found, the squares being more easily distinguished. A and B reactions are less frequent. Type D responses, however, increase. This shows that the child's resistance to intersection cannot simply be due to difficulty experienced in distinguishing the squares.

On the other hand, if a rectangular frame 3 × 5 cm is placed in a vertical or horizontal position on a frame 5 cm square, leaving equal 1 cm margins between the edges of the rectangle and the square, it is naturally easier for the child to solve the problem, as he has from the outset an intersectory figure with one shared part (the rectangle) and two unshared parts (the margins). From 6 years in 80 per cent of cases (though only 15 per cent at 5 years) the graphic image is correct when the rectangle is placed lengthways and the margins are horizontal, since it is only a matter of extending the margins. But if the rectangle is placed vertically so that the width of the right-hand margin has to be reduced and the left-hand one increased if the rectangle is displaced, then there is a failure rate of 60 per cent at 6 years and 20 per cent at 7 years. 20 per cent at 6 years and 10 per cent at 7 years modify the dimensions of the figures, while 20 per cent at 6 years and 10 per cent at 7 years suppress any intersection so that the square retains its surface entire.

It would seem, therefore, that the difficulties associated with intersection, and with conservation of boundaries considered from the interior of the figure, are systematic in their occurrence. The best proof of this is the final control test. This was as follows. The child was shown a red square. He was asked to copy it. The experimenter then took another square frame of the same size with three black sides and one red side; this he held in the air a little above the red square and to one side of it (1 cm). The child is asked to draw 'what you will see' when the two-colour square is put down. We began the drawing ourselves by marking in the red side of the black-and-red square. Now this red side is parallel to the right-hand side of the fixed square, at a distance of 1 cm. All that remains to be done, therefore, is to draw the intersection, as everything is visible and the overlapping section already drawn.

There are five types of reaction: $C\,1$, the two-colour square is drawn on the other side of the line given by the experimenter; $C\,2$, it includes the given line, but is placed outside the red square; $C\,3$, it includes the given line and is constructed against the red square, but as a narrow rectangle so that there is no intersection; $C\,4$, the intersection is drawn but the two-colour square is increased in size; $C\,5$, correct drawing. See Table 21 overleaf.

Although there is naturally some improvement, the control appears to be conclusive. The difficulty experienced in imagining the intersection seems to be due to a kind of pseudo-conservation tending to keep the surface area and perimeter of the base square intact. But we might ask whether this need for permanence is not perhaps

TABLE 21 *Reactions to an intersection already drawn*
(As % of the responses)

	C 1	C 2	C 3	C 4	C 5
5 years	29	14	14	29	14
6 years	0	34	29	0	37
7 years	0	17	17	6	60

fostered by the fact that the square is a good form. So we tried to find out what would happen if the same test were carried out using irregular forms. Accordingly we presented the subject with curvilinear figures, with random and asymmetrical curves, equal in size (in all particulars), and bordered with red. Now it emerged that the successes (type *E*) were distinctly more frequent. See Table 22 below.

TABLE 22 *Successes for the intersection of irregular congruent forms*

4,5 to 5,5 (N = 6)	5,6 to 6,5 (8)	6,6 to 7,5 (13)
17%	62·5%	93%

As for the errors, we found mainly juxtaposition (type *B*) and occasionally rejection of intersection – i.e. the interior side was not represented so that the fixed shape could remain whole. However, this difficulty is not so great in the case of the irregular figures. This seems to show that the pseudo-conservation, to which we may attribute the subject's reluctance to divide the fixed shape, is stronger in the case of a good form. On the other hand, when it is a case of an irregular figure a division into two appears to be more acceptable (though it must be remembered that it is also occasionally rejected).

Finally, two investigations on ten subjects – aged 5 to 7 years – designed to complement our information about the intersections of squares. The first one consisted in replacing the transparent squares by empty frames. No modification resulted. The second proved more instructive. Two empty or transparent squares with red borders were shown side by side but some distance apart. The child was asked to imagine what would result if they were gradually moved together. Only one subject aged 6,10 succeeded spontaneously in producing an intersection and finally a complete superimposition. Four others succeeded, but only after repeated suggestions made by the experimenter: 'Can't they go any further?', etc. As for the remaining five, they refused to go beyond the stage where the squares touch one another and have a common side. In other words, when the squares were shown initially apart, the children were disinclined to imagine an intersection which would have impaired the initial image of the non-segmented surfaces. So we see again how the reluctance to accept an intersection is linked with a sort of pseudo-conservation of the original given figuration. In particular we can see how the intersection problem is related to the boundary-taboo, since the child refuses both to exceed the external limits of the squares (apart and then contiguous) and to introduce internal boundaries into empty surfaces initially without them.

Configuration IV. The subject is required to imagine a circular frame (initially placed on a square frame) being displaced until it is half way out of the square. With one exception (*C*), the types of reaction observed correspond remarkably with the preceding ones: *A*, no anticipation of the displacement; *B*, the circle is separated from the square without any intermediate positions; *C'*, anticipation of the displacement of the circle, but with two difficulties associated with perimeters: either the circle remains in contact with the left-hand side of the square and is stretched out so that it projects a little beyond the right-hand side, or it breaks away from the left-hand side but is attached to the right-hand side in the form of a vertically oriented oblate ellipse; *D*, half of the circle is outside the square but the other half is not indicated (thus no intersection); *E*, correct drawing. See Table 23.

TABLE 23 *Reactions to the displacement of a circle inscribed within a square*
(As % of the reactions)

	A	B	C'	D	E
4,5–5,5 years	11	3	32	7	27
5,6–6,5 years	0	10	18	6	66
6,6–7,5 years	0	0	12	4	84

It should be noted first of all that the choice made by the child from among the prepared drawings more often than not corresponds to his own drawings, and does not show any systematic progress by comparison. It should be pointed out, however, that it is more difficult to copy a circle inscribed in a square than to draw the squares (no success until $6\frac{1}{2}$ years for circle in contact with the sides of the square). It is therefore all the more remarkable to find that successes are earlier for this configuration than for the preceding one (Table 20). The intersection problem (type *B* and *D*), however, appears again, though it is less marked than in the case of the squares. This is probably because the two intersecting figures are different.

But here as in section 1 we find a boundary problem (type *C'*). The two cases we have brought under *C'* are undoubtedly different but they both show the dominance of the base figure (fixed square). Thus the problem of the as it were additive boundaries occurs in proportion as the intersection is easier. This is a remarkable fact, which seems to us to indicate that the two types of reaction are related, although they are vicariant. In each case the respecting of the boundary lines regarded both from inside and outside the figure seems to be bound up with a kind of pre-conservation or pseudo-conservation of the base figure. 'But why (we asked one subject who had just produced a type *D* drawing) can't one see the circle? – *Because it's hidden behind.* – But look at that (the squares placed one on top of the other), you can see the circle there, can't you? – *Yes.* – So you *do* think one can see the circle? – *No* (he points to his drawing), *you can't see it: you won't be able to see the circle in the square.*'

Configurations II, III, V and VI. In these configurations the mobile part (square or circle) is considerably smaller than the fixed part (large transparent or opaque circle). The interesting thing about them is that the intersection difficulties disappear almost entirely, but are replaced (as we have seen in connection with Configuration IV) by external boundary difficulties – which thus constitute a kind of vicariant.

In fact we found that for these four configurations there are five different types of reaction, though of these the form *D* is unusual: *A* – the subject does not anticipate any displacement; *B* – immediate separation; *C* – the smallest of the figures is only displaced within the large square, is not moved beyond the right-hand boundary (and as a rule is placed up against it with consequent decrease in breadth); *D* – all positions accepted except straddling the limit (rejection of intersection); *E* – success. Table 24 gives the results obtained for Configurations II–III.

TABLE 24 *Reactions to Configurations II–III*
(As % of the responses)

	A	B	C	D	E
4,5–5,5 years	25	4	20	8	43
5,6–6,5 years	4	10	16	10	60
6,6–7,5 years	0	0	9	9	82

The occurrence of intersection difficulty is limited. But the problem of the external limit occurs more frequently. This is probably because the smaller of the two elements in these configurations stands out on the 5 cm square frame as a figure on a ground and not as occupying and intersecting a surface common both to it and the large square. This also explains why this displacement is easier to imagine than in the case of Configurations I and IV.

The small circles in Configurations V and VI present the same degree of difficulty as the small squares in II and III. They do not therefore call for special discussion.

Finally, in spite of their apparent complexity, the facts described in this section are referable to certain fairly simple laws. First of all, let us recall a fact brought out in section 1 – the tendency of the preoperational image to avoid overstepping the external boundaries of a figure in consequence of a kind of pseudo-conservation of the initial figurative data. The fact that the figures are superimposed and that they partially or totally intersect does not alone modify this phenomenon. For even when the figures are of very different sizes (II and III, and V and VI in Figure 7), the main problem, although solved more easily, is to avoid going beyond the external limit of the larger figure. However, when the superimposed figures are the same shape and size, the need to conserve (pseudo-conservation) the figurative aspect of the fixed reference element leads to a different boundary-effect: namely, the reluctance to introduce the internal boundary line necessitated by intersection into the fixed square, since such a division would spoil its form. Hence Tables 20 and 21 and the results of the numerous control tests. Now two facts enable us to confirm that it is not the intersection that is not understood. (Indeed it is successfully understood in graphic figuration of topological relations at the age of 3 years when the subjects can still only draw squares as closed curves.)[5] The image produced is in fact better when the figures are not the same shape and size (i.e. circle and square as in Table 23, or rectangle and square), and better still when the figures *are* the same shape and size but are irregular in form. In these two cases the intersection is easier to imagine. On the one hand this is because the initial properties are altered less and remain recognizable by their differences. On the other it is because the figures are not 'good forms', and their figurative non-conservation has fewer consequences for the image. In short, the nature of the reactions observed here is essentially related to the pseudo-conservation peculiar to the preoperational images. We have already seen this to be the case for external boundaries. This then is the interesting thing about these phenomena – which have occasioned a perhaps rather lengthy description which we hope the reader will bear with.

3. *The rotation of a rod about one end*

The situations discussed in sections 1 and 2 correspond to experiences with which the subject is familiar. Children are constantly seeing

[5] Piaget, J., and Inhelder, B., *The Child's Conception of Space*, Routledge & Kegan Paul, 1956, Chapter 2.

displacements of objects in relation to one another. Even so the corresponding kinetic reproductive images present a number of systematic difficulties which we have been able to relate to questions of perimeter or boundary lines. It is clear that the difficulties associated with the image are not connected with the representation of the movement as a whole, which is well known to the subject. They are connected rather with the representation of its adjustment in the form of particular relative positions, especially in so far as finishing points are affected. From this point of view the examples which we are going to study now constitute the converse of the preceding examples. Again we shall be concerned with a motion observed in everyday life. The 90° and 360° rotations of a rod round one extremity correspond to the fall of a vertical stick, to the movement of the fingers of a clock, to the movement even of the arms, and so on. It is difficult to conceive that the child will not possess a familiar mental image of such movements. But the numerous experiments carried out in collaboration with F. Paternotte, S. Taponier, E. Schmid-Kitsikis, D. Nicollier and M. Anthonioz have shown that the results, whether they were relatively good or whether they were astonishingly unco-ordinated, were not principally due to the boundary as finishing point of the movement. They were on the contrary due to concentration on, or neglect of, the starting point as a fixed pivotal centre. The results obtained vary somewhat, depending on whether the methods used stress the fixed point, or whether it is merely implied without being emphasized in any particularly explicit way. Normally, as the foregoing instances have shown, the child is inclined to centre his attention on the finishing points and to neglect the starting points, even when a pivotal centre is suggested. Now this question of the starting point, and of its fixity in the case of pivotal motion, deserves to be examined as attentively as the terminal boundaries or finishing points. What is in question here is the whole general problem of spatial co-ordination within the context of imaginal representations.

We shall start, therefore, by giving the results for those methods which did not particularly stress the fixed nature of the pivot, and then go on to those which made use of an apparatus that suggested it more strongly. In the latter case two methods were used. Either the child was asked for a preliminary drawing of the head of the nail used as a pivot. Or else we used a device in which a metal spindle was attached to one end of the rod and used to turn it from behind the cardboard base. The child was shown that the rod could be rotated by turning the end of the spindle behind the cardboard. This unexpected mechanism alone was often sufficient to focus the child's attention on the fact that the centre of the rotation was fixed (in a relative way, however, as we shall see). The methods not emphasizing this explicitly simply involved fixing one end of the rod with a small nail as a pivot. It made no difference at all to the younger children if one pointed out the nail, or told them verbally that the starting point was fixed. We shall see, for instance (Chapter Four, section 2, Table 45) that in the case of a square rotated about the apex of one of its corners fixed by a nail 5 cm long, 80 per cent of the 5-year-old subjects and 60 per cent of the 6- to 8-year-olds took no notice of the fixed nature of the pivot of the rotation.

The general plan of this rather long paragraph is as follows. Under I we shall examine the 90° rotation of a rod 20 cm long without any special devices to emphasize the fixity of the pivotal centre. Under II we shall compare the 90° and the 360° rotations of rods 5 cm and 15 cm long when the fixed pivot is made more obvious. Under III we again use 90° and 360° rotations and a rod 5 cm long, but this time with a right-angle mount and a metal spindle. The same rotations are used in IV for a 5 cm rod without the spindle and without the mount. After these controls we go back in V to the method employed in I, except that this time the rod is rotated through 360°. Under VI we examine the question of the length of the subject's drawings, and under VII the conservation problem in the case of rotation.

I. Let us begin then with an investigation we carried out with F. Paternotte. This concerns the 90° rotation in the horizontal plane of a rod presented in the sagittal plane (which we shall call here 'vertical'). The child was asked first of all to draw the initial and final positions of the rod. In a case like this the subject has no difficulty in imagining the result of a falling movement, although, as we saw in Chapter Two, section 4, there are generally some systematic errors concerning length (Figure 9).

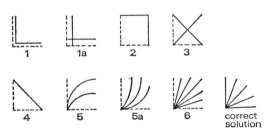

FIG. 9

First of all the child is shown a black vertical rod 20 cm in length and 2 mm in diameter, fixed at its base by means of a nail. Then the following questions are asked:

(1) The child is asked to draw the rod 'as it will be when it drops a little' (a gesture indicating the rotation about the fixed base). This is simply a question of representing an oblique line. If the child does not understand the question the experimenter starts the movement of the rod, but does not show it all.

(2) The experimenter gets the subject to draw the vertical and the horizontal positions of the rod, stressing the permanence of the fixed point marked by the nail. He then asks the child to draw how the rod will drop from the first position to the last. Several intermediate positions are requested.

(3) A bead is fastened to the free end of the rod and the child is asked to draw its path. He is asked also to represent this path by means of a gesture, since a rectilinear drawing is often only a simplification of the arc.

(4) The subject is presented with a stick with a large-headed pin stuck in one end. He is asked to draw the pin in its successive positions when the stick falls in the same way as the rod in 2.

(5) From three drawings – a straight line, a convex arc and a concave arc – the child is asked to choose the one representing the path of the end of the stick (question 4).

(6) The child is required to effect the actual movement of the initial rod (cf. question 2).

(7) The subject is shown a rod the top half of which is coloured red and the bottom half blue. He is requested to draw the successive positions of the rod and the two colours (cf. questions 2 and 4).

(8) He is asked to choose from five prepared drawings representing the rod's positions. The model drawings include types 1, 2 and 4 (two variants) of Figure 9, and the correct positions.

First, here are the reactions to question 1 (drawing of an oblique line):

TABLE 25   *Drawings of an oblique line (as % of the subjects) given the start of the movement (question 1)*

	No drawing	Wrongly placed lines	Curves	Correct
4–5 years ($N=18$)	21	7	22	50
6 years ($N=17$)	12	18	12	58
7 years ($N=17$)	0	12	0	88
8–9 years ($N=11$)	0	0	0	100

Correct responses are evaluated in terms only of orientation, independently of length. Table 26 gives the results obtained for question 2 (drawing of intermediate positions), question 8 (choice from given drawings), and question 6 (imitation of the trajectory, using the rod itself). The results for question 2 are numbered 1–6 as in Figure 9 (0 signifies 'no drawing').

The choice column and the imitation column give only correct responses. Incorrect imitations are difficult to classify. Incorrect choices are distributed more or less as the drawings themselves. Column 3 includes all inclined straight lines intersecting at some angle.

TABLE 26 *Drawings, choice from given drawings, and gestural imitation of the trajectories of a rod falling from vertical to horizontal position* (As % of the responses)

Reactions	Type 0	Types 1–2	Type 3	Type 4	Types 5–5a	Type 6	Correct drawing	Correct choice	Correct imitation
4–5 years (18)	5	24	5	8	5	30	23	21	7
6 years (17)	0	29	18	0	6	0	47	46	43
7 years (17)	0	0	18	11	0	6	65	81	87
8–9 years (11)	0	9	9	0	0	0	82	82	82

In Table 27 are given the drawings or gestures representing the trajectory of the rod's extremity and the choices made from the three given drawings.

TABLE 27 *Drawing or gesture indicating the path of the extremity of the rod (as % of the responses) and choice from three models*

		Drawings or gestures					Choice			
	0	Vert. horiz.	Square	Concave	Straight	Correct	0	Concave	Straight	Correct
4–5 years	11	35	29	0	20	5	20	10	33	37
6 years	0	12	6	6	17	59	0	7	20	73
7 years	0	6	6	0	34	54	0	0	17	83
8–9 years	0	9	0	0	27	64	0	0	0	100

In the choice column, 0 signifies inability to decide. We may group in a separate table (Table 28) the drawings of the successive positions of the two segments of the two-colour rod (question 7 = series *A*), and those of the pin attached to the stick (question 4 = series *B*). The drawings of these series *A* and *B* are reproduced in

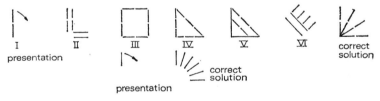

FIG. 10

Figure 10, and the numbering used there is also used in Table 28 (0 again signifying 'no drawing').

Summing up these four tables, one notices first of all that drawings of an oblique where the motion has been suggested are successful only at 7 years for more than 75 per cent of the subjects, but at 4 to 5 years for 50 per cent (Table 25). It was necessary, therefore, when posing the central questions of Table 26, to ask at the same

TABLE 28 *Drawings of the successive positions of the two halves of a two-colour rod (series A), and of the pin attached to the extremity of a stick (series B)*
(As % of the responses)

	0		I		II		III		IV		V		VI		VII (correct)	
	A	B	A	B	A	B	A	B	A	B	A	B	A	B	A	B
4–5 years	17	13	24	33	17	11	18	16	18	16	0	0	0	0	6	11
6 years	0	5	0	6	13	3	6	30	6	20	19	6	13	0	43	30
7 years	0	0	0	6	6	0	12	23	12	0	0	0	6	6	64	65
8–9 years	0	0	0	0	0	0	0	27	0	0	18	0	0	0	82	83

time for a drawing of the positions, for a choice from model drawings, and for a gestural reproduction using the rod. Now these three values remain fairly close together, with successful responses at about 7 to 8 years.[6] But, curiously, imitation at 4 to 5 years lags behind. This is no doubt because the child is being asked for an exact manipulation of the rod itself and not just for an imitative gesture with the hand. However, successful drawing of the trajectory of the end of the rod (Table 27) is (except at 6 years) only slightly behind that of manipulation. This is probably due to the fact that a certain degree of abstraction is involved. The choices from model drawings show better results than those in Table 26, and 73 per cent of the responses are correct from 6 years. The drawings of the two halves of the rod or of the pin in extension of the stick yield the same success score as do the drawings of the *whole* rod (at about 7 to 8 years), except for a lagging behind at 4 to 5 years (at 6 years for the pin). This retardation recalls that of the drawings of the rod's extremity, and the same kind of abstraction is probably the reason for it.

Now that we have established these facts for the successes, we may go on to interpret the systematic forms of the errors observed.

(1) The most elementary error, found frequently between 4 and 6 years for the successive positions of the rod (Table 26) and the trajectory of its free end (Table 27), was to imagine the rod taking a vertical, then a horizontal direction (Figure 9, I and Figure 10, I). This corresponds in fact to the initial and terminal positions of the movement. This reaction is equivalent to the absence of a kinetic image (RKM), since the only positions imagined are the starting and the finishing point. The subject confuses the movement itself with its result (RKP), as if the only thing retained from his perceptions were the static configurations corresponding to these states of

[6] It should be noted that the successes are helped by question 1, which was designed to test the graphic expression but which thereby also aids subsequent representations.

rest. When the child was asked how the rod or the bead was able to slide on its vertical axis and suddenly follow a horizontal path, it was clear that he did not put this question to himself in any clear way. One reason for this is that he does not give any consideration to a possible fixed pivotal centre.

(2) A slightly superior reaction (Figure 9), 1*a*, was to free the rods from their resting positions, and, still making them follow a vertical and then a horizontal path, to place them a few millimetres away from their initial and terminal positions, so that the paths intersect at right angles. This type of drawing was produced also for the trajectory of the extremity.

(3) Once dissociated from its initial and terminal positions, the moving rod again falls under their indirect influence. It is imagined as following horizontal and vertical paths as before, but this time in a symmetrical manner. The rods are thus felt to present a square trajectory (Figure 9, 2, corresponding to 11 per cent of responses at 4 to 5 years out of the 24 per cent in Table 26, and to 35 per cent in Table 27; and Figure 10, III, corresponding to 17 per cent and 11 per cent in Table 28).

(4) When the child finally represents the intermediate positions as oblique – in other words, when he starts to take account of the experience acquired or reacquired in question 1 – it remains open to him to differentiate and co-ordinate the trajectory of the free end and the positions of the whole stick, instead of stopping short at a failure to differentiate between states of rest and states of transition. Several solutions are possible in this situation (Figure 9, 3 to 6) which probably do not correspond to stages but to more or less contemporaneous types of solution from which the subject takes his pick. The least advanced is certainly form 3 (see Table 26), which shows no single central pivot. One might be tempted to attribute this simply to a belief, say, that some impact causes the rod to topple over, rather than a belief that it is rotated gradually. In Figure 9, 3, the rods are crossed, but with them may be grouped drawings not reproduced here in which the child makes do with parallel lines, not crossing and not possessing any single pivotal centre. But this form 3 is found again in IV of Figure 10 (and Table 28), and when one analyses the data given in this Table, series *A*, one sees that 41 per cent of the subjects at 4 to 5 years, 57 per cent of those at 6 years, 24 per cent of those at 7 years and 18 per cent of those 8 to 9 years give drawings of the two halves of the rod in which the top half is not in continuous extension of the bottom half – as if the two halves of a rigid rod could move about separately when the whole is rotated! The deficiency in imagination with regard to the pivotal centre thus applies also to co-ordination of the two contiguous segments of the rod itself. This demonstrates once again the difficulties of spatial co-ordination associated with the primitive kinetic image.

(5) Types 5 and 5*a* of Table 26, which represent the rotating rod by means of curves, clearly mark the beginning of differentiation and co-ordination between transitional states and initial and final states of rest. The curves symbolize the actual movement of the rod, though there is some lack of differentiation between the trajectory of the free end, which does in fact describe a curve, and the rod as a whole (cf. the number of curves as high as 22 per cent in the drawings of a single oblique line, Table 25).

71

Conversely, the younger subjects often imagine the trajectory of the free end (Table 27) as forming straight lines. This points to the same lack of differentiation, exemplified in reverse.

(6) Form 4 of Table 26, in which the rod is thought to follow the chord of the arc described by the extremities, shows the same lack of differentiation. But in addition there is confusion between the chord and the arc as a result of failure to take account of distances measured from the pivot. This lack of differentiation occurs again, though with a different kind of confusion, in drawings V and VI, Table 28, series *B*. Here the pin is thought to be displaced lengthwise and not as an extension of the rod, in consequence of a failure to differentiate between the rod and its extremity.

(7) Form 6, where oblique lines are inscribed within a square, is certainly superior to the forms discussed above, since there is a single stable pivotal centre and conservation of the rectilinear character of the rod. It is true that solution 6 is particularly frequent in the 4 to 6 age group (Table 26), but an analogous form (V) is found in Table 28 in 19 per cent of subjects at 6 years and in 18 per cent at 8 to 9 years. Although form 6, Table 26, indicates the oblique lines correctly, it remains tied to the square form of solution 2. That is to say, it again points to a failure to differentiate between the rod's course and its extreme vertical and horizontal positions.

Such are the reactions obtained when no special precautions are taken to ensure conservation of a fixed centre of rotation – when, in other words, one allows the subject to follow his spontaneous tendency to neglect the starting points and intermediary states to focus instead on the finishing points. In this connection four types of reaction can be distinguished.

(*a*) Lack of differentiation between the extreme static positions and the intermediary states. This is manifested in errors 1–2 in Table 26, and I and II in Table 28, with residual influence on types 6 and V.

(*b*) Lack of differentiation between the successive positions of the rod and the positions of its extremity. This is clear from errors 3–5*a* of Table 26, and II–IV–VI of Table 28.

(*c*) Absence of a fixed centre of rotation (errors 1–3 and I–IV).

(*d*) Lack of contact in the representation of the displacements between the two segments of the coloured rod, or between the rod and the pin (errors I–VI of Table 28). This reaction *d* is of the same kind as reaction *c*, both being tantamount to unco-ordination of starting and finishing points, and both disappearing at the same age. The correspondence between the ages at which success is achieved in Tables 26 and 28 is quite striking.

Now the controls the investigation gave rise to have shown that it is possible that success in the representation of the rotating rod may be slightly better from 5 years upwards. In order to interpret these reactions *a–d*, therefore, it is necessary to distinguish carefully all possible factors, so that we can analyse them by varying them in their distinct forms. There are at least six factors to take into consideration: (1) First of all, of course, there are the adaptations of the apparatus used to draw the subject's attention to the fixed pivotal centre. (2) The fact that a preliminary drawing of the vertical and horizontal positions is requested may be favourable to non-differentiation *a*. (3) A good rotation, which does not correspond to a 'good form', might be harder to imagine than a 360° rotation in which the intermediate stages, when drawn on a single sheet of paper, result in the regular, symmetrical form that the children called a 'daisy', a 'sun', a 'clock', and so on. (4) The fact that the experimenter indicates the start of the rotation by means of a gesture if the child cannot imagine it for himself may be favourable to non-differentiation *b*. (5) The results may differ depending on whether the drawings of the intermediate states are juxtaposed on the same sheet of paper or done on separate sheets. (6) The length of the rod (15–20 cm or 5 cm) may play a part, to the extent that it may be easier (at least from the drawing point of view) to represent the positions of a smaller rod.

II. To determine the part played by the factor of length and the factor of the size of rotation, we examined, in association with E. Schmid, thirty subjects aged between 5,0 and 7,2 years (twenty aged 5). We asked them (in the various possible orders) to do a drawing of the initial, terminal and intermediate positions of rods 5 cm and 15 cm long rotated through 90° and 360°.

The fixed nature of the pivotal centre was emphasized in two different ways at once. One end of the rod was fastened to the cardboard base by a large 5 cm nail, and the subjects were asked to indicate the head of the nail in their drawing – which they did by means of a small circle in the centre of the sheet.

The interesting thing about this particular test is that it shows some improvement, as far as accurate anticipation is concerned, compared with the preceding results: twenty out of thirty drawings, that is 66 per cent, and thirteen of the twenty 5-year-olds produced correct drawings for the 90° rotation. However, in spite of the noticeable effect of the devices used to stabilize the pivotal centre, four kinds of error are to be found which correspond to types 3–5 of Table 26. The first is a multiplying of the pivotal centres: 2 or as many as 4 distinct circles a few millimetres apart were drawn. The second consisted in drawing the successive positions as vertical or oblique parallel lines. This again led to an increase in the number of pivotal centres, which were not, however, represented as circles (there were 6 to 15 of these). The third consisted in drawing correctly the first 4 or 5 positions, and then a series of horizontal lines from the 45° diagonal. This recalls the squares (error 2) in Table 26. The fourth type of error involved the introduction of curves (cf. type 5).

To return to the two questions we set out to answer, the drawings with the 5 cm rod seem to be hardly any easier than the drawings with the 15 cm rod: eleven successes out of thirty drawings. The principal difference is the greater frequency in the case of the 15 cm rod of errors of the second kind described above (parallel positions not centred on a single point of origin). No such difference was found, however, between the 90° and 360° rotations. The latter showed 64 per cent success and the same number (eleven out of seventeen drawings), whether a 5 cm or 15 cm rod was used. The types of error are the same, but there is a further type that recalls the inability to differentiate between the path of the rod and the path of its extremity observed in Table 28. Instead of drawing a series of radii from the centre, the subject marked in a succession of very short strokes at a distance from the centre, and corresponding to the free end of the rod.

Finally, then, this inquiry brings out the importance of the factor focussing attention on the stable centre of rotation, but suggests that we need not take into account the length of the rod or the degree of the rotation.

III. After collaborating with S. Taponier in studying the rotation of a short rod 5 cm long at right angles to a rod 10 cm long (right angle figure, Chapter Five, section 3), it occurred to us that the same device might be used to analyse anticipations of the short rod rotating while the second remains fixed to a cardboard mount. In the experiment we then undertook the subject's attention was focused on the fixed pivotal centre by means of the mechanical device described above. A metal spindle to which one end of the moving rod is attached passes through the upper end of the fixed rod and through the cardboard mount. The experimenter can suggest the rotation without having recourse to gesture simply by telling the subject that the spindle can be turned behind the mount. The device is shown to the child beforehand by turning the cardboard mount round; this arouses his interest sufficiently to influence his subsequent behaviour. We studied two further groups of subjects. In one the drawings were juxtaposed on a single sheet (as before in I and II). In the other separate sheets were used for each drawing. Let us say right away that the difference was nil: 46 per cent and 45 per cent complete successes (360°) for the two groups of subjects aged 5 to 6 years.

Contrary to the results given in II, however, there is a distinct difference at 5 years at least between anticipations of the 90° and anticipations of the 360° rotations. This is no doubt due in the present case to the arrangement of the figure in the form of a right angle and to the presence of the fixed rod. It should be made clear that in the starting position the moving rod (i.e. the horizontal one) is at right angles to the fixed (vertical) one, so that the 90° rotation simply makes the former an extension of the latter. The 360° rotation, on the other hand, means that the mobile rod must cross the fixed rod (at 270°). This could hinder imaginal representation.

However this may be, one finds, always taking the child's first drawing, that there is a 52 per cent success score at 5 years for the imagining of the intermediate, initial and final positions of a 90° rotation, but only 24 per cent for a complete 360° rotation, whereas at 6 years 76 per cent succeed for 90° and 68 per cent for 360° rotations. Thus the measure taken to focus the subject's attention on the stability of the pivotal centre yields the same result as the procedure described in II: 64 per cent success score for all 5- and 6-year-old subjects taken together.

Before we go on to examine the types of error observed, here are the results we obtained using this particular technique for fifteen subjects aged 4 years. In spite of a demonstration of the actual rotation, five out of fifteen subjects, or 33 per cent, were unable to anticipate the position of the mobile segment in the first quarter of the circle; six succeeded for the second quarter, five at 180°, six in the third quarter and at 270°, and seven in the fourth quarter. Great difficulty, then, is experienced in imagining the rotation. At first the subjects persistently reproduce the rod in its original position and when they do get away from it (ten cases), they always return to the first quarter of the circle, which is the easiest. The most common error is to displace the starting point (in spite of the metal spindle), to the extent that sometimes the fixed segment and the moving segments are separated. The errors can further be classified into two categories according to whether the subjects succeed or not in representing the oblique positions. Those who do not succeed produce curious drawings involving right angles, which correspond to errors 1–2 examined in I. When he has done an initial drawing of the moving segment in its right angle position, the subject continues, moving on from the free end, and draws a second segment parallel to the fixed one, giving a ⊓ shape. Others even go on to close the figure with a third right angle, giving a square,[7] or replace the third segment with a curve in any direction to symbolize rotation. Those subjects who start off with oblique lines also frequently finish up with curves, which may even become *p*-shaped incurvations, or progressively displaced insertions. There is generally some underestimating of length, but quite often also the length is overestimated during rotation.

The errors observed at 5 years are quantitatively fewer with this method. But qualitatively speaking they correspond fairly strikingly to types 1 to 5 in Table 26. With the eighteen subjects aged 5 to 6 years who did not succeed in anticipating the 90° rotations (36 per cent of fifty subjects), we found the following:

[7] Cf. error 2 in Table 26. See Figure 9, 2.

(1) Five subjects failed to anticipate any of the intermediate positions, and simply reproduced the starting points, or both extreme positions (cf. types 0–1).

(2) Three subjects produced several varieties of closed figure representing the initial positions. In general the figure is triangular, but the principle recalls the square of type 2 (Table 26).[8]

(3) There were seven subjects, who like the last three (this gives a total of 20 per cent) gave drawings which did not conserve the fixed centre of rotation but which consisted of crossed strokes, parallel strokes, and (in two cases) lines extended according to a variety of angles. This corresponds to type 3 of Table 26.

(4) One subject joined the ends of the rod in initial and terminal positions, giving a triangle as in type 4 of Table 26.

(5) Two subjects produced drawings of intermediary positions with a common centre, but represented as curves, as in types 5 and 5a in Table 26 (curvilinear but non-radial lines were also observed in three cases in combination with error 3).

We thought it useful to point out the general parallels between errors 1–5 (they are found in similar form in the case of anticipation of 360° rotations), since they bring out two relevant points with some clarity: the force of the child's tendency to forget, in spite of the precautions taken, the starting point of the lines whose orientation he is supposed to be representing, and his tendency to introduce curves in consequence of lack of differentiation between the positions of the turning rod and the position of its extremity. We have now varied (in II and III) each of the six factors listed at the end of section I. We may now consider the tendency to neglect co-ordination of the starting point and the tendency to confuse the positions of the rod itself with the position of its extremity as the two dominant characteristics of the imaginal anticipation of rotations.

IV. It remains to check the result obtained in the procedure using the metal spindle for the case of a single rotating rod of 5 cm. This was done in collaboration with Monique Anthonioz in an experiment on fifteen subjects aged 4 years, and then on fifteen and thirty-four subjects aged 5 years, employing two sub-methods A and B. In A the child was shown a turning device and was then asked to do three things: (1) to copy the rod in a horizontal position; (2) to anticipate the successive positions of the rod up to 360°, using a drawing; (3) finally, the most important, if the child failed to anticipate the rotation, he was asked to represent it by means of gesture. In B, 1 and 2 were repeated, but in 3, if the subject got stuck, he was asked to copy the rod in oblique positions and try again.

(A) One subject (4,9 years) out of twelve aged 4 years managed a correct drawing with a single pivotal centre, and nine intermediate positions, six

[8] Further, in the decentralized drawings of the following type 3, three subjects gave square arrangements between the extreme positions, the square then being occupied by parallel uncentred strokes.

of which were oblique. One other subject gave all the positions, but displaced the centre. Six of the remaining subjects produced a series of varied positions without a common centre (there were up to nine scattered centres), generally with straight lines. Finally four subjects could do no more than repeat the copy without anticipation. When asked to anticipate the rotation by means of a gesture they merely indicated a circle with their fingers.

Out of fifteen subjects aged 5 years only one was immediately able to give a correct drawing. Another started with parallel straight lines, then drew oblique lines which had eight distinct points of origin. But when he was asked if the nail 'stays where it is', he arrived at the correct drawing. A third gave a drawing which would have been correct if the nail had not been replaced by a bar along and around which the lines were positioned at appropriate angles. Two other subjects also gave correct positions, but with several centres or nails (the heads of which were often drawn at the free end of the rod). Amongst the explicit errors we found the squares of type 2 in two cases, even though a 360° and not a 90° was involved. In other cases we found parallel lines, curves, etc. – in short, the whole series of the habitual forms of error. As for the gestures only the first five of the fifteen subjects gave correct paths based on the head of the spindle. The others gave circular forms, and one subject, whose drawing represented scattered oblique lines, even arrived at gestures indicating a square ('it is lying down, then standing up', etc.).

(B) In this sub-method, the subject is given practice in copying a 45° oblique if he fails to anticipate spontaneously. Using thirty-four subjects aged 5 years, we found the following:

(a) 32 per cent of the subjects managed a complete rotation with a fixed pivotal centre without the experimenter's intervention.

(b) 14 per cent managed recognizable but incomplete or erroneous rotations without the experimenter.

(c) Of the 54 per cent remaining only a third managed complete rotations after copying the oblique positions in the first quarter of the circle. The others failed to arrive at complete circuits or regular progressions.

It may be true that with this method of partial preparation we do not find the usual expected errors (loss of the particular direction of the rotation, right angles, etc., though curves are occasionally found). But one characteristic fact is to be observed. Namely, the difficulty experienced by certain subjects in actually initiating anticipation, in getting out of the first quadrant of the circle, or, if an oblique line has been copied into it, in going beyond it, or in going beyond the axes, etc.

Finally we asked sixteen subjects aged 5 years to copy all the principal successive positions of the 360° rotation. Now only nine gave copies without errors. The main reason for this low score was indifference towards the order of the positions. The neglect of order, along with the difficulty of actually getting started, clearly shows that this anticipation of rotation does not come naturally to the young child.

V. These controls have demonstrated above all the difference between the results of those methods explicitly stressing a single pivotal centre and those which merely suggest it, leaving it open to the subject to take it into account or not. As a comparison let us now take up the method described in I and apply it to the 360° rotation. This we did with the help of F. Paternotte, using twenty subjects aged 5 years, twenty aged 6, and ten aged 7. The method differed from the preceding one (in I) in four ways: the rod was 13 cm in length; it was shown in horizontal position; it was required to be drawn at the starting position only (instead of at the extreme horizontal and vertical positions); finally, and most important, the questions as to the paths of the red and blue halves of the coloured rods were separated. The subject was asked for a concrete indication of the positions occupied by the upper and the lower segments of the rod separately during the course of rotation (the segments are detachable), and then to draw these positions (in the majority of cases the drawings and the concrete anticipations coincide). We shall divide the reactions to the complete rod into five groups, thus: (*a*) no anticipation; (*b*) starting position surrounded by a circle or oval (=path of extremity); (*c*) no single pivotal centre, with parallel lines, divergent lines, or curves; (*d*) a single pivotal centre, but with curves to mark the rotation; (*e*) correct drawing.

For the drawings of the extremity of the rod the following types can be distinguished: (*a*) no anticipation; (*f*) drawings resembling types (*c*) and (*d*), but which confuse the trajectory of the extremity of the rod (although marked with a small red sphere) with the rod itself; (*g*) a successive series of small points in the shape of an oval – which is almost correct; (*h*) correct drawing.

Table 29 gives the percentage of these various types of reaction.

TABLE 29   *Rotation of a rod* (*360°*) *and of its extremity* (as % of the subjects)
(*N*=20, 20 and 10)

	Rod					Extremity			
	a	*b*	*c*	*d*	*e*	*a*	*f*	*g*	*h*
5 years	25	10	20	15	30	10	25	65	0
6 years	25	10	10	5	50	25	25	50	0
7 years	10	0	20	0	70	0	10	70	20

It can be seen that for the rod itself the successes are of the same order as those in Table 26 (90° rotation). It is difficult, however, to compare the trajectories of extremities with those in Table 27, as reaction *g* is almost correct.

The reactions to the questions concerning the two segments of the rod may be classified as follows. Upper segment: (1) no anticipation; (2) a horizontal line (the rod) surrounded by an oval; (3) numerous segments of parallel or extended straight lines grouped in a square figure (cf. type II, Table 28, Figure 10); (4) straight lines radiating from a single centre (=complete rods); (5) segments of straight lines arranged in an oval (=almost correct); (6) the latter arranged in a circle (correct figure). For the lower segment types 1–3 and 5 are found, type 4 being replaced by a form (7) that is nearly correct (oblique lines centred at the extremity of the rod), and form 8, which is correct. See Table 30 below:

TABLE 30 *Rotation through 360° of the two distinct halves of the rod* (In brackets: the lower segment) *and choice from prepared drawings* (As % of the subjects)

	1	2	3	4	5	6	7	8	Choice
5 years	15 (20)	15 (10)	10 (5)	10	45 (35)	5	(10)	(20)	45 (25)
6 years	10 (20)	5 (15)	0 (0)	15	60 (25)	10	(20)	(20)	60 (45)
7 years	0	0	0	0	80 (50)	20	(20)	(30)	100 (50)

It can be seen from this that the spontaneous successes (6 and 8) are less numerous for the complete rotation of 360° than for that of 90° (Table 28). On the other hand, when the child makes a choice from among the prepared drawings, which include the main errors as well as the correct solution, the success rate is of the same order as the spontaneous successes in Table 28. The chief difficulty in this test was encountered in distinguishing the respective paths of the distal and proximal halves of the rod (relative to the centre). The two halves tend to be confused in the spontaneous drawings, but are differentiated when the child is asked to choose from the prepared drawings.

VI. Let us now examine the question of the length of the drawn rods when imagined in their rotational positions. The two most remarkable aspects of the results obtained for this were, firstly, the variability of the estimations not only from one individual to another but from one group average to another, and secondly, the excessive character of these averages which frequently depart from the norms for under- and overestimation of length. These two facts have two causes that are ultimately reducible to one single cause. The first is the variable effect of the different techniques used. The drawings are influenced in different ways depending on whether the subject's attention is drawn to the fixed nature of the pivot or not. Thus he will either produce a drawing starting from the centre but under-estimating the length because he does not know where to stop the free end (exaggerated precautions to avoid exceeding the boundary point). Or he will draw lines which are too long, and which start from a variety of centres because he is aiming at fictitious limits, as in errors 3 and 5–6 in Table 26 where overestimation is almost inevitable. But behind this first cause there is a second, which is fundamental. If the subject is sensitive to the effects of the different methods, it is because he is normally inclined to neglect the lines' fixed starting point (the centre of rotation). Now the perimeter marked out by the free end of the rod in its different positions is a circle, and the child is unable to imagine in any clear way that its radius is determined by length of the rod itself. This means that the child oscillates between two possible types of unco-ordination – one relating to the starting point, and the other to the finishing point. Hence the excessive overestimation of length, which results from a fear of overstepping the bounding perimeter, and the unusual over-estimations, which are due to the influence of fictitious boundary points. In other words there is a mixture of variability and results quantitatively deviating from the usual norm.

M. Anthonioz measured an underestimation of -41 per cent at 4 years for the mobile rod (whereas the fixed 10 cm rod[9] is only underestimated by -14.2 per cent by the same subjects) and of -36.6 per cent at 5 years. Similarly E. Schmid found -40 per cent at 5 years for a 15 cm rod at 45°, while F. Paternotte obtained results of $+13.4$ per cent overestimation for positions below 90° with a 15 cm rod at 5 years, $+15.4$ per cent at 6 years and $+11.8$ per cent at 7 years.

As a means of comparison it might be useful to give first of all the results gathered by Tuât Vinh-Bang for the straightforward copy of an oblique line at 45°, and for indication of its length by pointing, without introducing any rotation. See Table 31.

TABLE 31 *Copy, and indication by pointing, of the length of a fixed oblique of 15 cm – averages of errors as % of 15 cm*
(Average length given in brackets) (10 subjects for each age group)

	5 years	6 years	7 years
Copy	$- 8.5$ (13·7)	-14.4 (12·8)	-15.2 (12·7)
Pointing	$+21.6$ (18·2)	$- 1.6$ (14·7)	$- 3.6$ (14·4)

	8 years	9 years	Adults
Copy	-9.7 (13·5)	-10 (13·5)	-2.6 (14·7)
Pointing	$+0.4$ (15·1)	$+ 6.3$ (15·9)	$+1.5$ (15·2)

[9] The long side of the right angle employed in III.

We find, then, the same laws of underestimation in the drawing and of overestimation in the digital assessment as are found for any straight line – though here development is less regularly related to age than in the case of the horizontal lines of Tables 1 and 3–7. But what would happen in the case of rotating obliques, with or without given reference points, and with stabilization of the pivotal centre?

At our request D. Nicollier examined twenty-four subjects aged 5,0 to 6,5 years in the following way. The children were asked to draw a 15 cm rod, imagining a rotation of 90° starting from a vertical position. The pivotal centre was kept constant by marking it with a large black point at the beginning of each drawing. In situation I the model rod remains in a vertical position. It is drawn in this position. The oblique positions are simply imagined and then drawn on the same sheet, the vertical acting as a reference. In II the drawings of the oblique lines are done on separate sheets: this suppresses the vertical reference. In III we introduce a horizontal rod which is fixed at the same point as the vertical rod. The child copies both, before going on to imagine and then draw the oblique positions. There are therefore two reference elements: the drawings are executed on the same sheet of paper, and the stability of the pivot is made clear.

The results presented in Table 32 give the percentage of underestimations, equalizations and overestimations of the average length of the oblique lines relative to the copy of the vertical. The lines may be curved to a lesser or greater degree, in which case their total length is measured – though results are exactly the same if the shortest distance between extremities is taken. The problem is to establish whether the absence or presence of reference elements modifies the image in one direction or the other. Lengths differing only 0·5 cm more or less were counted as equalizing.

TABLE 32 *Percentage of overestimations, equalizations and underestimations of the average lengths of rods rotated through 90° relative to the vertical*
(% of the subjects from 5,0 to 6,5 years)

	I	II	III
Overestimation	55	16	45
Equalization	25	26	45
Underestimation	20	58	10

It can be seen from this that even when the child is obliged to maintain a stable pivotal centre, the presence of the vertical reference leads to a majority of overestimation – which further explains the overestimations observed by F. Paternotte (Table 26, etc.). On the other hand, absence of this reference (II) leads to a majority of underestimations, because the subject does not know where to fix the terminal limits, although he can imagine the rod's positions.[10] Where there are two means of reference (III) there is a high proportion of overestimations, though they are evened out by equalizations (in consequence of the fixity of the pivotal centre).

But when neither reference nor fixed centre is imposed (the latter is of course implicit, but is not emphasized for each drawing), it is underestimation that is dominant. In the same way, M. Anthonioz finds that for a 5 cm rod rotated through 360° in these conditions there were 34 per cent overestimations relative to the copy up to 180°, 13 per cent accurate estimations (+ or − 1·8 mm) and 53 per cent underestimations; above 180° he found 15 per cent overestimations, 11 per cent equalizations and 74 per cent underestimations.

The diversity of the overestimations and underestimations observed for the imagination of the rotation of the rods, as opposed to the general underestimation of motionless vertical, horizontal and even immobile oblique lines (Table 31), is due to two systematic difficulties of co-ordination. On the one hand the child finds it difficult to stabilize the line's starting point, and on the other he finds it difficult to determine the terminal limit, that is the geometrical locus generated by the line's end points. It is due to his failure to grasp this geometrical locus that the subject frequently overestimates the length of the lines. He uses the vertical or horizontal references, the extremities of which he has a tendency to join up in a square shape − which necessarily entails overestimation of the obliques.

To turn to this geometrical locus, we note here that the following forms representing the external boundary of the figures corresponding to the 360° rotations were found by S. Taponier, F. Paternotte, E. Schmid-Kitsikis, *et al.*: a correct circle, partial circles (a quarter or, more often, a semi-circle, etc.), ovals (a particularly frequent figure, which, in cases where the pivot is kept constant, gives rise to overestimation in the lateral parts as well as to underestimation in the central part), kidney shapes (ellipse with concave segment on one side), irregular curvilinear forms, closed partly rectilinear, partly curvilinear forms, zigzag lines, and closed forms with horizontal and vertical rectilinear contours (rectangles and even squares). It is apparent that, depending on the figure or part of these figures, the lines representing the rotating rod will tend, even if they start from a common point, to be overestimated as well as underestimated. We thought it useful to emphasize this aspect of the question of rods in rotation. It shows that the generally predominant underestimations (see

[10] It should be noted that, contrary to the situation for Table 9 (Chapter Two, section 3), the positions are not indicated beforehand by tracing their outline with the finger.

Chapter Two, etc.), are not due to the purely graphical demands encountered in drawing, but rather to factors related to boundary points, since in the present case they occasion overestimation almost as often as underestimation.

VII. One last question is raised by the variable nature of the estimations of length – the question of conservation of length. It will be remembered (Chapter Two, Table 2) that in cases where the rod accomplishes a rotation of 180° and thereby places itself in extension of the starting line, conservation of the length is accepted at 5 years by 77 per cent of subjects, although only after hesitation and sometimes after vain attempts to discover evidence of non-conservation. In the present case non-conservations were more numerous.

The child was shown two rods 15 cm long, and that they were equal in length. One of the rods was set up in a vertical position, the other was gradually displaced from 0 to 90°. The child was asked whether they remained the same length or not. When necessary we occasionally enlarged on the question by saying that there are two ants running along the rods, and asking whether 'they have as far to go – '.

Now following this procedure, 67 per cent of twenty-four subjects aged 5,5 to 6,5 years, comparing one of the oblique positions with the vertical, affirmed non-conservation. This fell to 33 per cent, however, when the horizontal was compared with the vertical. For example Sor (6 years) said that '*the rod gets bigger when it turns round*'. (It was then turned slowly): '*Yes, it is longest here* (at 45°).' And Tea (6 years): '*The stick gets longer when it turns round and gets smaller again at the end.*' Cat (5,6 years) found that the vertical was '*bigger*' and reckoned that to make the rods equal it would be necessary to add 2 to 3 cm to the oblique line depending on the positions (this corresponds to the error type 6 in Table 26). Pal (5,9) reacted in the same way but judged the rods to be equal when they are both in oblique positions at a distance of 20° to 30°. As for the cases of conservation, Val (7 years) replied, '*It stays as it is!*' And Stra (7 years), '*The stick doesn't get any bigger!*'

VIII. It seems clear what general conclusions should be drawn from these facts (I–VI). Generally speaking, imaginal representation of a rod rotating about one of its ends raises no problems at 4 to 5 years, since the child is familiar with the movement. But in spite of this, difficulties start when he has to co-ordinate this rotation with one of the rod's extremities, be it the central pivot or the terminal point of the free end. Of the six intervening factors which we listed as possible in I, and which we checked in II–VI, it emerges that in fact only two are crucial, namely, those relating to the fixity of the pivotal centre, and those relating to the frame formed by the bounding positions of vertical and horizontal in the 90° rotation. On the one hand, unless particular care is taken to draw the subject's attention to the stability of the pivotal centre, he naturally makes the mistake of neglecting it, even if he can see (and is explicitly told of the fact) that the rod is turning round on a nail. Here lies our first problem: the reasons for this neglect of the initial boundary points. On the other hand, when the child's kinetic representations are guided by the emphasizing of the extreme positions of the rod (for the 90° rotation), the vertical-horizontal framework gives rise to other types of error combined with the first. This raises a second problem (which likewise arises from inability to differentiate between the trajectory of the rod's extremity and the successive positions of the rod as a whole – see the conclusions of I), namely, the reasons for the primacy of the terminal boundary points. It is true that it could be said that these two questions concern operational co-ordination of the displacements, and not the image as such of the rotation. But if it is not considered as spatial representation of the co-ordinations formed between the turning object's extremities and the positions inherent in the reference system, what exactly is the mental image? It is in fact the incomplete mental image characteristic of the preoperational level. And there can only be a complete image when it depends either on operations later acquired by the subject or on intuitive aids introduced by the experimental apparatus (as in II) – which necessarily produce artificially achieved results, in contrast to the spontaneous images of the young subjects.

All things considered, the upshot of this long analysis is that the image is closer to notions than perceptions, though none the less unique. Preoperational notions prompt ordinal rather than metrical assessment of length. This explains the importance of boundaries, the relative order of which provides the criteria (in terms of farther and nearer). But in order to have recourse to the boundaries, it is first necessary to imagine them. It is then that by a systematic simplification of the kinetic image oriented in the direction of the motion in question, the terminal boundaries associated with finishing points preponderate over the initial points. It is this that explains what is in fact the unity of the whole of the present results I to VI – as well as their compatibility with the preceding results (section 1 of this chapter) where the terminal boundaries were the main concern.

4. Gestural imitation of the trajectory of two fixed points on a rod rotated through 90°

The general drawback of the experiments described in the last section is that (apart from one or two attempts at gestural reproduction) they involve drawing. We thought it useful, therefore, to examine imitation effected by different means. In collaboration with

P. Mounoud we carried out an experiment in which the subject was required to use his finger to trace out the rotation of two luminous points seen through frosted glass. Behind the glass the points were attached to a rod 30 cm in length, which was lowered slowly from a vertical to a horizontal position.

Facing the opaque screen (50 × 60 cm) the child can see a luminous red point 30 cm away from the base, a green point 20 cm away from the base, and a white point, corresponding to the pivotal centre, on the base itself. The subjects were divided into two groups of twenty-eight and twenty-nine (seventeen aged 5, twenty-four aged 6, and sixteen aged 7). The first group were told what goes on behind the screen but were not actually shown the mechanism. The second group was given no explanation. When the red and green points had completed the 90° rotation (the white light was either switched on all the time or else only for a second rotation executed immediately after the first), the child was asked to point with his forefinger to the starting points and finishing points of the luminous marks on the screen. Then he was asked to trace out the paths of the points with his finger. The motion was repeated and the child asked to locate the green light for different positions of the red.

The child was then shown two partial rotations and was requested to indicate again the starting and finishing points of the trajectories. The request was repeated after a further complete 90° rotation. Finally, we established whether the white light was being imagined as fixed or mobile.

Four types of trajectory were obtained: A, rectilinear and varying inclination (complete or incomplete parallel); B, adumbrated but inadequate rotation; C, distortion and exaggeration of the rotational movement (sudden swerves, etc.); D, correct rotation.

For the location of the green light relative to the red we shall distinguish a type (a) no attempt at alignment, a type (b) abrupt haphazard attempts at alignment, a type (c) tentative trial and error, and (d) correct first time.

The results obtained from this experiment are set out in Table 33. The figures in brackets correspond to group II (where the mechanism is not explained), and the other figures to group I.

TABLE 33 *Gestural reproduction of complete trajectories*
(Group II given in brackets)
(As % of the subjects)

	Type A	Type B	Type C	D (success)	White point unmoved
5 years N = 9 (8)	44 (38)	44 (12)	0 (50)	12 (0)	22 (12)
6 years N = 12 (12)	17 (30)	33 (20)	25 (10)	25 (40)	75 (8)
7 years N = 7 (7)	0 (0)	30 (11)	0 (33)	70 (55)	86 (22)

It can be seen that even when the rod's rotation is explained (group I) gestural imitation of the trajectories is not successful until 7 years – at the same age, that is, as in the case of the drawings in Tables 26 and 29. Difficulty in keeping the pivotal centre in place is found at 5 years, even in group I; ability to maintain it is acquired at 6 years in group I, but in group II it has still not been acquired at 7 years.

At 7 years the general difference between the two groups is fairly clear (the development with age in group I being more regular), which would seem to indicate that some part is played by comprehension and concept at the level where the image is fully evolved. As the difference between the groups is less marked in the case of the test on location of the green point, and as fewer subjects were tested, we give the results for both groups combined (Table 34).

TABLE 34 *Location of the green light relative to the red*
(As % of the subjects)

	Type a	Type b	Type c	Type d	Types c + d
5 years (8)	38	25	38	0	38
6 years (17)	30	12	35	23	58
7 years (13)	0	22	62	15	77

We combine types *c* and *d*, since a correct response, albeit a tentative one, is obtained for type *c*. It then seems that the relations in question can be successfully imagined from the age of 7 years.

5. *The movements and positions of a snail on a path*[11]

The chief difficulties in imagining the reproduction of the movements considered in sections 1–4 were related to the boundary as finishing point, the internal boundary, or the fixed nature of the starting point (the centre of rotation, for example). It would therefore be of interest to turn now to movements which have no external boundary, which occur within a closed framework, and in which any problems will be related to the orientation and position of the moving body. Such a body would have to have anterior and posterior, and upper and lower parts – head and tail, back and feet. We first thought of using a model insect traversing the top and sides of a closed box. But in spite of the fact that they must have experienced this in everyday life, young children find it hard to imagine a fly moving about upside down with its feet to the ceiling and back

[11] In collaboration with M. Bovet, D. Nicollier and R. Droz.

downwards. In the end we used a plasticine snail with a magnet concealed in the foot so that it could adhere to a metal track in any position, with its shell pointing downwards, upwards or sideways.

The problems arising in this section will not then be concerned with the dimensional characteristics of translation or rotation, but exclusively with the three following topological characteristics: the orientation of the moving body in relation to the direction of its path (determinable by the position of the head); the general position of the moving body in relation to the frame (outside or inside, above or below); local positions of the moving body in relation to the frame (foot and not shell against the side, etc.). It will be of some interest to examine whether the image is more easily elaborated in the case of these elementary relations than in the case of those relations connected with displacements proper.

Two main procedures were used. In the first the subject was required to imagine the movement of the snail along solid metal strips in a square or circle, or else along tracks drawn in one plane. He was required to draw the positions, or better, to represent the snail in the required position by means of a small construction in three parts – head, shell and foot. (See Figure 11.)

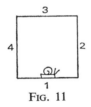

FIG. 11

In the second the child was required to imagine the snail's movement along four different metal strips with four distinct forms. The child was asked simply to place in positions *B*, *C*, and *D* a second snail identical to the first, which remained in position *A*. (Figure 12.)

I. In the first of these methods we began by getting the child to draw the snail diagrammatically in various positions, particularly in the upside-down position, but not inside the frame. We also made quite clear to the child that the snail can remain in any position whatever, by 'sticking' the magnetic model on a small metal plate. The experimenter placed the snail in position 1 and showed the child that it can only go straight ahead without turning round, and that it cannot pass outside the frame. The problem of interiority may be eliminated by colouring the interior and exterior of the frame differently; if the problem is interesting in itself, as it is for Figure 13, the frame can be left as it is.

The experimenter went on to trace out the snail's path on the frame with his finger, stopping at positions 2, 3, and 4, returning to 1. For each

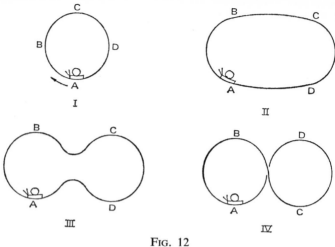

FIG. 12

position the child was asked to draw the snail (or to construct it, using his sectional model). The drawings were done sometimes on separate sheets of paper, sometimes on the same sheet; in both cases the frame was drawn for the subject in advance.

As a variation of this the solid three-dimensional frame was replaced by a two-dimensional drawing of a frame to be thought of as a window-sill along which the snail is moving.

When he had executed his drawings the subject was asked to justify them; other solutions were suggested, and the experimenter asked whether they were better or not; and above all the child was made to go round the track with the snail itself (stopping in positions 2, 3 and 4), and then to start his drawings all over again. A control test was carried out for comparison. It consisted in placing in different positions a flower which the snail was supposed to go and look at, but which was not to figure in the child's drawing.

In the first investigation, using seventeen subjects aged 5 to 9 years, eleven children made errors of orientation (direction of the path reversed) in position 3 (Figure 12), and four made similar errors in position 4. Six of the same subjects made errors of inclination in positions 2 and 4 (non-vertical positions). The most striking error was the reversal of positions relative to the frame in five of these subjects at position 3, in three at position 4, and in one at position 2. Instead of being upside down on the 'ceiling' (position 3), the snail was left in its usual position, so that its shell and not its feet (or the wings and not the legs when we used the fly) touched the top at position 3, or the sides in positions 2 and 4! Calculating the success percentage for the succession as a whole we found 52 per cent for position 2, 23 per cent for position 3, and 29 per cent for position 4. The 'ceiling' position is naturally the hardest, but of the two lateral positions that nearest the starting point is by far the easier, since it requires a 'shorter' or more immediate anticipation.

Examining seventy subjects aged 4–5 to 7 years with the two-dimensional technique, with drawings on separate and on single sheets,[12] and with and without the flower, we found that the types of error were the same – with two exceptions. The first of these was that there were fewer errors of position in relation to frame (the snail not upside down in 3), though such errors do still appear. The second was that errors of inclination were more frequent (snail horizontal on vertical side, etc.). The completely successful responses were distributed as follows (in brackets successes after demonstration of snail's circuit):

TABLE 35 *Successes for imagination of the movement of the snail (technique I)*
(As % of the responses)

	4–5 years (N=25)	6 years (N=23)	7 years (N=22)
Without flower	33 (50)	31 (62)	47 (90)
With flower	28 (72)	57 (85)	60 (87)

The first point is that the graphic representations of the snail's path (without flower and without preliminary demonstration) are no better than those of the displacements studied earlier. But when the subject has followed through the actual movement of the model, the image, which then becomes a simple delayed copy, is successfully achieved at 7 years, although at 4 to 6 years the success rate is only 50 per cent to 62 per cent. Another instructive finding is that when the flower is placed in positions 2, 3 and 4 the success rate improves appreciably at 6 years, especially when the child has seen the actual path of the snail demonstrated (at 4 to 5 years). In other words it is easier for the child to imagine the position and orientation of a moving body in relation to a fixed object than in terms of the movement – which once again shows the difficulty of kinetic images.

As for the number of successes for the position, the same result is found as in the initial investigation. Position 3 ('ceiling') naturally occasions the greatest number of errors. Particularly frequent was the placing of the snail above the frame rather than inside it (below the line). Although they are both lateral positions, 4 gave rise to 30 per cent more errors than position 2, the reason being that in the last case anticipation is at shorter range.

[12] There was no appreciable difference here, except perhaps that the younger children were slightly more successful when separate sheets were used – probably because some perseverations are thereby avoided.

The justification of the drawings received after testing gave some interesting results. First of all one notices the persistence of certain positional errors. For example Bes at 7,3 years still did not draw the snail upside down in position 3 ('ceiling') and fails to accept the correct drawing suggested by the experimenter, *'because here* (in the drawing) *the snail is standing on his head'*! And it remains true that the young subjects justify their drawings, even when correct, without referring to the snail's path. Their explanations run thus: *'because it is on one side and sticks'* (Mis 5,3); or again, *'because it is at the top and hangs down'* (Car 5,11). At 7 years, however, more than half the subjects do refer to the snail's path, thus replacing the initial static images with kinetic images. But the fact remains that in all three age groups errors of direction outnumber errors of position. And this will prove to be the case also for the circle in method II (Table 36).

II. We turn now to the results of method II, in which metal frames of four distinct forms were used (Figure 12; the oval and the figure of eight were presented in a horizontal position as they appear in the figure, but also in a vertical position). The questions put to the child were not concerned with graphic, but with direct anticipation: he was asked to reproduce the anticipated position by means of a second snail held in the air, and by means of a verbal description.

Several plasticine snails (red and black) with magnets attached to their bases were used. The metal frames were coloured black on both sides.

The test was in three phases: (1) The metal strips were shown to the subject (the order being varied from subject to subject), and he was allowed to confirm for himself that the snail could 'stick' head downwards to a ceiling (a metal box was used for this). The snail was then placed at *A*, and the experimenter explained that it was going to move round the track without turning back at all. Then the child was asked to describe *verbally* what the snail's *situations* would be at points *B*, *C* and *D* on the curve – whether they would be inside or outside the metal strip, above or beneath it, and so on. Then, starting again from *A*, the child was again asked to describe the *orientation* of the snail at *B*, *C* and *D* – the orientation of the head, that is, in relation to the direction of the circuit, etc. (2) In phase 2 we were concerned with direct indication. The *situation* of the snail is indicated by pointing with the finger. Then the subject is again asked to imagine the path traversed by the snail, and to indicate its imagined *orientation* by means of a second snail held in the air. (3) The snail's *situations* are again indicated on the metal track by pointing, and the *orientations* by this time placing the snail in position also on the track.

We examined sixteen children aged 4 years, twenty aged 5, twenty-one aged 6, nineteen aged 7, and fourteen aged 8. Further, twenty subjects were separately examined in order to observe eye and hand movements (digital, etc.) accompanying their attempts to reconstitute the snail's track. Table 36 above gives separately the results for the snail's situation, its orientation, and for both. Only those successes that were both verbal (phase 1) and gestural (phases 2

TABLE 36 *Successes for imagination of the movements of the snail (technique II)*

	4 years	5 years	6 years	7 years	8 years
Circle I:					
Situation	53	80	89	94	100
Orientation	45	66	82	76	100
Both	33	53	77	76	100
Horizontal Oval II:					
Situation	27	33		100	100
Orientation	36	48		85	100
Both	9	11		85	100
Upright Oval:					
Situation	33	77			100
Orientation	60	33			100
Both	28	11			100
Concave Oval III:					
Situation	33	47	65	88	100
Orientation	40	55	73	95	100
Both	6	33	55	83	100
Figure of eight IV:					
Situation	7	15	25	33	28
Orientation	23	52	61	61	64
Both	0	12	20	28	14
General averages:					
Situation	30·6	50·4		78·7	88·0
Orientation	40·8	50·8		79·1	80·6
Both	15·2	24·0		68·0	80·6

and 3) were counted, except for a certain number of 5-year-olds whose language was too vague compared with direct indication. It can be seen that direct anticipation (verbal and gestural) bearing on a circle results in better imagination of situation and orientation (taken together) at 4 to 7 years, than the graphic anticipation relating to the square figures of Table 35. However, if we go on from the circle to the other forms, we find that successes only begin to appear from 7 years onwards, and from 8 years in the case of the figure of eight. Further, in the case of the circle, it can be seen that situations have a higher success rate than orientations at all ages. On the other hand,

in the case of the elongated forms II–IV presented flat, orientations are more successful, since the direction of the movement is easier to imagine.

In about a quarter of the responses at 4 years[13] and more or less frequently up to 6 years, a qualitative analysis reveals a type − − + (i.e. B and C incorrect, D apparently correct). In other words the snail keeps its initial situation and orientation: above the metal strip (which is not necessarily the same as inside it), head turned to the left. For instance, Evi, at 6,0 years, said of the concave oval (III), point C: '*Its head is towards the window* (to the left) *because that's how the snail starts off* (from A).' Now when we analysed behaviour of those subjects who imagine these configurations as completely static, we noticed that their eyes did not follow the curve but jumped directly from A to B, from B to C, and from C to D, thus delineating a rectangle in the case of the oval and a quadrilateral with its long sides intersecting in the case of the figure of eight. One subject, Vil, aged 5,1 years, actually accompanied her eye movements with a gesture of her forefinger tracing a rectangle in the air for the oval. In short, at what is probably a primitive level, these subjects appear to be incapable of following the metal strip through, either with the eyes or mentally. The image consisting as it does of internalized imitation, this deficient motricity is translated into a static image of the distance covered, and the snail's situation and orientation remain unchanged accordingly. Here we are at the heart of what is probably the chief reason for the 'pseudo-conservations' of the static image, which in the reactions described in sections 1–2 leads to conservation of boundaries, and which in the present instance leads to conservation of positions.

It is possible to distinguish *semi-static* configurations due to the fact that the child's eyes succeed in following part and part only of the metal strip – for instance, the curve between A and B and between B and C in the regular oval and in the concave oval, and in certain sections of the figure of eight. There is then a conflict between the static or discontinuous tendency to pass directly or vertically between points A and B or C and D, and the new tendency to follow out the path bit by bit in its continuity. One of the most frequent types of such semi-static configurations is the type + + − for the orientation. It seems here – and we were able to establish the fact in some cases – that the subject is following the curve with his eyes from A to B and from B to C, only to jump directly from C to D. Hence the error for D, which is all the more paradoxical as in this case the snail at D would turn its back on the reference snail at A (in the case of the regular and the concave oval). Similarly, in the figure of eight presented flat, the subject was often successful as far as point C (where the snail is beneath the metal

[13] And in 4/5 of the subjects as against 2/3 at 5 years, 1/9 at 7 years, and in none at 8 years.

strip facing right), but then he would jump to D, conserving the snail's point C position, which is doubly erroneous. It is possible here, as before, to spot the child's error by watching his eye movements, and sometimes even his efforts to describe the course in the air with his forefinger.

There is another more advanced type of configuration in which the subjects understood the need for inversions and changes in orientation at certain points, but introduced them by jumps. Thus, for instance, we found a type $- + -$ (i.e. B incorrect, C correct, D incorrect), in which in the case of the figure of eight the subject passed directly from A to B, which means a failure to invert at B, from B to C, giving a correct result arrived at by an inexplicable route (a 'jump'), and finally went from C to D, a leap conserving the snail's position below the metal strip and facing right, which is a double error. Similarly in the error $- + +$, the subject moved directly from A to B, which produces an erroneous orientation at B as a result of the failure to follow the curve. But he then for no apparent reason introduced an inversion when moving from B to C, so that the result in C and D is correct. As the subject can always start again from A, these 'jumps' can be explained as a mixture of direct or discontinuous movements from one position to another and movements continuously traced out by the eyes along the metal track. The contradictions resulting from these two procedures remain unjustified by the subject, who gets out of it afterwards by saying that the snail has turned round and so on.

Unless they are purely fortuitous, it is no doubt to the mixture of these two procedures that we should also attribute the errors of the type $+ - +$ and $+ - -$. (The type $- - -$ did not occur in any consistent manner.)

The striking thing is, however, that the change-over from semi-static or semi-continuous configurations to correct, kinetic and continuous configurations is frequently signalized by gestural behaviour. This shows that in the case of the more difficult movements imaginal representation is not immediately internalized. Thus at 6 to 7 years the subject is often seen accompanying eye movements with finger movements, as if it were a question of *grasping* the path by means of a twofold ocular and gestural imitation. This twofold imitative activity, which yields correct answers, naturally takes a certain amount of time, in contrast to the rapidity of the younger children's reactions. It is also noteworthy that the verbal explanation of the 6- to 7-year-old subjects is sometimes vague or frankly erroneous, whereas their gestural imitations are correct, giving accurate situations and orientations.

At about 8 years imaginal representations are internalized, and there is a distinct decrease in gestural imitation. We observed a particularly interesting transitional phase, when the path traced out by the finger was reduced in size, as if the subject were delineating a miniature curve prior to purely mental anticipation. At the final stage, the child follows out the metal track correctly with his eyes, but at the same time simply holds his snail in the air, turning it round on a fixed axis without any further attempt to imitate externally its mentally imagined path.

To conclude, these experiments show that even for the topological relationships, as distinct from the dimensional characteristics of the displacements described in sections 1 to 3, the laws of the image remain generally true in their double aspect – the transition from static to kinetic, and the transition from physical to internalized imitation.

6. *The conservation of longitudinal order* (*before, behind*) *and transverse order* (*left, right*) *during circular motion*

The following investigation, which was undertaken with D. Nicollier and R. Droz, is a continuation of the snail experiments, but introduces questions concerning the order of moving bodies one behind the other or side-by-side. As snails are not in the habit of going about side-by-side or in single file, we replaced them with two airmen looping a loop equivalent to the circle in the previous tests. And as it is best if the movement constitutes a single and complete whole without any possibility of misunderstanding, we placed the pilots in the same aeroplane, on two seats either side-by-side or one behind the other. The problem is to conserve these positions during the course of the movement.

The apparatus used by the experimenter consisted of a small plastic aeroplane (25 × 25 cm) with three spaces for the pilots, two in front and one behind. It was coloured green on top and yellow underneath, and had two wooden pilots, one red, the other yellow. A metal strip in the form of a circle 1 metre in diameter represented the 'plane's path; it was held in a vertical position by means of a fixed suspension device which ensured that an exact circle was maintained. The child was placed at a distance of 1·50 metres so that he could see the model both in its details and as a whole.

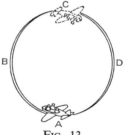

FIG. 13

The child was given a small magnetized plate symbolically coloured yellow and green to represent the 'plane. A metal propeller could be attached to the plate at any point to mark the front of the 'plane. Two small pilots made of iron wire, one red and the other yellow, could also be fixed anywhere on the plate.

The child was asked to do the following things: (1) To reproduce the trajectory in the air, using the metal plate and taking account of the top-bottom relations. (2) To reproduce the path of one pilot only without the metal plate. We placed a pilot in the model aeroplane, reminded the child of the trajectory, and then asked him to show the airman's position at points *A*, *B*, *C* and *D* (Figure 13), using one of his own pilots. After each question the pilot was put back on the table. After *D* the child was asked for the complete circuit, and, if necessary, for some intermediate positions for extra details. (3) Positions of two pilots one behind the other, without the metal plate. We put the yellow pilot in the 'plane behind the red one and asked the child to indicate by means of his own pilots the absolute and relative positions of the two airmen at points *A*, *B*, *C*, *D* and *A*. It is hard to ask for the reproduction of the complete movements, but we attempted this in some cases, also asking for some intermediate positions for the sake of precision. (4) Two pilots one behind the other, using the metal mount. The questions put to the child in 3 were repeated, and questions added concerning the absolute position of the metal mount, the position of the propeller in relation to the 'plane (the child attached it to one end of the mount at each of the points *A*, *B*, *C* and *D*), and the absolute and relative positions of the two pilots (to be attached to the mount at each point along the circuit). The child's model was taken to pieces each time. (5) The two pilots side-by-side without the mount; the same questions as 3. (6) As 5 but with mount. (7) Justification by the child, and, if necessary, counter-suggestions.

I. We found the following successes in twenty-three subjects aged 5 years, nineteen aged 6 years, seventeen aged 7 years and ten aged 8 years (Table 37).

TABLE 37 *Successes for the positions of the 'plane and its pilots* (As % of the responses)

	1 (plane)	2 (one pilot)	3 (one pil. behind the other without plate)	4 (one pil. behind the other with plate)	1–4 together	5 (pils. side-by-side without plate)	6 (pils. side-by-side with plate)
5 years	57	5	6	39	0	39	41
6 years	80	19	7	37	0	21	26
7 years	100	19	29	65	14	43	63
8 years	100	22	45	80	11	78	90

It can be seen that the positions of the 'plane alone (question 1, without propeller, so without before–behind relation but with top–bottom relation) are hardly any easier to imagine, except at 7 years, than the circular path of the snail (Table 36, I, both questions). Greater difficulty is experienced in imagining the path of the pilot alone (question 2), since this involves combining the relations of orientation (facing forwards) and position (to the right at B, pointing down at C, to the left at D, and constantly perpendicular to the arc).[14] The same difficulties were encountered in question 3, though learning influenced the result slightly at 7 to 8 years. In question 4 the introduction of the metal mount helped the responses by providing a reference. Questions 5 and 6 benefit from learning effects and from the fact that the left–right relation is maintained and not reversed.

The errors observed are very similar to those observed in the snail experiments: perseveration of the initial position and in particular failure to invert at the top of the curve position C. But in addition there are errors of order in questions 3 and 4, and of juxtaposition (non-conservation of the left–right relation) in questions 5 and 6. As in the case of the snails, there is a failure to invert at C: the airmen are placed above their aeroplane, the difficulty being to represent it as constantly on the inside of the curve. But up to the age of six and even seven we also found the following error for position C – an error all the more paradoxical as human beings and not snails were in question. The 'plane was correctly represented upside-down and within the curve above the pilots – but the pilots themselves remained upright, so that relative to the 'plane they were standing on their heads with their feet in the air.

But the most persistent difficulty as far as the pilots were concerned was to imagine them as constantly perpendicular to the arc. This explains the poor success rate for questions 2 and 3 as compared with question 4. The snail crawls – which facilitates representation of its positions in relation to the vertical or inverted parts of its course. But man remains vertical (standing or sitting). Thus we find that the pilot is drawn vertical at B and D (therefore not perpendicular to the arc), but lying down at C, whereas if the mount is brought in he is never drawn as if lying down on it. (On the other hand the 'plane is sometimes drawn vertical at C and the pilots lying down – i.e. perpendicular to the mount, not to the circle.) The total number of complete successes for the perpendicularity of the pilot in relation to the circle (questions 2–6) was as follows:

TABLE 38   *Successes for perpendicularity (questions 2–6)*
  5 years $= 9\%$ 6 years $= 13\%$ 7 years $= 14\%$ 8 years $= 23\%$

II. For a better analysis of the left–right relations, which were conserved in the four positions preceding (though this does not mean the young subjects did not frequently permute them), we carried out a further inquiry in

[14] These difficulties occur in spite of the fact that to make things easier the pilots are not bent in a sitting position, but are upright and hold their arms out in front of them.

collaboration with D. Nicollier and C. Fot. Questions 3 to 6 were put to twenty subjects aged 6 to 7, but were this time applied to a track in the horizontal plane as well as the vertical; so that left and right are reversed between *A* and *C* or *B* and *D*. The results are clear: (*a*) the errors of orientation (where the heads are facing in the direction of the movement), still frequent at 6 years, disappear almost entirely at 7 years; (*b*) the errors of order (questions 3 to 4, where one pilot is behind the other) also become rare at 7 years, in spite of the fact that they persist at 6 years, albeit to a lesser extent than orientation errors; (*c*) the errors concerning the left–right relation (where the relation between the juxtaposed airmen remains but is reversed relative to the subject in positions *C–A* or *D–B*), are still frequent at 7 years, although from 6 to 7 years they decrease by half.

Generally speaking, however, questions 3–6 are, as one would expect, much easier in the horizontal than in the vertical position. There was an average success rate of 52·3 per cent at 6 years for the horizontal, as against 22·7 per cent for the vertical position, and 84·5 per cent at 7 years as against 50 per cent. It is only all the more interesting, therefore, to find that the errors for the left–right relation persist right up till 7 years.

7. *Conclusion*

There is a definite conclusion to be drawn from the results of the probes examined in this chapter. However familiar the movements in question may be (squares displaced, a rod falling or turning as the hand of a clock, moving objects going round in a ring), the kinetic reproductive image can be formed only in virtue of a reconstruction involving anticipation. This means that there is in fact no fundamental difference between the kinetic images studied in the present chapter and those we shall study in the next chapter as 'kinetic anticipatory images'. We made the distinction in order to establish whether the kinetic image goes through more complex processes of elaboration if it relates to content with which the subject is not familiar. As far as the images considered in this chapter are concerned, there seems to be no simple relationship between familiarity of content and the stage of development at which adequate corresponding images appear, in the sense of the direct correlation that Egon Brunswick sought to show between certain perceptual structures and the probability of occurrence of corresponding configurations in everyday experience. For instance, at 6 years the child can anticipate the positions of a snail or an aeroplane describing a circular path in the vertical (Tables 36 and 37) whereas we had to abandon the idea of using a model fly, even though it is common enough to see an insect moving about upside-down on a ceiling. And, even though the snail's and the 'plane's circular path is correctly imagined at 6 years, the movement of one object overtaking another (as the squares in section 1), which is a far commoner sight, is not imagined until 7 years (Table 17), and the rotation of a rod not until 7 to 9 years, depending on the methods used.

The degree of ease or difficulty encountered in the anticipations involved in kinetic images is not simply a function of empirical frequency, but depends rather on the complexity of the relationships involved. The principal relationships involved in this way seem to us to be constituted by ordinal references (initial and terminal boundary points), internal boundaries in the case of intersections, references implicit in the frames (interiority, etc.), and polarized juxtapositions (left–right relation). Now this is where one of the principal problems of the mental image arises. If in the course of development these various relations give rise to a gradual and retarded operational elaboration, one might conceive of the image succeeding, independently of any intelligent or notional comprehension, in providing at an early stage a sufficiently faithful picture for these relations to be put in place correctly, although not accompanied by a satisfactory conceptual interpretation. Let us be clear that this is precisely what is successfully realized by perception. A young child can distinguish perceptually between the positions AB and BA long before he is able to *judge* that A is to the left of B in the former, and to the right of B in the latter. Why should he not in the same way be able to *imagine* correctly the relations AB, then $\frac{AB}{BA}$ then BA, and so on, for two bodies moving round a horizontal track, without *comprehending* why there is an apparent reversal? If the image were a direct prolongation of perception, we should expect it to be usual for the image to be ahead of the notion. This should be even more true in the case of relations as simple as overlapping or projection, where the subject quite clearly perceives that one solid projects beyond another, even though all kinds of problems are raised from the notional point of view (non-conservation, then conservation of staggered lengths; see Chapter Eight, section 6). Why then does the image of a square slightly projecting beyond another (section 1 of this chapter) burden itself with difficulties concerning boundaries? One understands that the intelligence might stumble against such difficulties, since its function is to pose problems that escape immediate experience, but perception is not affected by them, and an imagery based on perception could easily do without them for elementary reasons of economy.

The third important point arising from this chapter, then, is this. Although mental image and notion are quite distinct, they do have certain characteristics in common – whether it be that the former inspires the latter, as might be the case for preoperational notions, or whether the latter is reflected in the former, as one might expect at operational levels. It is striking that with the exception of the circular paths of the snail and aeroplane (success at 6 years), none of the various familiar elementary movements considered in this chapter gives rise to an adequate image until the level of concrete operations has been reached. And this is precisely because these images are a function of the intellectual complexity of the relations in question, and not of the degree to which the child is perceptually familiar with them – which was by no means self-evident. Therefore, in order to make a more extensive analysis of the possible affinity between kinetic images in general and the concrete operations, we first need to examine kinetic anticipatory images. In this way we shall be able to establish whether we have to deal with two distinct categories of image, or whether, as this chapter tends to suggest, kinetic reproductive images are in any case anticipatory. In other words we have to establish whether there is any fundamental difference between those anticipations involved in reconstituting the known and those involved in unfamiliar and unforeseen situations.

CHAPTER FOUR

Kinetic Anticipatory Images

In this chapter we broach the study of kinetic anticipatory images as opposed to simple reproductive images. Basically, the two categories are distinguished in that the latter bear on changes of position already familiar to the subject, and which need only to be recalled, while the anticipatory images bear on changes with which the subject is only slightly familiar or not familiar at all. In fact, the problem will arise, as we have just seen, to establish if these two sorts of images develop simultaneously or not. In other words, do they correspond to successive stages or are they both formed at the same stage in the child's development? In the latter case, we would have to conclude that all kinetic reproductive images (and *a fortiori* transformation images), where they are not simple copies, comprise an element of reconstitution very close to anticipation and, therefore, do not differ essentially from anticipatory images. The modification of kinetic reproductive images which we have said we think we can detect at about 7 to 8 years (displacements of squares, etc.; the falling of a vertical rod to the horizontal, etc.) seems to suggest that at the stage when concrete operations appear kinetic images become what are in essence figural imitations of the operations. Now these of necessity involve the intervention of anticipatory schemes. This would mean that an element of anticipation might be attributed to the reproductive image when it bears on movements, or transformations. So we now need to ascertain whether, if the subject is asked to imagine movements less familiar than those hitherto used, there will be any appreciable retardation in the formation of adequate images, or whether it is at the beginning of the concrete-operational stage that decisive progress is to be observed. The latter would, if found to be true, show that the generalization of operational structures is enough to render spatial images sufficiently mobile to allow of any elementary kinetic representation.

1. *Rotation, circumduction and overturning of square figures*

The investigation described in this chapter was carried out with the assistance of F. Frank and J. Bliss. It concerns displacements of a square familiar to the subject. But there is also an element of anticipation relating to the position of two adjacent sides of the square. One of the sides of the moving square has a blue border, and one of the adjacent sides a red border. When the square is set in motion the subject will then have to imagine the position of the coloured sides. The motions are of three different kinds: simple rotation (top and bottom faces not permuted), overturning (faces permuted), and circumduction.

The child was shown two 10 cm squares, one white and serving to demonstrate the movements, the other coloured blue along its left side and red along its bottom side (both faces) and remaining motionless. There were three types of question put to the child in the following order – not in order of difficulty.

A Rotation The white square was rotated through 90° and the child was asked to show on the same square where the blue and red sides would be if it were the coloured square. This was repeated for 360°, 180°, and 270°, starting each time from 0°, with the second square motionless. Rotations were in a clockwise direction but sometimes an extra rotation in an anti-clockwise direction was demonstrated to finish up with. These anticipations rest simply on imaginal representation of the result of the rotations. Two further questions were posed which in contrast presuppose operational generalization and which might be useful in comparing the subject's image with his deductive comprehension. (1) Is it possible, if we turn the square 'lots of times', to reach a position where the colours are opposite one another? (2) We showed the child any random position for the blue side and asked him if it were possible to deduce where the red side would be without knowing the number of rotations (but still going in a clockwise direction).

B Circumduction We began by showing the child a regular circuit (circular in the order: 1, down; 2, left; 3, up; 4, right) using the coloured square without pauses at the various positions. Then we put the coloured square in position 1 and asked the subject to say where the coloured edges would be if the square were stopped in positions 2–4. Finally, as a control, we occasionally showed an irregular circumduction of the white square (no rotation, of course), and asked the subject what the positions of the colours would be if the second square went through the same motion.

C Overturning We turned over the white squares sideways and asked the child to deduce the positioning of the colours on the second square when turned in the same way. As the square has red and blue borders on both its faces, and as the blue edge is on the left and the red along the bottom, the blue border of course changes place, while the red one stays where it is. This was repeated two, three and sometimes four times. Then a question based on operational generalization may be brought in. The subject was requested to predict the positions of the red and blue borders for a large number (even and odd) of overturning motions.

Finally, we in some instances demonstrated vertical overturnings, and asked the subject to predict the colours; this was then done for two such motions compared with one or three. To conclude we returned to the operational aspect, and asked the child whether the result would be the same for a sideways turn-over followed by a 90° rotation as for the same motions in the reverse order.

I. The first result obtained was that anticipation of the position of the colours is distinctly easier for the circumduction (B) than for the rotation (A) or for overturning (C). This was to be expected, of course, as the subject merely has to predict permanence. This permanence, however, has nothing to do with perseveration, as the success rate is only about 50–55 per cent at 5 years and 6 years, and the image is only correct in 100 per cent of cases at 7 years. Since rotation does not meet with success until about 9 years, circumduction does have a systematic lead. This explains why in the tests described above the subjects showed a systematic tendency to replace rotation with circumduction, which avoids oblique positions and allows the square to retain its characteristic image with vertical–horizontal sides.

See the quantitative results for ninety-nine subjects aged 5 to 9 years, Table 39. (The four positions correspond to the cardinal points of the circumduction.)

Imaginal representation of the circumduction is then especially easy as it conserves the relations unchanged. And this is what the successful subjects said clearly enough: '*It stays as it is because it isn't turned sideways*' (Bea 8,1), or, '*because you are not turning the square like that* (rotation)' (Urs 8,4).

TABLE 39 *Successes for the positions of the circumduction* (As % of the subjects)[1]

	Position 1	Position 2	Position 3	Position 4	Total success
5 years (N=18)	71·5	55	71·5	66	*49·5*
6 years (34)	84	78	78	72	*72*
7 years (23)	92·5	88	92·5	83·5	*83·5*
8 years (20)	100	100	95	95	*95*
9 years (4)	100	100	100	100	*100*

There are, even so, some errors, particularly in position 2 where the 5-year-old subject sometimes introduces a rotation and then maintains the new relations. The colours were also sometimes reversed, and in three cases at 5 and 6 years the colours were placed opposite each other (blue facing,

[1] Position 1 is the starting position, after a complete rotation.

and not contiguous to the red). At 7 years there were two cases in which circumduction and overturning were confused.

Operational generalization (circumduction with irregular or random circuit) was immediate. We found only one instance of complete success without this generalization: Dom (6,3) began by modifying the positioning of the colours for the circular motion, but corrected herself spontaneously. On the other hand, for the irregular motion, she said: '*When you turn it round in a circle it doesn't change, but apart from that* (i.e. this particular circuit) *it does*,' The other subjects, however, generalized immediately: Mar (6,4) '*For the colours to change, it would have to turn like this* (rotation)'. Nic (7,5), '*It will be the same all the time because you haven't turned it round.*'

II. For the *rotation* (*A*), the two principal results were these. The belated character of the general successes (for the four positions), which are scarcely to be found before 9 to 10 years, and the considerable difference in difficulty between the 90° position and the 180°, 270° and 360° positions. It is remarkable to find that we thus arrive at two of the results that we shall come across again in section 2, using a quite different technique. Table 40, in the present section, shows that the successes for the 270° position (*R*4) are somewhat lower than those at 90° (*R*1), although the square is in a vertical–horizontal position in both cases. Using the coloured square we find in fact that up to 7 years the results are generally more than twice as good for 90° as for 180°, 270°, and 360°, and that they do not equalize until over 10 to 12 years. This is no doubt due to the fact that the help of the operations is required in order to sustain the image beyond a certain degree of rotation.

TABLE 40   *Successes for rotation of a square with two coloured sides* (As % of the subjects)

	90°	180°	270°	360°	Total success
5 years (N = 18)	27·5	22	5·5	0	0
6 years (34)	51	25	15	27	9
7 years (23)	53	35	31	43	24·5
8 years (20)	80	40	40	65	30
9 years (10)	70	60	50	50	40
10–12 years (15)	86	73	47	73	40

From the qualitative point of view the chief type of error was failure to differentiate rotation and circumduction: the subject could not get away from the starting position and could not imagine the displacements of the two coloured edges, with the result that he left them as they were, as if it was a circumduction.[2] This error may affect all four positions, but it may also happen that the subject succeeds with the 90° and even the 180° rotation, only to revert to the starting position. Some subjects execute two rotations and then stick at the configuration they imagined last. Another interesting type of error was the reversing of the order of the sides, either right from the beginning or after one or two rotations. This reversal was no doubt due to a failure to differentiate between the two procedures that should have been distinguished. On the one hand there is the change in absolute position of a given side *a*, which during the rotation finds itself at the left, then at the top, then at the right, by a succession of inversions. On the other hand there is the conservation of the relative order of the positions of the sides one in relation to the other, side *b* always coming after *a* during the rotation, in spite of the absolute inversions.

The other error types are of little account. One side may be correctly, the other haphazardly placed, or the rotations may be correctly represented but fail to correspond to the number indicated by the experimenter.

It is difficult to distinguish these different types of error for each case. Table 41 below therefore only gives the distribution of objectively determinable errors concerning the contiguity of the coloured sides and the relations between them. Thus we shall distinguish the following four kinds of error: (1) permanence (i.e. circumduction instead of rotation); (2) the sides placed opposite each other; (3) the sides remain contiguous but in the wrong order; (4) the correct order is maintained but the number of rotations is wrong.

TABLE 41   *Distribution of error, types 1–4*
(As % of the responses)[3]

	(1) Permanence	(2) Sides placed opposite	(3) Contiguous but order reversed	(4) Correct order but not corresponding with number of rotations
5 years	22	13	20	47
6 years	18	7	43	27
7 years	9	4	29	27
8 years	0	0	22	22
9–10 years	0	0	32	13

[2] This fact is particularly interesting as those subjects who took the rotation test did not go through the circumduction test.
[3] Except for question 1 expressed as a percentage of subjects.

This leads us on to the two operational questions put to the children in addition to the representation of the positions. We began with the question asking whether the contiguous red and blue sides can be opposite one another after a large number of rotations. First of all one sees (Table 41) that quite independently of any question posed by the experimenter, 4 per cent to 7 per cent of the responses at 6 to 7 years (and 13 per cent at 5 years) consisted in spontaneously drawing the red and blue sides in opposing rather than contiguous positions. This is similar to a reaction we shall discuss later (section 8) where the child thinks that if a rod along which three beads are threaded is rotated several times through 180°, the middle bead will reach one of the end positions. This does not mean, however, that these subjects, when questioned in a general way, will always reply that it is possible to get the two coloured sides opposite each other. We would represent such a reaction thus: $D - Q -$ (i.e. error for drawing, error for the question). Indeed, it does happen that a correct reply to the question may accompany an incorrect drawing – so that we have $D - Q +$. Conversely, one may come across subjects who do not draw the red side and the blue side in opposition, but who nevertheless reply when asked that this is possible – so that we have $D + Q -$. Finally, correct responses to both parts we represent as $D + Q +$. The distribution of these four combinations is set out in Table 42 below.

TABLE 42 *Opposition of blue and red sides in drawing D and operational question Q*
(As % of the subjects)

	$D - Q -$	$D - Q +$	$D + Q -$	$D + Q +$
5 years (14)	16	21	21	42
6 years	9	9	26·5	55·5
7 years	5·5	0	28·5	66
8 years	0	0	0	100
9 years	0	0	0	100

This shows that it is not until 7 to 8 years that 75 per cent of the subjects judge it impossible to place the contiguous sides in opposition. '*They can't both lie down flat*', said Ano already at 5,5 years; '*They are stuck together*' (Aeb 6,5); '*Because the red one is always next to the blue one*' (Nic 7,5); '*No, they are fastened together all the time*' (Gil 7,3).

On the other hand, when we put the second operational question to the child the reactions were much more retarded. Asked whether it would be possible to predict the position of one colour given the position of the other, but not the number of rotations (always in a clockwise direction), we found that only 43 per cent of the subjects at 8 years could correctly solve this question. Certain subjects were successful in the drawing but not the questions; for others the reverse was the case. However, although at 7 years the situation is the same in both cases (27 per cent success), we find that at 5 to 6 years the drawings are to some extent in advance of the results for the questions. The latter usually lead to the assertion that several positions are possible for one colour when the other is given, whereas the drawings are sometimes correct for certain positions. But before we come to the conclusion that in this particular area correct imaginal representations are not directed by the operations, it should be pointed out that this second operational question is not simply a matter of engaging some specific operation. It calls rather on a generalization based on a preliminary *prise de conscience*, which is not without its attendant difficulties. Mag (8,8), for instance, gave completely correct anticipation of the rotations, but, when asked whether for any one position of the blue side there could be several for the red, she began by saying there could be, and needed to turn the square several times before coming to her conclusion: '*No, you can't do it.*' A correct response, then, such as Dan's (8,10), '*The blue and red are together*', or Sto's (9,8), '*The red one is behind the blue one all the time*', demand more than an operational deduction for each separate case. What is required is retroactive reflexion on the various rotations once they are actively or mentally executed. This does not in any way mean that the operations are not involved in anticipation of the rotations. Nor does it in any way prove that anticipation results from a mere succession of undirected images, as if it were enough to contemplate internally an unfolding of events without actively intervening.

III. The problems of overturning seem to be of the same order of difficulty as – or may even seem a little easier than – the problems associated with rotation. At 8 to 9 years 75 per cent of the subjects imagine correctly one or two lateral and also vertical turn-overs.

Below this age the principal errors observed consisted in placing the colours anywhere at all haphazardly, in placing them opposite one another (this was rare, but parallel to what we found for rotation), in confusing vertical and lateral turn-overs, in simply alternating the colours, in failing to change the initial order, and finally – this is the most persistent error – in making do simply with an inaccurate alternation of the red border (for the vertical movement).

The quantitative results appear opposite.

The operational questions bear firstly on the permanence of the position of the red side, and secondly on the alternation of the blue

TABLE 43 *Successes for lateral overturnings*
(As % of the responses)

	1 Overturn.	2 Overturns.	3 Overturns.	Success for all three (For two in brackets)
5 years (24)	35	39	27	18 (14)
6 years (41)	62	53	45	27 (50)
7 years (18)	49	66	36	18 (44)
8 years (25)	93	78	58	50 (69)
9–10 years (11)	91	83	83	83 (83)
11–12 years (10)	90	90	90	90 (90)

side. As before we distinguish two types of response. First there are the successful representational anticipations given by drawing or pointing $D-$ or $D+$, and second, the successful replies to questions $Q-$ or $Q+$. The permanence problem is easily classified. But in the case of alternation it sometimes happens that the child produces one or two irregularities in his anticipations. He finds particular difficulty in verbally expressing the 'regularity' of the alternation. In Table 44 following, we have classified intermediate results along with correct responses (this is legitimate since the large majority of cases are intermediate in both D and Q).

We no longer find that immediate reactions are ahead of the *prise de conscience* or vice versa. The errors observed were principally pseudo-conservation of the colours, incorrect reversal, and, in 20 per cent at 5 years and 4 per cent at 6 years, opposition instead of adjacency of the colours.

TABLE 44 *Relations between imaginal anticipation (D) and operational question (Q) for the case of permanence and alternation in lateral overturnings*
(As % of the subjects)

	Permanence				Alternation			
	$D-Q-$	$D-Q+$	$D+Q-$	$D+Q+$	$D-Q-$	$D-Q+$	$D+Q-$	$D+Q+$
5 years N (12)	25	33	9	33	28	17	17	38
6 years N (22)	13	7	17	63	10	22	18	50
7 years N (13)	16	8	38	38	16	14	18	52
8 years N (11)	9	9	9	73	7	12	9	72

The vertical overturnings show similar results but appear to be slightly more difficult. We shall just quote here two correct responses to the operational questions posed in relation to these movements. '*The blue one* (left side) *doesn't change, it turns round on itself –*' (Fra, who was as young as 6,2 years); '*The red will be at the bottom* (after two turns), *because it is always two plus two plus two –'* (Bea 8,1).

On the other hand, the combination of the 90° rotation and the lateral turn-over raises a curious problem. Out of nineteen subjects who were completely successful in both tests separately, only three managed to combine the two, thinking of them as interchangeable transformations.

2. Anticipation of the positions of a square rotating in relation to a fixed figure

In this inquiry (carried out with E. Schmid-Kitsikis) we were concerned with the displacements of a square in relation to a second square. It thus follows on from the inquiry described in the last section, and in sections 1 and 2 of Chapter Three. In the preceding experiments we investigated the simple translations of a square. These were most probably well known to the child from his own experience, and would consequently give rise to kinetic reproductive images. But the rotations we are now going to discuss are less common in everyday activities and may therefore be considered to require the intervention of anticipatory images, whose complexity we shall see shortly.

Fig. 14

We took a blue square, side 30 mm, attached to a frame (see Figure 14). At the apex of its lower right-hand corner was a nail 5 mm long passing also through the top left-hand corner of a red square side 30 mm, and acting as a pivot. We showed this device to the child, drawing his attention to the fixed nature of the blue square and of the nail, and indicating the direction of the rotation. Then (1) we asked him to imagine the positions occupied by the red square when moved gradually, and to draw these positions (up to 360°). Each time the child kept the drawing just done in front of him, but all those done previously were removed. He was also asked to show the exact position of the nail in each drawing. It is understood of course that the red square remains motionless throughout this and the following part of the test. (2) We next gave the subject drawings to choose from (four series for the four 90° sectors), which included the main error-types as well as the correct figure. (3) We displaced the *red* square step by step, and the child copied each successive position. This enabled us to judge retrospectively in what way the solutions given for 1 might be related to drawing difficulties, and also this cleared the way for the next part of the test. (4) We left the red square motionless as before, and got the child to imagine again, and draw, the successive positions as in 1. This allowed us to come to some conclusion about improvements due to 3, and to use the test as an analysis of the reproductive image after learning.

First, a statistical breakdown of the following: (*A*) the fixed position of the blue square (the younger subjects turn it round with the red square); (*B*) the invariant form of the blue square; (*C*) the fixity of the pivot – an important index, which when ignored, lies behind a number of errors; (*R*1) the position of the red square after a rotation of 90°, when it is right up against the right side of the blue square; (*R*2) the oblique position of the red square before 90°, or between 90° and 180°; (*R*3) the covering of the blue square by the red square (we counted the reaction as correct when indicated once, whatever the order); (*R*4) the vertical–horizontal position of the red square beneath the blue one at 270°; (*R*5) the oblique position of the red square before 270° or between 270° and 360°; (*T*) totally success-ful response.[4]

TABLE 45 *Anticipation of the rotation of a square*
(Successes as % of the subjects)

	A	*B*	*C*	*R*1	*R*2	*R*3	*R*4	*R*5	*T*
5 years (10)	50	60	20	40	20	20	20	10	*10*
6 years (10)	60	60	40	70	20	30	20	20	*20*
7 years (15)	73·3	60	40	73·3	66·6	46·6	46·6	33·3	*33·3*
8 years (10)	100	70	40	100	60	40	40	30	*30*
9 years (6)	83·3	83·3	50	100	66·6	50	66·6	50	*50*
10–11 years (8)	100	100	75	100	100	75	100	75	*75*

On the whole it seems that in the case of the blue square the easiest way to react is to conserve its position and form – though this reaction is not immediate as it is not acquired in 75 per cent of the subjects until the age of about 7 to 8 years. But conservation of the pivot comes later still. This suggests at once that there is a tendency to replace rotation by circumduction. And this tendency is met again in the reactions to the positions of the red square. On the one hand, the success score for 0° to 90° (*R*1 and *R*2) is higher than for positions above 90°, because the initial positions do not involve partial or complete covering. On the other hand, of the successes

---

[4] In this we did not take into account the factor of non-transparency in the case of complete or partial covering, since indication of transparency develops in an irregular way with age, and may be the result of various intentions (intellectual realism, negligence, or desire for clarity).

for $R1$ and $R2$, it is the former, $R1$, which appears first, and of the successes $R3–R5$, it is $R4$ which is the earliest, because in $R1$ and $R4$ the square remains in a vertical–horizontal position, as in circumduction, and is right up against the blue square (against its right side or below it) without intersection or partial or complete covering (there being no intersection either above 270°); but either comprehension of these final positions stays under the influence of that of previous intersections, or else the difficulty of imagining correctly increases with the degree of rotation.

In short, Table 45 would seem to indicate that there is a threefold tendency to substitute circumduction for rotation, to avoid intersections, and to avoid oblique positions. It is as if the imagination of the rotation were seeking to conserve certain characteristics of the figure in motion. Exactly what characteristics are conserved will become clear from the analysis of the principal types of error which follows.

1. First of all, there are the cirumductions proper. The red square is displaced round about the blue square, and in the main the sides conserve their vertical and horizontal positions (one in particular of the drawings represented the red square above the blue square, resting on its upper side). This error was observed in 60 per cent of the subjects at 5 years, 20 per cent at 6 years, etc., and still at 10 to 11 years in 12·5 per cent; it was often combined with the following error-type (2) (and assumes, of course, that there are changes in the position of the pivotal centre).

2. From 5 to 8 years, 10–20 per cent of the subjects produce errors analogous to the circumduction errors; but here the red square, instead of going round the blue square in a circle, is expanded lengthways into a rectangle, keeping its sides vertical and horizontal. This is tantamount to a kind of circumduction, by vertical and horizontal elongation and not by displacement (see Figure 15).

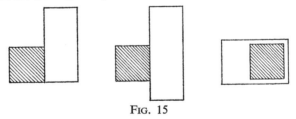

Fig. 15

3. Another kind of error, which is at a qualitatively higher level than the foregoing, but which is only to be observed from 5 to 7 years (indicative of similar tendencies to the above), consists neither in executing a circumduction nor in achieving a rotation, but in retaining simply the non-oblique positions of the rotation and in neglecting the intermediate positions.

4. An important form of error to be found in 10–60 per cent of subjects between 5 and 9 years, shows considerable progress over types (1) to (3).

The subject now seeks to imagine a real rotation of the red square, and not a circumduction, as is evident from the appearance of slanting positions and oblique sides. But this type of error remains essentially intermediate between circumduction and rotation, since the central pivot is not conserved but is displaced about the fixed blue square – so that one has circumduction and rotation at the same time (see Figure 16).

We shall not go into all the possible subdivisions of this type–distortion of the red squares, conservation of the square shape, intersection of the blue square, no intersection, and so on. The important thing is the general lack of differentiation that we have already pointed out.

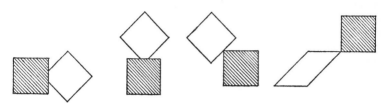

FIG. 16

5. The fifth type is still farther in advance of the last type. The pivot is conserved at the apex of the lower right-hand corner of the blue square. This is a decisive step towards the rotation. But there is a residual persistence of the tendency to produce a circumduction, as the red square is distorted in its oblique positions in such a way that at least one of its vertical or horizontal sides is maintained. The interest of this phenomenon – and it is a frequent one – lies in the fact that it accounts for why the subjects prefer circumduction to rotation and prefer to continue using the properties of circumduction for as long as possible (types 4 and 5). The reason is this – that in the spontaneous image of a square, the square stands horizontally on one of its sides and not on one of its corners (Figure 17). While true rotation conserves the square's geometrical form

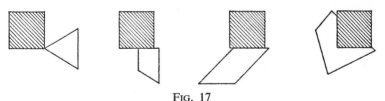

FIG. 17

(equal sides and equal angles) but modifies its orientation, the pseudo-conservation characteristic of the image seeks to maintain the horizontal-vertical positions (hence the preference for circumduction) by neglecting if need be the square's form, although it also tries to avoid intersections (which is always the case for types 1 and 3, and most frequently the case for types 2, 4 and 5) so as to maintain the integrity of the square to a maximum.

6. This is an error-type that is compatible with those already mentioned, but which is worth noting separately as it represents one of the still

partially unsuccessful efforts in the direction of the rotation (especially at 5 and 6 years). The blue and red squares are moved simultaneously, without a relative change in the pivotal centre, and with or without distortion of the figures.

7. Finally, mention should be made of a kind of reaction also compatible with those above. This consists in repeating the same drawing several times on the run.

There are two types of reaction which we shall not class as erroneous, because they increase with age, rather than decrease as those just described. The first is the indication of complete covering with a transposition of the normal order (covering at 270°). But the interesting point is that the subject comprehends that covering is necessary, and this is a sign that rotation has been mastered. The second is the indication of transparency when there is total or partial masking. The interesting point here is the mastering of intersection, which is bound up with the mastering of rotation.

Briefly then, the analysis of error-types, together with the analysis contained in Table 45, puts us in a position to see fairly clearly what are the similarities and differences between imaginal representations of a square rotating and those of a square translated in relation to a second, starting from 'superposition' or 'superimposition'. (Sections 1 and 2, Chapter Three.) In all three cases imagination of the mobile element remains at first subordinate to pseudo-conservation, but later approximates to the paradoxically distinct operational conservation. Operational conservation seeks to keep constant the shape of both the moving square, and the fixed reference square along with its associated properties (in this case the central pivot). But it accepts variation of the data as they are modified: positions, orientations, the crossing of perimeters, and intersections. Likewise the imaginal activity evidenced in our subjects tends to leave some characteristics unchanged and to vary others. But the underlying selection of characteristics is quite different – and here lies the nub of the problem. The characteristics that the child leaves unchanged are precisely those that are modified in the actual figures, while those that he then has to alter are in reality invariable. In the case of the translation with superposition the characteristic conserved is the external boundary, in the case of the translation with superimposition, the internal surfaces, which the subject avoids splitting up with new boundary lines. The same is true in the case of rotations, though more especially here it is the vertical and horizontal position of the sides that is conserved. And in all three cases it is the shape of the square and the position of the pivot that the subject sacrifices the more readily. At first sight one might think that these preconservations presuppose greater activity on the part of the subject, since they oppose the object both in what they conserve and in what they do not conserve, while the operational conservation might seem simply to copy these two aspects. But in point of fact the image limits itself to retaining the initial characteristics that seem to be the most simple, namely, the finishing point provided by the perimeter of the reference square, or its internal unsegmented surface in the case of translation, and in the case of rotation the internal surface and the vertical or horizontal positions relative to the line of regard. The imagination then evokes the suggested movements. But it does so only in so far as it hangs on to the simplest characteristics as a result of a kind of inertia, and modifies the others without any necessary regularity. And the sole reason is that they have not been retained as being any more complex (equality of the sides or of the corners of the square, stability of the pivotal centre presupposing a double system of left–right and top–bottom reference relations, intersections involving regular division, etc.).

TABLE 46   *Copies of square in rotation*
(Successes as % of the responses)

	A–B (invariance of blue square)	C (pivotal centre)	Oblique positions[5] (1)	Super-imposition[6] (2)	Total success
5 years	45	45	50	100	22
6 years	43	60	57	100	30
7 years	93	93	86·6	100	93
8 years	100	90	100	100	90
9–11 years	100	100	100	100	100

It is still possible that amongst the characteristics giving rise to these pseudo-conservations, some are more resistant than others. We saw in Chapter Three how persistent are the preconservations of boundaries. This is probably due to the fact that they partially coincide with the ordinal tendencies of the preoperational level. In the present case it could be that circumduction takes the place of rotation for reasons of economy – in order that those positions of the moving square may be conserved that are easiest to represent. In this connection it is instructive to examine the subject's selections from the prepared drawings and his direct copies of the movements. (See Table 46 above for the results of the copies.)

It can be seen that a rotation is given from 5 to 6 years in cases of superimposition, and that there is some progress for the oblique

[5] We counted as successful any quadrilateral containing oblique lines, as opposed to triangles, even if the form of the square is not conserved.
[6] We counted as successful any series including superimpositions, even if imprecise.

positions, whereas the reference elements (*A–C*) are not kept invariant until 7 years. The selection from prepared drawings gives a similar result, though it is better from the point of view of the oblique positions. The results for the repeat of the imaginal representation test after copying are set out in Table 47.

TABLE 47   *Imaginal reproduction after copying*
(Successes as % of the responses)

	A–B	*C*	*Oblique positions*	*Super-imposition*	*Total success*
5 years	45	15	50	45	15
6 years	50	50	66	50	50
7 years	93	66	66	66	66
8 years	90	66	90	88	66
9–11 years	100	66	100	100	66

In spite of learning due to the copy, the progress of the reproductive image is only relative, if it is compared with the anticipations of Table 45. In spite of the slight advance shown by the oblique and superimposed positions, the central pivot's lack of stability still does not allow us to speak, up till 7 to 8 years, of anything more than an intermediate form of imagination between rotation and circumduction.

Two final controls were carried out on thirty-seven and thirty subjects of 5 to 8 years of age. These are worth describing as well, since they confirm that there is some difficulty in imagining the rotation. A board 30 × 30 cm was divided into quarters. At the intersection of the co-ordinate axes a 15 cm square was attached at its top left-hand apex by means of a nail. (See Figure 18*A*.) A second board was used, similar to the first, except that it was not divided by co-ordinates, and that the right hand vertical edge of the smaller square is coloured red (Figure 18*B*). In these two control tests, then,

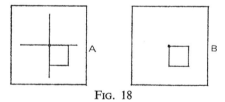

Fig. 18

we have a rotation relative this time not to a fixed square but to axes, or to a point.

The reactions to *A* were analysed from the point of view of (1) the stability of the pivot (in relation both to the axes and to the square) (2) successful responses for the vertical–horizontal positions (where the axes are not intersected), and (3) the successful responses for the oblique positions (where the axes are intersected). For *B*, we give the total successes both with and without correct positioning of the coloured side.

TABLE 48 *Rotation of a square relative to co-ordinate axes (A) or to a point (B)*
(Successes as % of the responses)

	A				B	
	Stability of centre	Horizontal–vertical positions	Oblique positions	Total success	Irrespective of colour	Respective of colour
5 years	12·5	50	0	0	0	0
6 years	26·6	53·5	13·3	13·3	33·3	27·2
7 years	75	62·5	36·5	36·5	33·3	33·3
8 years	83·3	100	50	50	83·3	66·6

Even when the rotation of the square is reduced to its simplest possible forms, only a slight improvement is obtained. In particular it is noteworthy that the fixity of the central pivot is not acquired until 7 years – even though the presence of the nail would seem to underline it with irresistible clarity.

3. Trajectories of various points on squares and other figures in rotation

It is possible to study the image of the rotations of a square by limiting ourselves, as we did in section 1, to asking the subject to imagine the internal relations within the sides of the square. This is successful at 6 years in the case of circumduction (because of the invariance), but not until after 9 years in the case of rotation (Table 40). At 8 years the child is aware of the impossibility of making adjacent sides opposite (Table 42). And the overturnings are successful at 8 to 9 years (Tables 43 and 44). But it is also possible to study the rotation of the square, as we did in section 2, in relation to a motionless figure (i.e. a second square or co-ordinates). This does not produce a successful response before 10 to 11 years (Table 45). It is also possible to study the imaginal representation of trajectories of various points on squares and other figures (rectangles or irregular figures) in rotation. And this is what we shall do in this section. The problem is to establish how and when the child will succeed in breaking away from square or irregular outlines and begin to

115

imagine all the trajectories of the points as circular and concentric. (The following inquiry was carried out in association with E. Schmid-Kitsikis.)

We took a rectangular mount covered with modelling clay. In the middle of this was fixed a metal peg 10 cm long. We ensured that the child observed its stability by showing him the screw holding it in place. The peg acted as a

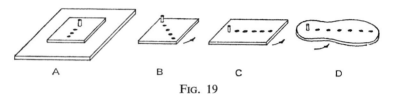

A   B   C   D

FIG. 19

pivot on which could be rotated four small wooden shapes (two squares with pivot-point at centre or one corner, one rectangle and one irregular curvilinear shape). See Figure 19. Finally, four differently coloured screws were fixed on to the boards in a straight line radiating from the pivot-centre. The child was asked to draw the paths of the different screws, when the board is turned from left to right. The subjects were divided for this into two groups, one starting the drawing with the point nearest the centre of the rotation, the other beginning with the point farthest from the centre (if the child fails he starts again with an intermediate position or with a single point). After these anticipatory drawings, the subject was asked to copy the paths following a demonstration either of a portion of the movement (the paths of the screws imprinted on the modelling clay serving as a model), or of the complete motion. After this the subjects were requested to imagine the paths again (deferred reproduction).

Table 49 below sets out the results of tests *A* and *B* (*C* and *D* gave the same results as *B*, by generalization or by learning). We shall

TABLE 49   *Successes (as % of the subjects) for the rotation of fixed points on square bases*

	Centre of rotation		Form of paths		Position of paths		Total success	
	A	B	A	B	A	B	A	B
5 years (*N* = 12)	0	0	8	0	0	0	*0*	*0*
6 years (12)	66	50	50	50	33	8	*16*	*8*
7 years (12)	75	25	50	66	75	16	*50*	*8*
8 years (12)	91	91	91	100	66	50	*66*	*50*
9 years (12)	91	66	66	50	75	33	*50*	*25*
10 years (12)	100	83	100	83	100	66	*100*	*66*
11 years (12)	100	100	100	100	100	75	*100*	*75*

distinguish reactions relating to the stability of the fixed centre of rotation, the form of the paths (circular or influenced by the moving element), and their position (one in relation to the other, and all in relation to the centre).

The first thing that can be seen from this table is that with two exceptions a successful response is more difficult in *B* than *A*. This is probably because the paths in *B* are external to the field in which the mobile figure of reference moves. The upshot is that complete success is not achieved till 11 years for *B*, as against 10 years for *A*.

Up to the age of 7 years for *A* and 8 years for *B* the fixity of the rotational centre again raises the kind of difficulty analysed in detail in Chapter Three, section 3, in connection with 90° and 360° rotations of a rod about one end.

The form of the paths was more unexpected. At 5 years it is in all cases, whether inside or outside the square, and whether in *A* or *B*, remarkably random. But one can discern a frequent tendency to distribute the points around the square, breaking away from it (see 1, Figure 20), following it (see 2), or even (in one case counted as correct) in a kind of circle inside the square (4), but not always with the pivotal axis as centre. At 6 years the

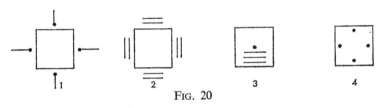

FIG. 20

square is taken as a reference in *A*, and, apart from one subject who took his reference from the rectangular base, the paths remain within the square. However, in six out of twelve subjects the paths take on a square or simple linear form. In *B* half the subjects make the paths circular, but the majority do not manage to get outside the square. The centre of rotation is generally given as the moving point in its starting position (without regard for the true pivotal centre at one of the square's corners). The paths are also often indicated without any consideration for their relations to one another (for instance, they may be represented as a series of small juxtaposed circles). From 7 to 8 years the paths are almost all curvilinear; any errors are connected with position and especially with the relation of the paths to the mobile frame of reference. What is particularly striking in *B* is that even those subjects who have understood the need to make the trajectories go beyond the square's perimeter[7] still stick to the boundaries and will go only a little way across them – with the result that they produce shapes

[7] It should be noted that in the drawings counted correct the square or reference figure remains fixed – the question concerns exclusively the trajectories of the coloured points, not the successive positions of the square itself.

which are elliptical rather than circular. It is only at about 10 to 11 years that representation becomes completely accurate.

It is also interesting to find that the copies of the paths in part or entire do not produce any improvement in the deferred reproductions until about 8 years. Either we just started the movement for the child, so that he could see what marks were left by the screws for the first part of a rotation. Or we went through the whole motion for him and got him to copy the impressions he saw in the modelling clay. In both cases it is not until after 7 years that the subject can utilize what he observes. Below this age the deferred reproduction merely repeats the previous errors (and in the youngest subjects even the copy shows these errors – absence of fixed centre of rotation, etc.).

These facts, as well as Table 49, demonstrate what we had good reason to expect – the close interdependence of the kinetic anticipatory images required in this particular case and the spatial operations enabling the movements to be comprehended. Slightly complex rotations may be perceived without being comprehended. But they cannot be imagined in anticipation or even in reproduction (as we have just seen from our control experiment with direct copies) unless the constituent relations are grasped operationally.

4. *Anticipation of rotations and superimpositions of triangles and other figures*

In section 1 it became clear that anticipation of the positions of the sides of a square (distinguishable by their respective colours) after rotation is less easy than one might have thought. Most of the subjects were inclined to treat the rotation as if it were a simple translation in the plane, or a circumduction. It may be of value to complete these data with those collected in another experiment carried out in collaboration with C. Émery. The experiment concerned triangles, and the points of reference were not in this case the sides, but the angles, in each of which was placed a distinct and significant mark. After the triangles various indeterminate forms were used in direct perceptual comparison.

I. *Method used for the triangle tests.* The investigation was carried out in two parts:

(*a*) In the first part, we showed the subject two equilateral triangles, both sides 5 cm, blue on one side, yellow on the other, each with markings in black (a small rectangle 10×4 mm) in the apex of one of its angles on both faces. Triangle A is static, triangle B mobile; both are in the same position, with the blue face uppermost and the black marking at the top (we shall call the yellow sides A' and B'). Then, after a detailed description of the two objects, the child was shown the two triangles in turn in the five different positions 1–5 in Figure 21. For each position we asked: 'How do you need to move this triangle (B or B') so that it is in the same position,

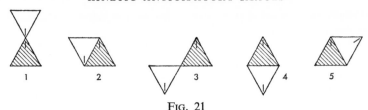

FIG. 21

exactly, as this one (*A*), and so that, if one triangle were put on top of the other, the black mark here would be on top of the other black mark?' We noted any anticipatory movement, and other movements made by the subject (rotations in the plane, turning motions in the air, etc.).

(*b*) In the second part we used the same triangles, with two additional factors. First, the fixed triangle *A* had, besides the black rectangle at its apex, two small drawings – a red house in the right-hand angle and a green tree in the left-hand angle. Second, the moving triangle *B* (or *B*') had the fixed drawn indication as before at its apex, but this time the child is given a green detachable tree and a red detachable house corresponding to *A* which he is required to put in the appropriate places. When this had been explained, the triangles were set up in positions 6–10 successively (Figure 22). For each position the subject was asked to 'put the house and the

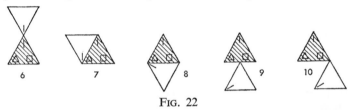

FIG. 22

pine-tree in the triangle *B* (or *B*') so that the black line is on the black line, the house on the house, and the pine-tree on the pine-tree, if one triangle is placed on top of the other one'. We also specified that the marks were to be imagined on the blue side all the time (even in 8 and 10). We repeated the instructions, of course, each time.

Out of sixty-two subjects aged from 5 to 8 years we found the following results for the first and second parts of the test. See Table 50 (results as percentage of the responses).

TABLE 50   *Successes for the rotation of the triangle (a) and for anticipating the position of its sides (b)*

	Part a						Part b				
	1	*2*	*3*	*4*	*5*	*(1–5)*	*6*	*7*	*8*	*9*	*10*	*(6–10)*
5 years	91	91	81	54	72	45	45	54	27	36	64	0
6 years	93	87	73	93	86	60	33	60	26	73	46	6
7 years	94	94	83	94	94	61	69	66	16	83	66	0
8 years	72	88	72	94	88	44	83	77	44	94	94	16

The columns headed (1–5) and (6–10) do not give the averages of the preceding columns, but the percentage of subjects successful in all the tests 1–5, and in all the tests 6–10. It can thus be seen that the development of reactions in part *a* is not, unlike anticipations for the rotated square (Table 40), a regular one advancing according to age. This is probably because the anticipations of the rotated square bear on a gradual progression from 90° to 360°, whereas questions 1–5 in the present test are posed in a scattered order. Even so the present questions are easier than the others (54–94 per cent as against 0–83 per cent). On the other hand, the questions in the second part (6–10), where reasoning has a greater share, produce an evolution more regularly related to development. If one examines the distribution of the number of correct answers, one finds two at 5 years (45 per cent of subjects with two correct answers), three at 7 and 8 years (33 per cent in both cases), and four at 8 years (66 per cent subjects with four correct answers out of five).

Analysis of the errors yields precisely what one would have predicted: incorrect reversals, errors by mirror inversion, etc. It is, however, interesting to note that when the subject was asked to indicate the paths followed by the markings during rotation he very frequently, up to 7 years, represented them as quite independent of one another, instead of travelling in one and the same rotational direction. We have here a reaction analogous to those we observed for the paths of the extremities of a rod rotating through 90° (Chapter Three, Table 28, Figure 10), and to those we shall observe in the present chapter for a somersaulting tube (Table 58, Figure 25). It is not until about 8 years that, probably under the influence of the formation of concrete operations, the general rotation of an object is represented by means of an image attributing one-way rotation or compatible trajectories to the various parts of the object.

II. The foregoing experiments – and especially the very widespread reaction imagining the rotations without attributing compatible or similarly directed paths to the parts of the object – are in contrast to what the perceptual constancy of the forms themselves would seem to imply. When, for instance, the subject has a three-quarter, rather than a full view of a square, so that he perceives it as a longer-than-broad parallelogram, but still recognizes it as a square, then he is effecting a correction, perceptually, in the frontal-parallel. And this procedure attributes remarkable invariance to the object and to the relations between its different parts. Now it is known that this kind of correction appears early in the child.[8] Furthermore, the

---

[8] E. Vurpillot has shown that at 5 years there are considerable 'regressions' with regard to the frontal-parallel which subsequently diminish somewhat with age.

young subjects can manage similar corrections quite easily whenever they look without any trouble at all at pictures wrongly orientated or almost upside down. The child's lack of concern about orientation was pointed out a long time ago in the lotto-tests of Decroly and Descoeudres. The subjects were found to place clogs or flags orientated to the left on clogs or flags orientated to the right, even though the choice was open, etc. Altogether these facts would seem to suggest the existence of a fairly fundamental opposition between the ability to effect perceptual corrections and the image's reluctance to represent them by evocation proper (of the paths, and even of the result of the motion).

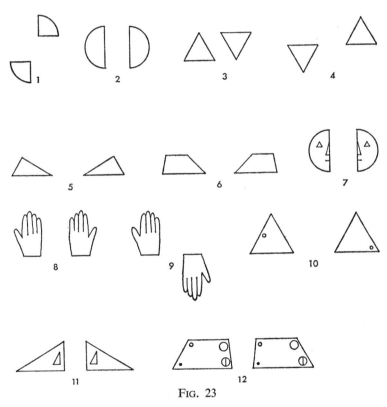

FIG. 23

We showed the subjects paired figures (Figure 23), some of which could (1–9) and some of which could not (10–12) be properly superimposed. The subjects were asked: (*a*) whether superimposition was possible; (*b*) how it could be done (rotation in the plane or in space (1–4 and 9), or only in space (5–8)); finally, (*c*) to do it for himself (1–9). Model 5 was shown to the child a second time after 6, but this time with the sides coloured (= 5′). so that the superimposition involves making the sides correspond.

As the child's gestures in carrying out these movements were so rapid, it was necessary for the sake of clarity to sort out the motions beforehand. We used a large sheet of cardboard with a recess. In this recess we placed one of the small square cards of Figure 24 (on this card is a figure in red: either a square, or triangle, a semi-circle or a trapezium); at the other side of the cardboard sheet we placed the corresponding free figure coloured green. We then asked the subject: (*a*) whether it was possible to put the green figure on top of the red one, and (*b*) to do this. The triangle was shown twice, once standing on one corner and once standing on a base.

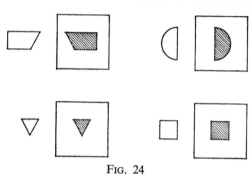

FIG. 24

The results obtained are given in Table 51. They are grouped in two categories according to whether the subject judged superimposition to be possible (or impossible for 10–12), and whether he actually succeeded in executing the superimposition (1–9). These two categories we designated *P* and *S* respectively. In brackets we give the successes after trial-and-error added to the immediate successes.

TABLE 51 *Successes for the superimposition of the models in Figure 24 (exercise) and Figure 23 (1–12)*
(As % of the responses)

	Ex.		1–4		5–9 (and 5′)		10–12
	P	S	P	S	P	S	P
4 years	91 (100)	67 (91)	100	100	97 (100)	40 (50)	60 (80)
5 years	100	83 (97)	100	100	100	85 (91)	23 (88)
6 years	100	86 (100)	100	100	100	66 (74)	31 (100)
7 years	100	88 (100)	100	100	100	91 (91)	70 (92)

It can be seen that these tests raise no difficulties comparable to those associated with the rotation of the triangle (Table 50, part *a*). At the most one finds that at 4 years the subject is a little awkward in realizing *S* for 5–9, and that there is some hesitation at all ages for the impossible superimposition 10–12 (although there is a correct response in 80 per cent of cases from 4 years). The plans or drafts of superimposition (question *b* for models 1–9) are nearly all on the same level as the actual execution (question *c* = *S*). But the younger children (4 to 5 years) generally fail properly to distinguish the two possibilities of rotation in the plane and rotation in space for 1 to 4.

It is therefore in a general way clear that the difference between the present tests and previous ones is that the latter concern perception rather than images. The task is to take stock of the given initial and terminal positions of the figure to be displaced, and then to 'perceive' it, as it were, in the position of the other figure, and to execute the superimposition all of a piece, instead of imagining it bit by bit in terms of its constituent relations. This behaviour is closer to the automatic perceptual corrections involved in the constancy of forms and the perceptual recognition of forms in various positions than it is to evocation by means of images and truly imaginal representation.

5. *Anticipation of the order of the sides of a rotated cube and of the development of four of its sides*

Having examined the image of the result of the rotation of various plane figures, it could be of value to study the case of a cube. The child may not be used to turning a square or a triangle for the purpose of noting the positions of respective sides which as a rule are indistinguishable. But a baby of only 12 to 18 months will explore the different and distinguishable faces of a cubic or parallelepipedal box. Could it be that an early experience of this kind might be translated into an ability to form anticipatory images relating to regular cubes more easily? We assume that this would not be the case, and that in this as in other instances one has to wait until the formation of the euclidean geometrical operations before the images are likely to become anticipatory. However, the problem remains, and we shall study it in this section, utilizing the material collected with C. Émery.

I. First we took two cardboard cubes with a side 5 cm, one white, the other differently coloured on each of its six faces. We gave the child twenty paper squares in the same colours as the second cube. We showed the coloured cube to the subject and demonstrated the three possible types of rotation (which we shall refer to as being in the plane or in space, the latter being parallel or perpendicular to the subject's frontal axis) in both possible directions. The cube was then placed in a fixed position in front of the child – green side facing him, blue side farthest away from him, and the red side uppermost. He was asked to recite the colours, including the black of the base. Then he was given the coloured squares, and was asked to place them on the white cube in the positions which would be occupied by the sides of the coloured cube if it were rotated. The coloured cube was left as it was, and the required rotation demonstrated with the white cube (for each question), so that the child could regard the coloured cube as he pleased, and place the coloured squares on the white cube in the positions corresponding to the rotation it had just completed.

The experimenter demonstrated some (but not all) rotations for each subject: 90°, 180°, 270°, 360°. Each subject was asked to imagine the results. Some questions were also put to the child about impossible solutions, such as turning the cube so that two adjacent colours end up apart and opposite, etc.

II. In the second part of the experiment the subject was shown a hollow cube of the same dimensions as before, but with two of its opposing faces removed, so that when 'unfolded' or developed the four remaining sides would give a long strip 20 cm × 5 cm divided into four coloured squares in the order, green, red, black and yellow. He was also given a white strip 20 cm × 5 cm with four blank compartments which he was required to colour in, and six strips also 20 cm × 5 cm with four squares in the same colours as those of the cube but in various orders, two of which were both correct but in reverse orders. The four-sided cube was placed in front of the subject in a fixed position – open face towards the subject, green face to the left, red face as base, black face to the right and the yellow face uppermost. The child was asked to imagine a break between the green and the yellow faces like the break in the cube already lying opened out on the table in front of him. There were three tasks: (1) a straightforward drawing: the result of unfolding the cube to be drawn, in colour, on a sheet of white paper; (2) enframed drawing: the white strip with the four compartments to be used and coloured appropriately; (3) selection of the correct order from the six previously prepared strips. The selection was to be justified, with the experimenter suggesting orders other than those chosen. In 1 and 2 the drawing was removed when completed.

Using forty-eight subjects we obtained the following results (Table 52).

TABLE 52 *Successes for anticipating the rotations of the cube* (As % of the responses)

	90°	180°	270°	360°	Double rotations	Impossible
4 years (N=12)	0	0	0	0	0	50
5 years (9)	0	0	0	0	0	57
6 years (11)	33	22	20	33	13	60
7 years (10)	50	40	33	50	33	84
8–9 years (6)	83	73	100	100	86	100

In spite of the fact that the rotation of a solid figure is doubtless more common than the rotation of a surface analysable in terms of its sides, it can be seen from this table that up to 5–6 years the successes lag somewhat behind those of Table 45. And they do not gain a lead until 8 years – the level of concrete operations.

Analysis of the errors shows that the child loses the tendency to confuse the planes (parallel or perpendicular rotation in space) more rapidly than his errors of direction. Of the primary type of errors the most curious are those relating to adjacency:

Eli (4,6 years) displaces the blue side more than the yellow one: 'Is it possible for one colour to turn less quickly than another? – *Yes.* – Why is the blue one there? – *Because it stops there.*'

Fuc (4,11 years): 'Do the blue side and the green side touch on my cube? – *No.* – Do they touch on yours? – *It's different* – You put the blue one down twice – is that right? – *Yes.* – Can you be here and in your classroom at the same time? – *No.* – And can the blue side be at the back and at the front at the same time? – *Yes.*'

Com (5,11 years) simply changed the order of the two contiguous colours: 'Is it possible for the colours to cross one another (gesture), and go in different directions? – *Yes.* – How do they do that? – *Because the green side goes to the white one's place and the white one to the green one's place.*'

Now adjacency is one of the most elementary relations of the child's topology, and order proceeds from a combination of adjacency and non-adjacency (if *B* is next to *A* and *C*, but *C* is not next to *A*, then one has *ABC* or *CBA*). If in the present case these relations do not allow the formation of better anticipatory images before 8 to 9 years, the reason must be that they are combined with difficulties peculiar to the kinetic image.[9] And the kinetic image is inadequate to the extent that the child accepts the possibility of crossing movements (Com), of unequal displacements (Eli), and even of loss of adjacency, or duplication (Fuc). Moreover, if the adjacencies were enough for kinetic anticipation, one would expect test II for the development, or unfolding, of the four successive sides to meet a successful response much earlier than test I. Now, this proves to be the case only to a very limited degree – see Table 53 overleaf (results given as percentage of the responses).

The results for the choice are lower than for the enframed drawing, because the six strips are presented all at once, not judged separately.

[9] We saw in Table 42 that conservation of the adjacency of two sides of a rotating square is a late development. Here there are several adjacencies to be considered simultaneously, and hence there is a need to conserve the order of the sides in its entirety.

TABLE 53 *Successes for anticipating the order of the four developed sides, taking the initial response of each subject*
(The figures in brackets are based on the final response after spontaneous corrections)

	4 years	5 years	6 years	7 years	8–9 years
Straightforward drawing	0 (0)	28 (28)	33 (44)	50 (70)	60 (83)
Enframed drawing	10 (25)	40 (40)	70 (60)	90 (90)	100 (100)
Selection	17 (50)	33 (44)	63 (50)	80 (89)	60 (100)

There is no successful response till 7 years for >75 per cent: it is clear that here also the image is not adequate until the beginning of the concrete-operational stage, although it is about a year ahead of the more complex questions of the preceding table.

6. *Imagination of the trajectory of a tube somersaulting in the air*

A tube was placed on a box with a fair part of its length projecting over the edge. The overhanging end of the tube was depressed, so that it rotated through 180°, somersaulted, and fell on to the table. The subject was then asked to describe the stages of its trajectory, by means of a drawing, by means of a gesture, or in words. We classify the images obtained in this procedure as anticipatory images. And this for three reasons: because this particular movement is less familiar than that of a rod falling through 90° on a fixed pivot (see Chapter Three, section 3), because the higher speed of this movement prevents its being perceived in detail, and because, if the child has tried somersaulting himself, other perceptual forms are involved – notably proprioceptive rather than visual perception. (Research conducted by Elsa Schmid-Kitsikis.)

(1) A cardboard tube 15 cm long was placed on a box, the projecting end being coloured blue, the other end red. The child was asked to watch carefully as he would be asked to draw what he had seen – and the tube was somersaulted.

(2) The tube was removed immediately, and the child was asked to draw the tube, in colour, 'as it was on the box', and then 'as it was on the table'. At this point nothing was said about intermediate stages (although the outcome of the somersault is a change in the order of the colours).

(3) We then went on to the drawing of the stages of the tube's path, and the subject was asked to draw the tube as it is just after it leaves the box, 'as it is a bit further on', and 'as it is a bit further still and so on until it lands on the table'. No further questions were asked, but the child was required to colour in the ends of the tube.

(4) Next we asked for the two extremities of the tube: 'Draw the way the

blue end goes to get from the box to the table.' The same question was put for the red end. (Indication simply by red or blue pencil strokes.)

(5) Only then did we ask the child to reproduce the movement using the tube itself. He was not allowed, of course, to make the tube somersault simply by tipping it up with one finger. He was asked to take the tube and reproduce its previous movement very slowly, holding it in his hand all the time. We insisted on having as far as was possible, a stage-by-stage reproduction, breaking the movement down.

(6) Quite often during these questions, the subject gave a spontaneous verbal description of the stages of the movement. When this did not occur we put various questions to him concerning the stages of the rotation. This was done only if there was no spontaneous description and only after all questions had been posed.

(7) We also used a completely white tube with a separate group of subjects who were asked to imagine the colour of the anterior and posterior extremities, and to indicate where the colours would be in the final stage of the movement.

Let us first of all examine the way the tube's path was imitated when the child reproduced it manually (question 5). We shall distinguish two types of reactions which are intermediate between a correct rotation and no rotation at all. The first are the reactions of those subjects who attempt a rotation unsuccessfully, but are nevertheless satisfied with their solution, and the second are those reactions consisting of incomplete attempts which the subjects themselves say are inadequate, without being able to improve on them. Table 54 sets out these results. In brackets are given the subjects who succeed in breaking down the rotation and reproducing it in slow-motion rather than at a constant speed (these figures are also included in the percentage of correct rotations).

TABLE 54 *Manual reproduction of the tube's path*
(As % of the responses)

	No rotation	Hesitation	Incorrect but subject not satisfied	Correct rotation (and breakdown)
4 years (N=4)	75	0	0	25
5 years (17)	41	18	18	23 (7)
6 years (19)	26	32	0	42 (32)
7 years (20)	25	20	10	45 (30)
8 years (10) –	10	20	0	70

For the drawings and verbal descriptions we distinguish three types of response: no rotation, intermediate reactions, and correct rotation. It should be made clear that a change in the order of the colours is not an adequate indication of rotation. In order to indicate such a change-over the child does not need to imagine how it occurs, and the tube may simply be represented as slanting, or in a series of almost parallel positions, and so on. The intermediate reactions consist of drawings showing curved trajectories (arc of a circle without rotation), curvature of the tubes themselves, and verbal expressions such as: 'It has fallen backwards', when it is not a rotation proper that is meant. Correct rotations are conveyed either in drawings or in words – in phrases such as: 'It has turned round', 'This end has come forward', and so on. See Table 55.

TABLE 55 *Drawings (D) and verbal descriptions (V) of the paths of the tube*
(As % of the responses)

	No rotation		Intermediate reactions		Rotations	
	D	V	D	V	D	V
4 years (4)	100	75	0	0	0	25
5 years (13)	100	41	0	0	0	59
6 years (11)	64	20	18	16	18	64
7 years (14)	36	20	22	5	42	75
8 years (10)	10	0	30	0	60	100

A comparison of the three sorts of reaction (Tables 54 and 55) is instructive from the point of view of the nature of the image. The best results are found for the verbal descriptions (*V*). This is because such a description can only translate the rotation into a notionally expressed fact, without imagining the details. So the notion would seem to some extent to precede the image. The source of this notion is, of course, to be found in the action. But gestural reproduction of the action (Table 54) is not identical, and constitutes an analytical slow-motion imitation. This brings in difficulties that explain why the motor reproduction lags behind the verbal or conceptual statement. The drawing or graphic image is less successful than the gestural imitation (from 4 to 6 years). Even taking into account the fact that the drawing may lag behind the mental image simply because of technical difficulties, it is none the less true that the tube itself is quite simple to draw and that its positions can be indicated symbolically as soon as they are imagined precisely enough. It would not be imprudent, therefore, to situate the mental image halfway between gestural and graphic imitation. This is tantamount to saying that the image is in fact an internalized imitation, and not simply a prolongation of primary perception, and that, further, it is an active reconstitution involving a certain amount of motor activity and a certain amount of comprehension. Both are equally important, the former imitating the action from which the latter also derives. At the level of human behaviour (as indeed also at the level of anthropoidal behaviour), imitation, which we have invoked as the source of images, in no way resembles anything like an automatic copy based on simple perceptuo-motor transfers. Imitation is closely bound up with the intelligence. It constitutes its accommodatory pole only, however. For, although the intelligence symbolizes its models by way of a motor reconstruction, it does so only to the extent that it seeks to express a comprehension which is not abstract or assimilatory, but which is concrete and accommodatory, or 'sympathetic'.[10]

We shall therefore examine how much of the rotation is comprehended, and at the same time try to solve the problem that arises constantly in connection with the problem of the image-concept relationship. Does imitative or imaginal comprehension precede and orientate notional or operational comprehension? Or, does the former on the contrary depend on the latter, complementing or defining it, but without directing it?

The examination can draw on three different sorts of evidence: (*a*) drawings of the paths of the tube's extremities, (*b*) drawings or verbal accounts of the change in colour order, and (*c*) drawn indications of the horizontal or vertical displacements between the tube's starting and finishing position. Now, *b* and *c* relate to the result or effect of the movement, whereas *a* is concerned with the movements as such. And it is interesting to find that the images relative to *b* and *c* are on average adequate at 7 years (70 per cent) – an age at which the child still fails completely in *a*.

Two different techniques were used for the permutation of the colours. In the first (questions 1–6) we used a coloured tube all the way through (blue at anterior, red at posterior end), so that the subject perceived the change-over during the motion or after it before the tube was removed, and so that he could indicate it in his first drawing (question 2). This first technique was used in order to establish the following points of interest: (1) whether the subjects would notice the permutation or not, and (2) whether they would draw from it the conclusion that a rotation of the tube had occurred. But the introduction of given colours makes it difficult to dissociate the factors of perception and imagination. So in our second method we used an entirely white tube, and asked the child to imagine the coloured ends in their starting and finishing positions. The results of both these techniques are set out in Table 56.

The first thing one sees from this is that the successes are fairly even. This would suggest once again that essentially the

10 See Finnbogason, G., *L'intelligence sympathique*, Paris, Alcan.

TABLE 56 *Permutation of colours*
(Successes as % of the responses)

	5 years (N=19)	6 years (N=21)	7 years (N=22)
Coloured tube	47	50	66
White tube	50	60	71

subjects register what they comprehend, and that unusable perceptual information is not taken in. It is also clear, however, that these results are considerably higher than the gestural or drawn imitations of the tube's path (Tables 54 and 55, *D*), and slightly lower than the verbal descriptions (Table 55, V). In other words, representation of the permutation of the colours is related to the kind of global comprehension of the rotation that is conveyed in verbal description, and is in no sense a detailed image of the rotation.

It is worth mentioning a piece of evidence which, though less clear, helps complete the picture – the horizontal and vertical displacements that the subjects put in their drawings spontaneously. Between the initial position on the box and its terminal position on the table, the tube is displaced simultaneously from left to right (horizontal displacement) and from top to bottom (vertical displacement). Now many of the subjects' drawings represent this somersault–motion as if the tube only fell from top to bottom (i.e. no horizontal displacement), or only moved forward without falling (no vertical displacement).[11] An adequate reproduction includes both displacements, though again this is only a global indication and not evidence that the details of the rotation are imagined.

TABLE 57 *Correct reactions to vertical and horizontal displacements*
(As % of the responses)

	Vertical displacement only	Horizontal displacement only	Both together
5 years	46	30	24
6 years	26	26	48
7 years	25	5	70

This shows that at 6 to 7 years the global indications reach approximately the same percentages as those in Table 56.

On the other hand, analysis of the paths of the tube's extremities (question 4) clearly confirms that the image lags behind the global

[11] The vertical displacement is, in fact, unlike the other, not a necessary one. But it is nevertheless a part of the given model and thus serves as an indication of the fidelity of the image.

comprehension found in the verbal descriptions (Table 55, V) or the colour-permutation tests (Table 56). We began by asking the subject to do a drawing in colour of the two extreme positions and then to indicate the paths of the ends of the tube in blue and red. (See Figure 25.) Between the primitive drawings excluding rotation

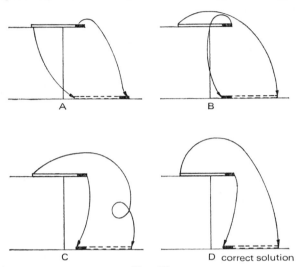

FIG. 25

altogether (Figure 25 *A*) and the correct drawing (Figure 25 *D*), we found a series of mutually incompatible paths (Figure 25 *B* and *C*). Both of these suggest rotation, but only symbolically, since to judge from the drawings the two extremities must be displaced separately (this we found also in Table 28 for the rod falling). This accounts for why the results set out in Table 58 are considerably behind compared with those of Tables 54 and 55.

TABLE 58   *Drawings of the paths of extremities of the coloured tube* (As % of the subjects)

		Intermediate reactions		
	No rotation	*Two paths incorrect*	*One path incorrect*	*Correct*
4 years (4)	100	0	0	0
5 years (16)	62	38	0	0
6 years (18)	28	44	28	0
7 years (20)	15	50	30	5
8 years (10)	0	10	30	60

In all, these various data show that notional and operational comprehension of the somersault is systematically ahead of the gestural image, and in particular of the graphic image (the mental image probably coming somewhere in between the two). However, correct imagination of the paths seems to constitute a necessary auxiliary in achieving operational comprehension. We found in fact that in spite of the colour permutation (Table 56) or global rotation (Table 55, *V*) the rotation does not acquire its strictly geometrical status unless it is represented at its various stages in space. Now such a concrete image does not precede notional comprehension but follows it, getting closer and closer to it. It is consequently difficult to believe that it develops autonomously, without the constant addition of contributory factors deriving from operational comprehension.

7. *Gestural reproduction of the paths of the extremities of a tube turning in the air*

The results we have just recorded (Table 58) raise a vital problem concerning the relationships between images and operational comprehension. The somersault movement is comprehended in a global sense from 7 years (Table 55: verbal reactions) and is correctly imitated from 8 years (Table 54: 70 per cent at 8 years) and the permutation of extremities is acknowledged at 7 years (Table 56: 70 per cent at 7 years). Why, then, is the image of the paths of these extremities so obviously retarded at all the ages examined, if it is not that organization of the image first requires an adequate act of comprehension? It is worth while taking this problem up in the context of the purely reproductive image – by showing the subject the paths of the extremities in detail and getting him to reproduce them by means of pointing with his finger, rather than by means of drawings.

The analysis that follows was undertaken with P. Mounoud. We used a system of spots of light (cf. Chapter Three, section 4). Behind a pane of frosted glass a mechanical device slowly lowers a horizontal tube 14 cm long with a red light attached to one end and a green one to the other through a rotation of 180°, so that the tube returns to a horizontal position with the lights in the reverse order. The child sits in front of the screen and can see the lights, but not the tube. He was asked to reproduce these with his forefinger on the screen exactly as he had just seen them. In this way everything is done to aid the formation of a reproductive image, either independently of comprehension, or in dependence on comprehension. In the former case the procedure just described is retained; in the latter the experimenter describes the drop of the tube behind the screen,

132

though the child is not shown the mechanism, which would distract his attention.

Then we went on to test the two groups of subjects (I, with explanation of motion of tube, and II without explanation) as follows: (*A*) A complete rotation was executed with the two lights. The child then had to show their starting and finishing points, by placing his two index fingers on the screen. and reproduce the paths separately or together. (*B*) A partial rotation was effected (the tube drops to a vertical position). The child reproduced what he saw. (*C*) A second partial rotation (¾ of the whole somersault) and the same questions. (*D*) The complete rotation was repeated and the subject was asked the same questions.

There were twenty-seven subjects in group I and thirty-four in group II aged in both cases between 5,0 and 8,11 years. Taking these 61 individual reactions to the situations and questions *A* – *D* we are able to draw up the following classifications of trajectories indicated. These serve for Tables 59 and 60.

Type 1. With his finger the child traces two more or less straight and parallel descending lines. In general he did not reverse the order of colours, and this produced paths looking like the correct trajectory without the curvature. However, when the subject was questioned (and this is always necessary), we realized that he did not think of the reversed final positions as the outcome of the trajectories, but rather as a simple given occurrence having no relation whatever to the rotation.

Type 2. The rotation begins to be drawn curved, but only correctly at the start of the path.

Type 3. Intermediate reactions. The end result of the trajectories is correct, but is only arrived at by the way of impossible intersections (observed also in type 2) which recall the drawings of Table 58 (see Figure 25, *B* and *C*).

Type 4. Complete rotation and parallel curves, but these were counted correct only if they were accompanied by the necessary reversal of colours – as it was in the case of the older children, though not in the case of the younger ones at 5 to 6 years.

Here are the gestural reproductions, classified according to type, of the complete trajectory (*A*):

TABLE 59 *Tracings of the complete trajectories of the red and green lights* (As % of the subjects, with permutation of colours given in brackets)

	Group I (with explanation)				Group II (without explanation)			
	Type 1	2	3	4	Type 1	2	3	4
5 years	75 (12)	12 (0)	0	12 (12)	50 (12)	12 (0)	0	37 (0)
6 years	50 (12)	20 (0)	10 (0)	10 (0)	42 (0)	16 (8)	16 (0)	25 (17)
7 years	40 (20)	0	20 (20)	40 (40)	33 (11)	22 (11)	11 (11)	33 (33)
8 years	25 (25)	25 (0)	0	50 (50)	40 (0)	0	20 (20)	40 (40)

Before we go on to interpret these results, we would also like to note, without going into details, the successful responses to *B*, *C* (partial), and *D* (second complete movement) for the two groups I and II (Table 60).

TABLE 60   *Successes (type 4), with permutation of colours given in brackets, for situations B–D*
(As % of the subjects)

	Sit. A	Sit. B	Sit. C	Sit. D
5 years	25 (5)	44 (5)	31 (12)	31 (5)
6 years	18 (9)	46 (46)	39 (35)	40 (31)
7 years	36 (36)	69 (52)	63 (52)	40 (32)
8 years	44 (44)	57 (35)	45 (45)	57 (35)

The first thing we notice in Table 59 is that the group II subjects who have been given no explanation of the apparatus do not develop very much with age, even from the point of view of successes (4). This is quite normal for simple imitation behaviour. The only clear development is in the attention brought to bear on the colour-permutation – which presupposes a conscious grasping of a relationship not noted at the outset. The group I subjects try harder to comprehend what is going on, since the test conditions encourage this. They start lower with poor comprehension, but overtake the other group slightly at 7 and 8 years.

On the other hand, if the trajectories are broken down (Table 60) there are improvements of two kinds. The one is local and due to greater ease in perception (*B* where the colours lie in a vertical line one above the other at their finishing point), the other general and characterized by learning between *A* and *D*. But since the breakdown of the rotation facilitates comprehension rather than learning by simple repetition, we have another indication of the part played by notional or operational factors.

The results obtained using the purely reproductive technique of imitation by pointing in *A* and *D* are better at 5 to 7 years than those obtained for the drawings in Table 58, which involve what one might call anticipatory reconstitution. But it is interesting to note that the final result of 57 per cent at 8 years for *D* coincides exactly with the 60 per cent at 8 years in Table 58. This fact would seem to suggest that at the level where the image relies on operational comprehension, gesture is not appreciably ahead of drawing, nor direct and reproductive imitation ahead of kinetic anticipation.

On the other hand, however, while gestural imitations are slightly superior to the drawings of section 6 at 5 to 7 years, the reverse is true for the alternation of the colours. If all the subjects are taken together for the four situations *A–D*, irrespective of the types of error or success 1–4, we find in fact that the colour alternation is noticed by 23 per cent of the subjects at 5 years, 39 per cent at 6 years, 64 per cent at 7 years, and 67 per cent at 8 years. Now, in the technique involving drawings of somersaulted coloured and completely white tubes (see Table 56), alternation of the colours is successful in 47–50 per cent of cases at 5 years, 50–60 per cent at 6 years, and 66–71 per cent at 7 years. Here, therefore, the 5- to 6-year-olds are ahead, and the gap closes at 7 years. Here also therefore one may legitimately speak of the favourable influence of comprehension on the image. In the technique used in section 6, 59 per cent of the 5-year-old subjects and 64 per cent of the 6-year-old subjects are already able to comprehend that a rotation takes place (cf. the verbal descriptions of Table 55), whereas in the present case it is in the main a question of brief incidental observations made by the subjects during the act of reproductive imitation. In other words, in the case of imitation, the subject does not centre on the result of the rotation but on the course of the red and green points perceived by him, while in the case of anticipatory reconstitution of the somersault the finishing-points are conceived of as functions of the overall process of the rotation, without, however, being immediately linked with the detail of the trajectories. We should bear in mind that in the present experiment the trajectories have no significance, and that the finishing points disappear immediately (there are thus no privileged states during the movement).

8. *The trajectories of three beads fixed on a rod rotated through 180°*

When studying the child's notion of movement, we devised a test for the subgroup of the rotations, using which it was possible to study the inversion of order (and inversion of the inversion, and so on.) Three differently coloured beads *A*, *B* and *C* were threaded in that order from left to right on to a rigid rod running through a cardboard tube or 'tunnel'. The task was to predict the order in which the beads would emerge from the tunnel first if it was not turned, second if it was turned through 180°, and third if it was turned twice, three times, and so on.[12] This experiment, however, dealt only with the operations involved, and not with the mental image of the trajectories of the beads during the rotation. P. Greco[13]

[12] Piaget, J., *The Child's Conception of Movement and Speed*, 1969.
[13] Greco, P., in 'Apprentissage et connaissance', *Études d'épistémologie génétique*, Chapter III.

took up the same test for the purpose of studying the child's learning of order. This led him to differentiate considerably the techniques used, and in particular to ask where appropriate for a drawing of the beads' trajectories. We realized that Greco was raising here a problem of imaginal representation, or kinetic anticipatory imagery, and that this was quite distinct from the problem of the composition of the operations themselves – so distinct, in fact, that good operational comprehension of the result of the rotation may quite easily be accompanied by an extremely inaccurate image of the trajectories.

It is this problem that we should now like to take up ourselves, and consider from the point of view of the images involved. For we have a particularly suggestive example here of relations between operational comprehension of kinetic transformations and imaginal representation of the movements in question. This inquiry was carried out with E. Schmid-Kitsikis in collaboration with A. Politi.

The basic technique (*A*) comprised the following five stages: (1) The child copies the starting order of the three beads threaded along the rod (he simply colours in a prepared drawing). He indicates their positions in the tube as soon as the rod is placed inside it. (2) The experimenter says to the child, 'Watch carefully what I am about to do; we want you to do a drawing afterwards', and then rotates the tube through 180° (horizontally on the table about an axis passing through the centre bead). The child then indicates the positions of the beads inside the tube, and draws their new order on a sheet of paper (the initial drawing of the starting order remains in front of him; the second drawing also consists of colouring in prepared outlines). (3) Then, with the first two drawings still in front of him, the child is asked to draw the trajectories of the three beads – the red (first), the blue (third) and the green (centre): 'Draw the path of this bead when it goes from where it was before to where it is now' (2 and 3*a*). This is repeated for a 360° rotation. (4) The child is asked to get hold of each bead in turn between thumb and forefinger, and to trace out with a gesture the trajectory imagined (we were careful to make a drawing of the subject's gestural trajectory). (5) Finally, it is useful to get the child to determine the relative positions of the beads in the rotation independently of the drawing (3), and the gesture (4). The experimenter takes the red bead and places it in four positions successively: 45°, 90°, 135° and 180°. For each one the child is asked to put the blue bead in position relative to the red one. In this question and in the preceding questions, it is helpful if from time to time the child is reminded of the direction of the rotation by being made to imitate the tube's general movement.

In the second technique (*B*) the subject was requested to draw the trajectories (3) before the final reversed positions (2). To complement this the subject was also asked for the following: (*a*) a global gestural reproduction of the movement of the tube with the beads inside it; (*b*) a slow-motion gestural imitation breaking down the beads' movement; and (*c*) a drawing of the trajectories, starting with the middle bead. Finally and most important (*d*), for the sake of comparison, we repeated the whole set of questions for a visible rotation (i.e. without using the tube). In order to determine the level of the image relative to that of the operations, it seemed useful to finish off by inviting the subjects to give a reasoned account of the trajectories and the changes of order.

The most remarkable general result to come out of this investigation is the considerable lag of the image of the trajectories, which is not successful until 8 to 9 years, behind the operational comprehension of the changes of order. The latter corresponds to the earliest of the operations – this goes for all spheres so far examined – and in the present case gives 75 per cent successes and above from 5 years for the single inversion, and from 6 years for the inversion of the inversion.

If we start with the subjects examined under method *A*,[14] and compare the successful changes of order for 180° and 360° with the successful drawings of the trajectories, we arrive at the table below (Table 61).

It should be made clear that the changes of order in question in this table were not obtained by questions of an operational kind (and we shall see later that the young child's comprehension is limited as far as the centre bead is concerned), but by means of drawings (drawings 2 and 2*a* of method *A*). Imaginal representation is therefore involved here, but is concerned only with the result or product of the rotation, as opposed to the movement as such or the trajectory

TABLE 61 *Successes for changes of order and for trajectories*[15] *– (technique A)*
(As % of the subjects)

	One rotation (180°)		Two rotations (360°)	
	Change of order	Trajectory	Change of order	Trajectory
4 years (12)	25	0	8·3	0
5 years (11)	73	0	18·2	0
6 years (13)	100	7·7	84·6	7·7
7 years (15)	100	13·3	80	6·6
8 years (9)	100	55	100	33·3

[14] In method *A* the child is asked for the change of order (drawing 2) before the drawing of the trajectories.
[15] Evaluation of the trajectories is based on complete success, bearing in mind the four criteria of Table 63: direction of the paths, circular shape, symmetry in relation to the horizontal axis, and the mere turning on itself of the centre bead.

(we are thus concerned here with an *AKP* not an *AKM* image, in the sense defined in Chapter One, section 1). Thus it is legitimate to conclude from this table that in the present case anticipation of the result of the rotation precedes representation of the trajectories themselves by 3 to 4 years (if the drawing of the trajectories bears on each bead individually, the drawing of the change of order must of course also be done in this way). The problem then is to account for this developmental displacement.

We note first of all that the successful responses to the questions concerning order and trajectories are not entirely independent in spite of the considerable gap between them. This emerges clearly if one compares techniques *A* and *B*. When the trajectory part of the test precedes that concerned with change of order (method *B*), the latter is more successful with the smaller children (54 per cent of the 4-year-olds as against 25 per cent in Table 61), because the attempt to follow the trajectories evokes the idea of the inversion.

Conversely, if the tests are taken the other way round, with the inversion of the order first (method *A*), then there is some improvement in the drawings of the trajectories – not in all their aspects but certainly in their circularity (25 per cent as against 18 per cent at 5 years, 83 per cent as against 30 per cent at 6 years, and 80 per cent as against 50 per cent at 7 years). And the reason for this is that the preliminary drawing of the beads' reversed position provides the child with points of reference which aid him in constructing the trajectories. In view of this relative interdependence of the two questions, the displacement of their respective developments is all the more surprising. We need therefore to try to analyse the difficulties involved in drawing the trajectories.

In this connection it might be useful first to draw attention to the relationship between the results for the gesture and those for the drawing, so that we can go on to determine what role is played by the purely graphical factor. With regard to the gesture, the question might arise whether the actual rotation of the tube as a whole (or of the rod with the beads) is comprehended at all ages. Now the global gestural reproduction of the horizontal rotation through 180° is successful in 75 per cent of subjects at 4 years, and in 100 per cent of subjects from 5 years upwards. In the case of the gestures reproducing the trajectory of each bead in detail, it is interesting to find that the drawing has a lead over the gesture which increases with age (Table 62).

In this case the drawing has an obvious advantage over the gesture: the drawings remain visible right through from the beginning, whereas the gestures do not, so the possibility of comparison in the case of the drawing facilitates execution of the three trajectories. The difficulties arising in imaginal representation of the

TABLE 62   *Comparing the drawings and the imitative gestures*
(As % of the responses)

Ages (and No. of subjects)	4 (30)	5 (28)	6 (29)	7 (31)	8 years (21)
Same result	80	64	69	58	43
Better drawing	10	25	21	26	48
Better gesture	10	11	10	16	9

trajectories are not, therefore, solely attributable to the graphic factor as such.

The final method (*d*), however, yielded a result that is important from all points of view. When the tube was not used and the rotations of the rod and beads were entirely visible, there was no significant difference between the results of techniques *A* and *B*! In other words, the perception of the rotation does not in itself entail the formation of an adequate image, even in those subjects who succeed (73 per cent at 5 years and 100 per cent at 6 years) in drawing correctly the change in order, or the inversion of the positions.

If we examine these images or drawings of the trajectories in detail (see Figure 26), a hypothesis is immediately formulable to explain why they are as surprisingly retarded as they are. It is this. Since the image is essentially a symbol, a subject who comprehends the order-reversal will for a long time make do with what is in essence a schematic symbol whose detail remains arbitrary (symbolic resemblance being global). One should be clear that, from the point of view of operational construction, comprehending a displacement as change of position (which only demands simple ordinal operations) is quite a different matter from comprehending a displacement as distance covered, with its various characteristics – direction, measurable size, shape, and orientation against reference systems or coordinate axes. Now the early representation of position-changes in Table 61 seems to correspond to equally early ordinal operations: in the same way it is very likely that imaginal representation of the beads' trajectories presupposes operational support provided by the operations of displacement, in the second sense of the term. If so, until these operations are formed at about 7 to 8 years[16] it would be natural for the child to make shift with very approximate symbolic images in order to draw the beads' trajectories. Such images serve simply to justify changes in order and fail to bear any close resemblance to the actual trajectories in question in their multiple aspects of size, shape and orientation.

Before going on to a qualitative analysis of the errors, let us first

[16] See Piaget, *The Child's Conception of Movement and Speed*, 1969, Chapter III, 3.

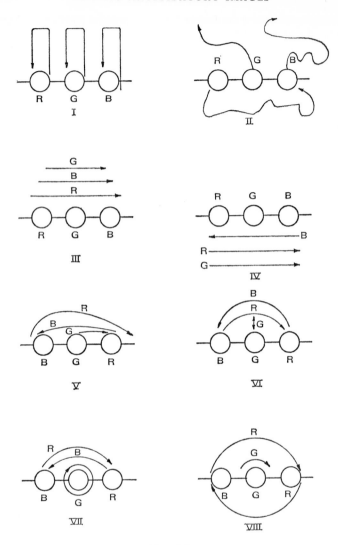

FIG. 26

test our hypothesis by giving a quantitative table of successes for each of these aspects, taking the different techniques together. In addition to change of order, we distinguish the following characteristics: (1) direction of the paths (left to right and vice versa); (2) shape of the paths (semi-circular as opposed to straight lines, or wavy or zigzag lines with various angles); (3) path of the centre bead (which is not displaced but merely turns on itself); and (4) symmetry of the paths of the outside beads in relation to the horizontal axis (as opposed to those drawings showing both paths on one side of the axis and those in which they pass arbitrarily from one side to the other). Table 63 sets out the results thus classified.

TABLE 63 *Percentage of successes for the various aspects of the drawing of trajectories*

	(0) Change of order	(1) Direction	(2) Shape	(3) Centre bead	(4) Symmetry
4 years (*N* = 30):					
(4,0–4,5)	22·2 ⎫				
(4,6–4,11)	62·3 ⎭	16·6	0·3	0	10
5 years (29)	79	44·8	20·6	6·8	13·7
6 years (30)	95	80	56·6	40	13·3
7 years (31)	100	90·3	70·9	45·1	22·5
8 years (21)	100	100	95·2	85·7	47·6

The first thing to be noted is that the direction of the paths (the red bead to the right, the blue to the left) is successfully recognized at 6 years (> 75 per cent) and from this stage on becomes simply a translation of the change of order. This does not mean that the paths are semi-circular (the shape of the paths is not successful until about 7 to 8 years). Nor does it mean that the centre bead stays in place (success at about 8 years). Moreover it does not mean that the child comprehends that when one bead describes its semi-circle on one side of the horizontal axis, the other does the same on the other side. The latter question is still unsuccessful at 8 to 9 years – probably because of some difficulty in grasping that when the tube or the rod goes through its constant clockwise rotation, the outside beads follow inverse but symmetrical paths.

We now go on to an analysis of the errors. Approaching them first of all by age, we distinguish three groups for the 4-year-old subjects. First, those in techniques *A* and *B* who fail to reverse the order. Either their drawings do not depict the trajectories at all (the beads turn on the spot, etc.), or they have vertical or tortuously curved trajectories turning back on themselves to their starting point. Second, those who do the test without the tube. In spite of the fact that the rotation is visible, several still fail to represent the change in order, and give drawings or make gestures similar to those found in the first group of subjects. Others manage the inversion, and occasionally produce crossed but rectilinear or curved but asymmetrical paths. Finally, there are those subjects in methods *A* and *B* who succeed with the inversion, but produce drawings of all the types just described, as well as rectilinear and parallel trajectories all going from left to right without doubling back, even for the 360° rotation. The gestures were similar. It seems evident, therefore, that for these subjects the image of the trajectory is merely a symbol signifying that something has revolved. But, apart from the rare instances of crossed paths, there is no real attempt to achieve the correct trajectory.[17]

At 5 years crossed trajectories begin to predominate. These are symbols of successful change of order; but the paths may also be rectilinear (even for the centre bead), square-shaped, capriciously curved, or correct but not symmetrical. All these drawings, apart from the few completely successful ones (7 per cent), appear to centre more on the final result than on the actual process of the transformation, which thus remains purely symbolic.

At 6 years there is some improvement as far as direction, the centre bead and the curves are concerned. But the predominant error is still the absence of symmetry. At 7 to 8 years, on the other hand, we meet with a clear attempt to co-ordinate the displacements of the outside beads in relation to one another, and even to some extent in relation to the horizontal axis. The symbolic image tends to become representative in intention. The errors can be said to be of a residual character in view of the difficulty of training constant attention on all the properties of this complex system of displacement at once.

To fix these ideas here is a table setting out the evolution of the errors (Table 64):

TABLE 64   *Types of path (all techniques combined)*
(As % of the subjects shown in Table 63)

	No path	Rectilinear	Near squares	Incorrect curves	Curves – correct but not symmetrical	Complete success
4 years	26·6	36·6	3·3	26·6	6·6	0
5 years	17·7	37·9	6·8	20·6	13·7	6·8
6 years	0	26·6	3·3	10	50·3	6·6
7 years	0	16·1	0	25·8	38·7	19·3
8 years	0	4·7	0	4·7	47	42·8
9 years	0	0	0	0	40	60·0

It remains to discuss the odd problem of the centre bead. Some time ago we studied the problem of these successive inversions from the operational angle. It was quite often found that some of the 4-year-old (and more rarely the 5-year-old) subjects, when asked

[17] We have already seen (Chapter Two, section 7) instances of gestural reproduction of trajectories similar to those involved here, and that they are on average successful around 6 years.

which of the beads *A, B* or *C* would emerge first from a 'tunnel', began by replying that *A* or *C* would come out first. But after several rotations, without any extra question or suggestion, they said it would be the middle bead *B*.[18] We had some doubts about this, and in 1953 one of us agreed to carry out some control tests. The same kind of thing was found again under the same conditions. On the other hand, P. Greco, in the study already mentioned (1959), did not observe any instances of this type. But W. R. Charlesworth took up the same experiments at the University of Minnesota using 200 kindergarten and primary school children. He used a standardized procedure and drew up the results according to a non-parametric statistical method. His conclusion was that significantly more older than younger subjects predict the displacement of the middle element in the direction of the extreme positions.[19] It seems, then, that this belief does in fact exist, but that in the Geneva area between 1940 and 1960 its upper chronological limit went down. Now this is not an isolated instance. Between 1930 and 1940 certain other reactions were commonly observed which are scarcely to be found nowadays. For instance one used to find that two rows of counters equal in length but unequal in number were estimated only in terms of length (space occupied) and judged to be numerically equivalent. (On the other hand one still finds that two rows equal in *number* but unequal in *length* are judged to be numerically or quantitatively unequal.) It is possible that the speeding-up of this development is due to more active methods of pre-school teaching. In any case it is of interest to follow such changes closely. Let us now examine the present results with this in mind.

These results are nicely graded. An inversion is comprehended by 25 per cent of subjects at 4 years and by 73 per cent at 5 years, a double inversion by 8–18 per cent at 4 to 5 years and by 85 per cent at 6 years – which is somewhat superior to our 1946 observations. In the change of order question (question 2, technique *A*, and question 3, technique *B*) we found no case of a subject asserting a modification of the middle bead's position. On the other hand, in the drawings of the trajectories, it is not until 8 years that more than 75 per cent of the children leave the bead in its place (40–45 per cent at 6 to 7 years) while at 4 to 5 years the large majority (see Table 63) are quite incapable of doing so. Table 65 expresses this in more detail.

[18] See Piaget, *Les notions de mouvement et de vitesse chez l'enfant*, 1946, 5–16, cases of An, Ros, Jac, Fran and Der.
[19] Charlesworth, William R., *The Growth of Knowledge of the Effects of Rotation and Shaking on the Linear Order of Objects*, Communication (duplicated) to the Minnesota Psychological Association Convention, 1962.

TABLE 65 *Paths of the centre bead*
(As % of the subjects, all techniques combined)

Ages	4 years	5	6	7	8
Paths identical to others	90	65·5	23·3	13	7·7
Paths smaller (centre)	10	17·7	36·7	41·9	6·6
No path (correct)	0	6·8	40	45·1	85·7

If the shortened trajectories returning to the centre are counted as correct, the question does not elicit a correct representation until 6 years (>75 per cent). It is true that the image is only symbolic. But if the child is asked what the centre bead 'really' does, there are three types of reaction. (1) Some at 4 years react as Sen (4,11): '*It is always in the middle: it can't come out first.*' (2) Others hesitate, start by assuming it can change position, and then correct themselves. (3) Others, like Man (4,10), say: '*If you turn it a lot it can come out first,*' or Ge (4,10): '*The green one can come out the first.*' Thus it can be seen that Hilbert's celebrated order axiom ('If *B* is placed between *A* and *C*, it is also placed between *C* and *A*') does not, as we have said before, seem to correspond to an *a priori* intuition. This intuition, which even at 4 to 5 years is still weak, seems rather to derive from a construction. At this level such a construction is almost completely formed: its beginnings will no doubt be found at 2 to 3 years – if ever we manage to study the preoperational thought of these early ages by means of techniques not dependent on language.

In conclusion, the foregoing facts are a remarkable illustration of relationships between mental images and operations. To the early-formed ordinal operations correspond the equally early imaginal representations of the result of inversions of order. And to the later-formed displacement operations correspond equally late images of the beads' trajectories. In the first case it is impossible to say, without an analysis of lower ages, whether the image precedes and prepares the operation, whether it is directed by the operation, or whether they are interdependent. The second, however, raises two noteworthy points. First, there is a difference of 3 or 4 years between the image of the positions and the image of the trajectories (these not being successful until after 9 years), while the displacement operations are formed at about 7 to 8 years. Now we can see that the latter will be more complex than ordinal operations (conservation of lengths, orientations). But it is surely surprising that there should be difficulty in imagining the beads' trajectories after their position-changes have been given. The second striking thing to arise from this investigation is that the representation of trajectories should remain symbolic so long and that the attempt to achieve an adequate representation should be so long delayed. It seems legitimate to draw the following conclusions from these two points. In the present case, the kinetic anticipatory image, in so far as it bears on the movement itself (*AKM* as opposed to *AKP*), cannot be formed without seeking support and direction in operational reasoning as such. The instance of the visible rotations in particular shows that perception of the process is by no means sufficient to ensure that it is subsequently accurately imagined.

9. *Anticipation of the positions of six elements on a rotating disk*

I. To complement the preceding inquiry, it would perhaps be valuable to examine a circular rather than a linear case. To begin with we used six elements, the aim being to find out whether permutation of diametrically opposed points would result in a change in the position of the four others while conserving the general order. (This first part of the experiment was carried out with C. Émery.)

The apparatus consisted of three sheets of cardboard 9 cm square and 1 cm thick. To each of these was attached a white paper circle 8 cm in diameter. Around the circumference of the circle for sheet I were six drawing-pins spaced at regular intervals (of 60°), each differently coloured (red, brown, white, black, yellow and blue, the red and the black being at the extremities of the diameter parallel to the table edge). The circle for sheet II was pierced with holes at the same regular intervals as for I. Into these the child could insert his own coloured drawing-pins. The circle for sheet III was similar to that for sheet I, but was provided with a rigid pivot enabling it to be rotated. A paper mask could be fitted so that only one drawing-pin would show.

The test was in two phases. The child was placed in front of sheet I. He was first asked to imagine the rotation of the circle in front of him and to anticipate the position of the colours after the rotation, a second lot of drawing-pins lay scattered on the table for the child to place in the anticipated positions on sheet II. The test began with the red drawing-pin – that is, with the left extremity of the diameter parallel to the edge of the table. Questions concerning rotation were put to the subject simply by indicating to him how far the red pin would travel. He was asked to imagine the pins' positions (*a*) when the red pin 'goes to where the black one is (= 180°) – so (gesture in clockwise direction),' (*b*) when it 'goes to the blue one's place (60° in the opposite direction)', and (*c*) when it 'goes to the black one's place', in the opposite direction to (*a*).

In the second part the child was shown circle III (with the red-black diameter in the same position parallel to the edge of the table). He ascertained that it corresponded to circle I – which could then serve as a check model or an aid to memory. Then the mask was put in position so that only the red pin was visible. The disk was then actually turned through the three rotations (180°, 60° in reverse, 180° in reverse) anticipated in the first

145

part of the test. The subject was required to reconstitute the positions of the five other drawing-pins that he could not see. (As before, he did this by placing his own drawing-pins on circle II.)

After each reaction, we asked the child to justify his response. The problem is therefore distinct from that dealt with in the last section. There it was a matter of imagining the positions of three beads reversing their linear order; here it is a matter of reconstituting the cyclic order of six points, given the displacement of one of them. In the last section the main task was to represent the trajectories. In the present experiment we did not stress this aspect – all the trajectories are in any case circular – but turned our attention to the results only of the rotations (except in cases where younger subjects imagined jumps between the red and the black drawing-pins while keeping the rest in position).

The solutions offered can be grouped into four types:

(*A*) None of the drawing-pins is left in its place (except, of course, the red one).

(*B*) The red and the black pins are correctly exchanged, but the others do not change position.

(*C*) The red and the black pins exchange positions, but the others simply change in pairs. This may occur in three different ways: (*a*) they cross over so that they remain on either side of the drawing-pin they surrounded at the outset (for instance: black, white, brown, red, blue and yellow); (*b*) those originally on either side of the red pin are placed on either side of the black pin, and vice versa; (*c*) a combination of (*a*) and (*b*) with one or two accidentally correct placings.

(*D*) Complete success.

Table 66 below sets out the quantitative results yielded by sixteen subjects aged 4 to 5 years, twenty-one aged 6 to 7 years and sixteen aged 8 to 9 years for a 180° and a 60° clockwise rotation. The results of the questions with and without the mask have been brought together, as they showed no significant differences.

TABLE 66 *Position of the six drawing-pins during rotation of 180° and 60°* (As % of the solutions)

	180°				60°			
	A	*B*	*C*	*D*	*A*	*B*	*C*	*D*
4–5 years	25·2	19·0	38·7	17·1	18·4	15·6	38·5	27·5
6–7 years	11·5	9·2	46·2	33·1	2·5	4·8	25·5	67·2
8–9 years	1·5	0	22·0	76·5	0	0	6·5	93·5

One sees from this that the representation of the positions of the six drawing-pins does not acquire any degree of accuracy until about 8 years (when the 60° rotation is a little ahead of the 180° rotation), whereas the linear order of the three beads is successfully inverted at 6 years. This difference is probably not only owing to the number of elements involved, but also to the specific difficulties connected with circular order. We give an analysis now of these difficulties in terms of the types of error *A–C*.

The initial behaviour (types *A* and *B*) involves the assumption that the rotation of the disk does not entail that of the elements it supports. But as the red pin occupies the place of the black one the child naturally puts the black one in the red one's place, in consequence of a sort of pseudo-permutation that is really only an imposed substitution. A situation of this kind is, of course, physically quite possible. For instance, if a vessel filled with water is slowly rotated, neither the liquid nor any objects floating on it move (at least not at the same speed) with it. The child needs to have learnt from experience, therefore, that drawing-pins stuck in a rotating disk will always move round with it.

This being so, some subjects (classed under *A*) modify the positions at random. But they soon begin to imagine regular modifications – which is tantamount to saying that there is some element of conservation. The first relationship to be conserved, however, is not that of order. At first the child merely affirms the permanence of a simpler relationship – that of proximity independent of direction (the direction in fact emerges as a result of co-ordinating the proximities). As we have tried to show in another work,[20] this relationship provides a basis for the relationship of order. For example, when the subjects see from the model that the brown and the blue surround the red drawing-pin, they put them next to it in its new position, but in an order contrary to that of the real direction of travel. The drawing-pin which was uppermost thus stays uppermost and is not placed 'in front of' the red pin in the direction of the rotation. In addition to conservation of proximity, then, there is imaginal pseudo-conservation of the upper and lower positions. This is not, however, always the case. The subject may proceed by crossing pairs of pins. While he reverses the positions of the red and black pin horizontally, he may do the same vertically with another pair of opposing pins.[21] The crossing changes may also be combined with conservations of proximity. The pins surrounding the red pin may, for instance, be put round the black one.

Now these various solutions *C* (none of which taken individually develops regularly with age) are on a par with a systematic deficiency in the imagination of the trajectories. It looks as if rotation of the disk gives rise

[20] *The Child's Conception of Space*, Chapter III.
[21] It should be noted that the symmetrical and equidistant arrangement which will be cut out in the next experiment (II) may introduce an artificial situation. But it is in itself interesting as it involves pseudo-conservations deriving from the image or from the configuration as such.

to a general all-change in which individual drawing-pins leap independently from one spot to another; moreover, some move in one direction and some in another – as the 4 to 5-year-olds explicitly affirm. For example Phi (5 years): 'Do they all turn? – *Yes*. – All the same? – *Yes*. – Do some go one way and some a different way (gesture)? – *Yes*. – How did the red one get there? – *It jumped* (gesture right across). – Can it do that? – *Yes*. – Did you see it? – *No, it didn't jump, it suddenly got there when it turned.*' And Der (5,7): 'Do they all change places? – *No, the blue, the red one and the black one do.* – What about the others? – *The drawing-pins at the top haven't changed.* – When I turn, do all the drawing-pins go the same distance? – *No, some of them go a long way, and some go a little way.*' This belief that the distances travelled differ in length persists till about 7 years.

The relations of proximity are the only constant elements in the initial general confusion. It is only in solution *D*, that is at about 8 years, that these relations are co-ordinated and ensure permanent order of succession. '*The one before the red one will always be in front*', Nic (7,10). '*The one that comes behind here (I) will be behind there (II) as well*', Mel (8,7).

The results obtained for the 60° rotation are successful approximately one year earlier (Table 66) than for the 180° rotation. It may be that this is due to the fact that in the case of the 60° rotations the child gets more guidance from the conservations of proximity and the step-by-step displacements. In the case of the 180° rotations on the other hand, representation of the positions seems to demand that the operations of order be brought into play in reconstituting a general shift of three stages (from the red to the black pin). And an operational kind of solution generally produces more errors before the correct solution is finally arrived at. Generally speaking, the overall retardation of the present anticipations compared with the order-changes of the three beads in the last section would seem to confirm the need for operational intervention. This also leads us to express some reserve concerning the analysis of the quasi-operational solutions of the younger subjects in the experiment with the three beads.

Finally, in the case of those subjects tested for a reverse 180° rotation, we found no difference between the anticipations of positions in the initial order and those in the reverse order. This is another piece of evidence in favour of the hypothesis that correct imaginal representations are here supported operationally.

II. The last lot of results concern an even number of symmetrically distributed elements. In any research into images, as into perception, it is important to take into account all the factors involved in the apparatus used. We thought it would be useful, therefore, to examine (with J. Pascual-Leone) the results obtained from a similar experiment with an *odd* number (five) of symmetrically (at intervals of 72°) and asymmetrically (intervals of 30°, 87°, 80°, 51° and 112°) arranged elements (see Figure 27). Some additional questions were introduced.

To begin with, here are the results of the comparison of the three different disks – one with six symmetrical elements (Table 66), one with five symmetrical elements, and one with five asymmetrical elements (Table 67). The test conditions were the same and the rotation was 180°.

TABLE 67 *Anticipation of the positions (after 180° rotation) of six symmetrical elements (6 SE), five symmetrical elements (5 SE), and five asymmetrical elements (5 AE)*[22]

	6 SE					5 SE					5 AE				
	A	B	C	D	C+D	A	B	C	D	C+D	A	B	C	D	C+D
4–5 years	25	19	39	17	56	50	31	19	0	19	25	50	25	0	25
6–7 years	12	9	46	33	69	50	25	19	6	25	8	33	58	0	58
8–9 years	1	0	22	77	99	0	21	29	50	79	6	6	50	39	89

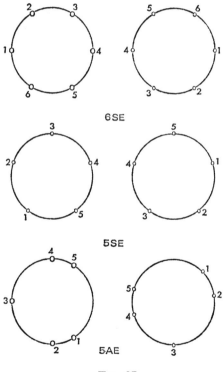

FIG. 27

It is clear from this that the disk with the six symmetrically

[22] The new subjects for 5 *SE* and 5 *AE* – sixteen and twelve aged 4 to 5 years, sixteen and twelve aged 5 to 6 years, and thirteen and eighteen aged 8 to 9 years.

arranged elements is appreciably easier than the other two. The main reason is probably this. In order to resolve the problem, there is no need for the change of order to be imagined step-by-step during the course of the rotations. It is enough to rely on one or two proximities and to reverse the left-right and top-bottom relations simultaneously (errors *A*, *B* and *C* generally arise when one and not the other of these relations is reversed). Consequently, once the subject has succeeded in determining the position of one element, he need only invert in order to find that of its counterpart. On the other hand, in the figures 5 *SE* and 5 *AE*, the correspondence can only be made obliquely, so that to imagine the permutations the subject must take the order into account by following the rotation step-by-step. Inversion can only give rise to an incorrect answer, though it yields a correct or apparently correct one in 6 *SE*.

Turning to the relationship between the disks with five elements, it can be seen that, compared with the asymmetry of 5 *AE*, the radial symmetry of 5 *SE* tends to some extent to favour the entirely successful response *D*. The *C* response, however, which shows that there is at least some comprehension of the problem, comes up more frequently in 5 *AE*. Hence a higher total for *C* + *D*. The reason for this seems to be that, except for cases in which the image is based on correct operational reasoning, the figural factor of symmetry offers the subject a deceptively easy way out, whereas the structure 5 *AE* exacts more reflexion since it is objectively more difficult to make its elements correspond.

The child was asked questions about 5 *SE* and 5 *AE* similar to those for 6 *SE*: (1) Have all the drawing-pins moved? (2) Do all the drawing-pins go the same distance? (3) Do they all turn in the same direction? (4) Which way do they go? (to get the child to judge the direction of the rotation). The percentage of correct answers to these four questions is given in Table 68.

Thus at least 75 per cent (or almost) of the subjects in all age groups accept that all the points are displaced when the disk is revolved. But it is not at all clear to the younger ones (nor even to the 6- to 7-year-olds in 5 *SE* and the 8- to 9-year-olds in 5 *AE*) that all the pins travel equal distances. This is particularly true for the asymmetrical arrangement. In the case of the younger children the reasons for this are related to figural factors; and in the case of the older children to the fact that a problem remaining unsolved at the operational level (Table 68) frequently gives rise to complicated hypotheses (in the present case, about the inequality of the intervals). Further, it is clear that the children are consistently more uncertain about the equal lengths of the drawing-pins' paths when the direction is anti-clockwise (results in brackets).

TABLE 68 *Answers relating to the anticipations of rotation 1*
(As % of the subjects)[23]

	5 SE					
	1	*2*	*3*	*4 (rot. +)*	*4 (rot. −)*	*4 (straight)*
4–5 years	86 (80)	62 (45)	46 (43)	63 (33)	31 (42)	50 (59)
6–7 years	88 (79)	38 (25)	85 (77)	80 (100)	33 (29)	27 (13)
8–9 years	92 (100)	100 (65)	91 (100)	100 (100)	14 (25)	0 (0)

	5 AE					
	1	*2*	*3*	*4 (rot. +)*	*4 (rot. −)*	*4 (straight)*
4–5 years	67 (78)	13 (43)	86 (25)	90 (100)	50 (89)	10 (11)
6–7 years	100 (91)	80 (55)	100 (100)	92 (100)	0 (40)	0 (20)
8–9 years	100 (94)	56 (53)	100 (100)	100 (100)	28 (11)	5 (0)

At 4 to 5 years the subjects are not yet certain that the points all move in the same direction. This is probably due to the inherent difficulties of circular order. On the other hand it is interesting to find that the frequency of straight trajectories is higher for 5 *SE* than for 5 *AE*. Similarly, a more detailed statistical analysis shows that there is also a consistently greater number of inversions for 5 *SE* than for 5 *AE*. This corroborates the fact that, confronted with a symmetrical arrangement, the child will be inclined not to utilize the rotation in order to imagine the displacements. They tend rather to make use of the left–right, and particularly of the top–bottom relations as in 6 *SE*, and even the 'facing' relation as in 5 *SE*. They continue in this way until they understand the necessity (unavoidable in 5 *AE* – hence its difficulty) of working on the basis of the circular order. At this point they are led to support imaginal representation with operational comprehension.

10. *Anticipation of the prolongation of movements of constant speed whose starting point has been perceived*

In most of the situations studied above one can well understand that operational comprehension and adequate imagery can be to a greater or lesser degree developmentally out of phase. For example, one can see that a somersault movement (section 6) may imply a rotation, that is, alternation of the object's ends, even though the details of the rotation may not be visualized in precise images. Turning now to an examination of images bearing on the velocity of a motion, we should like to analyse an instance in which image and operation seem to be much more closely interrelated, and possibly even interdependent. It should be recalled that children acquire a metric notion of time ($v = d : t$) at a very late stage, since it involves proportion and the relating of two different elements. Until this

---

[23] Anti-clockwise rotations in brackets.

stage children compare movement only in ordinal terms (overtaking, i.e. spatio-temporal change of order) or hyperordinal terms (in Suppes' sense, tantamount here to comparing the successive intervals between two moving bodies in so far as they increase, decrease or remain equal).[24] Now in the majority of cases these ordinal or hyperordinal comparisons are only possible if the continuation of the movement perceived is anticipated. A subject will only understand a *partial* catching-up movement if he is able to anticipate the subsequent movements leading up to a *complete* catching-up and eventual overtaking. In a case such as this it would seem that operational comparison must be supported by an image, since one would expect the act of anticipating the subsequent movements to demand some degree of imaginal representation. But conversely, an image of this kind may in turn rest on operational comprehension of the perceptual data preceding the anticipation – unless one accepts the view that the image is a direct prolongation of previous perceptions considered exclusively as such.

What we have here is an interesting problem concerning the relationship between kinetic anticipation and the operations. Its solution requires a separate study of the purely reproductive image, of the anticipatory image, and of the relations between them. And a study of this kind has been carried out by E. Schmid-Kitsikis and M. Boehme, as follows.

The moving bodies (small model cars coloured red and yellow) go along two rectilinear, parallel tracks 90 cm long. The last third of the paths is covered by a tunnel. The visible movements last 1·5 seconds at a constant speed. They include the following: (1) an overtaking (just before entering the tunnel); (2) a complete catching-up (at the precise moment of entry into the tunnel); (3) a partial catching-up (the objects actually catching up just after entry). The starting points are staggered, and one of the bodies – sometimes the red and sometimes the yellow one – is faster than the other. They both come to a halt inside the tunnel. The child is placed at the midpoint facing the paths. He has a strip of paper 180 cm long, without a tunnel (though the last third of the strip is, like the tunnel, coloured blue). The strip is marked every 10 cm., so that the experimenter can see whether the subject varies the intervals between the cars by reproducing, or by prolonging the movements perceived. This strip is 90 cm longer than the model trajectory to give the subject time to anticipate what goes on inside the tunnel.

The child was asked the following: (*a*) to prolong the movements perceived reproducing their visible phase and anticipating the continuation (but without a break, so that the movement is a continuous whole); (*b*) to estimate the speeds (this has nothing to do with the mental image but makes it possible to relate the level of the image to that of the kine-

[24] But independently of metric proportion.

matic operations); (c) to reproduce the movements seen as a whole without the tunnel; it is then a question of imitating the movements in their totality according to their respective constant speeds, without being limited to initial and terminal positions. (The movements are of course repeated for this question.)

Questions *a* and *c* deal exclusively with mental images – anticipatory in *a* and reproductive in *c*. And the method involves gestural imitation, not a drawing.[25] The child is not required in *a* and *c* (as he is in *b*) to estimate the speeds, but simply to reproduce what he has seen and to prolong it in a gestural anticipation. If this had produced a generally successful response, one might have suspected that it was simply a matter of perseveration. However, the interesting thing about the results (obtained from 161 children aged between 5 and 11 years) was that they demonstrated on the one hand that the reproductions themselves are far from being uniformly correct, and on the other that the anticipation, even when the reproduction is correct, does not derive from it as a simple continuation, but presupposes yet further original contributory factors.

To start with the gestural reproduction, it is striking to see the degree to which it accords first with preoperational and then with operational notions, rather than with the perceptual picture presented by the model. The criterion for fidelity of reproduction ought to be that it should not only respect the moving bodies' initial and final positions (ordinal reproduction), but that it should also at least symbolically express the continuity of the movement and the conservation of the speed. Now in the younger subjects, the order in which the bodies reach the finishing points has pride of place both in the reproduction and the notion. Their imitation of the movement proceeds by fits and starts and fails to keep the speeds constant: they tend to accelerate particularly before a catching-up and temporarily increase the interval between the objects just after an overtaking. Only at about 8 years do the subjects themselves observe that in order to reproduce the movements properly they need to show the objects 'driving along'. In other words they realize at this age that it is necessary to take account of the kinetic content (and conservation of speed) as well as the starting and finishing points. Thus in Table 69 we make a distinction between hyperordinal reproductions, which relate to the intervals, and ordinal reproductions, which only relate to the order of the objects.

On the reproductive as well as on the notional plane, then, the

---

[25] That is to say, the child uses his own movements, holding the cars in his hand, to reproduce the movements on his strip of paper. The movements of the model are operated mechanically so that they are exactly synchronized.

TABLE 69 *Successful hyperordinal reproductions of the movements of two moving bodies* (*without tunnel*)
(As % of the subjects)
(Ordinal reproductions given in brackets)

	5 years (N=15)	6 years (N=14)	7 years (N=14)
Overtaking	20　(40)	35·7 (71·4)	64·2 (85·7)
Catching-up	13·3 (20)	14·2 (57·1)	42·8 (64·2)
Partial catching-up	0　(26·6)	7·1 (30·7)	50　(50)

	8 years (N=15)	9 years (N=10)	10–11 years
Overtaking	73·3 (100)	100 (100)	
Catching-up	66·6 (66·6)	100 (100)	
Partial catching-up	46·6 (46·6)	60 (100)	80 (100)

easiest situation for the child to master is overtaking, since it involves change of order. Nevertheless, the success score does not rise to 75 per cent till about 7 to 8 years – till the stage, that is, where the notion of overtaking reaches the ordinal-operational stage and is no longer based on the predominant intuition of finishing points. Further, purely ordinal reproduction is in all three situations much easier than hyperordinal reproduction. It is of considerable interest to see that these sequences in order of difficulty at the reproductive level are repeated at the anticipatory level – even though anticipation is here simply a matter of prolonging the perceived movement, or, more precisely of prolonging the reproduction of the movement perceived before entry into the tunnel (question *a*). This anticipatory prolongation proves to be even less successful than the reproduction. While all the subjects capable of anticipation gave an accurate reproduction, the exact reverse is far from being the case. A certain number of subjects (the younger they are, the larger the number) reproduce the movements perceived without the tunnel correctly, but are unable to imagine the movements perceived *before* the tunnel as they are continued *inside* it – even though the movements after overtaking, etc., remain the same. Others fail altogether to imagine the overtaking and catching-up occurring out of sight: instead of prolonging the movements inside the tunnel, they continue the positions reached just before entry! We shall therefore distinguish two sorts of anticipation in Table 70: the purely ordinal anticipations – that is, those which only take into account the order ('in front' or 'behind') of the moving bodies, without considering the size of the interval between them; and the 'hyperordinal' anticipations – those which foresee that the interval between the objects will increase progressively after one has caught the other up.

TABLE 70 *Ordinal (0) and hyperordinal (Ho) anticipations relative to the number of correct hyperordinal reproductions*
(Figures in brackets refer to 0 + Ho as absolute %)[26]

Ages and no. of subjects [27]	Overtaking [28]		Catching-up			Partial catching-up		
	(Ho)	(Ho+O abs.)	(Ho)	O	(Ho+O abs.)	(Ho)	O	(Ho+O abs.)
5 years (29)	10·6 (7 s.)	(31·5)	0 (10 s.)	50	(18·0)	0 (13 s.)	15·3	(7·0)
6 (30)	22·2 (9 s.)	(53·2)	10 (20 s.)	60	(46·6)	16·6 (12 s.)	58·3	(43·2)
7 (24)	40 (15 s.)	(70·7)	22·2 (18 s.)	53·3	(49·9)	25·0 (8 s.)	25·0	(21·6)
8 (25)	43·8 (16 s.)	(72·0)	10·5 (19 s.)	57·8	(56·0)	15·3 (13 s.)	55·8	(52·0)
9 (34)	50·0 (20 s.)	(76·4)	27·2 (22 s.)	45·4	(50·0)	38·8 (19 s.)	55·5	(51·5)
10–11 (19)	76·5 (17 s.)	(89·4)	72·2 (18 s.)	16·6	(84·1)	77·0 (16 s.)	23·0	(81·2)

The first thing one notices – and this is a vital point – is the general backwardness of the anticipations as compared in terms of the absolute percentages with the reproductions (Table 69), when one might have expected a straightforward prolongation of the latter in the former.[29]

There are two other noteworthy results in this table. The first is the appreciable retardation of the hyperordinal anticipations as compared with ordinal anticipations. In other words, there is some considerable difficulty in anticipating the regular increase of the intervals after over-taking. The perception of speeds[30] does take the variation of intervals into account, as is proved by the effect of apparent acceleration due to under-estimation of the decreasing intervals. But the anticipatory image of the movements does not seem to reach the hyperordinal level until about 10 to 11 years in the three cases of overtaking, catching-up, and near catching-up. Now this is of some interest, since 10 to 11 years is the stage of tran-

[26] The reproductions in relation to which we have here calculated the *relative* anticipations are not the same as those of Table 69, which were observed in a test *without* the tunnel. In the present experiment *with* the tunnel the subject's reaction consists of a single complete movement, but can be considered as two parts (not, however, as two separate parts): (a) reproduction of what has been perceived outside the tunnel, and (b) anticipation of the continuation inside the tunnel. We calculated the *relative* anticipations of the table in relation to the reproductions (a). On the other hand the successful anticipations given in brackets as an *absolute* percentage were calculated without taking into account the successes for reproductions (a).

[27] The subjects were not always asked all these questions (7 s., 9 s., etc.).

[28] There was no need to anticipate orders (O) in the overtaking, as they are already given.

[29] It should be noted that Tables 69 and 70 cannot be compared directly, since in the case of reproduction before the tunnel the starting point was corrected by the experimenter, whereas in the case of anticipation without the tunnel (involving a partial reproduction of the visible part), there was no correction.

[30] Piaget, J., Feller, Y., McNear, E., 'Essay on the perception of speeds', in *Arch. de Psych.*, 144.

sition from ordinal operations (speeds estimated on the basis of changed order, or overtaking) to the metric operations (relationships of distance to durations in comparisons between successive movements). It is true that at 8 to 9 years, when comparing synchronous movements, the child is able to judge that the faster of two moving bodies will be the one which goes the further in the same length of time, or the one starting last or arriving first for the same distance. But here there is no question of measurement: ordinal indices relative to the extremities of the paths are an adequate basis for qualitative co-ordination of distance and duration, since conservation of speed is not involved. On the other hand, hyperordinal anticipations, formed at about 10 to 11 years (Table 70), imply conservation of the two speeds being compared. And while the conservation of speeds does not entail measurement as such, it does rest on an at least qualitative proportionality.[31] Now proportionality is a structure that is easily perceived (hence the hyperordinal character of the perception of speeds). But its imaginal representation seems not simply to be a matter of directly prolonging the perception. It relies rather on operational comprehension – and this is the interesting thing about the backwardness of the hyperordinal anticipations. On the other hand, ordinal anticipations simply involve predicting that one moving object will approach another, catch it up and overtake it, that catching-up leads to overtaking, and that overtaking increases (without any precise estimation of the intervals). Ordinal anticipations thus only correspond to preoperational intuitions before coming to rely on the ordinal operations.

The second interesting fact arising from Table 70 is this. Both in the case of the reproductions and in the case of the anticipations considered absolutely, the successes decrease as one passes from the overtaking to the partial catching-up. Further, one finds that the hyperordinal anticipations considered relatively to the reproductions have a clear lead in the case of overtaking over the other two situations. This fact supports the last in that it suggests some parallelism between the development of images and the development of the operations.

Let us take a closer look at this parallelism. It is, after all, the central problem raised by these kinetic anticipations, since it is on them, as we said at the beginning of this section, that the notional estimations of speed depend. One might, however, have thought of them simply as prolonging the perception of previous movements – though in fact it seems that the reproduction, and to an even greater extent the anticipation of these already perceived movements demands that they be operationally understood. It is essential, therefore, to look at this problem more carefully. This was the purpose of question b, which does not concern images as such, but comprehension.[32]

[31] See Piaget, *The Child's Conception of Movement and Speed*, Chapter X.
[32] Comprehension of this kind is, of course, based on the everyday experience of cars catching one another up, overtaking, and so on; this kind of experience gives rise to the ordinal notions.

Question *b* gave the following results (Table 70*a*):

TABLE 70*a*   *Successes for notional comprehension of speed (without tunnel)*

	Overtaking	Catching-up	Partial catching-up
6 years	44	8	12
7 years	64	24	20
8 years	64	32	24
9 years	88	64	68

It should be added that the reason why the success score is higher for overtaking without the tunnel than with it is that when the tunnel is present the subject centres on the finishing points rather than on the changes of order. On the other hand, in the case of complete and partial catching-up, comprehension of the speeds presupposes anticipation. This is facilitated by the presence of the tunnel and higher results are obtained.

Further, the operational comprehension dealt with in this table implies the interposition of lesser or greater gaps between the moving objects. Consequently it implies the existence of emergent hyperordinal estimation, without the continuous variations necessary for imaginal reproduction and anticipation. In the situation of over-taking, ordinal considerations provide an adequate basis for accurate reasoning. This situation is used in order to examine the relationship between hyperordinal imaginal anticipation and operational reason-ing, also taking account of hyperordinal progressions (see Table 71).

TABLE 71   *Relations between hyperordinal imaginal anticipation and hyperordinal reasoning in the case of overtaking*
(As % of the subjects)

Ages	5,0–5,5	5,6–5,11	6	7	8	9	10–11
Imaginal anticipation	0	5·2	6·6	29·1	28	29·4	68
Reasoning	0	5·2	16·6	33·3	32	52·5	73·6

The operations, then, are slightly ahead of the images. Similarly, in question *b*, of seventy-nine subjects aged 4 to 9 years, all those who achieve a correct anticipation (column *Ho* + O abs., except for one subject aged 5 and one aged 7 years, both for overtaking) also give a correct estimation of the speeds (with tunnel). But the reverse is not altogether true, since eight subjects (one for the overtaking, four for partial and three for complete catching-up) estimate the speeds accurately, but do not succeed in anticipation. On the other hand, the estimations of speed are less successful for the partial than for the complete catching-up, and less successful for the latter than for the overtaking. This fact also points to correlation between comprehension and anticipation. For, in default of the ratio $v = d : t$, comprehension of the partial catching-up rests on its continuation as complete catching-up, and comprehension of the latter on its continuation as overtaking. In the case of overtaking itself, on the other hand, it is sufficient to take in the change of order as perceived, in order to estimate the objects' speeds.

Now we have here two significant facts: the retarded character of imaginal anticipation, and an approximate correlation in which the estimation of speeds dependent on notional interpretation is slightly ahead of imaginal anticipation. These facts seem to us to demonstrate that imaginal anticipation is not merely a matter of a simple prolongation of perceptions experienced during the visible part of the movements before entry into the tunnel. It would appear rather that imaginal anticipation possesses some structuration contributed by comprehension. Now in the case of partial and complete catching-up, comprehension may depend on the subject's taking into consideration the lesser and greater gaps between the moving bodies, and may therefore imply the presence of emergent hyperordinal structuration. But it does not imply the continuous variation necessary in imaginal hyperordinal reproduction and anticipation. Thus one sees that comprehension may to some degree precede imaginal anticipation leading up to it and in turn utilizing it. The formation of the image, however – assuming that it cannot come about by means of perceptions alone – naturally has to wait until there is some operational comprehension of the relations involved. These are eventually translated into the *simili-sensible* symbolism characteristic of the image in its advanced forms, or possibly into the kind of gestural imitation we have been dealing with in the present tests.

11. *Conclusion*

The problem we posed at the end of the last chapter now seems to be solved. There is in fact no systematic difference between the formation or development[33] of kinetic reproductive images and that of anticipatory images *AK*. In the present situations, as in those considered in Chapter Three, it is less the fact that they are new than the complexity of the relations in question that explains why the

---

[33] This does not of course exclude subsequent differences: the adult distinguishes between imaginal evocation of a known movement and anticipatory representation of a new movement.

image appears at an earlier or later stage. For example, in the case of the square with two coloured sides, a circumduction is correctly imagined by 100 per cent of the 7-year-olds; but rotations and turn-overs only by 75 per cent of 9- to 10-year-olds. Now, in the child's day-to-day experience circumduction is probably a less frequent occurrence than a rotation in a plane or a turn-over in space (tests on these last two motions were included in the present chapter, which is basically devoted to unfamiliar situations, only for the sake of the analysis of the sides). If circumduction gives rise to a better image, the reason is not that it is more frequently observed, but that the relative positions of the square's sides remain unchanged. Similarly, anticipation of the order of the four unfolded sides of a cube is successful at 7 years (section 5), and the drawing of the result of a double inversion (section 8) is successful at 6 years. On the other hand, anticipation of speed relations by a simple process of pro-longing the movements perceived is not successful till 9 to 10 years. Now the latter situation (section 10) must be far more familiar to the child than any of the others. But it entails hyperordinal com-position, whereas the order of the sides of a rotating cube, and the double inversion, only involve simple order relations. Thus, at the end of the last section we found connections between the level at which images are formed and the notional complexity of the rela-tions involved. Otherwise one might have considered that certain cases could be imagined early, and their constituent relations com-prehended later on (in fact this does happen, though very rarely, as we shall see in Chapter Eight, section 1, and in Chapter Nine, section 2 – and this demonstrates the legitimacy of the hypothesis).

Having said that, we may assume that all kinetic images are essentially anticipatory (with the exception of the most common-place ones, such as the linear displacement of an object from *A* to *B*, though it would still be worth investigating the make-up of such an image at $1\frac{1}{2}$ to 2 years). What we still have not explained is why kinetic anticipations do not emerge until the formation of the con-crete operations – that is at about 7 to 8 years (and 6 to 7 years for order operations). Now, whichever way we look at it, whether the image is a prolongation of perception or whether it is, as the facts suggest, an internalized imitation, the problem remains. If it were only a question of perceptual origins, the problem would seem in fact to be insoluble. For there is early perception of movement which obeys the same laws (*Gestalten*, etc.) as perception of static forms. Why then, if they derive directly from perception, should the kinetic images be formed so late, and why should they involve any antici-patory reconstitution? If, on the other hand, the image derives from imitation, the particulars of the problem are a lot more complex, but a solution is possible if a certain distinction is made. With regard to objects relating to the body, we have seen already that, according to I. Lézine, the younger subjects find it easier to imitate an actual movement than to imitate its static end-product. With regard to *external* movements, on the other hand, the data collected in this present chapter tend to show quite clearly that it is easier for the child to imagine the product than the process, i.e. the movement as a trajectory (in those instances where we asked for both, which we did not always do). Thus in the case of the somersaulted tube (section 6) the alternation of the coloured ends is represented long before the trajectory itself. Similarly, in the case of the inversion of order (section 8) the inversion of the inversion is imagined (and drawn as product) at 6 years, but the beads' trajectory is still not imagined at 9 years, etc. These facts indicate that imitation of a movement external to the subject's body remains undifferentiated, as a symbolism working in a very approximate fashion (this can be seen constantly in the two examples mentioned). Above all they show that imitation only reaches any degree of precision by centring on the execution of the end-result. This being so, only the emergence of the concrete operations can provide the gestural or oculo-motor imitation of the movements with what it lacked – namely, comprehension of the relations involved and systematic utilization of the references in relation to which the movement in question is situated. Consequently kinetic anticipation at this stage need no longer rely on inevitably inadequate physical imitation, or on any rough-and-ready symbolism. Its instrument is now a more refined process of imitation resulting from the internalized reproduction of the operational manipulation, utilized not just to produce an end result, but to retrace the representational context across which this result is reached.

Thus the kinetic anticipatory image appears as an internalized imitation that goes beyond the elementary static reproductive image, and becomes mobile both from the point of view of the content to be imitated and from the point of view of the activity of anticipation. But it only reaches this point as a result of being orientated and supported by the nascent concrete operations. What remains to be seen now is whether the formation of these operations is promoted by the images at an earlier stage, or whether the aid given by the operations is entirely independent and external. In the next two chapters we go on to an analysis of transformation images which may enable us to establish an answer to this question.

CHAPTER FIVE

Reproductive Images of Transformations

A displacement is a change of position, a transformation a change of form. But changing an object's form means displacing its constituent parts. Conversely, when an object is displaced without its form being modified, the displacement is relative to other objects, so that the configuration of the whole changes. Between displacement and transformation, therefore, the difference is one of degree or of complexity only. This does not mean we cannot make a methodological distinction between kinetic reproduction images (RK) and transformation images (RT). We can establish later whether they belong to the same level or to different levels of development. Further, a transformation may be known to the subject, in which case the image will merely consist of a reproduction of it (RT). But if the transformation is new to him, he will have to anticipate it by imagination. This second distinction, useful from a methodological point of view, may, however, prove to be purely relative. For the question arises whether *any* reproduction of a transformation does not involve an element of anticipation.

1. *The transformation of an arc into a straight line and vice versa*

We shall continue to use only the most simple examples, so simple in fact, that in the present case one might at first glance think it merely a question of perceptual evaluation. The object of this present study is the image of the transformation of arcs into straight lines, considered from two points of view: the result of the transformation (RTP) – that is to say, the length of the transformed element in its terminal state; and the actual process of the transformation (RTM) – the intermediate states, that is, between the initial and final configurations. The investigation was carried out with F. Frank.

The child was shown three arcs 10, 13 and 24 cm in length (taken from a circumference of 26 cm), made of flexible wire. He was asked to do the following things: (1) to copy the arcs as they were (to get some idea of the extent to which the copying image (RST) might underestimate); (2) to draw the exact lengths of the straight lines resulting when the arcs are stretched out (this transformation is demonstrated with a somewhat longer piece of wire); (3) to indicate with both forefingers the length of these straight lines, while keeping an eye on the corresponding arc (gestural or digital, rather than graphic symbolization); (4) to follow an arc through with the finger-tip, and to trace out a straight line of the same length; (5) to choose from prepared drawings or straight pieces of wire those straight lines equivalent in length to the arcs; (6) to draw the stages of the transformation whereby the arc becomes a straight line (at least three drawings: two to represent the initial and terminal positions, and one at least, though more if possible, to represent an intermediate position); (7) to choose from prepared drawings those which best represent the stages of the transformation.

The same seven questions were asked for the reverse case – the transformation of a straight piece of wire into an arc, the child being left to choose the curvature for himself.

It is also useful to know the child's level of development with respect to the conservation of lengths. He was therefore shown two rods 11 cm long and asked whether they would still be equal in length if one was transformed into an arc. To control the validity of a verbal affirmation or negation of conservation we also got the subject to indicate the length of the straight line and the arc, using a piece of string or long wire.

Finally, we showed the subject an arc with its chord, and, leaving the drawing where the subject could see it, asked whether the chord was equal to the arc, or longer or shorter.

I. *Drawings of the results of the transformations.* We begin by examining the image of the results of the transformation of the arc into a straight line. To interpret this image, let us look first of all at the results for the straightforward copies of the arc.

TABLE 72 *Copy of the arcs of 10 cm, 13 cm, and 24 cm*
(As % of the objective length of the model; fifteen subjects for each age group)

	10	13	24	Average for age groups (10–24)
5 years	− 33	− 33·1	− 35·4	− 33·5
6 years	− 11	− 20	− 15·4	− 15·4
7 years	− 24	− 26·2	− 19·2	− 23·1
8–9 years	− 16	− 20	− 14·6	− 16·8
Average for copies	− 21	− 24·8	− 21·1	

They show a considerable degree of underestimation – even greater than in the case of the straight lines in Table 3. This is probably because the curve demands extra precautions concerning boundary points. We shall see later what part is played by the concerns of this kind.

In Table 73 below we set forth the results for the transformation of arcs into straight lines. These are given both as percentages of the objective length of the models and as percentages of the average length of the copies of these models.

TABLE 73   *Transformations of the arcs (10 cm, 13 cm, and 24 cm) to straight lines*
(As % of the objective lengths of the models, and as % of the averages of the copies shown in Table 72)

	10		13		24		Average (10–24)	
	% models	% copies	% models	% copies	% models	% copies	% models	% copies
5 years (N=15)	−43·0	−14·9	−48·5	−22·9	−57·5	−34·2	−49·6	−24·0
6 years (15)	−28·0	−19·1	−24·6	− 5·8	−43·3	−34·0	−31·9	−19·6
7 years (15)	−27·0	− 3·9	−30·8	− 6·2	−44·2	−30·9	−34·0	−13·6
8–9 years (15)	−15·0	+ 1·2	−23·8	− 4·8	−35·0	−23·9	−24·6	− 9·1
Av. 5–9 years	−28·2	− 9·2	−31·9	− 9·9	−45·0	−30·7		

Two instructive facts are clear:

(1) When the arcs are transformed into straight lines their lengths are underestimated to a greater extent than are the arcs copied as arcs. Even expressed as a percentage of the copy itself, the under-estimation remains appreciable.

(2) The more curved the arc, the greater the underestimation of the resultant straight line. This tendency was present already in the underestimation found in the copies in Table 72.

One sees immediately where we must look for our explanation of these facts. At 5 years the straight line imagined as the result of stretching out the arc approximates to the length of the chord in the case of the 10 cm and 13 cm arcs, and to the length of the diameter in the case of the 24 cm arc (which is almost a circle). In other words, it looks as if the transformation is at first imagined as a flattening out of the curve without the correlative lengthening. The chief concern of the younger children is to avoid overstepping the model's boundary points – the arc, that is (in the case of the 10 cm and 13 cm arcs), or the diameter (in the case of the 24 cm arc).

To verify this interpretation we used a further set of questions. The most important of these concerned the reverse transformation whereby the straight line becomes an arc. If our hypothesis is correct, there will be a tendency to make the chords of the arc equal to the model straight line and thus longer than they should be. But before we go on to examine these facts, let us first consider the simplest check – direct comparison of the respective lengths of an arc and its chord.

TABLE 74   *Answers relating to the lengths of the arcs (A2) and their chords (Ch)*
(As % of the responses)

	10			13			24		
	$Ch>A2$	$Ch=A2$	$Ch<A2$	$Ch>A2$	$Ch=A2$	$Ch<A2$	$Ch>A2$	$Ch=A2$	$Ch<A2$
5 years	22	44	33	0	44	56	0	11	89
6 years	0	25	75	0	12	88	0	12	88
7 years	0	20	80	0	10	90	0	0	100
8–9 years	0	10	90	0	0	100	0	0	100

The intervention of boundaries, which we adduce here as in Chapter Two, sections 1–3 and Chapter Three, section 1, raises a problem of general theoretical import relating to the nature of the image (is it a direct prolongation of perception or an initiatory symbolization representing notions?). This role of the boundaries derives essentially from an ordinal kind of notional structuration (longer = farther) and not from perception. In the case of the arcs and the straight lines, one might be tempted to compare the systematic errors of Table 72 with the perceptual overestimation of the curve and underestimation of the chord Piaget has studied with E. Vurpillot and which we were able to reduce to the law of relative centrations.[1] However, on the one hand, the perceptual errors and the imaginal errors are of quite different magnitudes, and do not by any means correspond for the particulars of the transformation. On the other hand, if the source of the imaginal errors were perceptual, it is apparent that in comparing chord and arc all the subjects would 'see' the former as shorter – whereas as far as the preoperational ordinal notions are concerned they should be equal because of the common boundaries. We therefore presented the subject with three drawings of arcs 10 cm, 13 cm, and 24 cm in length, coloured black, but their chords coloured red. We then asked: 'Is there farther to go along the red line or along the black line, or is it the same for both?' The results obtained for this from nine to ten subjects per age group are set forth in Table 74.

From this one can see that the metric estimation based on the distance between extremities (estimation therefore corresponding to the perception) does not appear in 75 per cent of cases for the 10 cm and 13 cm arcs until 6 years. Before this age evaluation based on boundaries plays the dominant role (except of course in the case of the 24 cm arc, where the chord is less than 2 cm and where the question concerned the chord and not the diameter). Two subjects diverging from the norm even judge the straight line (chord) to be longer than the curve (arc). This may have been due to the fact that the latter meets the limit-points only obliquely. It would seem clear, therefore, that it is these ordinal considerations based on the

[1] Piaget, J., and Vurpillot, E., 'La surestimation de la courbure des arcs de cercle', *Archives de Psychologie*, 1956, xxxv, 139.

extremities or boundaries that can be held to account for the images in Table 73. And it seems all the clearer as in this latter case it is not only a question of estimation but of imagining the result of the transformation – which in the absence of any other references makes the part played by the boundary points all the more important.

Here now are the reactions of the graphic image to the transformation of straight 15 cm to 16 cm lines into arcs. The results are expressed both as percentages of the objective lengths of the models and as a percentage of the average of their copies. These copies were obtained from a separate group of subjects as a check. It is not, however, worth reproducing them as they coincide with the results of Table 3 (Chapter 2) – underestimations of – 22 (5 years) to – 11 (8 years).

TABLE 75   *Straight lines transformed into arcs*
(As % of the objective length of the models, and as % of the copies of these straight lines)

	5 cm		11 cm		16 cm		Average 5–16	
	% *models*	% *copies*	% *models*	% *copies*	% *models*	% *copies*	% *models*	% *copies*
5 years (*N*=15)	+20·0	+76·5	−15·5	+ 4·5	−18·8	− 3·7	− 4·6	+28·6
6 years (15)	+ 2·0	+21·4	−19·1	−10·1	− 7·5	+ 2·1	− 8·2	+ 4·4
7 years (15)	− 4·0	+ 6·7	−12·7	+ 7·9	−21·9	+ 4·6	−12·8	+ 6·4
8–9 years (15)	+ 2·0	+13·3	− 5·5	+ 8·3	−10·6	+ 0·7	− 4·5	+ 7·4
Av. 5–9 years	+ 5	+29·5	−13·2	+ 2·6	−14·7	+ 0·9		

In the younger children, then, there is some slight overestimation of the arcs produced by bending the straight lines. But as the copy of these straight lines shows underestimation, the overestimation of their length when they appear as arcs is only visible in the values relative to the copies. The significance of the result, then, is this. When the younger subjects imagine a straight line bent into an arc, they tend to increase the length of the arc, so that its extremities or boundaries coincide with those of the straight line – so that the straight line, in other words, is made equal to the chord of the arc to be constructed. This is, therefore, the reverse of the phenomenon observed in connection with Table 73.

It is true that in the present case this overestimation is inversely proportional to the size of the models, whereas in Table 73 the underestimations increase according to the length of the arc. But it should be remembered that the models of Table 73 differ not only in length but also, and more especially, in curvature, whereas in the present Table 75 the curvature is left to the subject. The fact that the longest straight line (16 cm) does not give rise to any error (+ 1) simply means this – that the longer the line, the easier it is for the child to imagine that the initial boundaries are not affected by a slight curve.

Broadly speaking then, the imaginal effect of underestimation in the arc–straight line transformation is the reciprocal of that of over-estimation in the straight line–arc transformation, though the effect is less marked in the latter case. We attempted to complete these results by means of the following technique.

The child was given an arc 15 cm long (I), or two coupled arcs 20 cm or 30 cm long in all (II). The former type was marked with a large black point $\frac{2}{3}$ of the way along. The latter bore three marks: a black one at the point where the arcs were joined, and two red ones at a point $\frac{1}{3}$ of the whole length away from the free end of each arc. We asked the child to trans-form the arcs into straight lines, maintaining the lengths and keeping the marks in their original places, hoping that this would aid evaluation. Reciprocally, we presented the subject with three straight lines 10 cm long, with the following marked in the following way: (a) a black point in the middle, (b) a black point in the middle and two red ones $\frac{1}{3}$ and $\frac{2}{3}$ of the way along, and (c) a point $\frac{2}{3}$ of the way along. The subject was asked to transform them into single or double arcs, maintaining the lengths and the positions of the points.

The results for this are set forth in Table 76.

TABLE 76 *Transformation of arcs to straight lines and of straight lines to arcs with reference-points along the lines, using single arcs (I) and coupled arcs (II)*

(As % of the objective lengths of the models)

| | Arc–straight-line | | | |
	Mod. 15 (I)	Mod. 20 (II)	Mod. 30 (II)	Av. 15–30
5 years	− 41	− 52	− 54	− 49
6 years	− 18	− 29	− 40	− 29
7 years	− 37	− 30	− 42	− 37
8–9 years	− 40	− 34	− 33	− 36
Av. 5–9 years	− 34	− 37	− 43	

| | Straight-line–arc | | | |
	Mod. 10 (a)	I Mod. 10 (b)	II Mod. 10 (c) II	Av. 10 (a–c)
5 years	− 1	+35	+79	+37
6 years	− 6	+24	+24	+14
7 years	−11	+ 6	+11	+ 2
8–9 years	−10	+ 1	− 2	− 4
Av. 5–9 years	− 7	+16	+28	

In the case of transformation of arcs into straight lines, we found, with one exception at 5 years, no errors at all as far as the position of the marks is concerned. On the other hand 50 per cent of all age groups show errors in the reverse situation – the transformation of straight lines into arcs. It seems that the curve has the effect of pushing the points towards the extremities in the case of the two joined arcs (there was no error in the case of the single arc).

As for the lengths, it can be seen that the transformation of arcs into lines gives rise to results analogous to those of Table 73 (as percentages of the models). But the reverse case produces higher overestimation of the double arcs in the younger subjects. The reason is that the younger children are anxious to conserve the extreme boundary points of the original straight line, and are not concerned about the fact that two curves in place of one must modify the measurable length considerably.

II. *Control-test by selection and measurement.* Before we go on to examine the gestural symbolism, it remains to check the last lot of results, using the method of selection from prepared drawings and measurements carried out by the child.

The first control we tried on the transformation of arcs into straight lines was this. The experimenter himself traced out the straight lines step by step, and the child stopped him when he judged the length to be correct. See Table 77 below.

TABLE 77 *Estimation of the lengths of straight lines (from arcs), using lines traced out by the experimenter*
(As % of the objective length of the arc)

	Model 10	Model 13	Model 24	Av. 10–24
5 years	– 34·0	– 34·6	– 50·0	– 39·5
6 years	– 36·0	– 36·9	– 47·9	– 40·2
7 years	– 29·0	– 27·7	– 39·2	– 31·9
8–9 years	– 20·0	– 22·3	– 34·2	– 28·2
Av. 5–9 years	– 29·7	– 30·4	– 42·8	

There is relative agreement here with the results set out in Table 73. It is permissible, therefore, to conclude that underestimation of the length of graphic images was not due to technical (motor, etc.) difficulties involved in the act of drawing. This does not, however, prove that the underestimation is not bound up with graphic representation in general.

The same objection can be made in the case of selection from prepared drawings. We analysed it all the same, and completed it as far as two of the three values are concerned by introducing a selection test for straight lengths of wire. This meant that any graphic factor was completely excluded. We presented the child with three arcs made of iron wire, 5·5 cm, 6·5 cm and 11·5 cm long (taken from circles 4 cm in diameter). For the 5·5 cm arc the child was required to choose from four straight lengths of 3 cm (=chord of circle), 4 cm (=diameter of circle), and 5.5 cm (actual length); for the 6·5 cm arc he was asked to choose from lengths of 2 cm, 4 cm, 5·5 cm and 6·5 cm; and for the 11·5 cm arc, 1 cm, 4 cm (=diameter of the circle), 9 cm and 11·5 cm. The results are tabulated below:

TABLE 78   *Choice from drawings of straight lines (D) or from samples of wire (W) of a length corresponding to the arc in question* (As % of the responses)[2]

	Model 5·5			Model 6·5						Model 11·5					
	3 (=0·54)	4 (=0·72)	5·5 (=1)	4 (=0·61)		5·5 (=0·84)		6·5 (=1)		4 (=0·34)		9 (=0·78)		11·5 (=1)	
	D	D	D	D	W	D	W	D	W	D	W	D	W	D	W
5 years	40	30	30	60	14	30	71	10	14	30	28	60	71	10	0
6 years	0	80	20	60	30	40	70	0	0	10	30	90	70	0	0
7 years	30	50	20	40	20	60	60	0	20	40	10	60	70	0	20
8–9 years	0	56	44	33	22	56	67	11	11	22	11	78	66	0	22

The number of correct selections in all cases comes to less than 50 per cent (less than 25 per cent for the 6·5 cm and 11·5 cm arcs). Moreover, correct choices from the wire lengths are scarcely more numerous, and they are sometimes even less numerous (at 6 years for the 11·5 cm arc) than correct choices from the prepared drawings.

For the reverse transformation – from straight line to arc – the subject was given two series of arcs for a single straight line of 11 cm. Series I: slight curves; these include an arc (*A*) of more than 11 cm, but whose chord is 11 cm, an arc (*B*) of 11 cm, and an arc (*C*) of 4 cm. Series II: semi-circular; these included an arc (*A*) whose chord is 11 cm, an arc (*B*) length 11 cm, and (*C*) an arc length 4 cm (see Table 79).

The results of Table 74 repeat themselves. At 5 years the majority of subjects select an arc that is too long but whose chord equals the original straight line. From 6 years, however, almost all the subjects

[2] In brackets: length of the straight line as percentage of that of the arc.

TABLE 79 *Choice of the arc corresponding to an 11 cm straight line after bending*
(As % of the responses)

	Series I			Series II		
	A (chord)	*B* (=11 cm)	*C* (=4 cm)	*A* (chord)	*B* (=11 cm)	*C* (=4 cm)
5 years	62·5	25	12·5	50	37·5	12·5
6 years	20	80	0	0	100	0
7 years	11	89	0	0	100	0
8–9 years	17·5	82·5	0	0	100	0

pick out an arc of the right length. This shows that both in the selection test and in the drawing test it is easier to imagine the transformation of a straight line into an arc than the reverse. The reason for this is probably that when a straight line is bent into an arc, the ends of the arcs remain within the original line's boundaries, whereas the reverse process necessitates going beyond them.

But, except for the wire lengths of Table 78, these controls are not enough to enable us to dissociate the child's reactions from factors of graphic representation. It was important, therefore, to find a control test bearing on the result of transformations that did not require any drawing. We used the following experiment. The child was shown the same three arcs (of 10 cm, 13 cm, and 24 cm) as in Tables 73, 74 and 77. He was required to indicate the corresponding lengths on a straight piece of string 34 cm long. The request was formulated in such a way as to avoid explicit allusion to straightening, and was couched instead in terms of length. Thus: 'How much of this piece of string is needed to make this curve?'

The results (see Table 80) show a very regular evolution according to age. These now need to be compared with the drawings of Tables 72 and 73.

TABLE 80 *Measurements along a piece of string of the length corresponding to that of the arc in question*
(As % of the objective length of the model)

	Mod. 10 cm	Mod. 13 cm	Mod. 24 cm	Av. 10–24 cm
5 years (N = 10)	− 38·0	− 17·7	− 34·6	− 30·1
6 years (10)	− 19·0	+ 3·1	− 22·1	− 12·6
7 years (10)	− 7·0	+ 6·2	− 3·3	− 1·3
8–9 years (10)	+ 9·0	+ 4·6	− 6·2	+ 2·4
Av. 5–9 years (40)	− 13·7	− 1·2	− 16·5	

These averages would seem to show that the underestimations of Tables 72 and 73 are independent of the graphic factor up to the age of 7, and that they do in fact derive from imagining the product of the transformation. On the other hand, from 7 years the drawing and the selection from prepared models (Table 78) are both backward compared with the direct measurements represented here.

III. *Motor and gestural symbolism.* It is worth while analysing two further sources of information about the image of the results of transformation, before we finally go on to examine the way transformations are imagined as processes. The first is to get the child to indicate the length of the straight lines between the two index fingers, and the second to get him to trace out this length with his finger – not with a pencil.

In the first the child was presented with two more arcs (10 cm and 13 cm) in turn, held in the air by the experimenter. The child placed his index fingers on each end of the wire. The arc was then taken away, and we asked: 'Where will your fingers go when the wire is flat and straight (i.e. when we flatten it out to make a straight line)?'

In the second, we got the child to move his finger along the arc placed horizontally behind a curtain. He was then asked to trace out on the table with his finger the length of the line given if the arc was straightened.

Now these two questions produced very different results which it is instructive to compare. See Table 81.

TABLE 81 *Lengths of straight lines (transformed from arcs) indicated either between the two index fingers (I), or by tracing with one finger (II)* (As % of the objective lengths of the models)

	Model 10		Model 13		Model 24
	I	II	I	II	II
5 years	+11·0	−10·0	+ 4·6	−18·5	−46·7
6 years	+22·0	− 4·0	+16·2	−14·6	−27·9
7 years	+11·0	+ 6·0	+ 6·9	+ 0·8	−31·2
8–9 years	+21·0	− 0·1	+16·2	−17·0	
Average	+18·2	− 2·0	+10·9	−12·3	−35·2

From this it can be seen that if the lengths are traced out with the finger, underestimations occur that are very similar to those arising in the graphic method. When the distance is measured between the forefingers, however, it is consistently overestimated. This last result accords with Table 3 (Chapter Two). Static finger estimation (i.e. the distance as measured between the two forefingers) gives rise to over-estimation. This is probably due to the joint influence of the empty space and the absence of a continuous run (though the taut string used for Table 80 does, on the contrary, give the impression of a continuous course): consequently, the boundary effect is cut out. But as the present values (I) appear to be higher than those of Table 74, it is possible that a second factor is in play. The gesture executed by the child in this particular case is not just the symbol of a length, but of a straightening-out action ('Where will your fingers go to when the wire is flat?'), and an actual outline of such an action. With some rare exceptions, the child will place his fingers on the ends of the arc and move them apart. This means that he is acting correctly, although his graphic, motor (series II of Table 81) and probably his mental images still adhere to representations of the length to be covered and the boundaries to be respected. Now, this lead of action over image can be seen in many other instances. And it seems legitimate to assume that the same is true here, even though we cannot verify the hypothesis for this particular case. We make this assumption without more ado not simply because retardation of the image is common (in Chapter Three, for example, we saw what difficulties were experienced in imagining a square being displaced or a rod falling, while nothing is easier than pushing a square along or dropping a stick). We can make it also because, as we shall see in a moment, there is an even more striking lag between transformation images proper (i.e. the stages of the straightening of the arc) and the gestures adumbrated in series I of Table 81.

IV. *Images of the stages of transformation.* Now we have examined (in I and III) the images of the products of transformation, it remains to study the imagination of the intermediate stages between the arc and the straight line (or vice versa). This constitutes quite a new problem. It also provides us with the best kind of control for checking the foregoing interpretations.

The child was presented with the 13 cm arc. He was asked to copy it. Then he was asked to draw it 'when it has been pulled out a bit (gesture) but before it's completely straight'. When this had been done the experimenter said: 'If these were roads, would there be the same distance to walk from here to there?' (The lengths were referred to as 'roads' here in order not to evoke boundary points.) If the subject replied in the negative, we began all over again. Two or three intermediate stages were requested whenever possible.

For selection from prepared drawings, the subject was asked to state the reasons for his choices and rejections.

We observed eight types of drawings – see Figure 28. For the

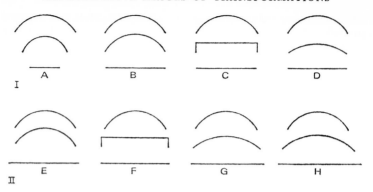

FIG. 28

frequency of occurrence of these, see Table 82. We reproduced these eight types as models from which the subject was requested to make a selection. The frequency of the choices made is set out in Table 83.

TABLE 82   *Drawings of stages in the transformation of the arc into a straight line*
(As % of the ten subjects per age group)

	A	B	C	D	I (ABCD)	E	F	G	H	II (EFGH)	BE	CF	DG
5 years	30	30	10	10	80	10	10	0	0	20	40	20	10
6 years	20	20	0	10	50	20	0	10	20	50	40	0	20
7 years	0	40	10	10	60	0	0	30	10	40	40	10	40
8–9 years	0	0	20	30	50	0	0	30	20	50	0	20	60

TABLE 83   *Choice from figures A–H (Figure 28)*

	A	B	C	D	I (ABCD)	E	F	G	H	II (EFGH)	BE	CF	DG
5 years	56	0	0	11	67	11	22	0	0	33	11	22	11
6 years	0	0	0	0	0	22	11	11	56	100	22	11	11
7 years	0	0	0	0	0	20	0	20	60	100	20	0	20
8–9 years	0	0	0	0	0	0	0	17	83	100	0	0	17

It is instructive to compare these two tables with one another, and with Table 73. First of all one finds that when the subjects attempt to imagine and draw in detail the arc–straight-line transformation, they represent the end-product less well than when it is the main object of the test. Solutions *EFGH* (final straight line correct) increase hardly at all with age. On the other hand, if a selection of model transformations is shown, they suggest to the subjects solutions

172

which otherwise they would have failed to translate into images at all, and 100 per cent at 6 to 9 years (as against 33 per cent at 5 years) select drawings in which the final straight line is longer than the chord of the initial arc (and there is a regular progression from 0–83 per cent for the correct stages *H*).

In other words, while symbolic action bears directly on the transformation (cf. Table 81, series I: the gesture of stretching out), imaginal representation bears first and foremost on the product of the transformation rather than on its successive stages. The image of the end-product is even somewhat better where there is no attempt to imagine the transformation itself – just as it is easier to get round an obstacle if one does not try to represent all the steps to be surmounted in detail. But as soon as the subject is given some help in forming a representation of the transformation, and is provided with all (from his point of view) possible models, then the situation changes. Once imagination of the process is promoted it can in turn improve representation of the product – at least from 6 years (at 5 years the selection procedure reinforces error *A*!).

All types of solution with the exception of *H* appear to be dominated by the question of boundaries, whether they are never in fact overstepped (*A–D*), or whether they *are*, but only in the last stage (*E–G*). But Tables 82 and 83 also make it plain that the importance of the boundary factors is linked up with the fact that the younger subjects try to imagine the product of the transformation independently of the transformation itself. The transformation-as-process is, of course, harder to get at by means of imagery, and consequently constitutes something of an obstacle until the transformation process and product are eventually co-ordinated. Only after this point is it really possible to speak of a transformation image.

In the case of the transformations from straight line to arc, or from arc to circle proper, we put the problem to the child in two parts. We first showed him a flexible rod 11 cm long and asked him to imagine and draw the stages it would pass through when curved to form a semi-circle (we indicated this with a gesture, and suggested it with appropriate comparisons – a 'tunnel', for example). In the second part the subject was asked what stages the semi-circle would pass through when curved still further to give a 'round'.

Now the results obtained for this do not constitute the inverse of the arc–straight-line transformation, since there is here no boundary to be respected. All the subjects thus produce a semi-circle with a diameter shorter than the initial straight line, since it remains within the initial boundary points. Adherence to these is found only in the rare cases when a subject begins by drawing slightly curved arcs whose chords are equal in length to the original straight line (or in the cases when they pass from a slightly curved to a slightly more curved arc keeping the same chord), or, much more frequently (90 per cent at 5 years), when they go from a semi-circle to a circle.

We observed the following types of reaction: (I) From straight line to semi-circle: A, inability and refusal; B, direct passage, without intermediaries, to a semi-circle whose diameter is shorter than the initial line; C, one or two intermediaries, which are, however, already semi-circles equal to the final one; D, from the straight line to a first and then to a second semi-circle with a shorter diameter; E, from the straight line to an arc less than 180°, and from this to a semi-circle whose diameter equals the chord of the preceding arc; F, correct answer with one case of a reaction intermediate to D and E. (II) From semi-circle to circle: A', inability and refusal; B', the diameter of the circle equal to that of the semi-circle; C', the diameter of the circle slightly shorter; D', correct solution – see Table 84.

TABLE 84   *Stages in the transformation of a straight line into a semi-circle, and of the semi-circle into a circle*
(As % of the responses)

| | Straight line–Semi-circle | | | | | | Semi-circle–Circle | | | |
	A	B	C	D	E	F	A'	B'	C'	D'
5 years ($N=14$)	0	29	35	29	0	0	9	91	0	0
6 years (11)	18	0	36	27	9	9	38	50	0	12
7 years (10)	0	10	10	0	50	30	0	86	0	14
8–9 years (10)	0	10	0	0	20	70	0	80	10	10

It seems, then, that it is easier to imagine the transformation of a straight line into a semi-circle than to achieve an adequate imaginal representation of an arc flattened into a straight line, or even of a semi-circle turned into a complete circle. First of all, these facts show that operations are not involved, since the transformations are the inverse, or the generalization of one another. What is involved is imaginal representation with its characteristic concentration on the product rather than the process of transformation. In this respect there is some similarity between reactions A–E of Table 84 and reactions E, F, G of Table 82, where the child succeeds in indicating a straight line longer than the chord of the arc, but only at the final stage, the intermediate stages retaining the length of the initial chord. The only difference between the reactions to the arc–straight-line transformation and the reverse is this: in the former there are boundaries which the subject believes himself obliged to respect, whereas in the second case the boundaries remain inviolate – which facilitates representation. The second case is also favoured by the fact that the child is probably more familiar from his everyday experience with the bending of a straight object than he is with the straightening of a bent one.

V. *Images and operations.* The retarded character of the transformation images analysed in this test with the arc would suggest that they are only formed under the direct or indirect influence of spatial operations. It is useful, therefore, to analyse the relationship between the different levels of the image and the different preoperational or operational levels to which they may correspond. We posed two sorts of question concerning conservation, since it is the most accessible of the operational structures.

(1) We showed the child two pieces of wire 11 cm long. We got him to compare them to ensure they were equal, and asked: 'Is it as far to go along one as along the other?' Then we bent one of these lengths, and asked: 'Is it still as far to go?' The results obtained are set out in Table 85 (eight to ten subjects in each age group):

TABLE 85   *Conservation of length between straight line and arc* (As % of the subjects)

	Straight line longer	Straight line shorter	Conservation
5 years ($N=10$)	70	0	30
6 years ($N=\ 8$)	12·5	0	87·5
7 years ($N=10$)	0	10	90
8–9 years ($N=10$)	10	0	90

Reading these results it might seem at first sight that conservation is achieved from 6 years. But in the question on the taut string (Table 80) one child of 7 years asked before indicating the length of the arc, 'Is it to make it straight, or to make it round?' We therefore introduced a second group of questions relating to conservation problems.

(2) The two 11 cm lengths were used again and their equality demonstrated. We bent one of them as before, and asked: 'Does one need the same length (of a flexible piece of wire 34 cm long) to make the arc round – like this, as one does to make it when it's straight – like this (gesture)?' When the child had replied we asked him to measure out the length for both cases – even, and especially, when he verbally affirmed that they were equal.

We found three successive levels of development: (I) the lengths are verbally declared to be unequal; (II) they are declared to be equal but measured out as unequal; (III) they are equal in both cases. See Table 86.

TABLE 86 *Verbal or measured equality of the lengths of wire necessary to reproduce an arc by bending, or the result of the same arc straightened out* (As % of the responses)

	Level I		Level II		Level III
	Straight > arc	Arc > straight	Straight > arc	Arc > straight	
5 years	50	0	50	0	0
6 years	25	0	25	0	50
7 years	0	0	25	25	50
8–9 years	25	0	12·5	0	62·5

It emerges that conservation is less good when the lengths are measured out than when the response is verbal. This is of some interest, and we might expect similar results for the other conservation notions (in those cases, at least, where measuring is possible). Here are two examples of non-conservation by measuring. They are taken from subjects who succeeded in conserving lengths verbally in Table 85, and again in the present test (II).

Sim (7,3): '*When it is straight, it is straighter, it is longer; when it is curved it does not need as much.*'
Char (8,3): '*When it is round it takes more – Oh! no, when it is curved, it is not as long, when it is straight, it is longer.*'

It seems, then, that in all the aspects examined in this section the image is closer to the notions than to the corresponding perceptions. It is inadequate at the preoperational level, and does not become adequate as a transformation image until the development of the operations and spatial conservations.

It might be objected to this that if the image merely expresses a notion, then nothing specific or even very interesting is being said about the image as such. But what in fact are the origins of the preoperational notions, starting with the boundary concepts? First of all there is the initial primacy of the ordinal considerations as opposed to the metric structures. These are notional in character, and have no direct relationship with imagery. In addition to this, we know (1) that ordinal relations at first only concern finishing points, (2) that 'far' does not simply replace 'long' in consequence of some semantic confusion, but that they are at first undifferentiated; and (3) that considerations of boundary play a general, not just an ordinal role, as we saw in the case of the displacement of a square (Chapter Three, section 2). So we conclude that notional ordinal relations

176

are not solely responsible for initial imaginal reactions, but that their marked prominence is precisely due to the fact that they are bound to images. And in general, the fact that preoperational thought relies on imagery does to a large degree explain its peculiarities. Thus we return to the problem of the image as image.

In the present case there is a curious paradox, which could only arise from the workings of images, and not from the notions. The notions in themselves do not normally get caught up in contradictions. The subject judges that the straight line deriving from the arc becomes longer in Tables 85 and 86, while the chord remains equal to the arc (except in the few cases where it is judged to be longer!) because their ends coincide (Table 74), and yet straightening the arc leads to a shorter line measuring at 5 to 6 years only 41–72 per cent of the objective length! What happens is that the image expands or contracts according to the situation, since there are no operations to ensure conservation of the lengths during transformations and to provide the image itself with the model of these transformations. The problem of images is thus a problem on its own and in its own right – since, before they are moulded by the operations, images, along with action, constitute one of the sole supports of preoperational thought.

The questions involved, then, are as follows: (*a*) At the operational level, how are we to explain the lack of co-ordination between actions and images? How are we to explain the lack of co-ordination, that is, between practical cognition of the transformations (cf. straightening the arc, or bending the straight line) and the representation of the states or configurations constituting the initial or terminal stages of the change? (This shortcoming is the clearest result of the foregoing analyses). (*b*) How are we to account for the improvement of kinetic and transformation images at the operational level?

We can try to answer this in the following kind of way. The operation transforming an arc into a straight line or vice versa is essentially an 'act'. This act has two main characteristics. First it realizes the transformation in a continuous process, and second, it conserves the length of the line throughout. Now it is easy enough to see that, however much of a mathematician he may be, not even an adult's mental imagery will be able to symbolize this operation adequately. Even when mobile, our images proceed only by fits and starts from one position to another. To use Bergson's celebrated phrase, mental images are confined to a 'cinematographic process' isolating stills in the *continu*, rather than grasping it as transformation. Bergson's account, we repeat, is a critique not of the intelligence in its operational form, but rather of imaginal representation. Furthermore, none of our images, however static, assures conservation with any degree of certitude. . . . These deficiencies of the essentially symbolic image unable to exhaust the resources of the operations are found again, multiplied tenfold, at the preoperational level: conservation is accepted by only 15 per cent of subjects at

5 years. The conclusions to be drawn concerning continuity are evident from Table 82 and Figure 28. The child is incapable of anticipating, and even of using his imagination to reconstitute the succession of intermediate states. And since he fails to imagine the transitions symbolizing continuity, his estimations are based simply and solely on the finishing points and the preferential character of the boundaries.

But at a later stage a new type of image forms under the influence of the operations. As the image is an internalized imitation, it develops under the influence of new external models provided by the intelligence as its overall functioning develops. The reproductive transformation image thus forms as a result of symbolic imitation of the operations. This leads to multiplying the stills to simulate the *continu*, taking conservations into account and approximately anticipating the extension of the sequences thus evoked.

2. *The transformation of angles into straight lines and vice versa*

The logical sequel to our preceding investigation would be an examination of exactly the same questions, but with particular reference to angles rather than arcs. As we have already analysed our observations of the arcs in some detail, we may spend less time on the question of the angles. We did in fact test eighty-three children aged between 5 and 8 years in one session and sixty in a second.[3] We shall, however, confine ourselves here to the points on which the results of the two inquiries differ.

A rigid length of wire or metal rod, 1 mm in diameter and painted black, was attached at its mid-point to a board 30 cm square. The length of wire was in two halves, each 7·5 cm, placed at an angle of 90°. However, these segments could be moved to increase the angle or to give a straight line. There was a second board 30 cm square with a further angle made of rigid wire lengths. The apex was not, however, in this case attached to the board. The board itself was fitted with a horizontal groove along which the free ends of the sides could be moved. It was found useful to bring in a third angle also with sides of 7·5 cm, but coloured differently, and two further right angles with 20 cm sides, one coloured black, the other in two colours. Two straight metal rods 40 cm long, one black, the other in two colours, were used to indicate the lengths independently of the drawing.

It was also found useful to show the child a series of five black and a series of five two-colour angles with the lengths (total length of the two segments) 13, 14, 15, 16 and 17 cm, and two series of straight, rigid rods similarly coloured with similar lengths. The purpose of this was to get the child to match the lengths without using drawings. When drawings were

[3] In collaboration with F. Frank and D. Nicollier.

made in the case of the boards presented at the beginning of the test, they were executed on sheets of paper 30 cm square.

The questions were as follows for six separate groups of children.

Group I. (1) We made it clear to the child that the angle is articulated. He was then shown an angle of 90° and was asked to imagine the stages it would pass through if it were transformed into a straight line. This was to be done by means of drawings: half the subjects did them on the same sheet, half on separate sheets. (2) We asked the subject to copy the right angle with the right dimensions. (3) Taking these dimensions into account, the subject then drew the straight line produced by folding back the angle. (4) The child was shown the larger angle (20 cm) and was asked to estimate, and indicate along its sides, the length of the sides of the model angle (7·5 cm). (5) He was shown the 40 cm rod and was asked to indicate on it the length of the straight line produced by folding back the angle with sides of 7·5 cm. (6) The child was presented with the 7·5 cm model and was asked to compare it to the six black right angles in the order, 15, 17, 13, 16, 14, and 15 cm. For each one he was asked which was the longer and which the shorter. (7) The angle with sides 7·5 cm was presented along with the straight black rods 15, 17, 13, 16, 14 and 15 cm in length. We asked for a comparison between the total length of the two sides of the angle and the length of the straight rods. (8) The subject was blindfolded. He was asked to trace his finger along the angle with sides of 7·5 cm. His finger was then dabbed in finger-paint and he was asked to reproduce the angle exactly as he had felt it. (9) As for 8, except that this time the child was requested to draw the angle as a straight line. (10) Taking the angle on the board we asked the subject to point with his finger to the positions which the free ends of the sides would occupy if the angle were transformed into a straight line.

Group II. Questions 1–9, for the reverse transformation – from straight line to angle. Question 10 was omitted.

Group III. Questions 1–10 using the grooved board.

Group IV. Same questions as II, but using the grooved board.

Group V. Questions 2–9, using the coloured figures. The subject was asked to draw first the red side and then the black side (for questions 2 and 3), or to compare one side to another (for questions 7 to 9).

Group VI. As V for the reverse transformation – straight lines to angles.

The two main results obtained from this were as follows:

(1) The product of the transformations is far easier to anticipate than the successive stages of the transformation itself. In other words, we no longer find the characteristic reaction of the arc test – the transformation of the arc into a straight line respecting the boundaries of the initial figure. (2) The stages of the transformation itself, however, point to a systematic difficulty encountered at about 5 to 6 years in modifying the angle, and more especially, in moving apart the free ends of the sides. Thus we return to the boundary problem. (For modifying a right angle to give another angle of 100°

to 130° is a different matter from transforming it into an entirely dissimilar figure such as a straight line.)

Let us start then with the question of progressive transformations. We shall limit ourselves to a purely qualitative analysis: that is, we shall neglect the objective dimensions of the model. Our central concern will be rather the plus, minus or equality variations between one drawing and the next, from the point of view of the angle (A), the distance between free ends of the sides (D), and the length of the sides (L). We found the six following combinations (out of a possible twenty-seven and a realizable thirteen): $A - D - L -$; $A = D - L -$; $A = D = L =$; $A + D = L -$; $A = D + L +$; and $A + D + L =$.

The last combination is the correct one: increase of the angle during the transformation, divergence of extremities, and relative equality of the length of the sides (though objectively speaking they may all be underestimated). There is a further category which does not fit in with the present criteria: the child draws the sides either as asymmetrical (one lengthened, the other reduced to nothing, giving a straight line), or as curvilinear. This is, however, fairly rare. We shall keep to the classifiable cases – i.e. those which respect the basic givens of the rigid elements of the apparatus. We are thus able to draw up the following table:

TABLE 87   *Qualitative successes for the transformation of angles into straight lines*
(As % of the responses)

	5 years	6 years	7 years	8 years
Angle varied	25	19	50	80
Corresponding distance between extremities	25	6	40	80
Length of sides constant	25	19	30	60

A similar kind of breakdown of the reverse transformation gave the following categories:

$A = -$ (n repetitions of the straight line and sudden change to right angle) $L = D =$; $A = D = L =$; $A = D + L +$; $A - D = L +$; $A = D - L -$; $A - D - L -$; $A - D - L =$ (correct).

Whence Table 88 (see opposite).

These developments advance fairly regularly with age. The only reversal of the trend occurs between 5 and 6 years in Table 87, and is no doubt due to the unclassifiable cases.

However, it is clearly easier to imagine a rod being bent from 180° to 90° than to imagine the transformation of an angle into a

TABLE 88   *Qualitative successes for the transformation of straight lines into angles*
(As % of the responses)

	5 years	6 years	7 years	8 years
Angle varied	25	75	90	100
Corresponding distance between extremities	50	63	90	100
Length of sides constant	33	44	80	83

straight line. Similarly, it appears that it is easier to represent a straight rod being bent into an arc (see Table 84) than the reverse (Table 82). On the other hand, if one compares Tables 82 and 87, or 84 and 88, one sees how much simpler anticipation is where angles rather than arcs are concerned, the reason being that the angles only involve straight lines.

These transformations may indeed be easier; nevertheless, one meets the same boundary laws. On the one hand it is not until 8 years that 75 per cent of the subjects go beyond the boundary lines of the angle to transform it into a straight line. At 5 and 6 years 60 per cent of the subjects keep the same distance between the ends of the sides (the remainder lessen it still more), and this is still the case for 27 per cent at 7 years. On the other hand, the response to the distance between extremities is better in Table 88 than in Table 87. This is probably due to the fact that in changing the straight line into the angle the distance between extremities is reduced and does not therefore require that boundary lines be overstepped.

The boundary problem, then, is still acute when the subject is faced with turning a right angle step by step into a more obtuse angle and finally a straight line. Be that as it may, the direct transition from angle to straight line does not, remarkably enough, meet with this difficulty. The reason is no doubt the dissimilarity of the two

TABLE 89   *Copy of the angle and drawing of its straightening out*
(Errors given as % of 15 cm)

	Copy	Transformation	Difference
5 years (12)	−4·6	−3·6	+1·0
6 years (18)	−3·2	−3·6	−0·4
7–8 years (5)	−0·9	−0·6	+0·5

figures. Indeed, if we take the results for the simple copy (question 2) and for the folding back of the angles into a straight line (question 3), as given by groups I, III and V, we reach the following conclusions:

181

the copy of the angles, as is the rule (see Chapter Two), slightly underestimates the lengths; but the drawing of the transformation of the angles into straight lines is somewhat less underestimated, contrary to the case of the arcs (Tables 72 and 73).

We found that there was no significant difference (− 0·2 per cent) between the copy of the straight line and the drawing of the angle resulting when the straight line is folded back on itself.

Anticipation of the final result of the angle–straight line transformation and the reverse does not, then, imply underestimation. We shall find that this same phenomenon is even more prominent in the case of the L-square figures in section 3. To a child an arc appears to contain a straight line (its chord), and the only difference as far as he is concerned is the curvature of the arc, which he disregards. The boundary difficulties thus implied are not present in the case of the 90° angles[4] and the child readily increases the gap between the extremities to make a straight line, provided he is not asked for the successive stages of the transformation (as he is for Table 87, where the boundary problem reappears, since the subject has to pass from one figure to a similar one next in order).

In the test where the child measures out the angle of the model (side 7·5 cm) on the larger scale (20 cm), and in the test where he uses the 40 cm rod to predict the length of the straight line resulting from the angle (questions 4 and 5), we found the following: for 33 subjects aged 5 to 6 years (groups I, III and V) the error is zero in the former (average 0) and insignificant in the second (average − 0·15 per cent, with a maximum variation of + 2·5 and − 1·9 for the groups). However, when the subject was asked to point to the positions of the extremities (question 10), there was, as one would expect, some degree of overestimation (+ 2·9 for twenty-five subjects aged 5 to 7 years). Once again, then, if it is a matter of indicating extremities and accounting only for the interval between them, rather than following through a trajectory, as is the case in the drawings, then error is reduced to nil or is reversed.

The same is true for the passage from the straight line (indicated on the 40 cm rod) to the angle (indicated on the angle with sides of 20 cm). For twenty-five subjects aged 5 to 7 years (groups II, IV and VI) the error is + 0·9 for the copy and + 1·4 for the prediction, both, therefore, tending towards overestimation. The choice from varied angles and straight rods yielded nothing of importance. But tactile-kinaesthetic copies and estimations (questions 8 to 9) gave two interesting (albeit imprecise) results. First, we found on average the same underestimations as we found in the case of the drawings. In both these cases the gesture traces out a trajectory and meets the attendant boundary problems. Second, the average error in

[4] When children aged 5 to 7 years were shown three isosceles triangles (*ABC*, angle *B* 45°, 90° and 135°), and were asked whether the path *ABC* is longer or shorter than (or equal to) the path *AC*, we found that *ABC* > *AC* for *B* = 45° in 100 per cent of cases, but for 90° only in 62 per cent, and for 135° only in 50 per cent of cases. What we have said concerning the neglecting of boundaries would thus not be valid for angles ≥ 135°.

182

prediction is equal to (or lower than) the error in direct copying. For thirty-five and twenty-five subjects the difference between these two errors was +0·2 for the angle–straight line transformation and +1·25 for the reverse. All these results present some coherence, therefore. But it would be unwise to give detailed figures for these tactile-kinaesthetic cases, as the test lacks precision. In particular, we noticed that when the child draws his finger along the model slowly, he tends to produce a longer finger-paint drawing than when he explores it more rapidly. The dimensions involved thus become spatio-temporal, and not exclusively spatial. This has considerable interest for the image problem, but complicates our findings.

3. *Transformation of a right angle with unequal sides into a straight line*

Now that we have established the difference between the transformations of arcs and angles, it would be informative to examine the transformation of a right angle with unequal sides, or L-square. We shall emphasize the product rather than the stages of the process of transformation.[5] The subject is requested to keep as closely as possible to the given lengths. This brings us up against the problem of underestimation discussed in Chapter Two, since the graphic overestimations which would have been at least theoretically possible do not in fact occur. . . .

When we were considering this sort of problem with S. Taponier in 1957, it seemed more closely related to questions of perception than to the mental image about which at that time we knew very little. We were led, therefore, to undertake a parallel investigation (on different subjects) regarding perceptual measurement. In this experiment the subjects were asked to compare a constant or standard L-square 65 cm × 35 cm with twelve variable straight lines each differing in length from the others by 4 mm. The comparison of these results will show the extent to which the graphic representation of the L-square–straight line transformation differs from the perceptual estimation (the results of which we need not expound here in detail).

To study the image, we used a cardboard base 74 × 54 cm at a gradient of 25°–30° (the slope of the school desks). On it was placed a sheet of white paper 37 cm × 27 cm, and on this was placed the L-square. There was a second sheet of white paper of the same size on the table for the child to draw on.

The squares consisted of cylindrical rods 2 mm in diameter and 20 cm in length, bent at *C* (See Figure 29) to 90° in the following combinations:

Rod 16 . . . . *AC* = 160 mm	*CE* = 4 mm
Rod 13 . . . . *AC* = 130 mm	*CE* = 70 mm
Rod 10 . . . . *AC* = 100 mm	*CE* = 100 mm

[5] See Chapter Three, section 3 (III).

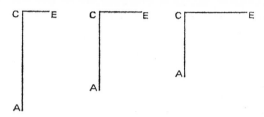

FIG. 29

Further, some of the rods 16, 13 and 10 cm were coloured black, and some (with the same lengths) had *AC* coloured green and *CE* blue.[6] Finally there were three straight rods 160 mm, 130 mm and 100 mm long for simple copies.

The subjects were asked to do the following:

(1) To imagine the black L-squares straightened out and to draw them thus (we demonstrated this beforehand with a differently sized L-square). The L-square is left so that the child can see it on the inclined base.

(2) To imagine the coloured L-squares straightened out and to draw them.

(3) To copy the black L-square (without transformation).

(4) To copy the straight rods of length 160 mm, 130 mm and 100 mm.

The copies (3) were done for two positions: (*a*) *V* = segment *AC* in vertical position (i.e. in the sagittal plane), while *CE* is horizontal (at the top of the sheet of paper facing the child); (*b*) *H* = segment *AC* in horizontal position, while *CE* is vertical (a little to the left of the child, to avoid direct transfer).

There were two groups of subjects for two different orders of presentation: *A*, drawing of the black rod straightened, then of the coloured ones, and then copies; *B*, copy drawing of the black rod straightened, and the same again for the coloured ones. Rods 16, 13 and 10 were presented in all six possible orders.

The averages for the errors in the imagined straightening of the L-squares are given in Table 90.

(The average error of – 17·5 at 6 to 8 years thus corresponds to a drawing of 165·2 mm instead of 200 mm and – 15·0 corresponds to a drawing of 170 mm.)

It can be seen that, in spite of variations due to the individual and to the experimental situations, the general average, *AE* completely coincide at 6 to 7 and 8 years, but differ considerably from the adult average. This is in the absolute, however, and what we need to do is to examine the relationship of these errors to those arising in the copies of the L-squares as they are either before or

[6] The margins were kept constant on the sheet supporting the L-square.

TABLE 90 *Drawings of L-squares straightened out*
(Errors given as % of the objective lengths)

	Black				Coloured			
	16/4	13/7	10/10	Av. AE	16/4	13/7	10/10	Av. AE
6–7 years (N=24):								
AC	−18·0	−17·1	−16·8		−18·4	−14·6	−16·0	
CE	+ 1·0	−17·3	−23·6		− 8·7	−16·0	−10·6	
AE	−14·3	−17·1	−20·2	−17·2	−16·5	−15·1	−13·3	−15·0
8 years (N=11):								
AC	−16·0	−17·6	−20·5		−15·5	−16·8	−16·1	
CE	−11·2	−10·4	−26·5		− 9·1	−13·8	−14·9	
AE	−15·0	−14·7	−23·5	−17·5	−13·7	−15·8	−15·5	−15·0
6–8 years:								
AE	−14·5	−16·3	−21·1	−17·5	−15·6	−15·3	−13·8	−15·0
Adults (N=24):								
AC	+ 0·4	+ 0·4	− 0·8		− 1·5	− 1·5	− 4·7	
CE	− 6·0	− 1·1	− 5·6		− 6·0	− 2·0	− 2·0	
AE	− 0·9	− 1·6	− 3·2	− 1·9	− 2·4	− 1·7	− 2·1	− 2·1

after the drawing of the imagined straightened line. Table 91 sets out the relevant data for a group of fourteen subjects aged 6 to 7 years and a group of eleven aged 8 years.

Three interesting facts emerge from this Table. (1) The underestimation in the direct copy is as great as in the straightening of the black angles when the copy comes *second*. (2) This underestimation in the copy is 1·2 to 2·1 per cent greater than in the straightening of the coloured angles, when the copy comes *second*. (3) The underestimation in the copy is appreciably greater when the copy is executed *first* (i.e. before the imagined straightening): it may exceed the underestimation of the straightened coloured angles by as much as 10 per cent.

If we take all the subjects who did the straightening test for the coloured angle (vertical and horizontal) and also the copies (before and after), and compare their underestimations from the point of view of the segments AC and CE, then we find a difference on the side of the straightening test of 5·2 per cent for AC and of 11·1 per cent for CE.

What we have here is an intensified form of the phenomenon observed earlier in connection with the straightening out of equal-sided angles. It would seem that copying is attended by underestimation due to the habitual boundary effects, whereas anticipation of the straightening-out actually reduces this effect. This is particularly so in the present case where one side can more easily act as a boundary in relation to the other.

TABLE 91 *Comparing the drawings of the straightened-out figures (lengths AE) with copies of the L-squares after and before straightening out*
(Errors given as % of the objective lengths *AE*)

I–Copy after

	Black straightened				Coloured straightened				Copy			
	16/4	13/7	10/10	Total	16/4	13/7	10/10	Total	16/4	13/7	10/10	Total
6–7 years (14)	−12·3	−15·5	−19·7	−15·8	−16·7	−15·1	−13·2	−14·3	−19·3	−17·6	−10·6	−15·5
8 years (11)	−15·0	−14·7	−23·5	−17·5	−13·7	−15·8	−15·5	−15·0	−14·8	−17·2	−19·6	−17·1

II–Copy before

	Black straightened				Coloured straightened				Copy			
	16/4	13/7	10/10	Total	16/4	13/7	10/10	Total	16/4	13/7	10/10	Total
6–7 years (14)	−13·5	−18·1	−12·7	−14·8	− 9·5	− 9·4	−14·0	−11·0	−21·8	−19·9	−21·7	−21·1

It should be noted at this point that in the horizontal position (*AC* horizontal and *CE* vertical), the L-square gives rise to less marked under-estimations both in the anticipation of the straightening out (black − 14·6 per cent and coloured − 7·9 per cent) and in the direct copy (− 9·0 per cent). This accords with what we have already seen in Chapter Two, section 3. The greater underestimation in the vertical case may be due to a perceptual effect (overestimation of vertical lines) relating to the drawing rather than to the model (cf. the frequency of the child's error in the case of the standard and variable lengths, where the error bears on the latter rather than on the former). That does not, however, mean that the boundary effects (even if they vary in one direction or the other for perceptual reasons) are in themselves due to perception.

However, the best way of bringing out the essential differences between the laws of the image and the laws of perception is to compare the last lot of results with those of the inquiry into the perceptual estimation of variable rectilinear lengths in relation to a constant L-shaped template. In the six-year-old child we find, in spite of considerable inter- and intra-individual variation, average errors of only − 5·2 to − 2·8 for the first of these right angles, and − 4·1 to + 3·3 for the second, in vertical position. In the horizontal position, these errors are − 1·0 to + 1·6 and − 3·0 to − 1·1 per cent. In the adult the difference between perceptual and imaginal estimation is, for the horizontal position at least, even clearer, going to the opposite extreme. For the vertical positions the average error is + 0·4 to + 3·0 and + 1·1 to + 3·3 per cent. These errors are of the same order as the errors normally found in adults for the image; but for the horizontal position there is a surprising degree of overcompensation: + 13·4 to + 17·7 and + 12·9 to + 17·7 per cent. This recalls the overconstancy in adult perception of dimensions in depth. Thus the child's perception of the relations between the L-squares and the lines resulting from straightening them out is considerably better than his imaginal reproduction of them, while adult perception, at least for horizontal positions, leads to errors which are appreciably higher.

4. *Spirals and concentric circles*

Take an underlying frame of reference, circular in form, whose diameter can be immediately and significantly increased – an umbrella, say, seen from above, closed and then open. To this extensible frame are attached elastic bands producing a configuration of spirals and concentric circles when stretched. To produce the concentric circles three coloured elastic bands are attached at appropriate distances around the umbrella's ribs (the covering is best removed, leaving the bare ribs of the umbrella – a child's umbrella with a handle 23 cm long, seven black ribs and a red tip). When the umbrella is opened, this gives three approximate circles (or polygons) with different diameters, and distinguished by different colours. For the spirals a length of elastic is fixed to the tip of the umbrella, wound round the ribs, and attached to the free end of one of them. If the elastic is attached at the appropriate places, this produces a more or less regular spiral when the umbrella is opened. The problem then is to establish whether the subject will be able adequately to imagine these concentric and spiral configurations. To prevent the question becoming one of the representation of the basic frame of reference, the child is provided with a drawing of the open umbrella seen from above. He is then simply required to inscribe in this framework the outline of the concentric or spiral bands.[7]

We shall see that the first of these questions is solved ($>$75 per cent) at 6 years and the second not till 8 years. In order to determine whether this is due to difficulties in imaginal representation or in perceptual discrimination, we need to begin with an examination of the latter. We began by getting the child to compare three concentric circles with a three-coiled spiral (see Figure 30 *A* and *B*).

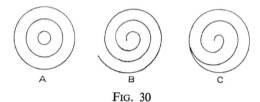

A   B   C

FIG. 30

This yielded 100 per cent discrimination at 5 years. We then went on to compare forms *A* and *C*, the latter being a 'closed' spiral starting from a small initial circle and inscribed in a larger one of the same dimensions as *A* (see Figure 30). Once the subject accepted the distinction between *A* and *C* we asked him to sort out ten cards bearing figures with increasingly more numerous and dense circles or coils. He was asked to classify them into two groups according to whether they resembled *A* or *B* (or *C*). The results of this were: for 270 individual choices (27 subjects from 5 to 8 years), 97 per cent successes for 5 years in the case of comparisons *AB*; 96 per cent at 6 years or 45 per cent at 5 years in the case of comparisons *AC*. Examination of the methods used by the subjects (and this is what we are particularly interested in) showed that they looked above all at the starting point and the finishing point, i.e. the centre and the circumference. If the centre of the figures was covered, or the centre and the external circumference, leaving only the intermediate lines visible, correct discriminations did not entirely disappear, but they were reduced by approximately 50 per cent.

Another useful piece of information was given by a device consisting of six concentric wire circles (or a spiral with six coils) along the circumference of which was threaded a bead representing a fly. We asked the child: (*a*)

[7] The experiment was carried out by D. Nicollier.

where the fly would be after one turn, two turns, and so on, right up to the centre, and (b) how many turns would be required for it to reach the centre. This experiment brought three things to light. First, at 5 years and even frequently at 6 years the subjects experience great difficulty in following the bead's path with their eyes. Because of the lack of visual adjustment they had to follow the path through with their fingers as well, in order not to lose the thread. Second, however, they all understood that in the case of the circles the fly would have to jump from one ring to another in order to get nearer the centre, and that on the spiral it can move gradually towards its goal without interruption. Third, although this part of the test always came after the first, questions (a) and (b) posed for the spirals resulted in half as many failures as the same questions posed for the concentric circles. This is no doubt due to the child's awareness of the spiral's continuity after tactile and visual exploration. In all, the successes were 33 per cent at 5 years, 78 per cent at 6 years and 91 per cent at 7 years.

It is thus established that from at least 6 years the child possesses all the instruments necessary for discriminating between spirals and concentric circles; and this especially in so far as he shows particular regard for the two fundamental points – the singularity of the curve and the two criteria provided by its starting and finishing points. We may now come back to our umbrella. One might have expected that a rubber band cut so as to give a linear rather than a circular form, wound round the ribs in an elongated spiral, and visible all the time, would make it easy for the child to anticipate the plane spiral resulting when the umbrella is opened, and which he has, moreover, already seen in the form of a drawing. But as Table 92 shows, the contrary is the case.

TABLE 92 *Successes for the graphic representation of concentric circles (3 elastic bands) and of a spiral (1 elastic band)*

	5 years	6 years	7 years	8 years	9 years
Concentric circles	60	87	81	83	100
Spiral	0	50	62	83	85

The obvious question arising from this concerns the influence of drawing problems. The most primitive reactions showed the elastic either as one or more non-concentric circles, or as a wavy thread running from top to bottom. But there was also a series of curves one inside the other with a common starting point or line. This indicates that there has been some attempt to differentiate spirals and concentric circles, but that the subject has failed to leave the extremities free. From a purely technical point of view, it would seem that it is easy enough to draw concentric circles – these are successfully executed at an early age – and to leave the extremities free. It is, however, striking to find that the criterion of extremities, which plays such an obviously large and early part in the perceptual discrimination and bead tests, is not, at 8 years, successfully translated into correct representation of the spiral.

We tried to counteract the difficulty experienced by the child in imagining the spiral, using a paper whistle which can be made to extend and curl round in a spiral by blowing down the tube in which it is contained. We asked forty-two subjects to reproduce by means of a drawing the four main positions of the whistle, including the half-rolled and completely rolled spiral position. But there was no improvement in the results and at 7 years there was still only 50 per cent success.

We shall go on now to examine a related but more precise problem.

5. *The imagination of lengths when a straight line is transformed into the circumference of a circle and vice versa*

Nearly all the facts described in this work relate to cases in which the mental image improves with age and consequently comes increasingly to the aid of operational functioning and the adequation of representation with reality. But one might conceive of conditions in which the progress of the image towards kinetic representation or representation of transformations produces, as secondary effects, errors that increase with age. Such errors might be due to some kind of over-compensation resulting from the transformations themselves. Cases of this kind would be comparable to those in which, on the perceptual level, late-emerging 'perceptual activities' (generally contemporaneous with the operations) engender 'secondary errors'. The latter arise from certain *rapprochements* induced by these same activities[8] (e.g. what has been called the 'size-weight illusion', which is due to erroneous anticipation).

An instance of increasing error in imaginal representation might be found in the transformation of a circumference into a straight line and vice versa. We do in fact know that a circle, although it is a 'good form' perceptually, occasions two kinds of regular error. First, the diameter will appear shorter than a straight line of equal length placed horizontally, and even shorter than a line placed vertically. Second (and here there is probably a mixture of perception and imaginal representation), the circumference will appear to be appreciably shorter than a straight line of equal length. This being so, when the subjects are asked to imagine the length of a straight line equivalent in length to a circumference, or the reverse, they tend to draw a line which is too short, or a circle which is too

[8] Piaget, J., *The Mechanisms of Perception*, 1969, Chapter III.

big, in order to compensate the perceptual error. The question then is to establish whether the errors in the image will increase or decrease with age. The perceptual illusions relating to the circle decrease with age.[9] So if the image error increases during the course of development, the reason would simply be this: that the initial images are not really anticipatory in character, and that the progress of the transformation image would allow the subject to engage, in consequence of 'unconscious precaution', in over-compensations (analogous to what may be observed in the case of perceptual overconstancy) that would be beyond the abilities of the younger child. This would be a good example of secondary error in the image actually due to the latter's acquisitions.

Madame Kathia Tyborowska, Assistant Professor at Warsaw University, kindly undertook to study this problem when she was in Geneva and to complete it on her return to Poland. The method used was as follows:

(1) The child was shown a piece of string 12 cm long, and was asked first to draw a straight line of equal length, and then to draw it imagining that it was made into a 'ring'. The question was repeated for a length of 24 cm.

(2) The subject was shown two pieces of string, first one 12 cm and then one 24 cm long, arranged in the form of a regular circle. He was asked (a) to copy the ring conserving the given size, and (b) to draw the string as he would imagine it rolled out in a straight line.

(3) The conservation question: is the string the same length when it is arranged as a circle as when it is made into a straight line? Two hundred children aged 5 to 16 years were examined (in groups of twenty for 5 to 13 years and one group of twenty 14 to 16-year-olds), as well as twenty adults.

Only 4 per cent of the subjects aged 5 to 7 years affirmed conservation of length for the transformation of the straight line into a circle. For the rest, some thought the string would be longer because 'it will take up more space'; some thought it would be smaller because 'it does not go as far' (pointing to the extremities of the diameter).

Up till 7 years, the subjects were little concerned with the accuracy of their copies of the straight line or the circle. This may have been because they were copying an empirically significant object (piece of string), and not just a model figure (straight line or circle). Consequently, we did not always find (especially at 6 years) the high underestimations which we analysed in Chapter Two: rather they were found to be lower and more persistent. From 8 years, on the

[9] See the inquiry conducted by J. Piaget and E. Vurpillot and summarized in Piaget, *The Mechanisms of Perception*, 47–51, Table 7.

other hand, we witnessed attempts at precision betokened by numerous alterations made to the initial drawing – which does not exclude the possibility of some degree of overestimation.

Here are the results obtained (Table 92*a*):

TABLE 92*a*   *Transformations of the straight line into a circle (I) and vice versa (II)*
(Given in cm and as averages of the subjects)[10]

Lengths	I 12			I 24		
	SCO	RIM	R/S	SCO	RIM	R/S
5 years	9·5	11·0	1·15	19·7	20·7	1·05
6 years	10·0	12·7	1·27	22·1	24·5	1·11
7 years	9·4	10·1	1·07	17·3	19·2	1·11
8 years	7·8	9·1	1.16	16·2	16·2	1·00
5–8 years	*9·2*	*10·7*	*1·16* (=16%)	*18·8*	*20·1*	*1·06* (=6%)
9 years	8·8	13·8	1·56	16·8	19·3	1·15
10 years	8·6	13·4	1·57	17·1	22·3	1·30
11 years	10·0	13·2	1·32	19·7	20·7	1·05
12 years	9·9	13·0	1·31	19·8	23·6	1·19
13 years	10·2	12·5	1·22	19·8	23·9	1·20
14 years	10·3	14·4	1·39	20·0	24·9	1·25
9–14 years	*9·6*	*13·4*	*1·39* (=39%)	*18·8*	*22·4*	*1·19* (=19%)
Adults	*9·9*	*13·2*	*1·33* (=33%)	*20·0*	*22·7*	*1·13* (=13%)

Lengths	II 12			II 24		
	RCO	SIM	R/S	RCO	SIM	R/S
5 years	10·5	9·6	1·09	19·6	16·8	1·16
6 years	10·5	9·8	1·07	20·0	19·5	1·02
7 years	9·2	7·7	1·19	19·2	15·6	1·23
8 years	8·6	7·5	1·14	16·8	13·4	1·25
5–8 years	*9·7*	*8·6*	*1·12* (=12%)	*18·9*	*16·3*	*1·16* (=16%)
9 years	9·7	6·8	1·27	17·9	12·4	1·44
10 years	11·0	7·4	1·48	20·3	24·0 (!)	0·84
11 years	10·4	8·9	1·16	21·1	16·2	1·30
12 years	11·1	9·3	1·19	21·2	17·1	1·24
13 years	11·0	9·1	1·20	21·4	17·6	1·21
14 years	12·0	9·0	1·33	23·9	18·5	1·29
9–14 years	*10·8*	*8·4*	*1·28* (=28%)	*21·0*	*17·5*	*1·22* (=22%)
Adults	*11·6*	*9·4*	*1·23* (=23%)	*22·2*	*18·4*	*1·20* (=20%)

[10] Abbreviations: *SCO* = copy of string when straight;
RIM = drawing of string imagined as circle;
R/S = ratio of circle to straight line;
RCO = copy of the string arranged in a circle;
SIM = drawing of circle imagined as straight line.
In brackets: the error as percentage of the imagined copy.

To start with the underestimations occurring in the copies of the straight pieces of string (*SCO*), we see that the 12 cm length is reduced to lengths of 10 cm to 7·8 cm between 5 and 8 years (with certain irregularities due to the circumstances already mentioned), and the 24 cm length to 22·1 cm to 16·2 cm. This yields average errors of − 2·8 cm and − 5·2 cm, or − 23·3 per cent and − 21·7 per cent (of the objective lengths). Between 9 and 14 years of age this drops to − 20·0 per cent and − 21·7 per cent (for the 12 and 24 cm lengths), and in the adult to − 17·5 per cent and − 16·6 per cent.

On the other hand, while at 5 to 8 years the copies of the circular arrangement (*RCO*) give the same degree of depreciation as the straight length (9·7 cm and 18·9 cm for 12 cm and 24 cm, or − 19·1 per cent and − 21·2 per cent), the error decreases considerably at 9 to 14 years (10·8 cm and 21·0 cm, or − 10·0 per cent and 12·5 per cent) and in the adult (− 3·3 per cent and − 7·5 per cent). It is important to note this fact, since it is at these ages that the transformation error R/S increases. But the drop in underestimation in the drawings of the circles does not explain the increase in the transformation error: for the latter is in fact more or less the same whether one starts from the straight line (*SCO*) or the circle (*RCO*). Taking the averages of these transformation errors R/S for 12 and 24 cm we have: $SCO \rightarrow RIM$ – 11 per cent, 29 per cent and 23 per cent at 5 to 8 years, 9 to 14 years and in the adult, respectively; and $RCO \rightarrow SIM$ – 14 per cent, 25 per cent and 21·5 per cent. These transformation errors, R/S, then, do not stand in relationship to the depreciation in the copies. If the copies of the circles show a lower degree of underestimation from 9 years upwards than those of the straight lines, the reason is this. At and above 9 years the subjects begin to concentrate more and become sensitive to any inequality in the case of the circle, since it is a surface, and any discrepancy in size is squared and all the more perceptible. Further, any perceptual error relating to the circle will affect the graphic copy as well as the model. All this means that we must turn elsewhere to discover the reasons for the increase in transformation errors.

If we measure the transformation error by means of the ratio R/S, whether it arises in imagining the circle after the straight copy or the reverse, we find first of all that the error is somewhat higher for the 12 cm than for the 24 cm strings (except at 5 to 8 years for imagination of the straight line). On the other hand, if one takes the averages for each age group and compares imagination of the circle with imagination of the straight line, then one finds no systematic difference (combining the drawings of the 12 cm and 24 cm lengths): 1·11 as against 1·14 at 5 to 8 years; 1·29 as against 1·25 at 9 to 14 years; and 1·23 as against 1·21 in the adult.

Although subject to considerable individual variation, the error is thus on average fairly stable, whether the straight line or whether the circle is the starting point. It is remarkable, therefore, to find that this error shows a marked tendency to increase with age. This is quite clear in the case of the 12 cm lengths, and a little less obvious for the 24 cm lengths where the errors are not so high (though they would be equally high for II 24 were it not for an aberrant group at 10 years[11] exceptionally reversing the error in passing from 12 to 24 cm, possibly because of some fear of a catch in the fourth test).

It is difficult to attribute this increasing error to a perceptual illusion. This is not only because, as we have pointed out, curve illusions diminish with age. There is a more important reason why one should look elsewhere for the sources of the error. It is possible to speak of perceptual activities when a magnitude or a relation is 'transported' at a distance in space or time from one subject to another, when there is anticipation, co-ordination, transposition of a form or a melody, etc. – but only provided that the perceived objects are not modified and that the transformation itself is perceptible. On the other hand if a circle–straight line transformation or the reverse is to be imagined without being directly perceived – if instead it is to be evoked without any sensory indication as to the change to be effected, then the resultant behaviour is to an appreciable degree outside the confines of perception. It is then necessary to go beyond the given and construct the required modification from scratch. It is, therefore, not possible to speak of perceptual anticipation here, since perception bears only on the starting point, while the desired result has none of the perceptible qualities of the object itself. One might reply to this that the subject does perceive his drawing and that he can compare it with the original object (the straight piece of string if he has drawn a circle, or the circular string if he has drawn a straight line). The objection would be valid (and then only with reservations) if the drawing were only a copy. But in fact it expresses the result of a transformation that has *not* been perceived, and thus presupposes a representation going beyond perception. Even a direct comparison between a straight line and a circumference is not purely perceptual, since it requires that the line be mentally curved, or the circumference mentally unrolled. And these processes cannot be realized merely by the activity of eye movement. Such activity may make it possible to range from one object to another, virtually right an oblique, restore the form of an object modified by perspective, and so on. But it is not equipped to transform the objective form of a solid, unlike the mental operations and the mental images in their dependent anticipatory form, which *are* able to do so.

Now it is remarkable that the younger subjects, while they depreciate the figures they are copying and while they always take the

[11] Apart from this group of 10-year-olds, we found an average error of 1·19 (= 19 per cent) between 9 and 14 years in II 24, as against 1·28 in II 12.

circumference to be longer than the straight line (in consequence of the perceptual error of underestimating the circumference), show at 5 to 8 years average transformation errors of only 6 to 16 per cent[12] (and at the same time frequently deny conservation of length). The older subjects (9 to 14 years), however, yield errors of 19–39 per cent (slightly lower in the adult : 13–33 per cent).

There seems to be only one explanation of this fact. The younger child's images are less anticipatory and more reproductive; consequently, they stick more closely to the apparent length perceived for the given model (allowing for the perceptual error). And one may recall from Table 84 that the individual stages of the line-to-semi-circle transformation do not begin to be imagined until 8 to 9 years (70 per cent success as against 30 per cent at 7 years), and that representation of the semi-circle-to-circle transformation is still poor at this age. At 5 to 8 years, then, the subject jumps, without attempting any gradual transition, from the starting point to the result of the transformation, thereby making it simpler, no doubt, to imagine the lengths in question. When the image becomes anticipatory and capable of representing the actual process of curving, resistance to the depreciatory effects of perceptual illusion is reinforced. This may lead imaginal representation to the sort of over-compensation we have seen (in relation, of course, to the drawn copy and not to the model), with the result that there are errors of up to 48–57 per cent at 10 years, that is, precisely at the age when anticipation of the curving process begins to emerge. (The errors are considerable; but there is, as we have seen, a reversal at 10 years with a jump from 1·57, 1·30, 1·48 to 0·84, as if the child were here trying out two extreme solutions in turn.)

A further word about arcs and straight lines (see section 1 of this chapter). The transformation of a circumference into a straight line or the reverse creates the same operational problem as the arcs and straight lines. Even so, it is clear that there is no link between the imaginal representations relating to these two situations, since the error arising in the case of the arc diminishes with age (Tables 73 and 75 to 78), whereas the present error actually goes up. The reason is that the error occasioned by the arc is dominated by the boundary problem, whereas the error occasioned by the circumference, though also indirectly connected with the same problem, is primarily the result of a reaction to the global perceptual appearance.

---

[12] The averages for each year range from 27 per cent (6 years, I 12) to 0 per cent (8 years, I 24). There is no regular decrease, however, from 5 to 8 years.

6. Conclusion

In the previous chapter we found that kinetic anticipatory images were not formed before the beginning of the concrete-operational stage. We went on to ask in our conclusion whether the part played by the operations in making the images flexible was a purely one-way affair. Are the displacement operations, etc., not perhaps themselves prepared by antecedent images? It is a difficult question to answer in the sphere of movements alone, and we shall take it up again on a general level in Chapter Eight. However, the present chapter does go some way towards providing a solution.

To begin with, the reproductive transformation images are no more capable than the reproductive kinetic images of organizing themselves in any adequate form. They too synchronize afresh with the beginning of the operational stage. Thus arc–line and line–arc transformations for a long time give rise to incorrect predictions, and intermediate stages are not successfully reconstituted until 8 to 9 years (and that only for the selection from prepared drawings, Table 83). Similarly for the transformation of angles into straight lines (Tables 87 and 88). The same is true also for the spirals (Table 92), and if this table shows successful responses to concentric circles at 6 years, the reason is that they involve not transformations so much as increases in size.

Now in the case of the transformations studied in sections 1–2 it is of course impossible to recount in detail the whole history of the image-operation interactions at their respective developmental levels. But there are at least two points that now seem established. In the first place, in order to produce a correct image (Tables 82–84 and 87–88), the transformation from arc to straight line and vice versa, and even the transformation from angle to line and vice versa, presupposes a frame of conservation assuring the invariance of the length of the rod or the sides of the angle. Conservation does in fact proceed by an interplay of inferences rather than by imaginal representation; further, it is bound up with operational reversibility, which in the present case the image does nothing to prepare. On the contrary, from 7 to 8 years, it is this operational reversibility that acts on the image, which it frames in a system permitting the structuration of the transformations.

Secondly, this influence of conservation on images is a probably genuine example of operational influence on the transformation image. But the facts collected in connection with the curves and angles furnish an equally clear example of the reverse action taking place at the preoperational level. The younger subjects' predictions as to the straightening of an arc into a line or the bending of a straight line into an angle manifest a constant concern with terminal boundary points that leads to distorted estimations. In this instance the image appears to function according to its own laws – pseudo-conservation of the boundaries and of the general qualitative appearance of the figures in question. And these laws almost certainly influence the notions of the corresponding developmental level – which enables us to account for the preoperational non-conservation of lengths.[13]

Generally speaking, preoperational thought may be thought of as a system of notions within which figurative treatment of states takes precedence over comprehension of transformations. Consequently, at this level images govern thought, while the situation is reversed at the operational level.

However, the picture would be far too simple if we were to limit ourselves to these two pieces of evidence. We would probably be able to understand the image's function at the operational level, since it would be brought in to correct the deficiencies of judgments still incapable of grasping transformations. But we would not arrive at any understanding of the image's role once it is subordinated to the operations at the next stage of development. Now, it is not a question of a functional reduction of its role. At the operational level, states are conceived of as end-products of transformations, and conversely, transformations as modifications of states. Consequently, the figurative role of the image, which bears primarily on states, remains indispensable even when states are subordinate to transformations; and in this kind of situation an accurate image of the states can promote comprehension of the transformations to the extent that approximately objective images of them may be formed. To verify whether or not this is the case, we now need to go on to analyse the anticipatory images involved in more complex transformations. The problem of the relationship between images and operations we leave to be tackled later (Chapter Eight).

---

[13] It will be recalled (Chapter Two) that the image does not explain the notional structures of order evaluation, but rather the primacy of terminal and initial boundary points within these structures.

CHAPTER SIX

Anticipatory Transformation Images

It will be recalled that we defined displacement as a change of position without modification of form, and transformation as a change of form accompanied by consequent displacement of the constituent parts of the figure or object. In Chapter Five we spoke of reproductive transformation images in those cases where the subject was felt to be more or less familiar with the transformation (e.g. the straightening of lines bent into arcs, right angles, etc.). In this chapter we shall speak of anticipatory transformation images when we can fairly assume that the transformation in question is not familiar to the child from past experience – no more familiar, that is, than the perceptual details presented in the experiment in hand.

But it goes without saying – we repeat – that this distinction between reproductive and anticipatory images (and the similar distinction between the two forms of kinetic imagery) is only valid as a methodological precaution. Only the facts can show afterwards whether the distinction has any basis in reality. It could well be that a reproductive transformation image involves anticipations that are as complex as when entirely new transformations have to be imagined. Tables 82 and 83 have already shown that in the case of the choice test for the arc-to-straight line transformation the correct intermediate positions H are not attained until 8 to 9 years (83 per cent), and are successfully drawn by the children themselves in only 10 to 20 per cent of cases. We need to know, therefore, whether anticipations bearing on new transformations are even more difficult, or whether the distinction between reproductive and anticipatory images becomes meaningless for transformations in general.

In this chapter we shall, then, attempt to analyse imaginal representation of some transformations with which the child is probably not familiar. These transformations will in principle consist of folding motions of varying complexity, beginning with the most simple. We shall also deal with the inversion of triangles and the location of their apices after change of position during rotation.

1. *Anticipation of proximities, 'surroundings', and the result of rotations after folding*

To approach the problems of folding in their simplest form we carried out the following investigation, with the help of F. Frank, A. Sella and P. Galindo. Our aim was to bring the subject's anticipations to bear on the most general topological relations, such as proximity and 'surrounding', in a situation where the rotational motion of folding would conserve or modify certain proximities and certain positions of a particular element in relation to the perimeter of a closed figure. This figure is said to 'surround' or not to 'surround', as the case may be, the element in question.[1] In order to make the intuition of folding more familiar, we used two transparent sheets, attached along the same rigid axis so that they could be laid together or separated like the leaves of a book (see Figure 31*A*).

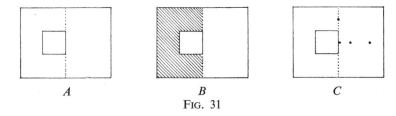

A B C

Fig. 31

We also used two opaque sheets in one of which a small square was cut out as a transparent window (Figure 31*B*), and not simply drawn as in *A*.

Our methods were as follows.

First of all we made certain that the child understood the words 'inside' and 'outside', by showing him a small red circle first inside and then outside the perimeter of a more or less circular closed curve. Similarly, using the 'book' *A* (Figure 31), we made clear what was meant by 'open' and 'closed'. In particular, we made sure the subject realized that only the left-hand part moves, while the right-hand part stays where it is. We then asked the following questions:

Technique I (*A and C*). (1) It was pointed out to the subject that the sides of the small 5 cm square in 'book' *A* are each coloured differently. He was then required to point to 'where the square will be when the book is closed', and to the positions of each of the colours in turn.

---

[1] To designate, for instance, the position of a small circle within the perimeter of a large square, we prefer the topological term 'surrounding' (*enveloppement*) to the term 'enclosure' (*emboîtement*). The latter seems to us to suggest rather class inclusions or wholes – in spite of Cantor's 'enclosed intervals' (*intervalles emboîtés*).

(2) We brought in the red point in the position 0/0 (the first figure refers to the vertical, the second to the horizontal axis. See 0 in Figure 31 *C*). The subject was asked to point to 'where the red dot will be when the book is closed'.

(3) Same question for position 0/2 (see *C*).

(4) Same question for position 0/7 (see *C*).

(5) Same question for position 4/0 (see *C*).

These five questions were posed first for 'direct anticipation' (verbal reply and pointing), and then for 'graphic anticipation' (the child was requested to draw the exact positions). On the basis of the drawings in particular are judged the four important cases of proximity: the positions of the colours; the square-rod, point-rod and point-square relations.

Technique II. The same questions (first 'direct', then 'graphic'), but for 'book' *B* coloured white.

Technique III. As technique II, except that the sides of the window are coloured.

The order of questions 2 and 3 was altered in each technique, but no differences were observed between the different groups of subjects.

We examined ninety-eight children aged 5 to 8 years, in groups of twenty-four or twenty-five according to age and further divided into groups of eight or nine for the three techniques. Before looking at the significance of the difficulties or errors from the qualitative point of view, let us first look at the quantitative results, starting with those provided by the rotation questions. Table 93 sets forth the averages for the successful responses to questions 1 (direct – *Dir*, and graphic – *Draw*), and for the successful indication of the colours in drawings 2–5 showing that the subject has comprehended that the square is rotated and not translated.

TABLE 93 *Successes for rotation questions 1 as direct (Dir) and graphic (Draw) indications – in brackets, successes for rotation based on the drawings for questions 2–5*
(As % of the responses)

	Technique I		Technique II		Technique III		Total	
	Dir	Draw	Dir	Draw	Dir	Draw	Dir	Draw
5 years	33	22·2 (13·8)	50	50 (53·1)	62·5	50 (50)	48·5	40·4 (38·5)
6 years	44·4	55·5 (44·4)	100	75 (75)	75	75 (81·2)	76·1	68·5 (66·8)
7 years	50	50 (50)	75	62·5 (62·5)	87·5	75 (68·7)	70·8	62·5 (60·4)
8 years	100	75 (81·2)	100	87·5 (87·5)	100	62·5 (94)	100	75 (87·4)

It is clear that at all ages the drawings are slightly less successful than the direct indications. But the image of the result of the rotation (only a reproductive kinetic image, of course, and not an anticipatory transformation image) is acquired from 8 years by 75 per cent of the subjects, with a fair approximation from 6 to 7 years (76 per cent at 6 years).

TABLE 94 *Successes for proximity questions 1 as direct (Dir) and graphic (Draw) indications – in brackets, successes for proximity based on the drawings for questions 2–5*
(As % of the responses)

	Technique I		Technique II		Technique III		Total	
	Dir	Draw	Dir	Draw	Dir	Draw	Dir	Draw
5 years	88·8	44·4 (51·7)	50	50 (47·9)	75	62·5 (56·0)	71·2	52 (51·9)
6 years	77·7	55·5 (50·8)	100	75 (76)	87·5	62·5 (70·7)	88·4	64·1 (65·8)
7 years	63·5	62·5 (66·6)	50	62·5 (76	88·5	62·5 (76)	67·3	62·5 (72·8)
8 years	100	75 (80·1)	100	87·5 (94·8)	100	75 (90·6)	100	79 (88.5)

The results for the proximities in Table 94 are parallel to the preceding direct and drawn results for question 1 (proximity of sides of square), and to the drawn results for questions 2 to 5 (proximity of square and rod, of red dot and rod, and of red dot and square).

It can be seen that these proximities, though sometimes conserved and sometimes modified during the rotation, give rise to better anticipations than the changes of position. It is true that almost all the proximities are conserved (although this does not mean that the graphic image is not attended by far more errors than direct indication). But the point-square proximity does vary. Here then are the particulars for the three proximities, questions 2 to 5:

TABLE 95 *Comparing modified proximities (point-square) with conserved proximities (techniques I–III)*
(As % of the responses)

	Point-square	Square-rod	Point-rod
5 years	48·0	52·1	55·8
6 years	66·6	62·7	68·3
7 years	82·1	62·4	73·9
8 years	91·7	82·1	91·6

There is almost no difference at all between the modified and the conserved proximities, except that from 7 to 8 years the position of the dots in relation to the square is more accurately observed than that of the square in relation to the rod. Let us now get down to the central issue – the direct or graphic anticipation of the proximity relations in questions 2–5. For 0/0 and 0/2 the red dot is surrounded by the square after rotation, and for 0/7 and 4/0 it is not. This leads to a useful comparison between the modified (questions 2–3) and conserved (questions 4–5) relations, and above all between the direct and the graphic anticipations (see Table 96).

TABLE 96   *Successes for anticipation of 'surrounding' (techniques I–III)*
(As % for the subjects)

	0/0		0/2		0/7		4/0		Total	
	Dir	Draw	Dir	Draw	Dir	Draw	Dir	Draw	Dir	Draw
5 years	92·5	48·6	96·2	44·4	92·1	71·2	88·5	71·2	92·3	58·8
6 years	95·8	65·7	100	69·4	92·5	84·7	100	95·8	97	78·9
7 years	95·8	87·5	100	87·5	95·8	91·6	95·8	95·8	96·8	90·6
8 years	100	87·5	100	87·5	100	100	100	100	100	93·7

Three interesting facts emerge from this table.

(1) Direct anticipation is excellent at all ages, and far better than the drawings at 5 years (for 4/0 the average of 88·5 is lower than the others only because of technique I; II and III give 100 per cent success). The difference between *Dir* and *Draw* narrows with age.

(2) In the case of direct anticipation, there is no significant difference between the successful responses to questions 2–3 (0/0 and 0/2) and those to questions 4–5 (0/7 and 4/0), that is, between non-surroundings transformed into surroundings and conserved non-surroundings.

(3) On the other hand, there is at all ages and particularly at 5 to 6 years systematic difficulty in drawing the red dot *within* the square (non-surrounding transformed into surrounding by the rotation) in cases 0/0 and 0/2, by comparison with the ease with which the red dot is left *outside* (conservation of non-surrounding) in 0/7 and 4/0 (questions 4–5).

These facts are clearly of some importance for a theory of the image. The child knows perfectly well when the red dot will be surrounded by the square and when not, since direct and verbal anticipation is successful as early as 5 years in 88·5 to 92·5 per cent of cases. And naturally the child is capable of drawing a round point in a square at 4 years. Yet in 51·4–55·6 per cent of cases the 5-year-old will not draw what he has only just expressed verbally – as if he were unable to construct an image adequate to his judgment. True, imagery may come into play in direct or verbal anticipation itself. But it does not have to be detailed and precise: it may be no more than a global symbolism even though corresponding to an exact judgment of topological relations. Then again, it may indeed be that drawing involves difficulties over and above those of the image; but in the present case there are, as it happens, no such difficulties (contrary to the questions of estimation of length, etc.).

To get a clearer picture, let us compare the results of the three techniques, which were varied precisely so that we should be able to dissociate the factors involved (Table 97). The difference between

TABLE 97 *Comparing the successes for the three techniques (drawings) in questions 2–3 (situations 0/0 and 0/2) and 4–5 (situations 0/7 and 4/0)* (As % of the responses)

	Technique I		Technique II		Technique III	
Questions	2–3	4–5	2–3	4–5	2–3	4–5
5 years	33·3	88·8	53·2	62·5	62·5	62·5
6 years	27·6	83·3	75	100	100	87·5
7 years	87·5	93·8	93·8	93·8	81·7	93·8
8 years	75	100	93·8	100	93·8	100
General average	55·9	91·4	78·9	89·1	84·5	85·9

the reactions to the two groups of questions is high in method I, low in method II, and negligible in method III. In I the square is a figure drawn on a sheet of transparent mica, while in II and III it consists of an open 'window'. In the latter cases, therefore, it is a patch of 'ground', rather than a 'figure'. Further, in II the ground is surrounded by white, and in III by coloured borders: which means that the space in III appears even emptier than in II.

Rubin's figure and the perceptual law of boundaries is well known. Now this states that when a figure stands out on a ground (as in I), or when a ground is cut out in a surface which then functions as a figure (as the cardboard sheet in II and III in which the square-ground is cut), the bounding outline *always* belongs to the figure and not the ground. Thus if a small dot is placed in the square in I, it means that the square's boundary is violated. In II, however, and more especially in III, while it would seem that the action or the drawing is essentially the same as in I, what really happens is that the circle is being placed in any empty space without its own boundaries (the boundary of the cardboard sheet is far less 'pregnant' than that of the square in I, as the square is a *good form*, whereas a sheet with a hole in it is not, or is to a much lesser degree, a good form). Thus the paradoxical situation in which subjects judge (direct anticipation) the red circle to come within the square but place it outside in the pictorial concretization of their image is yet another example of the boundary taboo which we have so frequently met in imaginal activity at the preoperational level.

We will give further details of the errors encountered in section 2 when we deal with certain other facts relating to that same situation. To conclude this section we shall just give a table of the completely successful responses to the three questions concerning rotation, proximity and surrounding. This enables us once again to assess the divergence between direct and graphic anticipations.

TABLE 98 *Successes for all questions combined*
(As % of the responses)

	5 years	6 years	7 years	8 years
Direct anticipation	56·9	76·8	75·8	100
Graphic anticipation	8	48	54	75

The difference between the two types of anticipation is much lower for the rotation (Table 93), higher for the proximities, at 5 to 6 years at least (Table 94), and very high for the surroundings (Table 96). Comparing Tables 93, 94 and 96, we find that at 5 to 6 years the topological relation of surrounding is anticipated best, the Euclidean relations of rotation are the least easy to anticipate, and the proximities come between these two in order of difficulty.

2. Anticipation of 'surroundings' and intersection after folding

The following inquiry was begun by S. Taponier,[2] who had collected together the reactions of forty-six subjects aged 5 to 7 years. The method used involved questions differing slightly from those of 1. The facts obtained by it will, therefore, serve as a control; but, more important, they will lead to an extension of the problem by bringing in intersection. Taking the apparatus of Figure 31 *A* with the 5 cm square on the mica sheet we replaced the small red circle a few millimetres in diameter by a second square with red sides. The size and position of this second figure were varied so as to introduce the following relations: the black surrounding the red square; the reverse surrounding relation; intersection of the two squares (see Figure 32).

I. We begin with the problem of the surrounding of the small red circle by the larger square (Figure 31 *A*). The apparatus is the same as in 1, method *A*, except that the rigid 'spine' of the 'book' is replaced by a piece of string. The subject was asked the following questions about the position of the red circle inside and outside the square.

We first checked that the child understood the terms 'inside' and 'outside', etc., and that he understood the folding motion and the transparency. We then requested direct and verbal anticipation of the position of the red circle at 0/0 and 0/2. If the child was unsuccessful, we proceeded

[2] It was continued by M. Antonini and L.-P. Poirier.

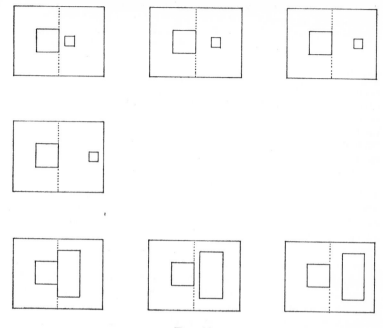

FIG. 32

to indirect suggestion. This consisted of putting questions concerned with proximity: 'Does the red circle stay near the string or not? Does the square?' etc. Then we asked again whether the red circle would be inside the square or not. Only two backward subjects failed again. The remaining subjects were then asked to draw the following, beginning with the square and going on with the circle: (1) Position 0/0 (cf. technique I, section 1); (2) position 0/2; (3) position 0/7; (4) position 4/0; (5) position 0/0 again; (6) position 0/0: a drawing first of the red circle in its constant position (straightforward copy), and then of the black square (we shall represent this as $R + B$); (7) an occasional repeat of 0/0, in the usual order (drawing first of the black and then of the red square: $B + R$). When any one of these seven drawings met with an unsuccessful response, we fell back on indirect suggestion, as in the verbal part of the test: 'Is the small ring near the string?' etc. We shall denote an inaccurate spontaneous drawing followed by a correct drawing after suggestion by the sign $\pm$.

The results are given in Table 99.

The first thing one notices here is that the difference between the reactions to positions 0/0 and 0/2 (surrounding) and to positions 0/7 and 4/0 (non-surrounding), which comes out so clearly in Tables 96

TABLE 99   *Successes for the drawings of 'surroundings'*
(As % of the responses)

	5 years			6 years			7 years		
	+	±	−	+	±	−	+	±	−
(1) 0/0	33·3	13·3	53·3	25	31·3	43·7	40	33·4	26·6
(2) 0/2	53·3	13·3	33·3	62·6	12·5	24·9	73·3	13·3	13·3
(3) 0/7	93·3	0	6·7	93·3	6·7	0	100	0	0
(4) 4/0	92·3	0	7·7	100	0	0	100	0	0
(5) 0/0	63·6	0	36·4	27·3	18·2	54·5	70	0	30
(6) R + B.	33·3	8·3	58·4	64·2	14·4	21·4	71·4	0	28·6

and 97 (I), is equally marked in this new group of subjects up to the age of seven.[3] But when question 0/0 is repeated after positions 0/7 and 4/0 reactions are improved slightly (at 5 and 7 years at least), as if comparison of the red dot in different positions made the subjects less scrupulous about crossing the boundary line. On the other hand, when the red circle is drawn (simple copy) before the square (question R + B) the 5-year-old subjects fall back to their earlier position (33·3 per cent in question 6 and question 1), whereas graphic anticipation is made easier at 6 and 7 years. The question (7) drawings, executed in the habitual order (square before circle), correspond to the order followed in 1 and 5 and do not affect the results.

These facts agree with those of section 1. We now need to give a brief analysis of the main types of error we come across, since such an analysis might enable us to verify the hypothesis that failure in questions 1 and 2 is due principally to a taboo on the boundary line. Now the chief error in question 1 (0/0) is to draw the circle outside the square. Most often the square is placed correctly against the axis, but the red point is placed just outside the square's right-hand side, and not, as it should be, up against its left side. Or the circle may be correctly placed against the axis but the square set a little to the right. Or the square may be placed correctly, and the circle displaced towards the top or towards the bottom, so that it remains outside the square. For 0/2 these errors may repeat themselves in exactly the same way; or they may be modified in accordance with the red circle's position.

When errors were made and suggestion failed we returned to the verbal part of the test. And it was interesting to find that the child would answer correctly as before, but still would not alter his drawing.

For example, we said to Ger (5,2) after he had drawn the red circle below the square against the string: 'If I close my book, will you see the red circle inside the square or outside it? – *Inside*. – Where is it in your

[3] These subjects have been successful in direct or verbal anticipation, the large majority without the correct answer having been suggested.

drawing? – *Outside.* – Then draw it as it should be.' (He starts again – and places it outside.) Isa (6,2) places the circle to the right of the square: 'Where is the circle in my book? – *By the string.* – And is it by the string in your drawing? – *No.* – Where is it in your book? – *The same place as in yours.* – Can you draw it by the string then? – *No, because the square's there.* – Can't you draw it there, by the string? (pointing to the square in its position after folding). – *No, you would have to draw it there*' (points to the square on the drawing).

With some subjects in test 0/0 we even ended up saying: 'Well, put it inside.' Naturally the child did this without any difficulty. Nevertheless, some subjects in the following question 0/2 drew the red circle outside the square, saying it was inside. . . .

II. To study the change from surrounding to intersection, we used mica sheets 20 cm × 15 cm with the usual 5 cm square with black sides on the left, and on the right a red square with red sides of 2 cm, or a similar one with sides of 7·5 cm, placed in the various positions shown in Figure 32. If the small red square is placed at position 0/5 and the larger one at 0/1·5 or 0/2·5 the result after folding is intersection with the black square; if on the other hand the small red square is placed at 0/1 or 0/3 and the larger one at 0/0 the result is a surrounding of the red by the black in the first case and of the black by the red in the second.

Now it is interesting to find that the twenty subjects (taken from the forty-six preceding) whom we tested on the intersection problem (from 5,1 to 7,3 years) gave appreciably better results for the surrounding of the red square in position 0/1 than for that of the red circle. On the other hand, the reverse surrounding – the left-hand black square inside the large right-hand red square at 0/0 – produced the same results as the small circle. See Table 100.

TABLE 100   *Graphic anticipation of 'surrounding' with small circle, small square and large square*

Small circle (0/0)			Small square (0/1)			Large square (0/0)		
−	±	+	−	±	+	−	±	+
25%	40%	35%	10%	10%	80%	35%	25%	40%

Thus, when a smaller figure is surrounded by a larger one, and both have the same form, the boundary taboo, which in Tables 99 and 100 prevented the subjects from drawing the circle in the square, is almost completely lifted! This is a good illustration of the heterogeneity of imaginal, perceptual, and operational laws. It is no harder to perceive the circle than to perceive the square inside the black square; but the circle inside the square is harder to imagine. Likewise, in direct anticipation all the subjects affirm that the small red circle, just as the square, will be 'inside' the black square. On the other hand, if the two figures in question are roughly the same size – as the 5 cm and 7·5 cm square are – the difficulties reappear. Their reappearance is, however, probably due to the fact that the situation is close to that of intersection.

III. In the case of intersection proper (small red square at 0/5, and large square at 0/1·5 or 0/2·5), the difficulties are the same as those analysed in Chapter Three, section 2, in connection with mobile transparent squares displaced relatively one to the other. Our account, therefore, can be fairly short.

As far as the small red square is concerned, only 15 per cent of the subjects were successful in spontaneously indicating the intersection at 0/5; the others placed the red square either inside or outside. When asked, 'Are you sure that it's completely inside (or completely outside)?', most answered in the affirmative. But when asked, 'Wouldn't it look partly in and partly out?', 35 per cent agreed that there would be intersection. The others jammed the small red square up against the right side of the black square, outside or inside, to avoid overlapping.

Only 15 per cent spontaneously succeeded in the intersection of the black square and the large red square. The others contrived to draw the squares small enough to be juxtaposed without crossing. This is particularly the case for position 0/2·5, where the size of the figures would make intersection unavoidable. If we persisted and suggested the right answer by introducing questions bearing on size and proximity, some subjects eventually indicated intersection at 0/2·5, but did not generalize the solution for 0/1·5, where intersection can be avoided. And when asked explicitly, 'Won't the red square be partly in and partly out?' they still answered in the negative.

Now we know that the child is able to copy an intersection, even when figures of different sizes are involved, at a very early age. We dealt in an earlier work[4] with the case of the three-year-old subjects who could not draw a square except as a rough closed circle, but who were able nevertheless to reproduce perfectly three oval figures – one containing a small circle, another having a small circle outside its periphery, and a third having a small circle on its periphery. They were even able to point out the intersection, using words such as 'half-out'. But in the present case intersection and surrounding appear to be far more difficult; and this is no doubt because the subject has to anticipate a transformation (simple enough to be successful on the mental level in direct or verbal anticipation) by means of images when in fact images as such remain for a long time static.

[4] Piaget and Inhelder, *The Child's Conception of Space*, 1956, Chapter II.

But we should not be too hasty in drawing any conclusions, as it is possible that there are here two factors combining to complicate intersection: (*a*) the fact that the intersecting figures are of different sizes might strengthen the need to safeguard the integrity of their boundaries; (*b*) the fact that intersection affects only that side of the square facing the line of fold might necessitate possibly difficult estimations of distances. Further, it could be that the difficulties observed in Chapter Three, section 2, are due to the situation of sliding that intensifies the boundary problems. In a situation of folding such difficulties would diminish, since here it is a question of all or nothing, a displacement *en bloc* of a complete portion, and not a gradual advance. We need to know, therefore, what results would be given by anticipation of the intersection of figures of equal size contiguous to the same axis of the fold (the intersection thus being lateral, rather than distal). This will be our task in the next section.

3. *Contiguity, intersection and superimposition resulting from folding*

Along with E. Schmid-Kitsikis we carried out an experiment in which squares and triangles were rotated about a common base – the line of the fold (see Figure 33) – in various ways to give relations of contiguity, intersection and complete superimposition. The figures were presented in two different ways: either on a transparent sheet of mica, drawn in outline and with differently coloured sides enabling us to judge the anticipation of the rotation; or on opaque coloured surfaces enabling us to see whether for the total superimpositions the child would take the masking into account or whether he would draw the whole by means of 'transparency' (in Luquet's sense). Each figure was shown to the child in turn. After explaining them, we asked him to draw the line of the fold and the figure that folding would produce. In particular the tests concerned the series *A* and *B* of Figure 33. Series *C* was brought in later to avoid having the triangles always drawn on their bases.

Using thirty-nine subjects aged 5 to 7 years (groups of 12, 17 and 10) we obtained the results set forth in Table 101. The successes under 'contiguity' were counted on a broad basis: all drawings were counted correct which indicated any kind of contiguity, as opposed to separation (or vice versa for *C*), even if it approached intersection. For rotation to be counted successful, on the other hand, there had to be accurate and detailed indication of the colours of the square's or triangle's sides. We have, however, included in brackets the cases in which the child merely indicated movement from one side to another during folding. The column 'intersections' gives the global

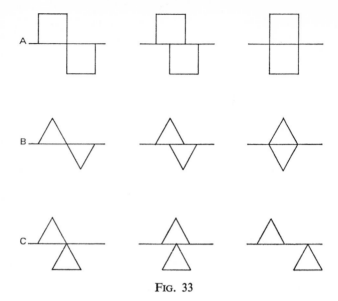

FIG. 33

successes, and in brackets the cases in which the child takes masking into account for the opaque surfaces instead of drawing the whole thing by 'transparency'.

TABLE 101 *Successes for contiguities, intersections, superimpositions and rotations*
(As % of the subjects)[5]

	Contiguities	Inter- sections	Super- impositions	Rotations	Complete successes
5 years	33	33 (0)	16	42 (42)	0
6 years	76	53 (0)	12	40 (65)	6
7 years	90	90 (60)		90 (100)	80

Two facts stand out. First, intersection does not raise the same difficulties here as in section 2 of this chapter or Chapter Three, section 2. And second, the real difficulty is now transferred to total superimposition. The subject rejects not only complete but also partial masking, as can be seen from the bracketed figures in the 'intersection' column (the 0 per cent at 5 and 6 years means that in the case of the opaque surfaces the subjects draw the outlines of

[5] For the superimpositions at 7 years *C* only was used, without total superimposition.

210

both figures, including the partially covered one, by means of 'transparency').

If we take these latter reactions to begin with, the first thing one notices is that on the notional level the 5-year-old subjects know perfectly well – and say so – that one of the figures obscures the other in the last two cases of *A* and *B* (Figure 33), and that all the lines are not visible in the case of the intersection of opaque surfaces. Nor can it be maintained that the difficulty is really connected with the execution of the drawing, since it is much easier, in the case of complete superimposition, to draw only one figure than to draw one set inside another with the sides more or less contiguous. We may say, with Luquet, that what we have here is 'intellectual realism', in the sense that the child draws what he knows about the figure and not what he sees. But it is difficult to apply this statement here, since the child also knows quite well that one of the figures is obscured, but still refuses to represent it. We would prefer to say, therefore, that this 'intellectual realism' in the drawing (and this might be true of all the cases) translates the imaginal representation rather than the concept. This does not, of course, mean that it is not 'intellectual', or rather, 'cognitive', but in a figurative not an operative, sense. In fact, one of the characteristics of the static image at the preoperational level is the pseudo-conservation of the boundary and contour of the figures. And it is this pseudo-conservation which usually hinders correct figuration of intersection and superimposition, and which in the present case remains in operation only for the latter.

The relative easiness of intersection in the present case is probably to be attributed, as we suggested at the end of section 2, to the following facts: the figures in question are equal in size;[6] intersection affects their lateral and not (as in section 2 of this chapter) their distal edge; and they are not (as they were in Chapter Three, section 2) displaced by partial sliding, but are rotated all of a piece.

These rotations are of an order of difficulty comparable to that of the rotations of Table 93.

4. *Folding and transformation of straight lines*[7]

When modifications of size and form are added to changes of position fold tests can become peculiarly complex, unless one keeps to the elementary models. We shall therefore only consider straight lines with two or three cross-strokes, whose relative lengths and shapes the subject is asked to anticipate after the sheet of paper on which they are drawn has been folded in two (along the dotted line – see Figure 34).

---

[6] This does not prevent certain subjects from sometimes reducing the moving figure and drawing the square as a narrow rectangle.
[7] With the collaboration of F. Frank and M. Anthonioz.

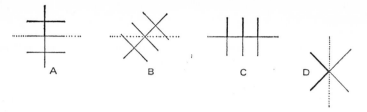

FIG. 34

We started the test with the following preliminary exercise. The child was shown a picture of a house with two windows and a door drawn on transparent paper. He was asked to anticipate verbally the form the drawing would take when folded horizontally. The drawing was then folded for him, and he was asked to explain the result: 'Why can you see only one window? Why this one and not that one? Why can you see the door?' etc.

Then we showed the child one of the forms *A* to *D* of Figure 34. We used four separate groups of subjects, each group seeing only one of the models, to avoid unwanted influences. There were seven questions.

(1) *Copy of the figure as presented.* Each of the three cross-strokes in *A–C* was coloured differently: likewise the two segments (above and below the fold) of the principal straight lines in *A* and *B*, and the four segments of *D*. The copy was done in black.

(2) *Verbal anticipation.* We folded the paper, which is transparent, and covered it with one hand. We then asked the child to list the colours he would see, and to give the forms, sizes and positions of the final figure.

(3) *Graphic anticipation.* We then asked the subject to draw the result of the folding in colour. To obviate memorization difficulties we either provided the subject with an unfolded figure as a check, or showed him the unfolded model at short intervals.

(4) *Explanation of the anticipation.* The subject was asked to account for the details of his drawing.

(5) *Selection from prepared drawings.* Four prepared drawings were shown to the subject (five for *B*) including, as well as the correct answer, the most frequent erroneous or incomplete ones. The child was asked to pick the most correct one.

(6) *Copy of the result of the folding.* The paper was folded again. The child was allowed to see the result and was asked to draw it.

(7) *Explanation of the result.* The child was asked for a detailed explanation of the transformations observed.

Using this technique we examined twenty subjects aged 5 years, nineteen aged 6 years, and twenty-five aged 7. With an additional group of twenty-four subjects aged 5 to 7 years we used a preliminary method comprising six figures, two of which were shown to each subject in various combinations. Now these apparently quite simple tests make it plain that anticipation of the modifications is surpris-

212

ingly difficult compared with the ease, albeit relative, with which the changes of position are imagined (sections 1 and 2). If we group all the errors into two large classes – viz. failure to change even the size of the figure (and its basic form) (I), and correct reduction of size but failure with shape and position (II) – then, taking the four figures together, we arrive at Table 102 (where the adult subjects are young apprentices).

TABLE 102 *Folding of the four figures of Figure 34 with graphic antici-pation and, in brackets, choice from prepared models*[8]
(As % of the responses)

	Error I		Error II	Successes	
5 years (80)	59·7	(22·2)	33·3	7	(24·9)
6 years (72)	38·9	(35·9)	61·1	0	(19·0)
7 years (75)	22	(18·9)	62·2	15·8	(36·1)
8 years (22)	17		30	53	
9 years (22)	7·5		10·5	82	
10 years (24)	3·5		7·2	89·3	
11 years (23)	0		14·5	85·5	
Adults (24)	0		4·2	95·8	

Anticipation is least difficult for *C* (the only figure yielding some successes – and that without the positions of the colours being taken into account). The reason is that the line of the fold coincides with the basic line, and that consequently only the cross-strokes have to be reduced in size. *B* is the most difficult (no successful response), as the fold transforms the basic line into two segments forming a right angle.

Although the selection test shows some improvement in antici-pation, it is a modest one. The copies of the result of the transforma-tions, and above all the subject's explanations which may throw some light on the cause of the errors, will be examined later on in this section. But first let us analyse these errors in more detail with the help of the verbal anticipations.

The most remarkable error (I) is an imagined pseudo-conserva-tion of the general shape and size of the figure. When the subject reproduces the model as found, as if folding did not affect it, the question might arise whether this is not due to laziness or to the perceptual pregnance of the given figure. In most cases, however, the child does have the impression that folding will obscure some part of the figure. But instead of reducing the lengths perpendicular

[8] The choice tests also showed rejection or acceptance of the whole set of proposed models in 25·9 per cent of cases at 5 years and 13·1 per cent at 6 years.

to the fold line, he modifies or suppresses what he can without changing either the lengths or the form of the whole. For instance, in figure *A* he removes the basic line but keeps the three cross-strokes and their respective colours. Similarly in *C*, with occasional modification of the colours (when they do not in fact change). In figure *B* one stroke is missed out and the basic oblique line is left, or the colours are changed. And in *D* the colours but not the form are modified, or the centre is missed out (= four arms without a point of intersection), or the X form may even be adjusted to +.

Now in verbal anticipation (taking place before the drawing) all the subjects except for 40 per cent at 5 years predicted shortening of figures *A* and *B*, although they were not always subsequently able to draw this. Almost all the subjects accepted that the cross-strokes in *C* diminish in length. But for *D* all verbal anticipations agreed with the subsequent drawings. As far as size is concerned, verbal anticipation appears to be well ahead of drawing. But this probably means that it simply expresses a global judgment without a precise image – whereas a drawing will necessarily involve a precise image, and will in any case be attended with practical difficulties. As far as the other aspects of the figures are concerned, verbal anticipation and the drawing are nearly always on a par, apart from some exceptional cases in which the former is ahead.

When the subjects do not make error I – when, that is, they do shorten the figure in their drawings – errors type II are found. The most frequent mistake is when the child understands that one figure is partly covered by the other after folding (except *B*), and succeeds fairly easily in predicting which colours are covered and which are on top, but fails to find the *position* of the top part, draws it in its original place, and cuts out the covered part. This was the case for the large majority of errors II in Figure *A* (apart from some subjects who drew the covered part where the covering part should be, and eliminated the latter), in Figure *C* (the cross-strokes were halved in length, but the covering half – the only part indicated – was left where it was, instead of being moved to below the horizontal), and in Figure *D*. In Figure *B*, which met with complete failure up to 7 years (inclusive), the top portion was drawn as given, while the bottom was suppressed, instead of remaining visible at right angles to the first. Another type of error interesting from the point of view of the image occurred in *B* and *D*, where the position of the fold was altered to make it perpendicular to the basic line of the figure because of the pregnance of the better perceptual form. Less interesting as far as the image is concerned is the tendency to eliminate the lines situated in the fold line itself, because, as one subject said of the basic line in *C*, 'it is hidden in the crease'.

Broadly speaking, then, imagination of the results of folding is far more rudimentary when a modification of shape and size is in question than in the case of the topological boundary line relations (section 1). The question is, therefore, whether this deficiency arises from the difficulties involved in comprehending the relations in hand, or whether it is due to the process of representation itself. A comparison of the spontaneous drawings and the selected drawings (Table 102) would seem to show that comprehension is ahead of the image, but does not lead very much further. However, selection of the right drawing from several possibilities evidences a mode of comprehension still bound up with graphic representation. To conclude the tests, therefore, we got the subject to copy the various results of folding the figures, and asked him to explain them. The copies present no problems (except for *B* and *D*). The explanations, on the other hand, are quite instructive. If we distinguish three responses – correct (+), incorrect (–) and intermediate (±) – we arrive at the following results (Table 103).

TABLE 103   *Explanations given for the results of folding, after copying* (As % of all the subjects)

	–	±	+
5 years	33·7	45·0	21·3
6 years	14·7	34·7	50·6
7 years	17·7	16·7	65·6

The hardest fold to explain was, of course, in Figure *B*. When the actual results of the transformations are given and there is no call for anticipation, a correct explanation is achieved by only 50 per cent of the subjects at 6 years and 65 per cent at 7 years. It is natural, therefore, that the anticipatory image should be even more difficult if the image is limited to translating comprehension of the process. But one might have considered the possibility that correct images exist before comprehension, providing a simple empirical preview on the basis of the perceived data and the experimenter's statement as to the folding. In fact we found this was not the case: on the contrary, the detailed image follows comprehension, rather than leads up to it.

5. *Anticipation of the modification of shape and size resulting from stretching the sides of closed figures*

The striking difference between anticipation of changes of size and form in section 4 compared with anticipation of changes of position (and of form, but without modification of size) in sections 1–3 prompted us to pursue our analysis of the question along with F. Frank and G. Voyat. The method used this time was more intuitive in character than the foldings, and was designed so that all details should be perceptible, or imaginable in an entirely perceptual mode. We used a single basic figure, a square, whose sides consisted of an elastic band held in place at the corners by four matchsticks stuck in a tray of modelling clay. The basic figure could be transformed into a trapezium, a rhombus, a larger square, or a triangle by moving two, four or one of the matchsticks. It is thus possible to get the subject to anticipate with the minimum of extraneous difficulty (*a*) the new form, by indicating the displacements of the matchsticks, and (*b*) the displacements of the matchsticks required to obtain a new form shown in a drawing. The question, then, is whether such elementary transformations are anticipated by correct images right from the preoperational stages, or whether it is necessary to wait until anticipations can be supported by the operations.

The apparatus consisted of a tray containing modelling clay. Four matchsticks were placed in it in such a way as to form the four corners of a square with sides 3 cm. We then showed the subject an elastic band, and asked him what figure it would make if placed around the four matchsticks. All the subjects found it easy enough to predict a square, since it was simply a matter of reading the figure off perceptually. Then we demonstrated (but not actually on the modelling clay surface) that the elastic band could change its shape and size, put it back round the matchsticks, and asked the following questions.

1. *Imagination of the form given the displacements.* It was explained to the child that we were going to displace the matches in certain directions (see Figure 35) indicated slowly and clearly with a gesture. In *D* the fact

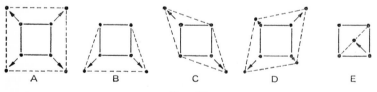

FIG. 35

that the matches were moved different distances was underlined verbally: 'This one goes a long way right to there, and this one goes a little way to here.' The child was then requested to draw the form taken by the elastic band when the matches were in their new positions.

2. *Imagination of the displacements given the form.* The child was shown five drawings in succession representing the five forms produced by moving the matchsticks (Figure 35). The drawings were actual size. For each one we asked: 'How do you need to move the matches so that the elastic band

216

is like that?' The child was required first to indicate by means of a gesture on the modelling clay how the matchsticks would need to be moved. Then we made it clear that each of the matches 'goes a little way', and asked the child to draw these short distances on a diagram representing the four starting positions by dots (the corners of the 3 cm square).

Here to begin with are the quantitative results (Table 104). For each of the five cases *A–E* of Figure 35 we distinguish anticipation of the forms (*F*) given the distances traversed by the matches, and anticipation of the distances (*D*) starting with the forms as given. The percentage of successes for the drawings are given without brackets. Within brackets are given the percentage of successful responses for gestural anticipation.

The first thing one notices is that, apart from *A*, these anticipations of transformation, although successful on average one year earlier (at 8 years rather than at 9) than in the case of the folded sheets (Table 102), are nevertheless more difficult than the anticipations of size transformations in sections 1–3. The reason for this is probably that the younger subject's imagery remains not only static but also bound to the initial configurations in consequence of the kind of pseudo-conservation that we have seen exemplified many times already. This being so, imagining a transformation at all is something of a problem (a problem which, as we have seen, becomes acute when it is required to *draw* surroundings and not merely to point to them). But having to imagine that this transformation modifies the size of the constituent elements as well as the shape of the whole will only doubly accentuate the tendency towards pseudo-conservation.

It is understandable, therefore, that the drawing of the square *A* should be superior to the drawings of the other figures – although normally the young subjects can draw a triangle – a 'roof' – just as easily. The reason is that transformation *A*, while increasing the size of the square, does conserve its original form. Strictly speaking, therefore, it is not a transformation at all in the sense we have defined for use in the field of images. One can also understand why anticipation by means of gesture, with two or three exceptions for the square and the triangle, is consistently better than anticipation by drawing (this has been observed already in sections 1–3, though it is not necessarily the case for pure kinetic anticipation or reproduction). The gesture, like the drawing, is effected by successive movements; but, unlike the graphic image, it does not leave any simultaneous and constantly perceptible result behind it. Consequently the things acceptable in gesture – the intersections, etc., in sections 1–3 and the transformations of size ratios in the present case – become much more disturbing in the drawing, where the outcome

217

TABLE 104 *Successes for the anticipation of the forms (F) resulting from given displacements, and of the distances (D) starting from given forms*
(As % of the responses)

	A		B		C		D		E	
	F	D	F	D	F	D	F	D	F	D
4 years (9)	56 (72)	23 (14)	0 (0)	0 (0)	0 (0)	0 (0)	0 (0)	0 (0)	0 (25)	0 (13)
5 years (9)	45 (55)	66 (66)	40 (33)	33 (48)	13 (0)	13 (0)	0 (0)	0 (0)	33 (60)	22 (25)
6 years (14)	54 (86)	79 (70)	39 (50)	42 (58)	0 (0)	30 (43)	10 (0)	30 (67)	46 (100)	18 (0)
7 years (12)	58 (83)	37 (55)	27 (44)	46 (60)	15 (25)	30 (56)	33 (34)	33 (63)	46 (80)	18 (17)
8 years (11)	91 (91)	87 (75)	73 (87)	75 (87)	58 (100)	87 (87)	46 (50)	86 (72)	44 (100)	86 (64)
9 years (8)	100 (100)	100 (87)	100 (100)	100 (87)	87 (72)	100 (100)	75 (80)	100 (100)	87 (100)	100 (100)

The Civic Quarter Library

www.leedsmet.ac.uk/lis/lss
www.leedsmet.ac.uk/lis/lss

Borrowed

Customer   Leather, Kerry

                                    Due Date
1 Mental imagery in   3/3/2010,23:59

                        17.02.2010 12:14:29

        Telephone (0113) 283 3106

is far more glaring and the pseudo-conservation characteristic of the younger subject's static imagery therefore increases its demands.

Turning to the relationships between anticipation of the forms F and anticipation of the distances D, it can be seen that in the case of the square A the former is on average the easier, for the reasons just mentioned. But in the following three figures $B–D$ it is anticipation of the distances that is superior. This may be due to progressive adaptation, since the question comes second; or it may be that the forms themselves are somewhat complex (but the higher success for the distances holds for the gestures as well as the drawings). In E it is anticipation of the form that is easier. The reason this time is clearly that the required displacement is not dual and symmetrical but singular, and that it does not connect to one of the triangle's corners but to the middle of one of the sides.

We note also the interesting set-back in some subjects at 7 years: 37 per cent in A (D) as against 79 per cent at 6 years; 27 per cent in B (F) as against 39 per cent at 6 years. Facts of this kind, frequently observed at about 7 years, would seem to point to a change of method in anticipation. The bringing in of operational reasoning may complicate representation before it comes to support it. This led us to examine the error types from a qualitative viewpoint, and to try thus to understand the mechanism behind the anticipations elicited. The present experiment allows the child's successive gropings to be more easily followed than the fold test.

The errors observed fall into three types: (*a*) failure to respond, or simple copying of the matchsticks stuck in the modelling clay, which comes to the same thing; (*b*) reproduction of the experimenter's demonstration of the movement of the matches (in F), when the resultant form is required, or reproduction of the shape as presented (in D), when the matches' movements are required; (*c*) responses intermediate between *b* and the correct answer.

Both this distribution and the analysis of responses *c*, would seem to show that anticipatory representation comprises three, rather than two, phases: (1) detachment from the situation of the moment (this is where the subjects fail in errors *a* and *b*); (2) back-reference, which is, as we shall see, the condition for 1 and 3; (3) reproduction of the process leading from the starting point up to the state given or observed, with modifications of the elements to be changed and conservation of those that can be transposed into the new situation. To vindicate this interpretation let us analyse two particular cases of groping which lead from errors *b* and *c* to the correct answer (Figure 36). At first the subjects cannot get away from the datum before them. They not only started with error *b* (1 – straightforward copy of the matchsticks' movements), but also, in 2 (I) and 2–4 (II), kept some of the angles and even complete sides of the square. How do they break away from the perceptual datum? Subject II threw light on this when he remarked, quite spontaneously, that 'you

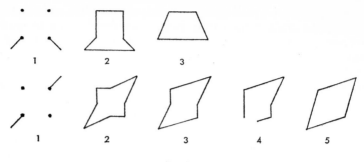

FIG. 36

need a straight line' for the left side in 4 (though he did not say the same thing of the right side). In other words, in order to detach himself from the square and at the same time imagine the new form, the child has to rethink the situation in terms of the taut elastic band, and not just in terms of the matches' position. This may seem little enough – but this solution does not become general until 8 years. Detachment from the given N in order to anticipate the result of the transformation R entails first comprehension of N as a function of prior transformations, and then application of this understanding of N to R. In short, it is necessary to return to the original position (O) in order to construct $O \rightarrow R$ by analogy with $O \rightarrow N$, otherwise the change from N to R offers any number of acceptable solutions (as in 2 and 2–4 in Figure 36). The anticipatory image cannot therefore be formed without the support of an operational process with its dual characteristics of reversible retroaction and progressive construction. Without such support there could be no anticipation of the result, because there would be no transformations in the strict sense – that is, transformations without which there is no 'comprehension' of states, only description. It is natural, therefore, that the anticipatory transformation images should not be constituted until 7 to 8 years and that until then the static images should show a fairly systematic preeminence.

6. Anticipation of n folds and n' holes

The preceding experiments involved a single fold, and anticipating it presented no problems. The same cannot be said of the results of folding, however, where it is a question either of purely topological transformations (proximities, surroundings, intersections: Tables 94–100), of Euclidean displacements (rotations: Tables 94 and 98), or of modifications of Euclidean dimensions and forms (short lines or cross-strokes shortened, obscured, or broken: Tables 102 and 103). Now the conclusions to be drawn from these analyses are fairly clear. Anticipation of the topological transformations is the least

220

difficult (particularly in direct anticipation, though there is systematic difficulty in translating certain of them into transformation images), followed closely by kinetic anticipation. But changes of form and size (section 3) meet with considerable resistance. It is of interest, therefore, to go on now to look at an example of the classic fold tests. In these it is required to anticipate (*a*) the number and position of the folds (where $n > 1$), and (*b*) the number and position of the holes made by cutting out a small piece from one of the creases after folding the paper *n* times.[9] This type of test will once again enable us to compare the image with operational judgment. The latter may in the present case result in the progressive induction or deduction of a proper law.

This inquiry was carried out with E. Schmid-Kitsikis at Geneva, and was taken up at Barcelona with Z. Mendez. Our methods were as follows.

Method A (4 to 8 years), *Question 1.* A sheet of white paper was folded in two while the child watched. The child was asked to draw it as it would be when unfolded, and to indicate the crease. This was repeated for a sheet folded in four.

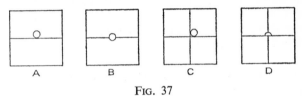

FIG. 37

Question 2. A small circle or semi-circle was drawn on the folded sheet (as in Figure 37). The child was required to imagine the positioning of this mark on the unfolded sheet (the crease again to be indicated).

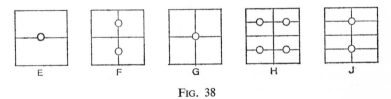

FIG. 38

Question 3. A piece was cut out of the folded sheet. The child was asked to draw the sheet as it would be when unfolded. The pieces removed were: (*a*) a semi-circle in the middle of the crease of the sheet folded into

[9] See, for example, the tests of Terman–Merril: tests for 9-year-olds, 14-year-olds and 'superior adults III'.

two (Figure 38 *E*); (*b*) a semi-circle in the middle of the principal crease of the sheet folded into four (Figure 38, *F*); (*c*) a quarter circle at the intersection of the crease lines of the sheet folded into four (Figure 38 *G*). In all these questions the child was asked to vindicate or explain his drawings.

Method B (8 to 15 years). We began with the questions above, but introduced a sheet folded into eight (three foldings). To question 3 we added the following: (*d*) a semi-circle in the middle of the principal crease of the sheet folded into eight – giving 4 holes (Figure 38, *H*); and (*e*) a quarter circle at the intersection of the crease lines of the folded sheet – giving two holes (Figure 38 *J*).

The subjects were also put through the following learning procedure. After each error, the sheet was unfolded and the child was asked to copy it. Then, when the subject had reproduced from memory the drawing that occasioned the error and subsequently the copy, we went on to the anticipation of the next sheet.

Finally, in order to determine whether he had discovered the law, we asked the subject to account for the number of creases and holes, stressing the difference between the pieces cut out in the middle of the fold lines and those cut out at the intersections.

Ninety-six subjects aged 4 to 11–15 years were examined at Geneva, and fifty aged 6 to 10 years at Barcelona. Here first of all are the results for question 1 with and without learning (Table 105, with the Barcelona percentage in brackets). The correct result is reproduced from memory:

TABLE 105 *Anticipation of the position of folds, with and without learning* (As % of the subjects)

	Without learning			With learning
	1 fold	*2 folds*	*3 folds*	*3 folds*
4 years	50	10		
5 years	85	73		
6 years	100 (100)	61 (44)	(33)	
7 years	100 (100)	78 (44)	(33)	
8 years	100 (100)	90 (90)	(77)	60
9 years	(100)	(90)	(90)	80
10 years	(100)	(100)	(90)	70
11–15 years	100			92

Anticipation of the positions of the creases poses no problems at 5 years in the case of a single folding, nor at 7 years (or a little earlier) in the case of a double folding, nor at 8 to 9 years for a triple folding. The reason is firstly that the transformations are known to the child, which means that the image is reproductive, and secondly that, as he has seen the experimenter fold the sheet, the child can more or less easily infer the number and the median position of the folds.

But, when we turn to the anticipation of the circle or semi-circle drawn on the folds, things naturally become more complicated, since a true anticipatory image is involved. Table 106 sets forth the reactions at 4 to 8 years to question 2, *A* to *D* of Figure 37 (as percentages of subjects, with the Barcelona percentage in brackets).

TABLE 106 *Anticipation of the position of circles and semi-circles drawn on the folds (Question 2)*

	A		B		C		D	
4 years	0		0		0		0	
5 years	13		33		7		0	
6 years	23	(40)	38	(40)	8	(0)	15	
7 years	64	(70)	93	(80)	36	(10)	7	
8 years	70	(60)	90	(70)	40	(10)	10	
9 years		(89)		(100)		(30)		(30)
10 years		(80)		(80)		(30)		(20)

There is naturally a big difference between anticipations for one fold (*A*, *B*) and anticipations for two folds (*C*, *D*). In the former case, it is easier to imagine the circle drawn on the crease (*B*) than drawn to one side (*A*) of it, and successes for *B* exceed 75 per cent from 7 years. The successful anticipations for the holes (question 3, Figures *E–J*) are given in Table 107.

TABLE 107 *Anticipation of the position of the holes*
(As % of success. Barcelona subjects given in brackets)

	Without learning										With learning				
	E		F		G		H		J		E	F	G	H	J
4 years	0		0												
5 years	20		6		6										
6 years	38	(60)	0	(0)		(0)		(0)		(0)					
7 years	78	(60)	7	(14)	14	(11)		(0)	0	(0)					
8 years	90	(100)	10	(10)	20	(30)	0	(0)	20	(0)	100	55	50	10	20
9 years	100	(100)	40	(40)	50	(80)	30	(0)	40	(30)	100	70	80	30	50
10 years	100	(100)	10	(20)	60	(60)	10	(10)	50	(20)	100	70	100	40	60
11–15 years	100		57		65		7		29		100	78	92	50	65

Two facts, the first of which is natural enough, emerge from this table: (*a*) anticipation is better when there are fewer folds: hence successes are in the order $E > F$, $G > H$, J, corresponding to one, two and three folds; (b) the success rate is higher when there are fewer holes, the number of folds being equal: hence $G > F$, and $J > H$, since G has one hole as against two in F, and J two as against four in H. These different orders ($E > F$, $G > H$, J, and $G > F$ and $J > H$) are found with and without learning, both in Barcelona and in Geneva. The $G > F$ and $J > H$ differences, however, signify that the holes' positions are anticipated more easily when cut out at the intersection of the creases than when cut out at the middle, since there are half as many holes as a result.

Now one would expect the successes to be inversely proportional to the number of folds. But the reason for the influence of the number of holes is not so immediately clear. On the one hand, it is hard to see why the position of two symmetrical holes should be more difficult to imagine than that of a single hole. On the other hand, the relation between the number of holes and whether they are cut out in the middle of a crease or at an intersection tends to suggest that this is the principal factor in the anticipation of the positions. And in fact, in the case of holes cut from the middle of the fold the most frequent error is to place the holes at the intersections, while in the case of holes cut out at the intersection the error is to locate them not in the middle of the lines, but (and sometimes in increased numbers!) at the corners of the sheets – the reason being that the intersection comes at the corner when the paper is folded. Before concluding, let us look at the table for the anticipation of the number of holes.

TABLE 108 *Anticipation of the number of holes*
(As % of the successes. Barcelona results given in brackets)

	Without learning					With learning				
	E	F	G	H	J	E	F	G	H	J
4 years	0	0								
5 years	20	0	13							
6 years	46	8 (0)	8 (33)	(0)	(0)					
7 years	57	7 (14)	14 (33)	(0)	(16)					
8 years	80	10 (10)	30 (70)	10 (0)	30 (33)	100	55	50	30	20
9 years	100	40 (40)	60 (90)	40 (10)	40 (50)	100	70	80	40	60
10 years	100	20 (30)	60 (70)	10 (20)	60 (50)	100	70	100	40	80
11–15 years	100	50	71	28	36	100	78	92	57	71

Like the table for the positions, this table shows the orders of successes: $E > F$, $G > H$, J, inversely proportional to the number of folds, and $G > F$, $J > H$, inversely proportional to the number of holes, with and without learning, and in Barcelona as well as Geneva. This amounts to saying, once again, that the number of holes is best anticipated when they are cut from the intersection ($=$ one corner of the folded paper) than when they are cut from the middle of the folds.

Here we have all the elements of the problem. On the one hand, the most frequent error, in the case of anticipation of the number of holes, is to anticipate one hole only because only one appears to be cut out from the folded sheet. The cases where a piece is cut from the intersection thus have the advantage because the result is fewer holes. On the other hand, when the piece is cut at the intersections, that is, at the corner of the folded paper where there are the most folds, the subject only needs to observe that this is so in order to be able to locate the holes correctly on the unfolded sheets. This usually leads the subject to give a single point for G (fairly good success rate), and two or three points for J (though the symmetry helps the subject in favouring two).

If these factors are accepted the order of the successes and their evolution with age in Tables 107 and 108 are sufficiently well explained, with the exception of a fairly frequent drop in the results at about 10 to 11 years in the situations without learning. But, it quite often happens that the level of the hypothetico–deductive operations the subjects err on the side of reasoning as a result of the new operational possibilities, and look for difficulties where there are none (for example, three to five holes instead of two for F and G, or a single hole with four side-branches, etc.).

However, the correct law determining the number of holes was discovered at 10 years by 20 per cent of the subjects both in the cases where the holes were cut from the centre of the crease and in those where they were cut from the intersections, and at 11 to 15 years by 28·5 per cent for the former and by 35·5 per cent for the latter situation. The other subjects, from 8 years on, thought they had discovered a law which consisted in anticipating a number of holes equal to the number of folds, equal to $n - 1$, to $n + 1$ folds, or to $n + 2$ and so on up to $n + 4$ folds. It is not until 9 years that the child makes any attempt to formulate multiplicative rather than additive laws, and at first he sticks at multiplying the number of folds by two.

All things considered, then, it seems that the anticipatory image in play in the tests examined in this section is formed, as before, in interdependence with the operations. However, one does see that the link between them may be more complex than in the earlier instances. If the anticipatory image requires the operational processes in order to be formed, may it not be that the operations in turn draw on the image here more than elsewhere in order to function? This is the question we now have to consider.

7. Conclusion

At the close of the previous chapter we asked what might be the role of the image at the operational level, when states are subordinate to transformations, and the figurative aspect of thought to the operative aspect. The fold experiments whose results we have just examined provide a ready answer – an answer which, although having reference to situations pertaining in particular to the present discussion, is true in general for any system of sequential transformations. In most of the situations we examined in order to assess the child's ability to comprehend and imagine transformations, we either considered one transformation only at a time (e.g. the change from arc to straight line) or more than one taken independently (for instance the tests in section 5 of this chapter, or in Chapter Eight, section 3 – change of shape of a ball of clay into a cylinder or disk, etc.). In these cases either the image governs the thought and results in operational non-conservation, or the reverse. If the latter is true, and the image is utilized simply to concretize ideas, then it is hard to see that it plays a necessary part at all. But in a succession of folds, such as those in Tables 105–108, we have a sequence of transformations, in which each one governs the following. This means that if a state $S(n)$ resulting from a transformation $T(n)$ is not known precisely enough, there can be no comprehension of the state $S(n+1)$ or even of the transformation $T(n+1)$. Now it is here that the image plays a role which, from a heuristic point of view at least, is indispensable. There may indeed be some abstract minds which, given a definition of the folds, can, by purely operational mental manœuvres, discover the requisite law without using an image. But one would still have to prove that their operational intuition is not supported by any prior imaginal symbolism – even if this is only a matter of indirect analogy. For the average unspecialized subject the image is necessary as an instrument in the representation of states, and in turn such representation is necessary for the comprehension of transformations.

The paradoxical thing about Tables 107 and 108 is that some difficulty is still experienced at 11 to 15 years (and also in the adults), in spite of the fact that the transformations in question are quite simple, and that a reproductive image of them is easy to evoke once their results are perceived (Figures 37–38). The difficulty occurs then only in imagining transformations. In other words, it has nothing to do either with the operation as such or with the reproductive image.

Rather it is related to the peculiar co-ordination of images and operations that go to make up the anticipatory transformation image. It is enough to say that in such cases there is a functional necessity for the images to be supported by the operations and reciprocally (a functional necessity, and not a logical one, since the image, though serving discovery, is quite unable to demonstrate). Hence we see the image playing a positive role at the operational level, and not just during the preoperational stages.

But, if this is the case, does it mean we still have to think of the image as a symbol, as we have done hitherto? Or does it mean that in such instances the image becomes an element of thought as an objective copy of the real? It seems to us that one must adhere to the thesis that the nature of the image is symbolic. And there are three reasons for doing so. First, however accurate the image may be in these instances, it is still incapable of rendering the continuity of a transformation, and is confined to symbolizing this kind of continuum by means of a succession of a few significant stages (Bergson's 'cinematographic' process). Second, although the image serves to illustrate deductions or inferences, it does not provide any kind of demonstrative proof. Thus, within imaginal representation itself we need to distinguish between the image and what the image represents – namely, the play of concrete (spatial, physical, etc.) relations between objects. Now, since these aspects of imaginal representation cannot both in the same way be constituent elements of thought, the system of relations must consist of a collection of signifieds and the images of a collection of signifiers. This is our third reason for considering the image symbolic. But, we repeat, a symbol is a 'motivated' signifier: that is, it resembles its signified. The fact, therefore, that the image is essentially symbolic does not mean that the image at the operational level is not increasingly true (in the case of space) to the relations (spatial) that it symbolizes visually.

This chapter has also demonstrated for the particular areas under discussion the relationship between the formation of the operations and the formation of the anticipatory transformation images. First, there are certain fairly striking synchronisms. For example, in Table 101 the complete successes rise from 6 per cent to 80 per cent between 6 and 7 years, which is hard to explain unless the operations intervene. Second, comparing the different areas of investigation, we find that there is a striking difference between the successful anticipation of folds in the case of changes modifying or conserving relations of interiority and proximity, etc. (sections 1–3) and the anticipation of changes of form and dimension (section 4). While the former are feasible from 7 to 8 years (>75 per cent), the folding of straight lines in Table 102 shows only 16 per cent successes at 7 years for the drawing and 36 per cent for the selection methods. Now, it is evident that if the latter anticipations are much further behind, it is because they correspond to operations deriving simultaneously from a measurement system and the utilization of reference systems.

If we now compare the whole of the results for Chapters Three to Six from the point of view of the level of success, we find first of all that there is no essential difference between reproductive and anticipatory transformation images. Both presuppose the intervention of anticipation or re-anticipation, whether the situations to be imagined appear familiar to the child or not. Thus we find that the same is true for transformation images in general as for kinetic images. Further, we are now in a position to conclude that there is no appreciable difference between kinetic and transformation images, not only because we know that both involve anticipation, but also because we know that neither is formed until the emergence of the concrete operations. As these operations relate both to changes of position (displacements) and changes of form (transformations) the corresponding images will as a whole naturally correspond to a real unity. Briefly the only major distinction is between the static images, or straightforward reproductions at the preoperational level, and the anticipatory images supported by the operations and including all the various kinetic or transformational types.

It remains to distinguish within this large category of anticipatory images certain levels differing in virtue of the complexity of the content to be imagined. As we pointed out above, the emergence of these levels coincides with the appearance of the corresponding operations. However, this increasingly close correlation between the anticipatory image and the operations by no means implies that there is progressive identification of the two. The operations carry out the transformations; the image represents them. Now, the representation of an operation remains figurative, and does not merge with the operation itself. However faithful this representation may be, it is still no more than an imitation of the operation. In the same way an imitative gesture imitates an action without being identical with it. Between the image – even when it is promoted to the rank of anticipatory transformation image – and the corresponding cognitive structure, there is, in spite of their increasingly close collaboration, all the distance that separates the symbolizer from the thing symbolized.

228

CHAPTER SEVEN

Static Reproductive Images and Action

If one accepts the view that the image results from active internalized imitation, and not from prolongation of perception (although it may be the occasion of re-afference or re-stimulation), then it is valuable to attempt to state precisely what relationship exists between the image and action. If kinetic images proceed from internalized imitation of a movement, and transformation images from the imitation of an operation, it goes without saying that such images are closely dependent upon action, and there is no point in concerning ourselves further with this. But is the same true of simple static reproductive images? This is the problem we now have to examine.

Our earlier treatment of static reproductive images was only brief, and was mainly concerned with the fore-image as involved in direct copies (Chapter Two). It is all the more important, therefore, to look further into the question. The difficulty is that the problem of reproductive images runs into the problem of memory, which is outside the very limited scope of the present work. But, although the question of the retention of the memory-image in time is outside our range here, the question of its formation and evocation after a short interval does concern us. Our particular concern is with the relationship between the formation of the reproductive image and action.

We all know that we discover and remember the lay-out of a strange town much better if we walk about in it on our own, and remain responsible for our own wrong turnings, rather than rely on a friend to show the way, although the perceptual data is comparable in both cases. The whole 'active' education theory rests on the hypothesis that a child will register the result of an experiment better if he carries it out for himself (so that it is an experiment – or experience – in the widest sense) than if he merely watched someone else perform it. Situations of this type differ from one term of the pair to the other, with respect both to affective motivation and cognitive structuration. However, in spite of their complexity, these were the sort of situations that inspired the investigations about to be described.

The general problem is this. Is the image of configurations, including static configurations, differently constituted according to the subject's role in the situation? That is, how is it constituted when the configuration is simply perceived by the subject as constructed by another person? And does it differ from the image formed when the subject constructs the configuration himself, either on the basis of a given model or (for the sake of comparison) as a free and spontaneous action? We shall take the simplest situations possible: those in which the three or four possibilities just mentioned are present. The only variables will then be the degree, or forms, of action, other factors being kept as far as possible constant.

We must now state the problem more precisely. It is not a question of directly verifying the hypothesis that the image is a product of internalized imitation, since each of the four modes of formation just given may include an element of imitation. To begin at the end of the list, if the subject spontaneously constructs a configuration and then reproduces it, his reproduction (which alone enables us to check production and fidelity of the image) constitutes a 'self-imitation', or imitation of the subject's own activity. If the subject begins by constructing his own copy of a given model and then reproduces it, we have in turn imitation of the model, and 'self-imitation'. If the subject watches somebody else construct the model and reproduces it, then we have both imitation of another person, and imitation of the model. Finally, if the subject simply looks at the model and then reconstructs it, there are several possibilities, related in particular to age, and consequently tricky to interpret. These are as follows: (*a*) an experienced subject may recognize in a particular model an analogue of already known structures, and may therefore assimilate the perceived datum immediately to possible action schemes – which means an element of self-imitation; (*b*) even if this condition is not fulfilled the subject may engage in active oculo-motor exploration – which, as Claparède has already pointed out, involves a kind of imitation of the object's contours, so that the resultant image would thus also be imitative; (*c*) finally, in the younger subjects, perception may remain more passive or 'syncretic', that is, without analytic activity, etc. This is the only case where imitation can be considered to be reduced to a minimum and the image to be affected accordingly.

The following investigations will not resolve the question whether the image does or does not derive from internalized imitation. They merely go some way towards establishing whether the degree of imaginal precision depends on the modes of the subject's activity. Nevertheless, it may be possible to shed some light – diffuse though it may be – on this essential point. And if so, it goes without saying that we may have an indirect means of defining the precise mode of imitation involved in the formation of the images linked with the activities in question.

1. *The formation of the image of an assemblage of cubes*[1]

The models to be reproduced in this inquiry are assemblages of cubes: *E* and *F* for children aged 4 to 6 years and *E'* and *F'* for those above. (See Figure 39. The figures refer to the number of blocks

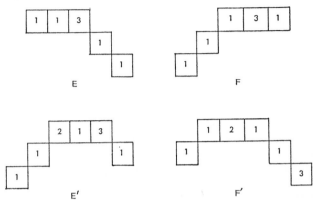

FIG. 39

piled vertically.) The images are not assessed as hitherto by means of a drawing, gesture or verbal description, but by reconstruction. This raises a minimum of motor or representational difficulties (for positions and numbers) if the retained image is accurate. It also enables us to make an approximate estimation as to the adequacy of the static reproductive image. But in dealing with the formation of the image three possibilities are open, with a fourth that is useful for control purposes. These are as follows:

(1) *Simple perception:* the child is limited to a given time (20 seconds) in which to perceive the model; the model is then removed and the subject has to reconstruct it.

(2) *Child's own action:* the child copies the model as he perceives it; copy and model are taken away and the child is asked for a reproduction.

(3) *Perception of action by others:* the experimenter constructs the model in front of the child (in 20 seconds, as in 1), and removes it as soon as completed, so that there is no time for a detailed perceptual exploration of the result (as there is in 1); the child then has to reconstruct it.

[1] Inquiry carried out with Françoise Frank, Joan Bliss, M. Levret, and L. Pecsi.

(4) *Free action:* the child is asked to invent a model, limiting himself to the given number of cubes; as in 3, the model is removed as soon as it is finished, and the child has to reproduce it.

I. We shall represent these different situations thus: *SP* (1), *CA* (2), *PA* (3), and *FA* (4). By comparing them we hope to obtain information about the relationship between the subject's mode of action and the formation of a more or less accurate image. In cases *FA* (4), *CA* (2), and even *PA* (3), the extent of the action involved is relatively easy to establish, but less easy, as we have already pointed out in the introduction to this chapter, in the case of simple perception *SP* (1). The only method here (and even this risks being inconclusive) is to analyse any changes in the relationship corresponding to age. Suppose, for instance, that *SP* yields lower results than *CA* in the smaller children, and equal or higher results in the older children. This would suggest that the subject's activity is modified in the meantime during perception itself, etc. But these are complex matters, and it is best to forge somewhat boldly ahead and analyse the facts collected carefully at a later stage, than to raise too many problems at the outset. Here then is the method we adopted.

The experiment was in two parts, I and II. All subjects were put through both parts: a group *A* in the order I–II, and a group *B* in the order II–I. A minimum of one week separated the two parts for the subjects aged 4 to 6 years, and two weeks for those aged 7 to 10 years (we eventually extended this latter interval to all subjects).

Part I. This was further subdivided into two stages: (I.1) *Simple perception* of model *E* (or *E'*) presented ready constructed. The child was asked to 'have a good look because afterwards we will take it away, and you will have to rebuild it'. We did our best to see that the child looked at the model for 20 seconds (but avoided clumsy turns of phrase suggesting obligation or boredom). Then we removed it and asked the subject to make it up again, offering him twenty blocks to do this. (I.2) *Perception of the experimenter's action.* The experimenter constructed model *F* (or *F'*) during 20 seconds. As soon as the last block was in place, the model was removed and the child was asked to reconstruct it (with the same instructions given at the beginning and with the twenty blocks).

Part II. (II.1) *Simple perception* of the model *F* (or *F'*) under the same conditions as model *E* in Part I.1, with reconstruction after 20 seconds. (II.2) *Action by child*[2] on *E* (or *E'*): model *E* was shown ready constructed and the child copied it. The copy and the model were then taken away and the child was asked to reproduce them from memory. (II.3) *Free action:* seven or nine blocks were shown to the child (seven at 4 to 6 years and nine at 7 to 10 years), and he was asked to construct some-

---

[2] Almost all the subjects aged 4 to 6 years began with II.2, going on to II.1, and then to II.3.

thing new for himself. As far as possible simple alignments of the blocks were not accepted. 'Make something like we made before, but something new.' As soon as the last block had been put in place the whole construction was removed. The child was then requested to reproduce it exactly.

Seven subjects aged 4 years, twenty-six aged 5, twelve aged 6, twelve aged 7, twelve aged 8 and fourteen aged 9 to 10 years were examined. The main difficulty in drawing up the results resides in the classification of the errors. Let us start, therefore, by getting a clear idea of the types of reaction and their classification:

(1) Negative reaction or simple alignment (horizontal, sagittal or diagonal).

(2) Height only: the blocks are piled on top of one another.

(3) Global form: the child retains the fact that some blocks are placed in a straight line, others diagonally and others vertically, but the structure is incorrect. In this category we include those subjects who make more than two errors of position, orientation or number, and those who reproduce the arrangement of the base blocks, but extend the vertical blocks in the horizontal, thus altering the overall structure.

(4) Orientation: the construction is correct, except for an orientation error involving one or more blocks. For example, the diagonal blocks may be replaced with a horizontal row attached to the lower free angle of the last block in the initial row.

(5) Number: the construction is correct in shape, but one or more blocks are omitted or added.

(6) Position: the construction is correct except that the vertical stack of blocks is in the wrong position.

(7) Completely correct construction.

II. We can now without contrivance classify the reactions into three groups: (a) errors 1–3; (b) errors 4–6; (c) correct constructions. Several errors may concur: the construction is then classed under a, if there are errors of types 2 and 3 as well as errors of number, orientation or position. Once this is established it is easy enough to determine whether a construction is reproduced better after simple perception (SP) or after constructive activity on the part of the subject (CA). Type b is considered correct as against type a, and type c as against type b or a. Table 109 sets forth the results of these comparisons.

In group A, where simple perception SP comes one or two weeks before CA, we find that the latter yields results more than five times higher between 4 and 7 years. At 8 to 9 years the responses equalize (nine subjects CA > SP, and ten subjects the reverse). This is no doubt because visual perception at this age is more immediately translatable into terms of action, as is shown by the group B results.

TABLE 109 *Comparing the reproductions (models E and E') after simple perception (SP) and after activity (CA)*
(As % of the responses)

	Group A (SP→CA)		
	SP = CA	*CA > SP*	*SP > CA*
4–5 years ($N = 28$)	32	64·5	3·5
6–7 years ($N = 19$)	31·5	58	10·5
8–9 years ($N = 37$)	48·5	24·5	27
	Group B (CA→SP)		
	SP = CA	*CA > SP*	*SP > CA*
4–5 years ($N = 28$)	73	13·5	13·5
6–7 years ($N = 19$)	61	23·5	15·5
8–9 years ($N = 37$)	40·5	8·2	51·3

(=) same level as
(>) better than

In this group, where activity *CA* precedes *SP* by one or two weeks, the results tend to converge between 4 and 7 years (high proportion of *CA = SP*, and *SP > CA* almost as high as the reverse). But at 8 to 9 years perception *SP* is a long way ahead of *CA* – which is the opposite of group *A* where *CA* and *SP* are fairly equal.

Both groups of results are instructive. They probably evince interference between learning effects and the effects of the predominance of activity. Here learning is not, as it often is elsewhere, a secondary factor that disturbs the principal effect, or is extraneous to it. Rather, it prolongs this effect and provides essential information about it. In group *A* it might be argued that the initial simple perception *SP* (first session) reinforces the reproductive activity *CA* (final session). This may well be the case. But the result is then a massive majority of *CA > SP* compared with the reverse, and even with the cases of equivalence *CA = SP*, that is, the active construction by the child leads to an image superior to that resulting from simple perception.[3] In group *B*, on the other hand, previous constructive activity (*CA*) (first session) improves the effects of the subsequent simple perception (*SP*). But how does this improvement come about? The

[3] It could be objected that the average length of time for constructions is longer than the 20 seconds for *SP*: at 4 years it was 28·4 s., at 5 years 36·4 s., at 7 years 35·6 s., and at 9 to 10 years 33·7 s. But it would have been impossible to make the time for *SP* longer, as after 15 seconds the subject hardly looks at the model, whereas the advantage of *CA* is that it induces the subject to look more carefully.

child has already constructed a similar model on his own. Consequently his perceptual exploration of the model is more active than the simple perception (*SP*) of a group *A* subject, and is carried on in terms of blocks to be manipulated according to certain perceptual and motor combinations. Thus the reproductive results of perception *SP* improve, but not beyond the effects *CA*, since the reproductions equalize and do not simply reverse the group *A* percentages. In other words the learning effect speaks in favour of the action effects *CA*, which modify and improve the power of perception *SP*: it does not, therefore, constitute a disturbing or inhibitory factor which would have adversely affected the *CA* results to the advantage of *SP*.

It is then worth examining more closely the effects of learning and of development with age. Let us begin by comparing the results of simple perception *SP* for models *E* and *E'*, those for *F* and *F'*, and the results of the child's reproductive activity *CA*. We will be concerned this time with complete successes – reaction 7, or type *c*, and not with partial progress. The responses of groups *A* and *B* will be taken together, that is to say, we will not take into account the I–II or II–I order involving learning effects (Table 110).

TABLE 110 *Complete successes (c) for reproductions after perception (SP) of models E, and E' and F, F', and after activity (CA) bearing on models E, E'*
(As % of the responses)

	4 years	5 years	6 years	7 years	8 years	9–10 years
SP for *F, F'*	0	39	45	8	8	43
SP for *E, E'*	29	31	50	50	42	42
CA for *E, E'*	72	85	75	75	67	72

Two important facts stand out:

(1) Whether activity *CA* promotes perceptions *SP* for models *E* (4 to 6 years) and *E'* (7 to 10 years) or whether the reverse, the successes after action are on average always higher than after simple perception, in ratios of between 3:2 and more than 2:1.

(2) Models *E* and *F* (4 to 6 years) or *E'* and *F'* (7 to 10 years) are comparable as far as reproduction difficulties are concerned (see Figure 39). But the success rate for *E* and *E'* is on average higher than for *F* and *F'*. The difference is due to the fact that some of the reproductions after *SP* for *E* and *E'* are promoted by the learning effect resulting from action by the subjects *CA*. On the other hand, reproductions after *SP* for *F* and *F'* can only be influenced by perception of the experimenter's action *PA*, without copy activity on the part of the subject *CA*. We shall return to this point later.

Before we move on to the *PA* effects, however, let us first look more closely at the *SP* effects for *E*, *E′* and *F*, *F′*. Table 111 gives the necessary details. The reactions to models *E*, *E′* and *F*, *F′* are compared in terms of the types *a* (errors 1–3), *b* (errors 4–6) and *c* (complete success), which are further classified in terms of subject groups *A* (order I–II), *B* (order II–I), or both together.

TABLE 111   *Reproductions after simple perception (SP) of models E and E′* (As % of the responses)

Types	Group A			Group B		
	a	*b*	*c*	*a*	*b*	*c*
SP of *E* and *E′*:						
4–5 years (*N*=28 and 22)	44	42	14	5	31	64
6–7 years (*N*=19 and 13)	37	26	37	0	30	70
8–9 years (*N*=37 and 37)	5·5	54	40·5	0	16	84
SP of *F* and *F′*:						
4–5 years (25 and 19)	20	52	28	36	26	38
6–7 years (19 and 12)	26	47	27	25	42	33
8–9 years (37 and 37)	11	48	41	16	32	52

Comparison of groups *A* and *B* clearly shows a learning effect in the case of models *E* and *E′*, due to the preceding action by the subject *CA* in group *B*. In group *A* perception *SP* does not have this advantage. The results for *F* and *F′* are more or less equal in both groups. Now, if the reproductions after *SP* of *F* and *F′* were improved by learning based on perception of the experimenter's action (*PA*), then one would expect them to be more successful in group *A* (second week). But this is not the case. Type *c* successes are even slightly higher in group *B*, as if the sight of the adult hindered the child's direct perception (see below, Table 113)!

There is no point in giving a more detailed analysis of the reproductions after *CA* than we have already given in Tables 109 and 110. These reproductions do not develop with age (see Table 110 *CA* for *E* and *E′*), nor do they show any clear-cut learning effects from perception *SP*, though there is an exception to this at 6 years, when type *a–c* reactions are respectively 0 per cent, 40 per cent and 60 per cent for group *B* (first week), and 0 per cent, 14 per cent and 86 per cent for group *A* (second week).

III. Let us now examine more closely the reproductions of models *F* and *F′* after perception *SP* and after perception of action by the experimenter *PA*. A global comparison (groups *A* and *B*) of these two kinds of reproduction is given in Table 112.

236

TABLE 112 *Complete successes (type c) after simple perception (SP) and after perception of the experimenter's activity (PA) bearing on models F and F'*
(As % of the responses)

	4 years (F)	5 years (F)	6 years (F)	7 years (F')	8 years (F')	9–10 years (F')
SP	0	39	45	8	8	43
PA	0	7	36	8	16	29

Table 113 is a detailed comparison along the lines of Table 109.

TABLE 113 *Comparing reproductions after simple perception (SP) and after perception of the experimenter's activity (PA)*
(As % of the subjects)

	Group A		
	SP = PA	*PA > SP*	*SP > PA*
4–5 years (14 and 11)	35·7	14·3	50·0
6–7 years (13 and 10)	30·8	23·1	46·1
8–10 years (16 and 10)	25·0	6·3	68·7

	Group B		
	SP = PA	*PA > SP*	*SP > PA*
4–5 years (14 and 11)	27·3	27·3	45·4
6–7 years (13 and 10)	20·0	40·0	40·0
8–10 years (16 and 10)	50·0	30·0	20·0

(=) same level as
(>) better than

The results of these two tables converge exactly. Without the partial learning due to the subjects' own action *CA*, reproduction of models *F* and *F'* (after *SP*) is inferior to that of models *E* and *E'* (cf. Table 110); but reproduction of the same models *F* and *F'* after perception of their construction by the experimenter (*PA*) is even lower. This simply means that it is easier to retain the end product of a process of construction than to retain the process itself. This is obvious enough when the model is external to the subject. But when an imitation relates to the subject's own body, the contrary is the case. Irène Lézine has shown that young children are able to imitate a movement (for example, the placing of a forefinger on the forehead) more easily than the result of the process. This is not so for the external models F and F' in the present case: if the subject perceives only the process (the activity of another person), he does not have the same view of the model as a whole that he has if he perceives the resultant construction.

It is all the more interesting, therefore, to note that in the case of CA, where perception both of the result (the model to be copied) and of the process of personal action (CA) are involved, the latter factor considerably improves the perception of the result (SP: Table 109).

But in spite of the relatively weak effect of PA, one finds in fact that perception of the action as performed by another person, not only progresses with age (Table 112, allowing for the difference in difficulty between models F and F'), but also gives rise to some learning effect. Thus the result $PA > SP$ is higher in the second session (group B), whereas the predominant $SP > PA$ percentages diminish from group A to group B. But, contrary to what is the case for $SP - CA$ relationships, it is the result for PA that is improved by simple perception (SP), and not the reverse. In other words, test PA yields better results in the second week, because perception of action by another person has been improved by the preceding perception of the result (first week). In the case of CA, on the other hand, it is precisely the subject's own action that improves perception SP from one week to the next. This interesting effect comes out even more clearly in Table 114.

TABLE 114　*Reproduction after perception of the experimenter's activity* (PA) *bearing on models F and F'*
(As % of the responses)

Types	Group A			Group B			Group A + B		
	a	b	c	a	b	c	a	b	c
4　years	75	25	0	33	67	0	57	43	0
5　years	40	47	13	18	81	0	31	62	7
6　years	43	43	14	0	25	75	26	36	36
7　years	50	33	17	17	83	0	33	58	8
8　years	25	62	13	25	50	25	25	58	16
9–10 years	50	50	0	0	33	67	29	42	29

There is a small degree of learning in almost all instances between the first (group A) and second week (B). This confirms the difference between the reactions to PA and the reactions to CA which show no comparable effect based on simple perception SP.

IV. It remains to compare the results of personal action (CA) with those of free action (FA). The results for the latter are contained in

Table 115 (it will be remembered that the 4- to 6-year-old subjects have seven cubes only, while the 7- to 10-year-olds have to arrange nine cubes).

TABLE 115 *Reproduction of a spontaneous model after free activity (FA)* (As % of the responses; groups *A* and *B* combined)

	4 years	5 years	6 years	7 years	8 years	9–10 years
Type *a*	28	11	0	8	17	21
Type *b*	57	50	17	50	50	43
Type *c* (success)	14	38	83	42	33	36

The drop in the successes between 7 and 10 years is not simply due to the fact that nine blocks are being used, but to the fact that the subjects produce increasingly complex constructions which are less easy to reproduce from memory.

Thus, apart from an exceptional average success at 6 years (seven blocks), the results obtained here are systematically less good than when the subject's activity is purely reproductive (*CA*) (cf. Table 110, *CA* for *E* and *E'*). This is not at all surprising as the spontaneous construction is taken away by the experimenter as soon as it is finished. There is thus no overall perception of the final product, whereas in the *CA* tests the model to be copied remains throughout where the child can see it. This phenomenon is comparable to what we found in III (Tables 112–114): it is easier to reproduce a model if the subject perceives it as a whole than if he only perceives the process of construction in its successive stages.

But if we compare now *c* (complete successes) in Table 115 with the last column (type *c*, groups *A* and *B*) in Table 114, one sees that the *FA* results are two to five times better than the *PA* results: 0–36 for the latter, and 14–83 per cent for the former. This underlines once again, and conclusively, the prime importance of personal activity. The 'active' school is not wrong, therefore, in its assumption that a pupil retains something he has discovered for himself much better than something he has seen from experiments performed for him, or *a fortiori* from lessons in the form of lectures in which he is all too often steeped, when he should be allowed to work on his own with a minimum amount of discreet direction.

2. *The image of a row of coloured surfaces*[4]

The last experiment concerned entirely homogeneous cubes. But what would be the position if we used differently shaped and coloured

[4] With the collaboration of Tuât Vinh-Bang.

surfaces, presented in an arbitrary series with only rudimentary symmetry? (See Figure 40.) The same model is used for reconstruc-

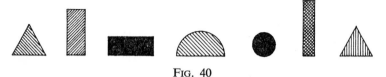

FIG. 40

tion after perception (*SP*) as for reconstruction after a preliminary copied construction by the child (*CA*). There is a fortnight's interval between the two sessions. The model is placed beneath a screen, and the child is told that he will have to look carefully at, or copy, what he is about to be shown, so that he will be able to reproduce it from memory afterwards. He is given 30 seconds for both these tasks, and provided with twenty-one distinct shapes from which to reconstruct the model.

We classified the subjects' reconstructions into four types: (*a*) omissions, inversions, additions; (*b*) correct figures (allowing one omission) but with changed order; (*c*) one mistake (colour, omission or inversion of two neighbouring elements); (*d*) correct. See Table 116 (seventy subjects).

TABLE 116   *Reconstructions after simple perception (SP) and after active copy (CA)*

	Simple perception (SP)											
	1st Session				2nd Session				Together			
	a	*b*	*c*	*d*	*a*	*b*	*c*	*d*	*a*	*b*	*c*	*d*
4 years	25	0	75	0	70	29	0	0	55	18	27	0
5 years	70	20	10	0	54	27	19	0	62	24	14	0
6 years	30	40	30	0	25	25	50	0	27	34	39	0
7 years	27	18	54	0	22	44	33	0	25	30	45	0

	Active copy (CA)											
	1st Session				2nd Session				Together			
	a	*b*	*c*	*d*	*a*	*b*	*c*	*d*	*a*	*b*	*c*	*d*
4 years	57	14	29	0	25	0	75	0	45	10	45	0
5 years	36	19	45	0	50	0	40	10	42	10	42	5
6 years	50	12·5	12·5	25	40	20	30	10	43	17	22	17
7 years	11	33	33	22	9	36	27	27	10	35	30	25

The first thing to note is that there are hardly any learning effects, although the same configuration is used in both sessions: learning affects the active copy slightly at 4 years (errors *a*, *b* give way to *c*), but the reverse effect is found in the case of simple perception; slight, equally variable effects are found at 5 to 7 years.

The low value of these learning effects, compared with those in the preceding investigation, corresponds to a less marked difference between the reconstructions done after active copying and those done after simple perception. The former yields some completely correct results (*d*), while the second yields none at all. Column *c* suggests a similar kind of divergence. If we analyse the difference in terms of the subject percentages we find the following (see Table 117).

TABLE 117   *Superior results for active copy (CA > SP) or for simple percep-tion (SP > CA)*

	4 years	5 years	6 years	7 years
CA > SP	36	48	33	50
SP > CA	27	19	44	19
CA = SP	37	33	23	31

The absence of any great difference between the two procedures of image formation can be explained in two ways. One possible factor is that the active structuration elicited by the given configuration is less good than in the case of Figure 39 – if by active structuration we understand not the action of a good perceptual form, but the estab-lishing of relationships bringing out the peculiarities of the model (such as the asymmetry both in the plane and the vertical of Figure 39). And in fact complete successes (*d*) are far less frequent in Table 116 than in Table 117: this being so, there would naturally be a diminution of the difference between the results for the copy and those for the perception. The second possible factor is that simple perception yields better results here than in the case of the cubes in section 1. The reason for this may be strictly perceptual (rudimentary symmetry of the two end triangles and the two vertical bars next to the ends). Or it may be that at the outset perception induces assimila-tion to schemes of action involving the first factor mentioned above. Now this second possibility is excluded for reasons already adduced. As for the first, the presented row of figures does not constitute a good form; the rough symmetry is involved hardly at all in *a* and *b* reconstructions; and, more especially, the absence of complete success (*d*) in the perceptual method shows that there are scarcely any strictly perceptual pregnances. We can thus with a fair degree of probability attribute the lower *CA > SP* effect, and indeed the lower learning effect (compared with those of section 1), to weaker intervention of the active structurations as defined above.

3. *The image of five squares arranged in order of size*

The cube experiment (section 1) showed a fairly clear-cut difference between the effect of simple perception and the effects of imitative activity in the formation of the reproductive image. The figures arranged in arbitrary order (section 2), on the other hand, gave a low result for this. It is necessary, therefore, to go on to examine assemblages which are better structured than the two preceding and which even call for an operational seriation principle. As the image of a number of squares ordered in a straight line would have been too easy for the subject to retain, we decided to use a series of superimposed squares. We made this more complex by introducing two extra, arbitrary factors: different colours for each position in the series, and central or off-central arrangement. The experiment was carried out with G. Voyat.

We used cardboard squares with sides of 5, 4, 3, 2, 5 and 2 cm, with a hole in their centres or in one of their corners. There were two tests. The first (*A*) involved five differently-coloured superimposed squares. The smallest was on top, and a vertical axis (a nail) ran through the holes (Figure 41 *A*), which were in the centre. In the second (*B*) all the squares were red. The first two were placed centrally and the other three off-centre, in order of size (Figure 41 *B*). To reconstruct the model the child had at his disposal thirty squares in the five different sizes, each size coming in six different colours – brown, black, blue, yellow, green (test *A*) and red (test *B*).

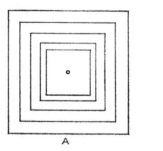 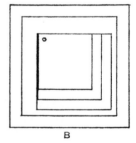

A   B

FIG. 41

The subjects were divided into four groups for four different procedures. The experiment began either with simple perception of the model or with an active copy prior to reproduction from memory, and involved either apparatus *A* or apparatus *B*.

Group One. In the first session the child looked at series *A* for 20 seconds. The model was then taken to pieces and the child was requested to reconstruct it. A fortnight later he was shown the same series, and asked to make a direct copy. The model and the copy were then dismantled and the subject was required to reconstruct the latter.

Group Two. Same procedure the other way round, with active copy at the first session and simple perception a fortnight later.

Group Three. As group one, but using apparatus *B*.

Group Four. As group two, but using apparatus *B*.

Further, at the second session, when the subject had completed his construction, he was always asked to repeat it in the inverse order (ascending if the first was descending, etc.).

One hundred and twenty subjects aged 4 to 9 years were examined in this way, in age groups of twenty. Tests *A* and *B* yielded exactly the same results (with variations of 0 per cent to 5 per cent and a maximum divergence of 10 per cent at 9 years). This means we may take them together and concentrate on the essential point – the order of the two kinds of reproduction, namely reproduction after simple perception at the first session (I) or at the second (II) or after the child's own action in (I) and (II). In the results below (Table 118) we make a further distinction between the child's initial and his final, spontaneously corrected reproduction, which is the only version he himself finds satisfactory (first-time successes are bracketed).

TABLE 118 *Total results for tests A and B*
(Initial results given in brackets)
(As % of the responses)

	4 years	5 years	6 years	7 years	8 years	9 years	Average
Perc. I	0 (0)	0 (10)	0 (0)	10 (10)	10 (10)	30 (20)	10 (6,6)
Act. I	10 (10)	20 (10)	10 (10)	60 (20)	40 (20)	70 (50)	35 (20)
Act. II	0 (0)	20 (20)	30 (30)	40 (40)	60 (50)	80 (70)	38 (35)
Perc. II	0 (0)	20 (20)	40 (30)	50 (50)	80 (70)	100 (100)	48 (45)

At the first session successes are higher after active copying at all ages, and in particular from 7 years, than after perception only. But most significant is the fact that the difference between the activity results in the first and those in the second session is slight. This means that when active copying is preceded a fortnight earlier by a simple perceptual inspection of the model (Perc. I), any learning effect ensuing is minimal compared with that given by direct copying (Act. I) without the reproduction after perception (Perc. I). But if we compare the successes after mere perception in the second session (Perc. II) with the corresponding successes for the first session, we find that there is considerable improvement; these improved results (Perc. II) are even higher than those for action in the second session (Act. II). This fact is instructive from two points of view.

In the first place, of course, it shows that the effect of learning produced by active copying at the first session (Act. I) on simple perception at the second is far stronger than that discussed above (for Perc. I, Act. II). In other words, the child has learnt to analyse the model by virtue of the fact that a fortnight beforehand he has executed a direct copy followed by a reproduction from memory. By simply looking at the model he is thus able to take in the constituent relations (here, seriation) in a more comprehensive way than if he had had no previous practice.

But the fact that success in reproduction of the model from memory is higher at the second session after simple perception than after active copy also deserves comment. It should be pointed out to begin with that this is only the case from 6 to 7 years upwards – at the beginning, that is, of the concrete-operational stage. Now what the subject has to do is discern in the model a seriation structure. We may therefore take it that if Perc. II after Act. I yields better results than the reverse (Act. II after Perc. I), the reason is that the 20 seconds of perceptual examination (Perc. II) then creates the possibility of simultaneously restructuring what has already been constructed step by step during the active copying. That is not to say, of course, that perception is in all cases superior to action. On the contrary, the initial perception (Perc. I) yields lower results than the initial action (10 as against 35 on average, whereas between Perc. II and Act. II we find 48 as against 38). After preliminary activity the overall perceptual examination of the model makes possible a synthesis and a simultaneous apprehension which constitutes a positive supplementary factor, but which is dependent for its effectiveness precisely on this previous activity.

In fact, if we examine the different kinds of error affecting the serial order, the colours, the central or off-central position of the squares, and the number of the squares, then we find (it is not necessary to give a detailed table here) that the latter kind of error diminishes more or less regularly with age. On the other hand, the reactions to the seriation are of some significance. In Perc. I seriation is observed by only 10–35 per cent of the subjects up to 8 years inclusively (at 9 years 70 per cent). In Act. I, however, there is a sudden jump from 20–30 per cent to 60–85 per cent from 7 years, and in Act II, and especially in Perc. II, a rise to above 50 per cent from 6 years and 70 per cent from 7 years. It is, then, the serial aspect of the model that is established by the child's own activity at the operational level and observed in simple perception at the second session – though not at the first session until 9 years. This is the more remarkable as we systematically included in the test a reproduction in reverse order, and as the subjects who succeeded with the first order also succeeded with the second.

4. *The image of an assemblage of heterogeneous surfaces and volumes*

The following investigation (carried out with D. Nicollier) is concerned primarily with collections of figures devoid of regular relations and everyday meanings (Figure 42). The subject was required

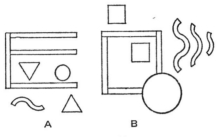

A   B

FIG. 42

either to look at them or to copy them, taking as long as he liked in both cases. To make the copy the child was presented with a collection of cardboard shapes greater in number and variety than was actually necessary. He was finally asked to recontruct the model from memory using the same method.[5] About half the subjects did the *SP* test, perception and reconstruction, at the first session, and the *CA* test, active construction and reconstruction, a fortnight later. The others were put through these tests in the reverse order.

The subjects' reactions fall into four types: (*a*) no memory, or pure invention; (*b*) some elements of the figure, but without correct relations; (*c*) all elements but one, or one element turned round; (*d*) correct figure.

Using twenty-three subjects aged 5 to 6 years the results were as in Table 119, overleaf.

This table, unlike Table 116, shows a relatively clear-cut learning effect in simple perception *SP* at the second session under the influence of the active copy at the first session, and also in the active copy (second session) under the influence of the previous perception.

Possibly related to the fact that learning is better here than in section 2 is the greater difference observable between reconstructions carried out after active copy and reconstructions carried out after simple perception: 41 per cent and 42 per cent of type *c* and *d* for *CA* as against 19 per cent and 17 per cent for *SP*, and 0 per cent and 17 per cent of the inferior types *a* and *b* for *CA* as against 14 per cent and 50 per cent for *SP*. The reason for this greater difference between

[5] The subject was told in advance that he would be asked to do a reconstruction from memory afterwards.

TABLE 119 *Reactions a–d to reconstruction after simple perception (SP) and after a previous construction (CA)* (As % of the subjects)

	SP				CA			
	a	*b*	*c*	*d*	*a*	*b*	*c*	*d*
Figure *A*:								
1st Session	23	54	8	15	0	10	60	30
2nd Session	0	44	33	22	0	28	14	58
Together	14	50	19	17	0	17	41	42
Figure *B*								
1st Session								
2nd Session								
Together	0	50	33	16	0	0	0	100

CA and *SP* would appear to be that the configurations of Figure 42 give what we have termed active structuration much more to get hold of than the configurations of Figure 40. They are not 'good forms'; but they are figures in which the asymmetric elements are, with a little effort, easy to situate in relation to an overall framework of partial symmetry.

But there is only one assemblage of shapes for a double experiment: that is to say, the same shapes appear at the second session as appeared in the first, and are used both for the reproductions after direct copy and for the reproductions after simple perception. It might therefore be argued that it is natural and necessary that a copy from memory after a direct copy should be better than after perception alone. In the first case perception is involved to an equal extent; but there is also the motor memory of the movements in copying the model direct. It is true that together these two factors make it plain that an improved result is highly probable. But things are not as simple as that. For the subject knows in advance that he is to produce a reconstruction from memory, and it could well be that during the simple perception he assimilates what he sees to action schemes – in other words, that he perceives the model from the outset in terms of movements to be carried out. Pierre Janet said that to perceive an armchair is to see an object in which one is about to sit. And V. Weizsäcker likewise held that when a 'real' house is perceived, it is not the house that enters the subject's eye, but the subject who gets ready to enter the perceived object. It is not all that self-evident, therefore, that the reconstruction of the assemblages after active copying should be better than reconstruction after perception alone and two facts show this.

First, there is the difference between the results for *CA* and for *SP* in the preceding experiments (sections 1–3, and the present section 4). We need not dwell on this. But the second fact is more instructive. There are cases in which no difference is observable at all between the reconstructions after active copy *CA* and the reconstructions after simple perception *SP*.

So let us now take a look at one of these cases investigated with D. Nicollier. We used a collection of differently-shaped volumes joined together by metal rods (Figure 43), and taken from a well-known children's game ('Matador').

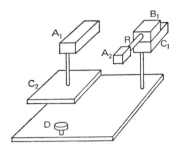

FIG. 43

Without having any particular signification (although one of the subjects did call it a 'mill'), the model in a general way induces much more active (and much longer) construction than those preceding. It is of particular interest to describe this example, because the reconstructions done after simple perception are just as good as those done after direct copying. And that in spite of the different impression periods: 4 minutes (3' 55", to be exact) for the copy, whereas we got no attentive perception after 20 to 30 seconds.

We did not, therefore, fix any time limit for the tests. There was an interval of a fortnight between the first and second sessions, and the procedure was as before. We examined twenty-five subjects aged 7 to 10 years in two groups, one for the order *CA–SP*, the other for the reverse order. We were able to base our figures on the fact that the different parts of the construction (*A*1, *A*2, *B*1, etc., Figure 43) give rise to distinct success scores that are very similar after *CA* and after *SP* – which makes it possible to weight them and derive from them a relatively objective evaluation of the reactions.

That said, out of twenty-five subjects ten gave better reconstructions after direct copying *CA*, thirteen after simple perception *SP*, and two gave equivalent reconstructions. But if we take the average of the results after *CA* and after *SP* for the same twenty-five (the order being reversed for thirteen of them), then we have a weighted success score of 61·2 per cent after direct copying (average of individual scores), and 60·0 per cent after simple perception – which is strictly equivalent.

247

But the equivalence of the two different kinds of reconstruction (a fortnight apart, it must be remembered) comes out even more strikingly when we examine the separate successes for each part of the construction (see Table 120).

TABLE 120   *Successes[6] based on correct choice of blocks*
(Neglected blocks given in brackets)
(As % of the responses)

	A1	A2	B1	C1
After *CA*	76 (12)	88 (12)	28 (28)	44 (8)
After *SP*	56 (32)	68 (20)	40 (28)	56 (20)

	C2	D	R	General averages
After *CA*	72 (16)	76 (24)	92 (0)	68·0 (14·3)
After *SP*	68 (16)	80 (12)	88 (4)	65·1 (18·9)

The general averages were the same. If the two sets of results are expressed graphically, the curves have the same peaks at *A2* and *R*, and the same minimum at *B1*. The two types of construction are thus very similar.

But beneath this similarity between the individual score averages (61·2 per cent and 60·0 per cent) and the average reactions for the separate parts of the construction (68·0 per cent and 65·1 per cent) lies hidden an essential fact which will give us the key to this surprising convergence. This fact is expressed in Table 121.

TABLE 121   *Averages of the scores (based on blocks employed or not employed) in the 1st and 2nd sessions*

	1st Session	2nd Session	Difference
Direct copy	51.4	69.2	17.8/51.4 = 34.6%
Simple perception	44.0	80.4	36.4/44.0 = 82.7%

Perception improves the initial result of the direct copies (51·4) by 34·6 per cent. The direct or active copy, on the other hand, improves the initial result of the perceptions (44·0) by 82·7 per cent. Furthermore, one sees that behind the deceptive general averages 61·2 for the direct copies and 60·0 for simple perception lay the crucial fact that the simple perception results are better than the direct copy results at the *second* session. But the reason why they are better is that they

[6] For twenty-five subjects aged 7 to 10 years.

have the advantage of learning due to CA in the first session, whereas the second session direct copy profits much less by the first session SP! In other words, learning in the direction $CA \rightarrow SP$ and in the direction $SP \rightarrow CA$ are not symmetrical, as we have seen already in sections 1 and 3. If there is some degree of learning in the direction $SP \rightarrow CA$, then it is only half as effective as the reverse.

We can see, therefore, why this test does not show the general average differences favouring the direct copies as previous tests did (sections 1–3, and present section). In discussing in section 2 the reasons for the differences between the results from one test to the next, we considered several possible factors. On the one hand, lack of opportunity for adequate active structuration would weaken the part played by direct copying. Or the perceptual 'reading' would be reinforced if the subject were dealing with pregnant structures, or if he were able to translate what he perceived (SP) immediately into action schemes. Now in the present instance it cannot possibly be argued that the configuration under consideration does not induce active structuring, since it involves varied, not previously known combinations, causing all possible relationships to be brought into play. This fact favours direct copying – and the importance of this mode of reproduction is the learning effects. If, in the last analysis, the results of the procedures CA and SP are equal, the reason is not that the action CA diminishes. It can only be that SP increases in strength. Now, Figure 43 contains no perceptually pregnant 'good forms'. On the other hand, the apparatus was known to the children from the game. One might have predicted, therefore, without Table 121, that perception of the model Figure 43 would be immediately assimilated to action schemes, and that it would produce results at the first session which would be almost as good as those for the direct copy. But we can learn more than this from Table 121. It shows that after a fortnight the effect of the active copy CA on SP is almost twice as high as that of SP on CA. The table thus gives tangible proof of the ability acquired by perception to assimilate the data to action schemes and thus to translate the visually perceived into terms of possible manipulation. (The facts indicate that this capacity is indeed an acquisition, or partly an acquisition.) It will perhaps be replied that perceptions intervene in the active copying CA – even for the duration of the average 4 minutes – and that these perceptions, converted into memory-images, reinforce the simple perception SP a fortnight later. But one must not overlook the fact that if the perceptions involved in CA are more effective than those we have qualified as 'simple' perceptions SP, the reason is not that they last 4 minutes rather than 20–30 seconds, since nothing is to be gained by lengthening the time for SP (in any case unrestricted). The reason is, in fact, that the perceptions involved in CA are framed in action from the outset, and thus belong to a general sensori-motor context, rather than to an exclusively oculo-motor one. The upshot of Table 121 is, then, that it is possible to transfer the sensori-motor schematism over a period of a fortnight to the subsequent 'simple' perception SP. At this point, it ceases to be 'simple' and acquires, from the moment of oculo-motor exploration,

249

the capacity of sketching in outline the action to follow. Thus it integrates oculo-motor activity in a more general sensori-motor activity.

It is not possible, therefore, to argue in favour of the exclusively perceptual origin of images by drawing on the superiority of the effects *SP* in the present experiment. In the first place, the facts show once again that all perceptions cannot be placed on one and the same plane. Some perceptions evidence more, some less perceptual activity, and, after the initial sensory contact, are accordingly more or less active or passive. Some perceptual activities, on the other hand, are to a greater or lesser extent integrated in more general sensori-motor, representational or operational activities. Let us turn to the image itself. Even if we accepted that first session 'simple' perceptions *SP* were prolonged as memory-images without reference to the subject's previous *actions* (and this is surely improbable in the light of the facts described in this chapter, always bearing in mind that they could have been foreseen in accordance with the most widespread and commonplace views on the subject), even then the fact would remain that the image prolongs not primary perception considered as sensory organization, but the perceptual activities considered as oculo-motor imitation of the object's contours. But, once the gap is bridged between the perceptual activities and the sensori-motor activities in general, the image appears not as a prolongation of, but as a copy or imitation of the perceptions – which is not the same thing; and, more widely still, it appears to be an internal imitation of the result of the actions in which the perceptions are incorporated. If in the second session (Table 121) the perceptions *SP* produce excellent reconstructions (80·4 per cent), this is in consequence of an extremely rich extra-perceptual contribution, the image retaining only its imitative or imitable aspects.

5. *The image of a simple configuration discriminated in a perceptually complex structure*[7]

I. Take the complex figure *G* (see Figure 44) within which the subject is required to discriminate a simple figure *F* sufficiently clearly to be able to reproduce it as a drawing (though he is not told in advance that he is going to be asked for a reproduction from memory). Will the subject arrive at the same results when he follows the outline *F* himself (*CA*), as when he merely perceives the movements of the experimenter tracing the outline for him (perception of the experimenter's activity, *PA*)? This test, then, turns on the comparison of the results of *CA* with those of *PA* rather than on *CA* and *SP* (as in sections 2–4 and part of 1). We have touched on this problem already in section 1.

Figure *G* is 40 cm square, and is placed on a sheet 360 cm square. The outline *F* is coloured blue, the rectangle red, the triangle on the right

[7] Inquiry carried out by M. Bovet.

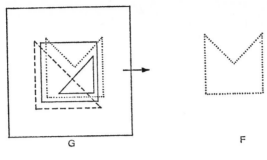

FIG. 44

brown and that on the left green. The subjects were divided into two groups. One group worked in the order $PA \rightarrow CA$ (with a week's interval), the other in the reverse order. In PA the subject simply watched the experimenter demonstrate the outline by going round it with a toy car, starting at the lower right-hand corner and moving up. First, however, we familiarized the subject with this kind of question by showing him a simplified structure and going round one of the outlines for him. When the experimenter had completed the outline F, the whole thing was covered, and the subject was asked to do the following (without forewarning): (1) to reproduce the 'blue road' (that is, the shape F irrespective of the movements used to draw it) with a blue pencil on a sheet of paper the same size as that used for the model; (2) to reproduce outline F as distance covered starting from the same point and maintaining the direction and continuity of the displacement: this was done gesturally, the child indicating the path with his finger on a sheet of paper of the same size as in 1.

In CA (a week earlier or later), the method was the same, except that the subject himself went round the outline F in figure G using the toy car. He was asked to begin at the lower right-hand corner (this was just pointed to), and he was told the direction of travel.

At the end of the second session (whether CA or PA) we requested for the sake of supplementary information (useful later) a direct copy of G, or, failing this, a direct copy of F alone (but from figure G).

The reproductions of F may be classified in four categories: (*a*) open figures corresponding only to part of the model; (*b*) closed figures without the indentation; (*c*) closed figures generally quadrilateral in shape, but with a not entirely successful indication of the indentation along the upper side; (*d*) correct figures.

Using fifty subjects grouped in three classes, I, II, III, according to their educational level (I = about 5–6 years, II = about 6–7 years, and III = 7–8 years), we found the following global results (the two groups together, Table 122). It can be seen that the results increase considerably with age. This complicates the analysis. But if we compare the

251

TABLE 122 *Distribution according to educational level, of the reconstruction of types a–d in configuration F*
(As % of the responses)[8]

	PA						CA					
	a	b	c	d	a-b	c-d	a	b	c	d	a-b	c-d
I	10	45	20	25	55	45	5	45	30	20	50	50
II	15	21	36	28	36	64	15	7	21	57	22	78
III	12	19	31	38	31	69	6	13	25	56	19	81

differences between columns *a–b* (clearly inadequate drawings) and *c–d* (*c* drawings are almost correct – that is, they indicate the general shape and the indentation, though the latter is clumsily drawn), we find that they increase more rapidly after *CA* than after *PA*: −10, +28 and +38 for *PA*, and 0, +56, and +62 for *CA*. The memory image is, then, formed slightly more easily if its starting point is personal action (*CA*).

But we found nothing like this for the path *F* (as opposed to the configuration *F*) when indicated by hand rather than by drawing, perhaps because the gestural procedure is easier. There is no point in giving the details of this here. But one point is of some interest. The subjects who were unsuccessful in reproducing the configuration or the path *F* in the direct copy made at the end of the final session went through a further exercise to improve their performance. Now, with these subjects, notably in the case of the path *F*, we obtained better results for *CA* than for *PA*. Further, when we analysed the drawing methods of thirty-one subjects who managed to reproduce the configuration *F* exactly, we found that twenty-four moved their pencil in the same way as the path; this was particularly marked (sixteen out of nineteen) in the case of those subjects whose reproductions came after active imitation *CA*.

Table 122, then, indicates that activity on the part of the subject *CA* has a slight advantage when the model is reconstituted as a configuration, though this is not the case when it is reproduced as a continuous path. But we still need to know whether acquisitions are made in the direction *CA→PA* or the reverse. Table 123 will provide an answer to this in terms of the comparison of the results (*CA>PA* signifying better results after *CA* than after *PA*, etc.).

The situation as regards the configurations is clear enough, and is comparable (though the differences are lower) to the relationship between *CA* and *SP* in Table 109 (section 1). When the subjects begin

[8] *PA* =perception of *F* as the distance traced out by the experimenter. *CA* =perception of *F* as traced out by the child himself.

TABLE 123 *Comparing reconstructions after exploration of the form (F) by the child himself (CA) and after perception of its exploration by the experimenter (PA)*
(Border-line cases given in brackets)
(As % for the overall responses)

	Order PA→CA		
	PA > CA	CA > PA	CA = PA
Configuration	4	50	40 (6)
Path	7	46	40 (7)
	Order CA→PA		
	PA > CA	CA > PA	CA = PA
Configuration	15	15	57 (13)
Path	26	13	53 (8)

with *PA* and finish (at the second session) with *CA*, the results for the latter are better (50 per cent as against 4 per cent with 46 per cent equal). But, even if this result for *CA* were reinforced by previous perception *PA*, it could not be accounted for entirely by this fact, since, in the reverse order, the situation is not inverted but merely equalized: 15 per cent as against 15 per cent with 70 per cent equal. Thus, from the point of view of the configurations, the present Table 123, like Table 109, speaks in favour of the pre-eminence of *CA*, though the effects are less marked.

Two things still remain to be explained: why the perception *PA* at the second session equals *CA* at the first, and what is the nature of the learning, or the transfer reinforcing *PA* after *CA*. To begin with it should be noted that perception of another person's activity *PA* is quite different here from what we called *PA* in section 1. There the subject watched the adult construct an assemblage of blocks without perceiving the final result: hence the difficulty experienced in imitating it. In the present case however, the subject watches the experimenter follow a blue line, and at the same time perceives this path as the configuration *F*. The only difficulty is discriminating this within *G* (Figure 44). It is much easier, therefore, to imitate the adult's movements in the present case and it is even surprising that *PA* and *CA* are not equal in the first group of subjects also. But imitation is easier still in the reverse situation. When the child first of all traces out the blue line for himself (*CA*) and a week later sees the experimenter engage in similar explorations, he will naturally project – or more precisely, *introject* – his behaviour by direct assimilation into that of the adult. This is still imitation, but in reverse. It is thus quite natural that there should be a transfer of *CA* on to *PA*, resulting in equalization.

In its general workings the situation is the same for *F* as a path (as opposed to *F* as a configuration). But, since in this case it is a question of the kinetic and motor aspects of *F*, the imitation and introjection already in play when *F* is considered as a static configuration are reinforced. The order $CA \rightarrow PA$ tends to reverse the proportions obtained in the opposite order, so that the general averages no longer show any difference between the results of *PA* and *CA*, as we saw above. In other words, when the subject begins with *PA* (first session), *CA* has the lead, being reinforced more or less by the imitation resulting from *PA*. When he begins with *CA* and ends with *PA*, this second method has the lead, though it is this time reinforced by introjection resulting from *CA*. True, we referred earlier to the fact that the youngest subjects who are unable to produce a direct copy turn out to be better equipped if they start with *CA* than if they start with *PA*. But this in no sense means that more advanced subjects will not assimilate *CA* to *PA* just as well as *PA* to *CA* by means of a combination of introjection and imitation. Finally, the frequent similarity between the methods of drawing and the reproductions of the path by gesture only underscores the part assumed to be played by this two-way imitation.

In short, it is no more possible here than in the preceding investigations to separate with any degree of accuracy the motor aspect and the role of the perceptual models in image formation. On the contrary, the present inquiry shows once again that in those cases where one might be tempted to overestimate the influence of the models in their perceptual aspect, there is, on analysis, an important degree of motor activity. Motor elements do, of course, intervene in perceptual activities, in so far as such activities remain, in contradistinction to operational movements, figurative in function, and orient them towards oculo-motor imitation of the object's contours. But in addition to this, those perceptions playing a part in the formation of images are constantly being integrated in imitational contexts at a higher level. In the case of the perceptions *PA* the subject imitates another person. But more important is his self-imitation, his reproduction of his own activity, arising when exploration *CA* promotes his perceptual probes and is prolonged as internalized imitation, that is, as an image.

II. The last inquiry yielded some positive (Table 123) and some non-significant results (the paths). It might, therefore, be useful to compare it with the investigation about to be described. The results of this investigation may seem negative – but it is instructive to try to find out why this should be so.

As before, we used a complex figure (Figure 45), 12 cm × 20 cm and drawn in blue. Three tasks were set for ninety subjects aged between 5,11 and 8,11. They were in three groups of thirty (ten for each age). Each group undertook one only of the tasks and then did a drawing from memory. The subjects were asked:

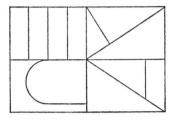

FIG. 45

(1) to 'look carefully' at the drawing for about 2 minutes;
(2) to go over all the lines in the drawing (blue) with a yellow pencil;
(3) to colour yellow all the surfaces contained by the blue lines.

Now, we did not analyse the effects of any one of these procedures on the others, since we were working with separate groups. Consequently, we observed only a trivial difference between the reactions to 1 and 2, and for 3 a distinctly lower result.

Here are a few examples of the reactions. The general framework and the axes were missing in two cases out of thirty in question 1, in five cases in 2 and ten cases in 3. The occurrence of badly placed parallels was 6/30 for 1, 5/30 for 2 and 10/30 for 3. The diagonal in the upper section was left out in 17/30 cases, 20/30 and 19/30. But in those cases where it was indicated it was poorly connected more often in 3 than 1 and 2 and in 2 it was poorly connected in only two cases out of thirty, and four out of thirty in 1, etc. In the light of the foregoing results (sections 1–4) these facts (gathered at the beginning of the present inquiry) are easy enough to explain. Procedure 3 gives lower results because the subject's active involvement is restricted to colouring in 'ground' surfaces: the lines themselves – the 'figures' – are neglected. It is natural, therefore, that the structuration of the model should be inadequate, and that the copies done subsequently from memory should be inaccurate. Procedure 2 calls for better structuring activity on the part of the subject, but there are two handicaps that prevent it improving on 1. In the first place, (a) it is not a question of activity in the full sense of the term, since the subject is asked merely to go over lines already drawn in (the visual exploration in 1 can be just as 'active', depending on the amount of effort put in by the child). And in the second place, (b) the question merely requires the subject to proceed line by line, and demands no preliminary overall plan (in contrast to the active copies in sections 1–3). Method 1, on the other hand, enables the subject to concentrate on the whole as well as on the particular details. Thus one can see why method 2 did not have higher results than the simple perception 1. The fact is that just as much activity may be involved in following the lines with the eyes as in following them with a pencil.

Finally, and above all, what we learn from the lack of significant difference between the results of 1 and 2 combines with what we learnt in I from the lack of difference between *PA* and *CA* results for the paths. The subject's active involvement leads to a better performance in image formation in the case of simple perception. But this is not just due to the fact that motor activity is brought more extensively into play, since it is already present to a high degree in the perceptual activities themselves. What counts in the subject's action is that the cognitive factors (perception, motor and postural adaptation, comprehension and imitation), and the affective factors (interest and effort) are integrated into a single whole. The subject's activity reinforces the formation of the image, because the internalized imitation which constitutes the image is a function of the whole action schematism, not just of the perceptual activities (although these too are equally reinforced). But this level is attained only when there is a complete action. That is, when there is an obstacle to overcome or a problem to solve. It is precisely this element that is lacking when the child merely goes over the lines of the drawing with a differently-coloured pencil. On the other hand, the discrimination of forms in the preceding complex figure (Figure 44) presents problems. And this is even more obviously the case in the active copies of sections 1–4.

6. Conclusion

At the end of Chapter Six we were led to the view that the great natural dividing line separating image categories falls between static images formed at the preoperational level and anticipatory images bound up with the operations and embracing both kinetic and transformation images. Further, anticipatory images occur in two forms: they bear either on the result of a transformation or movement, or on the modification itself in its successive stages. Now, it is always easier to imagine the results than the modifications or movements themselves (except in the case of imitations relating to the body of the subject himself), since an anticipatory image relating to an actual modification presupposes a greater degree of internal imitation of the operations.

This dichotomy of static and anticipatory images suggests a similar bipartite classification for that other figurative function, perception (the three basic figurative functions being perception, imitation and image). The perceptual mechanisms can be classified as primary processes or field effects, and as perceptual activities from which the secondary effects derive. The two dichotomies are analogous. In the case of perception, as in the case of the image, the second class of the dichotomy contains processes more dynamic than the first that are also capable of being increasingly directed by levels above that of perception, right up to the operations. Now, after having put forward the hypothesis that the primary effects are genetically primitive, we have arrived at the conclusion that they too result from earlier perceptual activities, which are themselves probably integrated into the overall action schematism.

256

The partial analogy between the two dichotomies gives the cue for a similar interpretation, *mutatis mutandis*, of the image categories. If the anticipatory images are formed and orientated with the aid of external contributory factors, and if they depend in consequence more or less directly on the progress of the operations, then will not the static reproduction images also be actuated by some earlier dynamism anterior to the operations, but genetically equivalent? This is what led us to look for possible links between the formation of static reproduction images and the subject's personal activity. And this chapter has shown us that such links do indeed exist.

Now several facts make this hypothesis all the more likely. While the perception relies on itself alone, the image appears to be formed as a result of internalized imitation. Imitation itself is characterized by the primacy of accommodation to the object, and thus represents the accommodatory pole of action. The static reproductive image is facilitated if the configuration reproduced is the result of the subject's own action. Less favourable are configurations that merely call for exploratory perceptual activity. Again, it follows that in the case of simple perception the perceived configuration is retained in image form much better if the perceived datum is assimilated to action schemes, than if the perception remains, as it were, external to activity. In other words, the more imitable the actions with which the image is linked, the more accurate it will be. But this amounts also to saying that oculo-motor imitation (in the double sense of eye movements imitating the contours of an object in perceptual exploration, and of the same movements reproduced in imaginal evocation imitating those occurring in perception) is reinforced to the same extent as it is integrated in the schemes of the activity as a whole. Thus our analysis of the relationships between the static reproductive image and action links up with what we have said about the relationships between primary perception, perceptual activity, and action.

CHAPTER EIGHT

Mental Images and Operations

One of the things that has emerged from the preceding chapters is that mental images apparently do not develop autonomously. Both the transition from reproductive to anticipatory images and the relative mobility ultimately achieved seem to be due to the formation of the operations and to their gradually acquired capacity to direct imaginal representation, to subordinate figurative states to transformations, and to promote approximate imagination of such transformations. But even if these hypotheses prove correct, two big problems remain concerning the relationship between images and operations.

The first problem is to establish whether images at the preoperational level, however static and however unanticipatory, amount to a preparation for the operations. If not, then do they at least constitute a necessary, or even a merely useful, prior condition for their formation? We have constantly recognized the image's functional, symbolic property, and have seen that imaginal representation is a predominant characteristic of preoperational thought. Both these facts lead us to conjecture that representation with all its attendant blanks and systematic errors (boundaries, etc.) actually has a positive function in the composition of operational thought, and does not merely throw up obstacles on the way. But what precisely is this function?

The second question is this. When it is ultimately structured and oriented by the operations, does imaginal representation merely conserve the positions acquired at the preoperational level? Or does it react, and take on new functions, by progressive interaction of figurative and operative processes? This problem is similar to the first; but its terms are renewed once the operational structures are fully formed.

The best way of answering these questions is to resume some of our habitual operation tests (on conservations, etc.), and to get the subjects to anticipate the transformations in question (transfer of liquids, stretching-out, etc.) by means of imaginal representation before the experimenter actually demonstrates them. Thus one can elicit an anticipatory image, on the one hand, and on the other, after demonstration, an operational or preoperational explanation. It is then possible to determine the relationship between the two.

1. *Anticipation of the levels of liquids, and conservation of their quantity*

Our first example of this method shows right away the kind of unexpected results it can produce. The usual test for the conservation of liquids consisted in showing the child two glasses *A1* and *A2* of the same shape and size filled to the same level. The contents of *A2* were poured into a wider glass *B*, or into a narrower glass *C* (the heights being the same). The child was then asked if there would be the same quantity to drink in *A1* as in *B* and in *C*. The results showed that up to 6 to 7 years the children refused to accept conservation because of the change in level. From 7 years on, however, 75 per cent or more of the subjects[1] arrived at invariance by dint of operational arguments.

We turn now to the anticipation of the transfer, with a view to examining the role that may be played by imaginal representation. The subject was required to anticipate the outcome of pouring *A2* into *B* or into *C*. The vessels themselves were left empty. Or, better, they were covered with a fine opaque sheath: this aids imagination of pouring, since the liquid is actually being poured but remains invisible. We compared the results of these anticipations with the reactions when the glasses were left uncovered and the act of pouring was visible. More explicitly, we posed the following four questions.

(1) The subject was asked to anticipate the level of the liquid in *B* and then in *C* (only *A1* remaining visible).

(2) He was given glasses *A* and *B*, then *A* and *C*, empty and uncovered. Then he was asked to pour the liquid into these glasses, two by two, in such a way as there would be 'just the same to drink'.

(3) *A1* and *A2* were filled to the same level. *A2* was poured into *B* and then into *C* (these remaining empty and covered). The subject was asked whether, when poured into *B* or *C*, the liquid would conserve its quantity (anticipation of conservation, not just of the levels as in 1).

(4) *A1*, *A2*, *B* and *C* were taken as before. *A2* was poured into *B* or into *C*, the receiving vessels this time remaining visible. The usual conservation questions were posed.

It should be noted that these four questions are relatively independent. It is possible to have correct anticipation of the liquids' levels (1) in a child who fails to equalize the quantities, (2) because he puts the levels at the

---

[1] The results of Vinh-Bang's and Bärbel Inhelder's standardization for conservation of the liquids were: 4 per cent complete success at 5 years, 18 per cent at 6 years and 74 per cent at 7 years.

same height in B or C as in A. And one may find anticipation of conservation (3) in a child who will deny it when the pouring is visible (4), because the anticipated conservation implies a level that is also constant! The present technique of imaginal anticipation does in fact yield the following new and surprising results. (a) The youngest subjects expect some kind of generalized conservation or pseudo-conservation that includes levels. They abandon this only when they actually see the liquids being poured (question 4), since they can then observe that, contrary to their expectations, the levels are different in B, C, and A. (b) Subjects in the middle age group (5 to 6 years), on the other hand, quite often succeed in imagining the correct levels in B and C when the liquids are poured out of sight. But at the same time they anticipate non-conservation, as conservation of the liquid's quantity still implies for them the permanence of its level. (c) The subjects at the most advanced level (those who affirm conservation when they can actually see the liquid poured) anticipate correct levels as well as conservation of the quantity of the liquid, the variation in level being understood as due to a process of compensation.

I. Here first of all are the reactions classified by age to question 1 (anticipation of level of liquid) and question 2 (equalization of quantities). See Table 124, for which, together with the next three tables, we are indebted to S. Taponier.

TABLE 124   *Anticipation of levels and equalization of quantities*[2]
(In glasses B and C; as % of the subjects)

	Question 1			Question 2		
	$A=B=C$	$A=B$ and $A<C$ or $A>B$ and $A=C$	Correct	$A=B=C$	$A=B$ and $A<C$	Correct
4 years ($N=4$)	75	0	25	100	0	0
5 years ($N=17$)	52	24	24	76	6	18
6 years (29)	31	31	38	62	4	34
7 years (11)	12	24	63	37	18	45
8 years (7)	0	28	72	28	14	58

This confirms that the anticipatory image of the levels (question 1) has a lead over the equalizing of quantities (question 2). But the classifiable (non-intermediate) subjects may be split into four categories $(-L-Cp; +L-Cp; -L+Cp; +L+Cp)$ depending on whether they are successful $(+)$ or not $(-)$ in anticipation of the levels (L) or in conservation when the pouring is visible (Cp) (question 4). We then arrive at Table 125.

[2] The sign $=$ indicates equal levels in 2 and in 1.

TABLE 125 *Relating anticipation of levels (L) and operational conservation (Cp) for the same subjects as in Table 124* (As %)

$-L-Cp$	$+L-Cp$	$-L+Cp$	$+L+Cp$
30	22·5	5	42·5

As we have suggested, there are three main categories of subject: (*a*) Those who fail the anticipation of levels, because they believe them to be permanent, and who consequently also fail the conservation when the pouring is visible ($-L-Cp$). (*b*) Those who are successful in the anticipation of levels, but who do not believe the conservation ($+L-Cp$). (*c*) Those who are successful in both ($+L+Cp$). A very few subjects manage the conservation without going through the anticipation of the levels (5 per cent $-L+Cp$). These subjects anticipate the levels incorrectly, and discover the conservation there and then when they observe the unexpected variation in level and interpret it in terms of compensation (it could also be that these subjects are on the brink of understanding conservation, though only on the basis of simple identity, without realizing the implications for the levels of the liquid).

Here is an example of category *a*, which corresponds to the most elementary stage.

Grou (4,10) sees that $A1 = A2$. $A2$ is poured into B (covered). – 'Is there as much to drink? – *Yes.* – Why? – How far does it go up here (B)? (She points to the same level on the cardboard sheath as in A.) – ($A1$ is poured into C covered.) Is there as much to drink? – *Yes.* – Why? – *Because you put a bit in.* – Up to where? – *Up to there!*' (She points to the same level on the sheath C as in A.)

Question 2. 'We are going to put the same amount to drink in here as in there (A and C uncovered). How far up will we have to make it? – (Shows the same level.) – (The liquid is poured.) Is there the same amount to drink? – *Yes, you put some in and it is smaller* (i.e. narrower). – Then is there just as much? – *Yes.* – Why? *Because you put it in up to there.*' (Shows the same level.)

Conservation without sheath (question 4). (Grou ascertains that $A1 = A2$, then pours $A2$ into B.) 'Is there just as much to drink? – *No, it is higher there* ($A1$). – Have I got more or less (in B)? – *You've got less.* – Why? – *This glass is bigger.* (B, wider.) – So? – *It's smaller* (i.e. the level is lower). – ($A1$ is poured into C, B having been put back in $A2$.) – Is there as much to drink? – *No you've got more.* (In C.) – Why? – *The glass is smaller* (i.e. narrower). – Well what does that do? – *It makes it higher.* – So I've got just as much to drink? – *No.*'

Wil (5,3) reacts in the same way, but in question 4 he says that there is less to drink in B than in A because '*it's smaller*' (i.e. the level is lower). –

'And how do you make it the same? – *You have to put some more in.*' And in *C* he says: '*It's not the same.* – What shall we do, then? – *You have to put it up to here* (level in *C*) *like in there* (level in *A*).'

These initial reactions are very coherent, and are informative from several points of view. The first thing they tell us is that pre-operational non-conservations are not due to an attitude oriented in advance towards expectation of change. It is rather that, as long as the transformations are not too obvious to avoid, the young subjects arrive by way both of assimilation and perseveration or economy at what we shall call primary pseudo-conservation[3] or 'persistency'. In the present case the child can see that the liquid is being poured from *A* into wider or narrower vessels (*B* and *C*), and says so explicitly. He therefore has to accept that the column will vary in width. But he starts off by postulating the 'persistency' of the rest, of the quantity, that is, and of the level (height), the latter being his gauge for the former. Thus it is only when the liquid is visibly transferred (question 4) that the subject feels constrained to accept non-conservation of the quantity, since he can no longer believe in the persistence of the levels, and since he uses the latter to gauge the former and is incapable of dissociating them. And this is the second thing we learn from these reactions – that initially the level is the yardstick for the quantity (question 2). Probably we should see this as a particular case of the ordinal estimation (from the point of view of judgment) and of the submission to the terminal boundary point with which we are already so familiar. Just as this dual influence works so that the length of a straight line is, at the pre-operational level, frequently estimated with regard to its finishing point irrespective of its starting point – so the quantity of the water is at first estimated by the upper limit (level) of the column, irrespective of the breadth.

This brings us to the third important thing revealed by these facts. The subjects have doubtless often been able to observe that a liquid poured from a wider into a narrower glass shows a higher level (see type *b* subjects, $+L-Cp$). Nevertheless, the subjects in category *a* imagine the levels in terms of notional implications (same quantity implies same level), rather than in terms of any previous perceptions. This is contrary to what we find in subjects of type *b*.

The subjects in this category (we hesitate to speak of 'stage II' as it is by no means proven that all the intermediate cases between the notional stages I or *a* and III or *c* pass through reaction *b* as far as

[3] This is to distinguish it from operational pseudo-conservation, which occurs when the child who has reached the level of operational conservations extends them to the wrong cases – as in the pseudo-conservation of the surface area of a square transformed into increasingly narrower rectangles with perimeters of a constant length.

the image is concerned) continue to believe that the quantity of the liquid can be gauged by its level. This is clearly shown by their replies to question 2. But they are able – probably as a result of past experience – to foresee the levels by imaginal representation. They consequently anticipate a non-conservation, and persist in this view when even the liquids are poured in front of their very eyes.

Aeb (4,11). Question 1: *A2* is poured into *B* (covered): – 'Is there as much to drink? – *No, because it's wider.* – How is that? – *There's less juice here because it's wider.* – (*A* poured into *C* covered.) Is there the same amount to drink? – *No, because it's smaller* (i.e. narrower.) – Which has the most? – *There* (*C*) *because it's smaller.* – How does that happen? – *There's more because it's not as wide. It's bigger* (i.e. taller); *there's more in.*' Question 2: 'Will you tell me how far up you need to pour the liquid to have just the same amount to drink in both glasses. (*A* and *B* visible.) – *Up to here.*' (He indicates the same levels and is of the same opinion after the glasses are filled. Similarly for *A* and *C* uncovered.) We go straight on to question 4, where the subject sees the liquid being poured. He is first required to anticipate the levels (confirming what he has already said for question 1). For the pouring of *A2* into *B* he anticipates the (lower) level correctly, and says after the liquid has been transferred: '*There's less; it's wider.*' For *C* he anticipates a higher level and says: '*There's more here because it's smaller, it's higher.* – But is there as much to drink? – *No.*'

Dec (6,0). *A2* into *B* covered: 'Is there as much to drink? – *Yes ... No* – Yes or no? – *No, because that one* (*A*) *has more.* – Why? – *Because that one* (*B*) *is fatter* (i.e. wider), *it makes half.* – But is there really as much to drink, or not? – *No* – And there (*A1* in *C*)? – (He takes a long look at the cardboard case.) *No* (he points to a higher level). – Why? – *Because this glass* (*C*) *is smaller* (i.e. narrower). – Which has the most? – *There is less in that one* (*A*) *and more in that one* (*C*).' Question 2 (equalization of levels). He indicates the same levels. Question 4 (invisible transfer of the liquid). In *B* '*it gets smaller* (i.e. lower), *because the glass is fatter* (i.e. wider).' And in *C*, '*You* (*C*) *have the most.*'

Clo (5,5). Same reactions; anticipates a higher level for *C*, and concludes: '*That will make more because it is a small* (i.e. narrow) *glass.*' Clo anticipates a lower level for *B*, and concludes. '*It's not as much because you put it in a big glass.* – What difference does that make? – *It means you don't have very much.*'

These subjects are interesting in connection with the problems of the mental image. They anticipate the levels more or less correctly but continue to think that they can use them to measure the quantity of the liquid. And quite logically, whether they anticipate in advance or actually see the transfer, they conclude that there is no conservation. The central questions, then, are these. Where do these anticipatory images originate? Do they or do they not constitute a preparation for subsequent conservation operations?

Two facts lead us to believe that these anticipations of the liquids' levels are based on a straightforward application of reproductive images acquired from past experience, and that at this stage there is no compensation in the operational sense of the term. The first of these facts is the frequency of the errors (equalities mixed with inequalities or temporary reversal of the relations narrower × higher or wider × lower), not in the cases quoted but in most of the others (including Clo in the parts of the test not recorded above). The second and principal fact is that although these subjects in the main anticipate that a liquid will rise higher in a narrower glass and will stay lower in a wider one, they are of one mind in unhesitatingly setting the levels at the same height when estimating equal quantities (question 2). Consequently, in questions 3 and 4 they all conclude that the quantity is not conserved. Thus their more or less correct imaginal representation is far from being able to lead them to an operational compensation of the type 'narrower × higher = same quantity'. That is to say the image is limited to representing a legalistic relation ('when a glass is narrow the water rises higher, etc.'), and fails to grasp the causal relation that would constitute conservation. In other words, these subjects merely imagine what they have seen during previous liquid transfers. But it is one thing to manage a correct description of the relationships in question, and quite another to comprehend them.

The fact remains that even if representation of the liquid levels is not a sufficient condition for operational compensation, it is nevertheless sooner or later necessary, and will act as an indispensable auxiliary. It is therefore natural that there should be intermediate cases between the clear-cut cases of type *b* subjects and those of type *c* (the stage of operational conservation and compensation). In these intermediate cases correct description is prolonged in comprehension and thus leads to compensation. But, as we shall see from the protocols below, such cases only occur when the subject arrives at conservation actually during questioning. An important problem then arises. Is it the image that leads to the operation? Or is it due to operational progress that the originally descriptive imaginal representation is able to be completed with comprehension of compensation?

Ost (6,10) starts with a type *a* reaction: If *A2* is poured into *B* there will be the same quantity to drink, and the levels will be the same. But for *C* he reacts according to type *c*: '*There will be more in here* (*C*), *because that one is narrower and takes more* (!) – What difference does it make if it's narrower? – *It makes the juice go up.* (!) – But will there be the same to drink or not? – *Yes.* – How far up does it go? – *It's higher.*' Ost then wavers between reactions *b* and *c* for question 2 (*A* and *B*): '*You have to put it in to the same height* (to have the same amount to drink). – Will we have as much to drink? – *No.* – What do we need to do? – *Put half of it here (B).* – Why? – *Because there (B) it's wider and there (A) it's narrower, it takes more.* – And here (*A* and *C*)? – (Anticipates a higher level in *C*.) *It's narrower here (C) and wider here (A), so it's the same.'* – Question 4 (conservation). *'It's the same amount, because you poured the same, you just poured* (without adding or removing any of the liquid).'

Obr (6,10) moves from reaction type *a* to type *b*, and then to type *c*, starting with question 1: (*A2* is poured into *B* covered.) *'There will be the same amount to drink.* – 'How far up does it go? – (Indicates the same level reaction *a*.) – (*B* is poured back into *A2*.) Is that the same? – *No, you've got too much.* – And now? (*A2* poured into *C*.) – *No, not the same to drink, because it's smaller.* (*C*, narrower.) – How far up does it go? – *There.* (Higher in *C* – reaction *b*.) – Who's got the more to drink, you or I? – *No, both the same: there (C) it is smaller, so it goes up higher* (= reaction *c*, since we now have conservation alongside difference in levels).'

Tac (7,3) starts with reaction *b* (questions 1 and 3 combined). He does not move on to reaction *C* until question 2, and this is maintained in question 4. Questions 1 and 3: (*A2* is poured into *B* covered.) *'There will be less because the glass is fatter.* – How far up does it go? – *Lower.* – Why? – *Because it's fatter.* – So? – *There's less.* – (*A1* poured in *C* covered.) – *There'll be more because it's smaller* (i.e. narrower). – How far up does it go? – *Higher.'* Question 2: Tac anticipates that the same levels in *B* and *C* as in *A* will give equal quantities to drink; but when he actually pours the liquid in, he sees that he has made a mistake and pours more into *C* to get equal amounts, saying, *'Because that one is smaller* (i.e. narrower) *you have to pour it higher.'* Question 4 (conservation) gives rise to a correct reaction with the same explanation by reference to compensation.

Chab (7,10) moves rapidly in questions 1 and 3 from reaction *a* to reaction *b*, and then to reaction *c*. When he has anticipated the correct level for *C* (for *B* he still anticipated equal levels), he replies thus: 'Is there the same to drink? – *No . . . er, yes, no, yes, yes, because the glass (C) is narrower and it makes no difference if the juice is higher.'* Questions 2 and 4: correct.

Rio (8,1) same reactions for questions 1 and 3: progression from type *b* answer to type *c*. Question 2: *'Higher* (in *C*). – How do you know? – *I did it with my mummy; once my sister had a glass like that* (narrow). *So she took it* (thinking she would get more): *she didn't realize!'*

Each of the subjects manages to foresee the levels correctly; and this is almost immediately followed by comprehension of compensation type *c* (narrower × higher = same quantity). They are thus distinct from the clear-cut type *b* subjects. But, given the age of the subjects (6,10 to 8,1), the type *b* reaction represents only a temporary phase which they rapidly leave behind. Sometimes they even jump directly from type *a* to type *c*, as Ost in questions 1 and 3. It is difficult to see how the image alone could be responsible for the development whereby correct imaginal representation of the liquid levels is overlaid by comprehension of compensation and thus progresses from purely legal description to causal interpretation. For the operation is already in process of formation and asserts itself immediately after, whereas in the clear-cut type *b* cases (Aeb, Dec and Clo), the image is obviously far from able to bring about the kind of operational elaboration in question. In other words, these subjects are on the threshold of the operational stage and of conservation, so that the type *b* reactions are merely a rapid transitional, or even residual, phase. It is thus the nascent operation that enables them to interpret their correct image of the levels from the viewpoint of compensation. This does not mean that the image of the levels is itself due to the operations, since the existence of the clear-cut cases type *b* shows that the image can be formed independently under the influence of past experience alone; but it does mean that the correct image of the liquid level does not itself incorporate a compensation scheme, and that such a scheme depends on the operations. Nor does it mean that the correct image of the levels is of no use at all in the formation of operations and compensation; it simply means that even if it constitutes a necessary condition – and this is doubtful, as there are apparently cases of a direct jump from *a* to *c* – it is certainly not a sufficient condition. The image appears rather as a useful auxiliary, aiding knowledge of states, but powerless to master transformations.

Finally, here are some clear-cut cases of reaction *c* – the operational stage.

Vui (7,7). (*A2* is poured into *B* covered): '*That makes the same amount to drink. –* How far up does it go? – *Here* ($\frac{1}{4}$ below the level of *A*). – Why? – *Because the glass is fatter. –* And if we put it back in here (*A*)? – *Higher* (correct level). – Is there as much to drink? – *Yes, because you haven't put any of the juice back. –* (*A2* is poured into *C* covered.) – *There is just as much, but it will be higher.*' Question 2: correct indication of difference in level.

Pri (8,2). (*A2* poured into *B* covered): '*It's fatter, wider, and there's the same amount. –* How far up will it go? – *Lower. –* (Liquid poured into *C*.) – *It's narrower and it goes higher. –* Is there as much to drink? – *Yes.* Why? – *It's the same quantity* [sic].' Questions 2 and 4: both correct.

Such, then, is the final level of achievement at which both operational interpretations and anticipatory images are exact.

II. It remains to say a few words about a control experiment carried out on 23 subjects aged from 5,0 to 7,5. We used six glasses *B* and *C* with different heights, instead of the two with equal heights used before.[4] Questions 1 to 4 were retained, but were posed in the following standardized manner:

Question 1: (anticipation of levels) with cover and pouring out of sight. Order: *B1, B2, B3, C1, C2, C3.*

Question 2: (*id.*) without cover and without pouring. All the glasses (*A* glasses three-quarters full, *B* and *C* empty) were on the table. After each anticipation of level an elastic band was put round each glass as a reminder of the level indicated. This enabled the child to make a general comparison. When the results had been taken down, the rubber bands were removed. Taking the *B* glasses, we asked the subject whether the levels would be the same in *A*, and, if not, which glass would have the lowest level. The same was done for the three *C* glasses and the subject was asked which would have the highest level.

Question 3: anticipation of conservation (with cover and the pouring not seen by the subject) for *B1, B3, C3* and *C1.*

Question 4: conservation, with actual transfer of the liquid.

The results showed good correlation[5] between the anticipation with and without the cover, and between the reactions to the *B* and to the *C* glasses. On the other hand, given the number of the glasses to be compared, there was a high proportion of intermediate reactions between type *a* and type *b*. This proves that correct anticipation of the levels (reaction *b*) does not emerge all of a sudden, but during the course of a series of transitions. These intermediate reactions are even more numerous than the clear-cut cases of type *a*. Most of these subjects foresee persistence of the levels and quantities for three out of the six glasses. The other glasses give rise to fluctuations (unfortunately affected by perpetual illusions making what is assumed to be equality of the liquid level difficult to estimate).

It is only all the more striking to see that in the first place there is excellent correlation between the reactions to question 2 (equalization of the quantities *E* in the six different glasses and in the *A* glasses) and the reactions to question 4 (conservation when the liquids are actually seen poured *Cp*). See Table 126.

This means, then, that all those subjects who fail the conservation test reckon that approximately similar levels are required in the six glasses *B* and *C* in order to have the same amount to drink in each

---

[4] As before, the *B* glasses were wider and the *C* glasses narrower than *A*. But the widths were as follows: *B1 = B2* and *C1 = C2*, but *B3 > B2* and *C3 < C 2*. And the heights: *B1 = A = C1*: *B2 = B3* and *C2 = C3*, but *B2 < B1*, and *C2 > C1*.

[5] Contingency. Between the two methods we find 86·2 per cent of cases + + and − −, as against 13 per cent of − + and + −, and between the two kinds of glasses we find 76·2 per cent of cases + + and − −, as against 23·8 of − + and + −.

TABLE 126   *Relating equalization (E) and conservation (Cp)*
(As % of the subjects)

$-E-Cp$	$-E+Cp$	$+E-Cp$	$+E+Cp$
53·8	3·9	0	42·3

one.[6] In the same way there is perfect correlation between the three B glasses and the three C glasses ($-B-C=57\cdot7$ per cent, $+B+C=42\cdot3$ per cent, as against $+$ $-$ and $-$ $+$ $=0$). The initial law of the preoperational stages ('same quantity = same level') is thus confirmed.

In the second place, if one tries to discover the relationship between anticipation of the levels L (question 1) and equalization of quantities E (question 2), which correlates closely with the final conservation, one finds that the former is in the lead – and this is the distinguishing feature of type b reactions:

TABLE 127   *Relating anticipation of levels (L) and equalization (E)*
(As % of the subjects)

$-L-E$	$+L-E$	$-L+E$	$+L+E$
30·7	26·9	5·9	36·5

All in all, this control with the six glasses does in fact verify the conclusions drawn earlier.

2. *Anticipation of the levels, and conservation of the quantity of beads transferred from one receptacle to another*

We used the same receptacles A, B and C as before, this time filled with beads, and analysed reactions to the same set of questions. We carried out this experiment with F. Paternotte, using thirty-four subjects aged from 5 to 7 years. We lay no great emphasis on these results, since, in spite of the additional glasses (glasses B and C as in section 1, glasses D = four small narrow glasses, and glasses E = three to six small but wider glasses) involving four transfers from A to $B-E$, we found the same reactions as regards anticipation of the levels (see Table 124 in section 1): 28 per cent success-rate at 5 years, 37 per cent at 6 years and 60 per cent at 7 years.

But the relationship between the anticipation of the levels, similar in the case of the beads and in the case of the liquids, and the con-

---

[6] The one subject who had $-E+Cp$ discovered the conservation during the experiment.

servations is quite different. It is on this point that we should like to say a few words. Since the Vinh-Bang–Inhelder standardizations we know that conservation of the beads in the case of a simple transfer is acquired at an early age. The overall results are as follows:

5,0	5,6 to 5,11	6,0 to 6,5	6,6 to 6,11	7,0 to 7,5
25%	25%	47%	75%	94%

It follows from this that anticipation of the levels is, in this particular instance, behind conservation, not ahead of it as in the case of the liquids. But one may ask whether conservation without compensation constitutes a true conservation, and whether there is not in the case of the beads more or less complete continuity between what we have called (see section 1) 'persistency' or primary pseudo-conservation and conservation proper. When we got the child to anticipate conservation or non-conservation in the A to $B-E$ transfer we did in fact find 62 per cent 'persistency' or conservation at 5 years, 80 per cent at 6 years and 100 per cent at 7 years. This is tantamount to saying that between the type a reactions of section 1 (persistence of quantity and level combined) and the type c reactions (successful anticipation of levels and conservation) we must expect to meet only a few type b reactions (correct anticipation of levels and non-conservation). And indeed, if we determine the relationship between anticipation of the levels L and anticipation of the conservations C (be it a question of 'persistencies' or of conservations proper), we find the following (Table 128):

TABLE 128 *Relating anticipation of levels (L) and anticipation of conservations (C)*
(As % of the subjects)

$-L-C$	$+L-C$	$-L+C$	$+L+C$
7·3	6	49·2	37·5

It can be seen that the category $+L-C$, which corresponds to reaction type b, is here only 6 per cent as against 22·5 per cent in Table 125 (and there it was a question of operational conservation in particular, not C in general) and 26·9 per cent of Table 127.

The reason for this difference between the beads and the liquids is undoubtedly to be sought in the fact that the beads are fixed in form, discontinuous, and countable.[7] It is thus easier to make do with phrases such as '*all the beads are poured in*' (Ris 6,1), or '*you always have the same number of beads*' (Pid 6,5). These subjects are halfway between persistency and conservation. As anticipation of the levels is just as hard for the beads as for the liquids, and as conservation is easier, it is only natural that type *b* reactions ($+L - C$) should be far less numerous. From the point of view of the image-operation relationships these differences and similarities between the bead and liquid situation have the following implication: they confirm that the anticipatory images are not the source of the operations involved in conservation and compensation, since two distinct operational evolutions correspond to one and the same image development. It is none the less true, however, that the image of the levels, probably acquired as before from past experience, can play an auxiliary role in the constitution of operations and compensations. But in the present case, this role is not so much one of preparation (since conservation precedes rather than follows the anticipation of the levels) as one of consolidation and completion within the structurations. What the image does is to further the transition from conservation by simple identity to conservation by compensation, elaboration of the latter presupposing a framework of operational conservation.

3. *Anticipation of shape-changes of a ball of clay. Conservation of the quantity of clay used*[8]

In the two preceding situations (transfer of liquids and transfer of beads) the youngest subjects spontaneously adopt an attitude of generalized pseudo-conservation or 'persistency', which they apply to the level of the content if the containers differ in shape (the dimension of width being neglected). If a ball of clay is taken, and the subject asked to anticipate its transformation into a sausage shape or other form, the initial reaction is the contrary of this. The child will anticipate non-conservation of the quantity of matter or substance, because the given change affects one dimension only, while the other (width, etc.) can be neglected. We are dealing with a quite new situation, therefore. But the central concern of our inquiry will still be to establish the relationship between image and operation, considering whether the image varies one, two or three of the dimensions affected.

The technique used was as follows: (1) The subject was told the ball would be transformed into a sausage shape, a pancake shape, or into small

[7] Whence a background of recurrence.
[8] With the collaboration of H. Niedorf.

pieces. He was asked to anticipate the forms and dimensions of these (*a*) verbally, (*b*) by means of gesture, (*c*) by means of a drawing[9] and (*d*) by a choice from prepared drawings. (2) He was then asked to anticipate whether there would or would not be the same amount of modelling clay in the ball when transformed (and during the intermediate stages) as in its original state. (3) We then gave the subject (*a*) a sausage shape, a pancake, and a collection of small pieces of clay, and (*b*) three differently sized balls to choose from. We asked him to say which of the three one would get if the sausage, etc., were transformed back into a ball. In this question the problem is inverse anticipation, not conservation, since the child has not seen the ball that the sausages, etc., came from. (4) Finally, we asked the usual conservation questions, transformation being carried out visibly in front of the subject.

These were the principal results: (1) The anticipations of the forms and dimensions at first take only one dimension into account and neglect the rest. Not until 8 years (the age of conservation) do they finally give an adequate image in 75 per cent of cases. (2) Inverse anticipation is even more difficult. (3) Initially the subject anticipates non-conservation, not 'persistence', as was the case for the liquids and the beads.

Here to begin with are the anticipations of forms (or relative dimensions) as expressed verbally, by drawing, and by choice from model illustrations (the gestural indications turned out to be very poor and difficult to interpret). The anticipations are not easy to deal with numerically, and we give three values: (1) Broadly counted successes, including even those instances where the child gives the two dimensions one after the other (for one transformation, and for the one following) and not simultaneously, since it is necessary to take simple concentration difficulties into account. (2) In round brackets ( ) we give the simultaneous successes. (3) In square brackets [ ] we give only the strict successes, abstracting any which might have been suggested by the formulation of the question. For inverse anticipation the figures in brackets indicate three correct responses for the three presentations (making nine in all for the sausage, the pancake and the small pieces); the first figure is the average for two successes out of three presentations. Broadly speaking, the successes given in Table 129 are the averages for the successful responses to the sausage, the pancake and the fragments, and the criterion for a success hinges on qualitative compensation. Thus there is a success when, in the case of direct anticipations, the child indicates that two dimensions vary in opposite directions: elongation and narrowing of the sausage, flattening and broadening of the pancake, increase in

---

[9] We asked for three successive drawings corresponding to the continuation of the transformation.

number and decrease in size of the fragments. In the case of inverse anticipation, a success is determined on the basis of the subject's selection from the three differently-sized balls of clay. Finally, a success in anticipation of conservation is judged from the verbal answer.

In all three methods of analysis and in all five questions a 75 per cent success score is reached only at 8 years, after an intermediate plateau at 6 to 7 years. It also emerges that the verbal expression of representational anticipations is more successful than the drawing. This is understandably due to weaknesses in drawing technique. The subject has to represent variation of two dimensions, and finds particular difficulty in drawing the disk shapes (otherwise anticipation is equally difficult whether bearing on the cylinder, the disk or the fragments). The choice from prepared drawings[10] elicits better answers, in that they suggest to the subject what he had not previously imagined for himself. Even so, a score of 75 per cent is reached only at 8 years (an average of 70 per cent at 6 to 7 years).

TABLE 129 *Successes for anticipations of form and of conservation* (As % of the responses for the three forms)

	5 years (N = 3 × 31)			6 years (3 × 24)		
Verbal	22·5	(5·3)	[5·3]	69·4	(63·8)	[23·6]
Graphic	7·5	(5·3)	[5·3]	35·9	(33·3)	[28·2]
Choice	47·2			73·6		
Inverse anticipation	20·4	(4·3)		44·4	(31·9)	
Anticipation of conservation	16·6			33·3		

	7 years (3 × 23)			8 years (3 × 8)		
Verbal	60·8	(60·8)	[52·7]	91·6	(91·6)	[75]
Graphic	38·6	(38·6)	[38·6]	100	(91·6)	[91·6]
Choice	66·6			100		
Inverse anticipation	52·1	(44·9)		100	(83·3)	
Anticipation of conservation	66·6			100		

The inverse anticipations and the conservation anticipations appear to be fairly closely interlinked. It is of some interest, therefore, to establish the relationships between them, and the conservations of question 4. Table 130 below provides the details. We have grouped the two relations together thus: *Ca* = anticipated conservation;

[10] It should be pointed out in this connection that the illustrations need to be of a good quality, particularly in the way they represent depth.

Cp = operational conservation in the presence of the actual transformations; Ai = inverse anticipation.

TABLE 130 *Relating the reactions Ca and Cp, and Ca and Ai*
(As % of the responses)[11]

N	$-Ca-Cp$	$-Ca+Cp$	$+Ca-Cp$	$+Ca+Cp$
132	52·2	0	1	46·8

N	$-Ca-Ai$	$-Ca+Ai$	$+Ca-Ai$	$+Ca+Ai$
105	40·9 (37·1)	10·5 (10·5)	3·8 (13·3)	45·7 (39)

There is perfect correlation between anticipation of the conservation (Ca) and the final conservation (Cp), and it is still good between (Ca) and the inverse anticipation (Ai). The first of these correlations shows that conservation in the strict sense, and not 'persistency', is involved here. This explains why, compared with conservation of the beads (section 2), they are retarded in character. Inverse anticipation embodies a quantitative element (dimensions of the ball to be selected) and is consequently successful shortly after direct anticipation, which relates only to form. Its relative correlation with conservation goes without saying, if the latter is based on reversibility. Further, in the eighty-six subjects examined, the conservations are slightly ahead compared with Vinh-Bang's averages (complete success + intermediate cases = 16 per cent at 5 years, 32 per cent at 6 years, 36 per cent at 7 years, 76 per cent at 8 years and 88 per cent at 9 years). This is probably due to the fact that preparation for a correct solution is provided by questions 1–3.

It remains to settle the central issue: namely, the relationships existing between anticipation of shape or dimension (question 1) and anticipation of conservation. Table 131 sets forth those relationships first for all the subjects (as in Table 129 a distinction is made between broad and strict assessment of successes, the latter being placed in brackets), and second for the 5-, 7- and 8-year-old subjects (the 6-year-olds are excluded). We shall see the reason for this division in a moment.

TABLE 131 *Relating direct anticipations of form (Ad) and of conservation
(Ca)* (As % of the responses)

	$-Ad-Ca$		$+Ad-Ca$		$-Ad+Ca$		$+Ad+Ca$	
5–8 years	19·8	(47·7)	35·2	(8·1)	9·9	(21·6)	35·1	(22·5)
5 and 7–8 years	28·0	(31·6)	5·3	(1·7)	8·8	(26·3)	57·9	(40·3)

[11] The numbers in brackets correspond to three out of three successes for Ai (see Table 129).

If we count the successes on a broad basis (including successive not simultaneous compensations, and successes possibly due to help given by the questions) 54·9 per cent of cases show correlation ($+ +$ and $- -$), as against 45·1 per cent that do not. Of these 35·2 per cent are of the type $+Ad - Ca$. That is to say anticipation of the forms is ahead of anticipation of conservation, as was also the case for anticipation of the levels of the liquids (type b). Now this lead is found almost exclusively at 6 years, before the move towards conservation. At 5, 7 and 8 years the $+Ad - Ca$ cases and the $-Ad + Ca$ cases fall to 14·1 per cent, and the correlation cases ($- -$ and $+ +$) go to 85·9 per cent. On the other hand, if we take only those imaginal anticipations Ad successful in the strict sense, then the cases of non-correlation ($- +$ and $+ -$) are 29·7 per cent, while the cases favouring correlation are 70·2 per cent. This time it is anticipation of conservation Ca that is ahead of anticipation of the forms Ad: 21·6 per cent as against 8·1 per cent (and 26·3 per cent as against 1·7 per cent at 5, 7 and 8 years).

These facts are of considerable interest for the theory of the image–operation relationship. In general, they are parallel to what we have already found in the case of the liquids (section 1). They show, on the one hand, that images may to some extent precede the operations – probably under the influence of past experience. But such images are not accompanied by any proper comprehension of compensation, and they remain relatively imprecise and vague even for images. This is the point of broad assessments in Tables 129–131. It is clear that as soon as the operations and conservation appear, they both act on the image, and the image gains in precision under the influence of the compensation framework that they provide. Hence the reversal of the relations when one considers only the strict method of assessment and the most accurate anticipations.

Finally, to illustrate this evolution, we give some examples of these three stages, starting with the level at which there is not even any vague conservation or anticipation of the change of shape.

Far (5,2) makes an elongating gesture and draws the sausage just as thick as the ball and slightly longer than its diameter. 'And if I roll it out a bit more? – *It will get bigger.* (Draws it longer and just as thick.) – And if I roll it more still? – *Bigger still.*' (Draws it longer, but thicker than before.) Pancake-shape: 'What happens if I press on it? – *It's like that* (Draws a circle of the same diameter as the ball.) – And if I press it more? – *It's smaller.* (Draws a circle with an even smaller diameter.) And if I press it still more? – *It's smaller still.*' (He draws a circle with an even shorter diameter than the preceding one.) He imagines the pellets increasingly smaller, but does not increase their number. In inverse anticipation he selects three balls in ascending order of size for the sausage, the pancake and the pellets respectively (the second being correct, though only accidentally).

So (5,9) anticipates that the ball will be transformed into a sausage 10 cm long (gesture), and draws it as 13·5 cm by 4 cm. 'What happens if I go on rolling it? – *It will get smaller, no bigger.* (Draws it 16·5 cm by 5 cm, increasing both dimensions.) – And what if I roll it more still? (gesture of rolling the clay on the table?) – *It will be like that but round.*' (Draws it 17 cm long by 5–6 cm, one side straight, the other curved.) From the illustrations he picks the thickest. For the pancake-shape, So reacts in the same way as Far: he says of the pellets that they are *'very small'*, then that they are *'very, very small'*, and finally that they are *'very tiny'*, but he does not bother about how many there are. In inverse anticipation he selects one ball for the sausage, a *'bigger one'* when it is rolled out further, and a *'very big one'* when it is still further elongated. For the pancake and the pellets he also chooses balls of increasing size: *'It's very big* (the third ball) *because there are a lot of little bits.'*

Com (5,0) anticipates that the ball will be transformed into a thinner sausage: *'maybe like that.* (Draws it the same length as the ball's diameter, but narrower.) – And if I roll it more? – *Thinner.* (Draws it same length but thinner.) – And if I roll it still more? – *Even thinner.*' (But draws it only as long as before.) Similarly for the pancake: Com gives three successive drawings all having the same diameter, but getting *'flatter'*. Inverse anticipation: 'I'm going to make a ball out of the sausage. Will it be like that? – *No, fatter.* – And that one? (Sausage twice as long and twice as narrow.) – *A bit fatter than the first one.* – And now? (Even longer and narrower sausage.) – *Fatter than the second one.*' – Similar reactions for the pancake. Finally, he is shown four fragments, then eight, and then sixteen, and he anticipates three balls of increasing size.

Here is an example of an intermediate case. There is no conservation, but the subject does anticipate the shapes, which points to an emergent appreciation of the simultaneous variation of the two dimensions.

Bel (6,1): 'If I roll this ball into a sausage, will there be the same amount of clay? – *No, because the sausage is longer.* – And what if I make it into a pancake? – *No, in the ball there's more, because the pancake is thin.*' – 'And if I make it into little pieces.' – *There's more in the ball, because the pieces are small.*' (This in anticipation.) Anticipation of the forms: *'The sausage will be long.* (Gesture: 40 cm.) – And if I roll it more? – *Very long.* (Gesture: 60 cm.) – And what will it be like? – *Thin.* (He draws it thick.) – Why have you made it thick? – *I want to do it again.* – What like? – *Long and thin.*' The pancake: *'Flat and round* – And if I press on it more? – *Bigger.*' (Gesture indicating breadth), etc. In inverse anticipation Bel agrees that the extreme models give the same ball of clay, and thus seems to be getting close to compensation, but negates this in the intermediate cases. For instance, in the case of the first lot of fragments, he says: *'Yes, you can make the ball because the pieces are big and there are only four.*

275

And with these (the eight fragments)? – *No, that won't do, because there is more clay* (in the eight fragments). – And with these (sixteen)? – *Yes, that's the same because they're small and there are a lot.*' Similar reactions for the three sausages and the three pancakes.

This type of subject anticipates the shapes more or less correctly, but by dint of descriptive images rather than understanding of compensation: hence his failure to anticipate conservation. Here, for the sake of comparison, is an example of a superior level of attainment.

Gan (7,11): anticipation of conservation: '*It will make the same amount because it's the same clay.*' – (Shape: sausage.) – '*It will be longer but not thick!* – (Pancake?) – '*Flatter and bigger* (i.e. broader). – Will there be as much clay? – *Yes, because before they're the same.*' Inverse anticipation (sausage): '*The sausage (3) is longer and thinner, and that one (1) is shorter but fatter, and that one (2) is also longer and thinner: That makes the same ball because there's just as much clay.*'

Thus anticipatory transformation images acquire a greater degree of accuracy; and at the same time, within a framework of conservation for which they themselves are not actually responsible, they come to signify compensation.

4. *The anticipation of one-to-one correspondence between rows of counters*[12]

The amazing thing about our earlier experiments on numerical equivalence by correspondence is the apparent weakness of imaginal representation. The 4- to $5\frac{1}{2}$-year-old child can see that 8–9 red counters are equal in number to as many blue counters if they are opposite one another in two parallel rows of equal length. But as soon as the blue counters are displaced by about 3 or 4 mm, he seems unable to imagine that it is possible to put them back as they were in order to check that their number has been conserved! Yet the child perceives the displacement. Does this mean that the mental image is so poor at preoperational ages that it cannot represent a shift back of only a few millimetres? It is true that the child's difficulty is not connected with anticipation so much as with a tendency to estimate quantity or even number in terms of space occupied (length of the rows). But, even so we do not get away from the problems of the image. The young subjects reckon the length of one row in terms of the extent to which it exceeds the limits of the other. This they turn into a criterion for numerical increase, while ignoring the density of the row. The reason is probably that they fail to anticipate not so much a return of one element to its original position as a contraction

[12] With the collaboration of S. Taponier.

of a row extended beyond the limits of another, or more generally, modifications in length of a row as such, at a development level where length notions are primarily ordinal. Now, as we saw incidentally in Chapters Two–Three, the ordinal character of these notions is in part attributable to the part played by the image.[13]

Another important question arises from an experiment carried out with A. Morf.[14] The subject had to compare two rows of 4 elements with and without joining lines between them. We found that the younger subjects were uninfluenced by the presence of the lines. But from 5 to $5\frac{1}{2}$ years the joining lines o prevailed over the difference in length of the rows. Now why is the image incapable of playing the same role as the lines?

What we needed, then, was a device with the following characteristics. It would have to present two rows of different lengths with the members of each corresponding one to one; it would have to be such that the subject could imagine displacements; and he would have to be able, simply by inspecting paths traced out in advance, to represent the outcome of placing the members of one row in visual correspondence opposite the members of the other row. So we used the apparatus shown in Figure 46: a fan-shaped frame with twelve sections, those in the centre being 24 cm or 50 cm long (models I and II), and

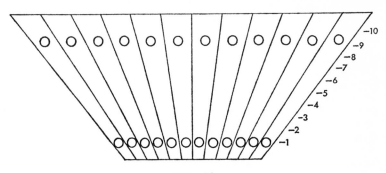

FIG. 46

each one being 5 cm (I–II) or 7·5 cm (III) wide along the top edge and 1·5 cm wide along the bottom. These sections are separated by string (I) or, better, are partitioned off by means of cardboard strips. At the top of the frame is a fixed row of 12 counters F all the same

[13] We would note, however, that a few subjects, particularly at 6 years, occasionally judge that the shorter rows contain more counters. These subjects also attach importance to the density of the rows. This is a step towards the two factors involved and is an indication of the operational level.

[14] *Étude d'épistémologie génétique*, vi, Chapter III, 'Logique et perception', Presses Universitaires de France, 1958.

colour; at the bottom is another row of movable counters M all a different colour. Depending on the model used there are six or ten possible positions between the short movable row (position 0) and the longer fixed row at the top (position 10). The problems to be solved are these. On the one hand we have to establish whether by simply examining the apparatus the subject can recognize immediately the numerical equivalence of F and M. And on the other hand we have to determine the extent to which the subject is aided if the M counters are moved along the lanes (positions 1, 3, 5, 6 to 9 next to row F at 10).

The results showed that at the preoperational level the lanes aid discovery of conservation hardly at all. We therefore concentrated less on drawing up statistical tables of success (for which see section 5) than on making a qualitative analysis of inadequacies of the image. These inadequacies are probably due to the fact that the subject attaches more importance to the different lengths of the horizontal rows than to the vertical lanes connecting individual counters. We employed several different techniques, which from a qualitative point of view are complementary, but whose results are heterogeneous from the quantitative or statistical point of view.

Method I (fan I divided into six successive levels) incorporated the following four questions. (Question 1) We first asked the subject if there were or were not as many red buttons in position 0 as black buttons in position 6. (Question 2) If the subject's reply was in the negative, we moved one red button to position 1, and indicated where it would end up if we went on moving it. We asked the subject to predict how the red buttons would be if they were all pushed until they were opposite the black ones (position 6), just below the black buttons. The child was given extra red counters to line up beneath the black ones (in certain cases we at first masked the intermediate positions; but this only proved to be an unnecessary complication, and we discontinued it). (Question 3) He was then asked whether there were as many red as black counters in position 6. As the red row is a little shorter than the black (particularly in fans I–II 24 cm high – for which reason we changed to model III, height 50 cm), the child may think the red counters are fewer in number. In these instances when he did, we asked whether 'each black counter has a red one with it', and then asked again whether the two rows were equal in number. (Question 4) The child was asked whether there were or were not as many red counters in position 0 as black counters in position 6, and why.

Method II (model II with ten different levels) is similar to method I, except for a modification in question 2. Here the subject was asked to move the green counters himself from position 0 to the next position. Green counters were used this time, as red, it appears, sometimes leads to overestimation of the number simply because the child prefers the colour. The subject thus has to imagine the distribution of green counters in position 9 opposite brown counters at position 10, and to compare them

278

quantitatively. Even then it seems that the subject did not actually go on to anticipate the paths of the counters along their individual tracks (in spite of the cardboard partitions used here instead of string). He was content simply to line up his markers (pieces of paper, coins, yellow counters) in position 9 irrespective of the paths.

Method III A was an attempt to remedy this negative reaction (which is, however, interesting in its own right). (Question 1) The green counters were placed in position 0 and the brown counters in position 10. The subject was asked to compare the quantities and to vindicate his reply. (2) Without actually moving the counters, we asked the subject to antici-pate the distribution of the green counters in position 9. We pointed to each counter in turn and asked the subject where each one would finish up (we noted his gesture, or eye movement from 0 to 9). He was asked to place a yellow counter (a 'tiddleywink') at the finishing point. At the eighth counter the subject was asked whether it was correct to put a yellow counter in the place he indicated, and which green counter it corresponded to. (Question 3) The subject was asked to estimate whether the brown (position 10) and the yellow (9) counters were equal in quantity. (Question 4) The subject was asked to anticipate the distribution and quantity of the green counters in positions 1, 3, 6 and 9. He was required to indicate these positions clearly by gesture (the brown counters remaining at 10 and the green counters at 0). (Question 5) If there had been no con-servation during the preceding anticipations, then we began again with a numerical estimation at 0 and at 10 ('just as many or not?'); and the green counters were moved up by the experimenter to positions 3 and 10 and then to positions 6 and 9, etc., until the subject eventually accepted or rejected that they were equal in number (and explained why).

Method III B is a repetition of method III A in descending order. (1) The green counters at 9 and the brown counters at 10. The child was asked if there were as many or not. (2) Anticipation of the displacement of the green counters from 9 to 0, the child being asked to place the yellow markers at 0. (3) Quantitative comparison between 9 and 0. (4) As question 4, III A, but in the order, 9, 6, 3 and 0. (5) As question 5 but in the order, 9, 6, 3 and 0; then, if required, in ascending order.

I–II. The initial reactions elicited by methods I and II in the case of the younger subjects are of some interest. These subjects do not isolate the individual elements and relate them one by one, but concentrate on the image of the rows as they stand.[15] Consequently, when he has to anticipate the red or green counters going up from 0 to the top position (6 or 9), the child reacts in one of the following two ways. Either he does not bother with the lanes at all and simply places his markers opposite the top row (black or brown) – which

---

[15] Cf. Elementary level of classification (Inhelder and Piaget, *The Early Growth of Logic*, 1964, Ch. I) at which the subject produces 'figural collections' before classes or non-figural collections, the collections being characterized by a figure in space (rows, surfaces, etc.) irrespective of the properties of its members.

does not always, however, mean that he sees that the collections are equal (since the black row remains objectively a little longer because of the fan shape). Or he does take account of the lanes (especially if the mask is removed), but does not dare to ensure that all the lower counters are moved up for fear that the anticipated row of red and green elements should exceed the boundary points of the lower row from which they started out! Here are some examples of the first reaction.

Mei (5,10): 'Are there as many or not (of black at 6 and red at 0)? – *More black ones because it's bigger* (i.e. the row is longer. – Look, you can move them up (four moved into position 1); can you do it? (He moves the rest up to 1.) – Look carefully and show me how they will be when they get right to the top (the cardboard cover is put in place, covering positions 2 to 5). – (He establishes a one-to-one correspondence at 6.) – Are there as many red ones (at 6) as there are black ones? – *More black ones.* – Why? – *It's bigger* (the row of black counters is 1–2 cm longer than the row of red counters at 6). – Are there any black ones without red ones? – *No.* – Any red ones without black ones? – *No.* – Are you sure? – *Yes.* – Then there must be as many red ones as there are black ones? – *More black ones and more red ones.* (Which no doubt means that the subject does not want to commit himself, but also that he thinks there are more red ones at 6 than there were at 0.) – And what if you bring the red ones down (the cover is removed and the counters moved down one or two positions)? – *More black ones.* – Why? – *Because it's bigger.* – And what if you go right up (they are moved back to 6)? – *More black ones and more red ones.* – But are there as many, or not as many? – *More black ones.* – Why? – *Because it's bigger here* (points to the ends of the black row) *and here* (the red row at 6) *it's smaller.* – Are there some missing? – *No.* – Then there must be just as many? – *More black ones and more red ones.* – And when the red ones are at the bottom? – *More black ones.* – And what about the red ones? – *Less.* – And the red ones at the top? – *There will be more.* – And at the bottom? – *Less.* – Have some been taken away? – *No.* – How can there be more at the top and fewer at the bottom? – *Because it's smaller.* – If you haven't taken any away how do you know there are fewer? – *It's smaller.*'

Thie (5,10): Black at 10, Red at 0 (without cover). – '*There are more black ones.* – Why? – *There are a lot.* – And the red ones, look (he is shown the guide-lines). – *There aren't a lot.* – Look, you can move them up (the first red counter is placed in position 1, then 6 and then 7). You go on. – (He brings them into correspondence at 9 with the top row.) – Are there as many? – *More black ones.* – Why? – *There are more* (the row is 1–2 cm longer). – Is there still a black one for every red one? – *Yes.* – And are there any black ones without red ones? – *No.* – And are there any red ones without black ones? – *No.* – Then are there as many after all, or not? – *More black ones.*'

Tea (6,0): '*More black ones.* – Why? – *It's bigger.* – Look, you can move them up, etc., etc. – (He puts 12 red ones opposite the 12 black ones in position 9.) – Are there as many? – *No, more black ones.* – Is there still a red one with each black one? – *Yes.* – The red ones were at the bottom, do you remember? – Yes, there were less. – And what if you move them up? – *At the top there are more of them.*'

Evaluation of the quantity of the elements by reference to the length of the row is, of course, a well-known phenomenon. In the present case of the fan, this mode of assessment is as active as ever; but in the perceptual experiment mentioned above (the one carried out with A. Morf) the bars connecting the elements soon came to play a greater part than the length of the rows. Now the reasons for this are these: (1) in the present case there are twelve guide-lines and two sets of 12 elements, whereas in the other experiment there are only four lines and two sets of 4 elements (with 5 or 6 the part played by the lines already begins to diminish); and (2) Morf's lines were closely bound to the circular figures they connected (the children compared them to 'dumb-bells'), whereas in the case of the fan the role of the guide-lines is not figurative but purely kinetic. The remarkable thing about the foregoing reactions is that all representational and anticipational activity (in so far as it intervenes at all) is concentrated on the transverse (or horizontal) dimension, the length of the rows, and almost totally neglects the longitudinal (or vertical) dimension. Such longitudinal anticipation of the paths to be followed does not in fact present the slightest difficulty. But, as far as the child is concerned, that is not the point. It seems that the subject attaches no importance to the identity of the individual elements, and takes into account only the row as such. Hence Mei sees that nothing has been taken away, but from the point of view of the transverse row, 'it's smaller'. Similarly Tea knows that the red counters remain the same, but 'there were less', whereas if they are moved up, 'there are more'.

There are two problems here: one concerning conceptual structuration (non-conservation), the other concerning imaginal representation. With the first we are already familiar. Once it is accepted that the whole is not equivalent to the sum of its parts or elements, it is no more difficult to accept that a lengthened row increases in total quantity independently of its density than it is to accept that a rod moved relative to another becomes longer because it goes beyond the end of the other irrespective of its starting point (see section 5 below). But from the image point of view, it is quite impressive to find that this attitude should continue to dominate in a test designed to aid longitudinal anticipation and imaginal representation of the elements individually. Now, either this longitudinal anticipation is entirely neglected by the subject (which might be what happens when he puts the red counters at 6 and 9 and forgets those at the bottom). Or else such anticipation does indeed occur, but is outweighed by *transverse* anticipation bearing on the length of the rows. This latter mode of anticipation arises from what for the child is the only important consideration – namely, whether one of the rows does or does not go beyond the limits of the other.

FIG. 47

The pregnance of the boundaries has become clear during the course of nearly all our foregoing analyses (Chapters Two–Five). But in the present situation this preoccupation is so strong that the children fail to accept that the counters are equal in number, even when they are touching, because the upper black row extends very slightly beyond the bottom row (Figure 47). It makes not the least difference that the child can see there is a black counter for every red one, and vice versa: he still denies that their total amounts are equivalent.[16] This paradoxical judgment may be due simply to the fact that the upper row extends slightly beyond the lower; or it may be due to the fact that once the red counters have been judged inferior in number in the lower positions, they retain this status relative to the black counters at the higher positions, although at the same time they themselves are felt to become more numerous. Hence Mei's evasion, 'more black ones' and 'more red ones', and his insistence that there are, all the same, more black counters.

A second group of subjects showed the contrary reaction (particularly when the intermediate positions were not covered). At first their general tendency is to anticipate the lengthwise displacement of the counters from the bottom to the top of the frame. Consequently they affirm that the red counters in the upper position are equal in number to the black ones. Nevertheless, they deny the fact firmly when the counters are at 0. Moreover, initial anticipation of the displacement of the red counters is associated with a concern not to overstep the limits of the row as it stands at position 0.

Cer (5,6): 'Do you think there are the same number (black at 6; red at 0)? – *No, there are less red ones and more black ones.* – And when we put all the red ones here (position 1)? – *It will be very big.* – Show me how it will

[16] P. Greco has shown that in such cases (rows of different lengths but $X = Y$) the judgment 'more X' may mean inequality as regards *quotiety*, or inequality with respect to *quantity* with equality as regards *quotiety* (see *Études d'épistémologie génétique*, Chapter I, Presses Universitaires de France, 1962).

be. – (He puts the red counters in position 1 but stops at the ninth counter, opposite the end of the preceding row at 0.) – And if I take all the red ones (placed back at 0) and move them up to here (position 2)? – *It will be very wide.* – (He puts them in position but stops at the seventh, so that he will not go too far beyond the line at 0.) – And if I move them up to here (top row 6)? – *It will be like the black ones.* – (But he does not pair them off, and his row is 28 cm long instead of 60 cm!) – But if I take them all and move them up like that (along the tracks). – (He does this himself so that the counters are seen to correspond.) *It's the same.* – (The red counters are moved back to 0.) Are there as many? – *More black ones.* – And if I move them up? – *The same.* – And when we go down? – *More black ones.* – And when we move them up again? – *The same.* – So do you think that there are as many at the top and not as many at the bottom? – *Not as many.* – Why? – *Because here* (6–6) *I put them in the same place and there* (6–0) *the rows are not in the same place.* – But are there as many when they are there (6) as when they are there (0)? – *No, because there are more black ones and less red ones.* – Why? – *Because you have put more black ones and less red ones.* – And here (6–6)? – *Just as many.* – And if I move them down, that makes less? – *Yes.* – Why? – *Because . . . you have put less of them.* – Have any of them been taken away? – *No.* – Have some been added? – *No.* – Then there are just as many – *No, more black ones.*'

Gre (5,1) says that in the higher positions '*the red ones will be underneath the black ones*'. But he only puts 10 in a row 24 cm long, so as not to go too far beyond the original row at 0. Then he moves them all up and accepts that there are just as many red as black counters. 'And if you move them down?' – '*More black ones.* – Why? – *Because it's longer*,' etc.

Subjects of this type, then, think that the red row at O and the black row at the top are unequal in number; what is more, they think that this state of affairs should be conserved when the bottom row is moved up! To begin with longitudinal anticipation results in over-short rows, owing to a desire not to exceed the ends of the initial lines. The child then accepts the numerical equality of the counters at the upper position, only to deny it as soon as they are moved down.

The large majority of 5- to 6-year-old subjects react in this way. Subjects of type III do not experience any difficulty in foreseeing at the outset that the numbers will be equal in the top position; but they rigorously maintain that this equivalence gives way to difference in all the other positions.

Tis (5,6) 'What can you see? – *Red and black buttons.* – And what else? – *Lines.* – What are they like? – *Leaning over.* – What will happen if you move the red ones up? – Like this.' (Counters put in corresponding pairs at 6.) Red counters return to 0. – 'If all the red ones are moved up, will there be any missed? – *No, because they are all on the lines.* – Are there as many of the red ones as of black ones? – *More black ones.* – Why? – *They are at the top and it's wider, and at the bottom it's smaller.* – And if I move the red ones up? – *There'll be the same number.* – Same number of what? – *Of red ones and black ones.* – So there is the same number? – *There are more black ones, but if you move the red ones up it's the same.* – Then are there just as many, really, or more? – *It's the same if you move them up, and more black ones if you leave them where they are.* – Why? – *Because the lines are leaning.*'

Mos (5,10) starts off in a similar way for 6 and 0: '*More black ones.* – How do you know? – *There are more buttons here* (black). – Look, you can move them (to position 1), do you see? – *Yes.* – You go on. – (He puts the red counters in position 6 and, after hesitating at the ends, affirms that they are equal in number.) *It's the same.* – And is it the same number if they are moved down? – *No, more black ones.* – Aren't there as many red ones? – *Less red ones.* – Why? – *Because some are taken away.* – You move them down. (He brings them to position 0.) Did you have to take any away? – *No.* – And is it the same number or not? – *More black ones.* – And at the top? – *The same number.* – And at the bottom? – *Less red ones.* And what if you counted them? – *Not the same number.*'

Mon (5,6). Same reactions: '*Less red ones, it's small, and more black ones, it's longer.* – If the red ones are moved up, where will they be? – (He indicates correspondence.) – Is there the same number? – *Yes.* – And at the bottom? – *More black ones, less red ones.* – Have some been taken away? – *No.* – And if one counted them, would there be less? – *Yes.*'

Lec (6,1): '*There aren't as many* (at 6 and at 0). – What do you need to do to have as many? – *Move them up to the top.*'

Dun (6,1): '*More black ones.* – And if the red ones are moved up? – *It'll be the same.* – Why? – *Because some more have been put on.* – Some more what? – *Some red ones.* – Who's put them there? – (——) – Well? – (——) – And what if we move them down? – *More black ones.* – Why? – *There is more room at the top.*'

In these cases – the most frequent of the three initial types – there is evidence of clearly outlined longitudinal anticipation. Subjects of this type do not foresee how the red counters will be distributed in the upper position, and draw the conclusion that the type I subjects failed to draw and that the type II subjects only drew with difficulty and after some hesitation: namely, that in the upper position the red counters are equal in number to the black ones. But such anticipation does not yet take in the identity of the individual elements (thus Mos says, 'some have been taken away', and Dun thinks 'some more have been put on'); nor does it take in the identity of the rows as totalities. All the child predicts is that the red rows will get longer or shorter when moved. Thus the outlined longitudinal kinetic image remains dominated by transversal considerations, and the rows are felt to increase or decrease in quantity and frequently even in number. This is shown remarkably clearly by Tis when he says that the number of red counters varies (because the lines are 'leaning').

This interpretation is borne out by the fact that there is a fourth intermediate type of subject who starts off with the same semi-longitudinal and semi-transversal anticipation, but who finds as he goes on that the red and black counters are permanently equal, and eventually bases his judgment on their longitudinal displacement.

Wi (5,8); 6 and 0. '*More black ones, because it's small there* (0) *and it's big there* (6). – Look, you can move them up. – (He puts them at 6 after 1; positions 1 to 6 screened.) – Are there as many? – *Yes.* – And what about when they are moved lower down? – *Less red ones than black ones.*' We start again: 'For the last time now, is there the same number of red ones as black ones? – *Yes.* – And here (at 0)? – *You have brought them lower down: that makes them less.* – Less or the same? – *It's the same.* – Why? – *The lines!*'

Vol (5,10): '*More black ones.* – Why? – *There are more lines* (!) – Why? – *They are leaning over.*' Then he moves the red counters up to 1. The cover is put in place, and he anticipates them as they will be at 6.'Will that give as many or not? – *Yes, because the black ones are at the top and the red ones are at the top.* – And, if we bring them down? – *More black ones because there are less red ones.* – You do it. – (He slides them over the cardboard cover following the order of the guide-lines underneath.) – Now is that the same or not? – *The same number, because at the bottom it is closer together and at the top it is wider. I saw under the cardboard!*'

Eg (5,11): Same reactions; ends up by affirming equivalence, '*because there are the strings*' (the pieces of string used to mark the sections in fan I).

Ael (6,7): At first says that there are more black counters '*because it's wider*', and that the red counters increase as they are moved up and decrease as they are moved down. Then when he has moved them himself (with the cover) he turns his argument round and says '*it's the same number because there* (at the bottom) *it's smaller and there* (at the top) *it's wider*'.

Thus type III anticipations are quite suddenly transmitted into strictly longitudinal anticipations. This comes about as soon as the subject subordinates the length of the rows to the individual displacements of their members or to their density. Wi and Eg end up saying, 'There are the lines', or 'the strings'; and Vol says that the counters are 'closer together', and Ael that they are 'wide'. In other words, the static image of the rows suddenly gives way to a kinetic image of the longitudinal paths. This only occurs, however, after a long preliminary phase corresponding to the preceding types of reactions.

Finally, type V subjects. These subjects anticipate from the outset in longitudinal terms, and do not hesitate to affirm that equal, or as in the control tests, different numbers of counters, are conserved.

Hen (6,1): 6 and 0. 'Are there as many? – *Yes, because there it's close together and then not close together there.* – And if we make the red ones go up. – *It's the same, because it's one in each line* (10 red and 12 black counters); *less red ones, because there aren't any there* (track No. 1) *and not there* (track No. 8).'

Per (6,2): (10 red at 0 and 12 black counters at 6.) '*More black ones because you've put less red ones down.* – And if they are moved up? – *Don't need to: each one has its own line.* – (12 and 12.) *That'll make the same; some have been put back.*'

From now on immediate perception of the model acquires the force of the longitudinal type of kinetic anticipation.

III A and III B. Methods III *A* and III *B* were intended as a control for the preceding results. The object was to get the subject to concentrate on longitudinal anticipation by isolating the elements and their paths, dissociating the anticipations pure and simple (questions 2 and 4) from the displacement itself as demonstrated by the experimenter (question 5). The results obtained were slightly better than those for the previous methods. This indicates that longitudinal anticipation is within the reach of children of 5 to 6 years. Nevertheless the success score remains modest, which shows that in spite of previous practice this form of anticipation gives rise to certain systematic difficulties. Out of the twenty-six subjects aged 5 to 6 years to whom we were able to put all of questions 1–5, method III *A*, 23 per cent (six, that is) accepted that the counters were equal in number in question 1 (conservation); out of the remaining twenty subjects, ten (38·5 per cent) succeeded in question 3 (anticipated equivalence – six subjects) and question 5 (equivalence accepted after actual displacement – four subjects), and ten (38·5 per cent) failed in the same questions, in spite of the part played in them by repetition and practice. The results for method III *B* are similar, but differ from those of methods I–II.

There is no point in going back to the subjects who affirm conservation in question 1 (comparison of brown counters at 10 and green counters at 0), since they come under the type V reaction which we have just examined (subjects Hen and Per). We therefore return to the question in which the fixed elements at 10 are compared with the mobile elements at 9. In methods I and II the type I subjects deny that the counters in these positions are equal – either because the visual correspondence is not exact or because the mobile row has been judged inferior in number at 0. A comparison of methods III *A* and III *B*, makes it possible to establish three different kinds of result:

(1) Using method III *A*, with the brown counters at 10 and the green counters at 0 we asked the subjects to anticipate the movement of each green counter right up to position 9 where a yellow counter was placed as a marker. We found that 90 per cent of the children (while not acknowledging equivalence for positions 10 and 0) recognize that the brown counters at 10 and the yellow ones at 9 are equal. This is due to longitudinal anticipation of the course of the green counters and perceptual concretization achieved with the aid of the yellow counters (question 3).

(2) Still using method III *A*, and with the brown counters still at 10 and the green ones still at 0, we asked the subject to anticipate the movement of each green counter for positions 1, 3, 6 and 9 without employing the yellow one at 9 (and without, therefore, any perceptual concretization: question 4, with gestures to indicate the positions). This time we find that positive anticipation of equivalence for the brown counters at 10 and the green at 9 drops to 50 per cent! It is the longitudinal anticipation that falls short here for lack of concretization. This means that the factor of imperfect visual correspondence (upper row at 10 extends slightly beyond lower row at 9) is precluded. Consequently, the only way to explain the failure of 50 per cent of the subjects to affirm equivalence is to attribute it to a pseudo-conservation resulting from insistence on the initial length difference between positions 10 and 0.

(3) But besides this factor, which we have assumed operative in type I reactions to methods I–II, there remains the factor of imperfect visual correspondence. This is shown in method III *B*. Here positions 9 and 10 are given at the outset before any comparison is made between the brown counters at 10 and the green ones at 0. We find that successful appreciation of the equivalence of the brown counters at 10 and the green counters at 9 drops to 65 per cent (against 90 per cent in 1), and that 35 per cent of the twenty-eight subjects examined declare the numbers unequal. Several of them (Cê 5,1, Du 5,4, etc., and even Fra 6,5), after counting the 12 brown counters, reply, when asked to guess the number of green counters: '*I don't know*' or '*there aren't twelve*' or '*there'll be less*'. etc. We would further note in this connection that we managed to compare reactions to imperfect correspondence of elements on the fan-shaped frame with those to a similar arrangement of staggered pairs of buttons set out in rows on the table. In the former case the subject denied that the counters were equal in number, but said that they were in the latter case. It would seem, therefore, that the sections of the fan are a hindrance rather than a help!

Let us now examine the other reactions to question 4 with respect to the numerical equivalence between the brown counters at 10 and the green anticipated at the intermediate positions from 0 to 9. There were six subjects who did not recognize equivalence at their initial examination of the apparatus (question 1), but who did accept it after being asked to anticipate the paths and the positions (question 2). When reference is made to the intermediate positions (question 4) these subjects are all of one mind in adducing the guide-lines: '*Because there are the lines.*' (Bla 5,3); '*Because they are in the same line*' (Bu 5,10), etc. But it is interesting to note some initial hesitation in certain of the subjects between transverse and longitudinal anticipation. To begin with, they stress the horizontal length of the row in position 10, but go on to discover that '*there are no* (vertical) *lines missing*' (Mu 5,3), that '*the lines go towards the green buttons*' (Bi 6,3), or that although the tracks are wider at the top than at the bottom, the counters '*are in the same triangle, at the top and at the bottom*'. On the other hand, fourteen 5- to 6-year-old subjects, while anticipating correctly the paths and positions of the green counters (question 2), fail in question 4, because they do not change transversal considerations for a longitudinal viewpoint. They therefore come under the type III reactions examined earlier (variation of the number of green counters). Of these fourteen subjects only four were shaken in their conviction that the numbers differed by actually seeing the counters run along the tracks (question 5). And then it is because there is '*one button per line, not two on one line*', etc. The ten remaining subjects remained unshakeable:

Dar (5,2), for example, thinks that the green counters moved up to position 3 give '*more green ones*' than in position 0, and that if they are moved back to 0 '*there are not a lot of green ones*'. – She counts 12 black counters in position 10. – 'And how many green ones are there (at 0)?' – '*You can't tell, not the same, there are more black ones.*'

Lur (6,3) gives the same variation in number for the green counters whether they are moved up or down. – '*There are more black ones because they are more apart.*' The experimenter picks up the 12 black counters at 10 in one hand and the 12 green counters at 0 in the other. Lur concludes that there are more buttons in the first than in the second.

Turning to the reaction to method III *B*, we find eight to nine subjects out of twenty-eight who in question 3 succeed in seeing that the black counters at 10 and the green at 0 will remain equal in number. To these must be added another five subjects who hesitate or vacillate. Out of the remaining fourteen subjects, eight who fail to anticipate equivalence in question 3 succeed in question 4, where they have to anticipate the intermediate positions between 9 and 0: only then do they discover the significance of the guide-lines. Finally, the remaining subjects two succeed in question 5 (actual displace- and the behaviour of the others is principally characterized by vacillation. These different reactions are thus very similar to those observed using method III *A*.

In conclusion, these various facts are instructive from three points of view: the images, the operations leading to conservation, and the relationship between the images and the operations.

As far as images are concerned, we have been obliged to distinguish two kinds of representational anticipation. These are completely interdependent after a certain level of development. But before it they are extraordinarily independent – to the extent that, as type IV subject Vol said, there appear to be 'more lines' at the top of the tracks than at the bottom, simply because they are oblique, or 'leaning'. These two kinds of anticipation are, namely, *transversal* anticipation, or representation of the horizontal extension of the rows, and *longitudinal* anticipation, or representation of the paths of the counters along the vertical or oblique tracks. Now, although these two modes of anticipation are not co-ordinated until about 7 years, imaginal representation of the movement of the counters does not in fact present the slightest difficulty. Question 2, method III *A*, which concerns the paths as such, is successfully answered by 100 per cent of the subjects at 5 years. It is not, therefore, the basic data of the problem that cause difficulty (as it is when the subject is asked to anticipate the levels of transferred liquids or the widths of the elongated balls of clay). Thus the failure to co-ordinate transversal and longitudinal anticipations is not so much due to intrinsic difficulty as to the fact that the young subjects simply do not utilize them or carry them spontaneously into effect. The root cause of this unco-ordination is that the images involved in transversal and longitudinal anticipation are fundamentally incomplete. Instead of being brought to bear on the length and density of the rows simultaneously, they relate only to the former (or very exceptionally the latter – in which case the former is neglected). And this for two reasons. The first reason concerns the laws of the images as such (boundary considerations: hence the importance of length), and the second the corresponding notional structure: the whole is not yet conceived as the sum of its constituent elements, and the image, therefore, does not attempt to isolate them.

In the operational context the present facts make it clear that non-conservation is not due to a total inability to imagine the paths of the counters, but simply to the child's lack of interest in them. And this in turn is due to a lack of additive ability that would lead to isolation of the individual elements within an overall representation of the whole as their sum. It is precisely this ability that appears on the scene at the level of conservation operations, and it should be pointed out that the anticipatory image of the trajectories, with the practice or reinforcement due to questions 2 to 4 of method III *A*, does promote this faculty of additive conservation.

The child is capable of such images from the outset (since there is 100 per cent success score for question 2), although they are not put to use and consequently not elaborated. It seems that, except where practice is a factor (as in methods III *A* and III *B*), these images are not actually formed until the operations emerge and exert their influence by providing an additive framework that rouses interest in the individual elements. Thus once again it is the operations that appear to orient the images at the level where they become adequate to their object. On the other hand, at the preoperational level of non-conservation and subordination of longitudinal to incomplete transversal anticipation, the reverse is probably the case. The early images in their dual static and global aspect oblige the subject to focus his attention on boundaries as a criterion for estimating lengths and quantities in general. They are thus in all probability responsible for the non-additive character of the notional structures of this level that hold back the formation of the operations and conservation.

5. *The anticipation of one-to-one correspondence when the counters are moved simultaneously*

The results of the last section are so surprising that it is only proper to go on to the only control-test enabling us to eliminate any doubt or misunderstanding in the child's mind about the meaning of the questions put to him. So we took the fan-shaped set-up (Figure 46) and, without bringing in the cover or any other complications, we moved the 12 counters simultaneously by means of a mechanical device. This made possible a direct perception of the counters being placed in correspondence. The experiment was undertaken with M. Aboudaram. The point is that it may be questioned whether in the experiment in section 4 the individual processes of pairing counter by counter and lane by lane are really enough to enable subjects, such as those at the preoperational level who do not believe that the whole equals the sum of its part, to symbolize visually the term-by-term correspondence of the two wholes (12–12). But if the 12 green counters (green to avoid the red–black contrast) are moved up simultaneously until they are right against the 12 upper counters, both anticipatory image and direct perception become so pregnant that the questions lose any ambiguity they may previously have possessed. If the 4- to 6-year-olds react here in just the same way as before, the reason will be that the image is indeed unable to set operational comprehension in motion within a context characterized by other interpretative assumptions.

The apparatus is the same as that used in section 4, with the following exception: each lane is fitted with a narrow longitudinal slot through which the lower movable counters are fixed to a transverse (horizontal) bar behind the apparatus, so that the experimenter can displace all the counters at once for any distance required. The device is divided lengthwise into ten equidistant positions (0 at the bottom to 10 at the top). The subjects were asked the following questions.

(1) Twelve green counters at 0 and twelve black counters at 10. The subject was asked whether or not there were as many green as black counters, and why.

(2) We asked the subject (as in section 4) to anticipate the positions of the green counters at 9 without actually moving them, and then to indicate where each of the green counters would end up by means of a yellow counter.

We noted the child's eye-movements and the path followed. After the seventh counter we asked him if what he had done was correct, and which of the green buttons would 'end up there' (8th place at position 9).

(3) We asked whether there were or were not as many yellow counters at 9 and as many black counters at 10 (or green at 0), and why.

(4) We asked the subject to anticipate the positions of the green counters at 1, $3\frac{1}{2}$, $6\frac{1}{2}$ and 9, and to estimate each time (except 1) whether the quantity of green counters in the anticipated position (without their actually being seen there) would be the same as the quantity of black counters at 10.

(5) Finally, all the green counters were moved simultaneously to $3\frac{1}{2}$, $6\frac{1}{2}$, 9 and 10. Each time the subject was asked if the green and the black counters were numerically equivalent or not, and why.

(6) The green counters were brought back to 0. The child was asked as in (1), whether the green counters at 0 and the black counters at 10 were equal in number.

For 77 subjects the quantitative results were as follows (Table 132, overleaf; question 2 was, of course, solved at all ages).

This table contains a number of instructive facts. To begin with (question 1), we find that as usual it is not until 7 years that 75 per cent of the subjects see that the longer and the shorter rows are equal in number: and this in spite of the fact that the term-by-term correspondence could have been taken in earlier, and could, as here, be observed from the perceptible device of the fan's sections. (It will be remembered that question 2 is successfully resolved at all ages: that is to say, each subject sees that it is possible, by following the lanes, to make one green correspond to one black counter and one only.)

And then we find that, in spite of the practice afforded by the series of 8 questions and sub-questions 3–5, it is only at 6 years (question 6) that the comparison of the green counters at 0 and the black at 10 gives rise to the judgment that they are numerically equivalent. We therefore have to wait for the subjects to reach the

TABLE 132   *Anticipations (3–4) and judgments made from direct perception (1 and 5–6) of numerical equality between the green and black counters (As % of the responses)*[17]

Questions		1	3	4			5				6
Positions		0	9	3·5	6·5	9	3·5	6·5	9	10	0
4 years (*N*=16)		12	47	31	38	42	41	59	71	81	33
5 years	(30)	10	37	23	32	39	33	46	52	77	33
6 years	(18)	56	72	67	72	76	67	73	89	94	80
7 years	(13)	77	84	92	92	92	92	92	100	100	92

threshold of the stage during which the concrete operations are formed. It is not until then that the fact that he has seen the green counters simultaneously displaced (question 5), then paired against the black counters and finally brought back to their starting point will convince him that they are consistently equal in number.

As for question 5 – the question that the present investigation was principally designed to examine – we find that its results are much the same as those of question 4. In other words, the subject may indeed perceive the twelve green counters move simultaneously off down the twelve tracks to be matched one by one against the black counters: but this improves hardly at all the anticipation of the individual paths from the point of view of the numerical equivalence of the two rows. It is at 4 and 5 years that the difference is most marked, i.e. that a surprise effect occurs most clearly. This is probably due to some insufficiency in anticipation in question 4, or to its insufficiently vivid nature. But in spite of the slight progress it is still only at 6 years that 75 per cent of the subjects accept the equivalence of the green and the black counters at position $6\frac{1}{2}$ (though not at $3\frac{1}{2}$).

We saw from the section 4 experiments that anticipation of the paths of the counters failed to convince the subject that the green and the black counters were numerically equivalent. And in our commentaries on the experiments we were led to attribute this to the fact that the anticipation in question remained essentially transversal rather than longitudinal – that it was brought to bear on the length of the horizontal rows rather than on the actual paths of the counters. We now see that this tendency to dwell on the transversal is so strong that even direct perception of the simultaneous movement of the counters can only slightly weaken it. Thus

[17] This table shows an apparent set-back at 5 years compared with 4 years. But as there are thirty 5-year-old and sixteen 4-year-old subjects, it is more likely that the 4-year-old group should be considered as ahead. It is unfortunately difficult to examine as many 4-year-olds as one would wish, and we have not been able to make a check by doubling this total of sixteen subjects.

there are more black counters, according to Isa (4,9), at $3\frac{1}{2}$, $6\frac{1}{2}$ and even 9, *'because it's longer'* (i.e. because the black row is longer), and (Jer. 5,5) because the green ones are *'closer together'*, or again, *'because the black ones are a bit wider'* (Mar 5,8), *'because in the black ones there are more lines'*, *'because there is a bigger space'*, and so on. The correct answers generally base themselves on longitudinal comparison: *'the same, because it's in the same lines'* (Oli 4,10), *'because there are some in all the lanes'* (Iea 5,5), etc.

In conclusion, one or two extra observations are also worthy of comment. And to begin with, the preoperational subjects who refuse to accept that the green and the black counters are equal. The majority of these subjects think that the black are more numerous because their row is longer. But as we have already pointed out in connection with other experiments, there is also a minority who judge quantity by density. Thus Pie (4,11) says of position $6\frac{1}{2}$: *'there are more green ones, because they are nearer together'*, while for position 9 he says: ' – *because they are not apart'*. Now, the existence of this minority proves that non-conservation of the numerical aggregate is not a consequence of some semantic confusion affecting number, quantity and spatial length. For we find that non-conservation is sometimes (and most frequently, in fact) justified on the grounds that the lengths of the rows are unequal; but it is sometimes also justified by adducing the opposite criterion. The two dimensions involved are in fact complementary (longer = less dense), and the common characteristic of all non-conservations is precisely that they retain one dimension and neglect the other. This corresponds exactly to what we saw in the case of the anticipations relating to the clay ball. The ball transformed into a sausage is said to contain more clay generally because it is elongated (the fact that it is also thinner being ignored), but sometimes also because it is thinner (the fact that it is *longer* being ignored).

Another case worth quoting is that of the subjects who add extra elements in order to make the two collections equal. For example, in question 3, Mic (4,7) puts eighteen yellow counters down in order to obtain a row equal in length to that of the black counters. Also worth noting is the fact that, in the case of direct perception (question 5), some subjectss, a we have already seen, refuse to accept that the green and the black counters are equal, even in position 9, unless they are actually touching: *'They need to touch'* (Mar 5,8), and *'They need to bump together; then it's the same.'*

Finally we mention a curious reaction frequently observed when the child was anticipating the movement of the green counters towards the top. Quite a large number of younger subjects, instead of aligning the counters horizontally, arrange them in an arc: *'it'll be round because the pieces of wood are leaning* (i.e. the sections of the fan are oblique) *and in the middle they get there more quickly'*, and, *'because it's straight* (i.e. vertical) *in the middle and at the ends it's leaning'*. This reaction has no direct repercussion on the conservation of numerical equivalence. Nevertheless, it is of interest in several respects – even if all it shows is that a notional centration lies behind the younger subjects' essentially transversal (rather than longitudinal, in the senses defined above, section 4) anticipation. And this does not in any way mean that there is no vivid concrete image of the counters' movement at all, since it is expressed in this distinctive incurvated form.

6. The image of staggered parallel lines of equal and of unequal lengths[18]

Two sticks are first juxtaposed to show they are equal in length, and then one is slid slightly ahead of the other. The 4- to 8-year-old subjects generally react to this by maintaining that the displaced rod 'has become longer'. One might, of course, raise the question whether this is a genuine case of non-conservation, in the sense that the examples discussed in sections 1 to 5 above are cases of non-conservation. Is it not, perhaps, really a semantic question – a confusion in the child's mind between the terms 'longer' (*plus long*) and 'further' (*plus loin*)? But the many facts described in Chapters Two–Five of this work are already enough to reassure us in this respect. In the first place we have seen the part played by boundaries in spatial representation, and in the second place we have seen that for a long time ordinal and metric estimations of lengths are not differentiated, and that the reasons for this reside not only in the notions and characteristic inferences of the preoperational phases, but also in the peculiar nature of the early spatial images. It seemed, therefore, to be of particular relevance to try to define the part played by the image both in non-conservation and the formation of positive conservation of length. When we were working with S. Taponier a while ago,[19] we found that non-conservation could not be imputed to perceptual factors, since the 5-year-olds were able to estimate the relative lengths of two equal but staggered horizontal lines with a greater degree of precision than 8- to 11-year-old subjects. But although we can say that perception does not account for the notions, we still need to determine what influences are exerted by imaginal representation.

To this end we got the subject to imagine, both reproductively after perception and in anticipation, three basic details, all of which come into the conservation question: (1) the actual lengths of the rods B and E, laid side by side with their ends corresponding, or staggered (the lengths to be anticipated with varying degrees of stagger); (2) the projecting lengths c (B projecting beyond E), and d (E projecting beyond B); (3) the lengths of the empty spaces a and b corresponding to the distances in 2 (see Figure 48). Using 242 subjects

[18] With the collaboration of S. Taponier, A. Papert-Christofides, and M. Bovet.
[19] See Piaget, J., *The Mechanisms of Perception*, 1969, Table 117.

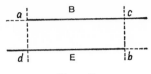

FIG. 48

aged 5 to 9 years, Vinh-Bang has found that the arguments introduced to vindicate non-conservation referred for the most part to (I) the movement of the displaced rod, (II) to the projection of the leading end, and (III) to alleged non-compensation of the projection of rod B to the right by the projection of the rod E to the left and vice versa. It is worth while quoting the numerical results as standardized by Vinh-Bang. (See Table 133. As percentage of subjects.)

TABLE 133   *Successes for conservation and justification of non-conservations* (*Vinh-Bang*)

	Successes	Movement	Projection	Non-compensation	Other answers
5 years ($N=25$)	0	44	20	12	24
6 years (50)	10	18	40	20	12
7 years (67)	40	11	12	37	
8 years (50)	60	8	24	8	
9 years (50)	94	0	2	2	

In the first place, it emerges that this form of conservation comes surprisingly late[20] (and it comes even later – sudden success at 9 years – in the case of conservation of the length of straight lines transformed into broken lines by a rearrangement of segments). This seems to show that in these cases the operational problem is subordinate to, or closely linked to, questions of imaginal representation and the concomitant attitude towards boundaries. In the second place, non-conservation occurs in the majority of cases when the subject thinks that the displaced rod becomes longer because it has been moved (this is particularly the case at 5 years), or because – and this amounts to almost the same thing – it projects beyond the other (this is particularly the case at 6 years), or (the two projections being compared at about 7 years) because the extent of projection of the leading end c appears greater than the other d – 'it's less here (d)', etc.

It is of some interest, therefore, to study the imaginal represen-

[20] It should be remembered that standardized tests always give late results. As there is no free conversation, it is not possible to elicit the subject's maximum potential.

tations connected with these conservation problems. Our main focus of attention will be the image the child makes for himself of the projections c and d (question 2) and of the empty spaces a and b (question 3). This is, however, going to bring us up against a some-what paradoxical situation – and we point this out right away, since it may well explain the surprisingly backward nature of apparently simple forms of conservation. The paradox is this. In the sphere of preoperational judgment we shall see that the child shows a marked tendency to overestimate (notionally) both the displaced rod B and the projection c. On the other hand, in the sphere of imaginal representation, he none the less systematically underestimates (imaginally) the elements exceeding a boundary point – that is, the rod B or its projecting portion c. This is a very instructive situation. From a general point of view it brings out the dual nature of the images and the operations (or preoperations); and in this particular case it explains the otherwise incomprehensible difficulties that we shall see the subjects experiencing in co-ordinating the data provided by imaginal representation with the reasoned arguments that eventually lead to conservation.

Method I. The first thing to investigate is the way the child by means of gesture or drawing presents the length of a line so that it is equal to a second line but in a staggered position.[21] Our problem, then, is to give the results for a series of methods corresponding to the successive approximations of the inquiry.

The subject was presented with successive sheets of paper 21×15 cm. On the first I.1 there is drawn a model horizontal line 8 cm long M between points M1 and M2. At M1 the line M starts from a small square representing a house (M being a 'road'). 2 cm above M1 and the square is a second square. This is the child's house, and from here he has to draw a line C imagining a road of the same length as, and parallel to, M. As point C1 is above M1 the subject will have no trouble in tracing a line to C2 above M2.

Sheet I.2 is as I.1, except that the child's house and point C1 are displaced 2 cm to the right. The question is, will the child, in order to make the roads 'just as long', stop C2 above M2, or will he be able to take it the corresponding 2 cm ahead of M2?

On the third sheet, I.3, the point C1 and the child's 'house' are displaced 2 cm to the left. The child thus has to stop point C2 this side of M2.

Sheet I.4 repeats I.2.

In sheet I.5 C1 and the 'house' are 6 cm to the right of M1 – that is, three-quarters of the way along M.

On sheet I.6 point C1 is 4 cm to the right – that is, halfway along M. The child was shown each of these sheets in turn, and told that he was

[21] With the collaboration of S. Taponier.

going to be asked to draw the lines C so that they would be the same length as M. But before actually executing the drawings he was asked to indicate on each sheet in turn how far his line would go by pointing with his finger. Then we went on to the drawing, 'properly this time'. After each drawing we asked the child if he had been successful: 'Are our two roads just as long? There isn't one longer than the other?' When the child admitted that they were not equal, we asked him how this could be remedied without displacing the houses at $M\,1$ or $C\,1$. If the child made mistakes at first, and then corrected himself during the course of the experiment (for example, in the long displacement in I.5), then we went back to the first sheets for more drawings. And if the errors persisted, we said after drawing I.6: 'One little boy started off just like you, but he didn't think the roads were as long as one another; and he went up to there (the experimenter draws the line as he speaks). Is he right?' If the subject came round to the right answer, he was asked to repeat his earlier drawings.

When this part of the test – which is concerned with imaginal representation – was completed, we went on to the operational problem of conservation. The subject was presented with four sticks, two 16 cm, one 14 cm and one 18 cm in length. He was asked to choose the two equal sticks. Then, (1) the two equal sticks were placed horizontally on the table 4·5 cm apart, with extremities corresponding, not staggered, and the subject was asked to note that they were equal; (2) the top rod was slid 5 cm to the right and the subject was asked: 'Are they both just as long as one another, or is one longer than the other?' If he replied in the negative (non-conservation) he was asked for an explanation and the sticks were again placed one above the other; (3) the lower rod was then displaced 5 cm to the left and the questions were repeated; (4) finally, the sticks were put back in their position one above the other; one was then moved 2·5 cm to the left and the other 2·5 cm to the right: the questions were repeated and the child asked to justify his answers.

The following table (Table 134) gives the results for anticipation of the lengths by pointing and by drawing for tests I.1 to I.6 combined. The symbol $+$ designates complete success, and $-$ failure for I.2 onwards (the staggered positions); the symbol $\pm$ designates success only in I.5 and I.6 for pointing, or only after the supplementary questions and corrections for the drawings. In addition we give the reactions to the conservation tests. Here $\pm$ means that there is a successful response to question 4 only (double displacement).

First, it is interesting to see that pointing is less frequently successful than drawing. Generally speaking, one finds the reverse (cf. Chapter Two, Tables 3–5, and Chapter Five, Table 81), and usually there is overestimation in pointing and underestimation in drawing. But when cases of the former have arisen the subject has only had to reproduce the length of a single isolated rod, and the only boundaries involved have been the rod's own extremities indicated

TABLE 134 *Anticipations, by pointing and by drawing, of the lengths of staggered 'roads' I.1–I.6, and reactions to conservation*
(As % of the subjects)

	Pointing			Drawing			Conservation		
	−	±	+	−	±	+	−	±	+
5 years N = 18	94	6	0	39	22	39	68	5	27
6 years (18)	61	17	22	22	22	56	50	0	50
7 years (20)	40	25	35	10	20	70	30	30	40
8 years (19)	26	11	63	0	16	84	21	5	74

simultaneously and without starting and finishing points (whereas the drawing starts at one end and finishes at the other). In the present case, however, the subject has to indicate the length of a path staggered in relation to another – which means that there is a boundary external to the line to be constructed, and that the child's problem is to decide whether it should be exceeded or not. Further, the starting point of the required line C is already fixed at $C\,1$ and the problem is to choose a finishing point $C\,2$ in relation to $M\,2$: this means that there is a virtual movement from $C\,1$ to $C\,2$, rather than simultaneous indication, and that the ensuing difficulties are comparable to those met in drawing. This explains why pointing is not more successful. But why is it in fact as inferior as it is? Probably because the drawing, during or after execution, consists of a continuous line C that can be compared perceptually with the model M, so that assessment of the lengths can be checked or corrected simply by reference to $M\,2$. When the length is merely traced out with the finger, on the other hand, the starting points $M\,1$ and $C\,1$ may be neglected.

The second noteworthy fact is the lateness of successful responses to these tests both in the case of the drawings (75 per cent not until 8 years) and, more especially, in the case of the gestures. The initial attitude, of course, consists in cutting short the drawing of C at a point above $M\,2$, and in then maintaining that C and M are equal because they stop at the same place. The intermediate attitudes consist in producing the same drawing and discovering afterwards that the lines are not equal, or – and more often – in being seized by uncertainty in test I.5 (three-quarter shift along M).

And the third remarkable fact is the correlation of the results for the representation tests with those for the conservation tests. The correlations may be tabulated thus (Table 135). It should be pointed out that in the present case the gestures and the pointing and drawing tests I.1–I.6 constitute a training in conservation that gradually liberates the child from his concern with the finishing points alone.

TABLE 135   *Relating imaginal anticipation and conservation at 5 to 8 years*
(As % of 75 subjects)

	Non-conservation $(-C)$	Conservation $(+C)$
Unsuccessful anticipation $(-A)$	65 $(-A-C)$	5·5 $(-A+C)$
Successful anticipation $(+A)$	1·5 $(+A-C)$	28 $(+A+C)$

The conservation tests 1–4 are themselves sufficiently numerous to give the subject practice. Consequently the success score for conservation is slightly higher here than in Table 133, and even higher if we include the cases of initial failure and ultimate success (this gives 32 per cent at 5 years, 50 per cent at 6 years, 70 per cent at 7 years and 79 per cent at 8 years). Thus we find not only that successful conservations come mid-way between the pointing and the drawing successes, but also that at 8 years the same subjects successful in anticipation are also successful in conservation (with the exception of one who managed the former but not the latter, and one who managed the latter but not the former).

Method II. In a second investigation we dealt with exactly the same problem. But, instead of getting the subject to compare two pencil lines ('the road'), one of which he has drawn himself, we used two rods (lengths of wire), which we placed either directly above one another or in a staggered position arrangement. One of the rods was almost completely covered by a case (or 'tunnel'). The subject was required to indicate by pointing how far the rod under the cover would move, and to reproduce both the rods in a drawing (one being completely visible, the other covered along 19/20 of its length). The experiment was performed as before, with the following exceptions: the child has to fix the starting points as well as the finishing points in his drawing (in I the starting points were given), and to determine for himself the value of both c and d (Figure 48; in I one of the projections c and d was given). We shall thus be able to compare the lengths of the drawings of the rods B and E as well as those of the projections c and d, before we go on to investigate their relationship to the successful responses of the conservation tests.

The apparatus consisted of two rods 10 cm long, one 12 cm and one 8 cm long (bicycle spokes), and of two cases, or 'tunnels' (metal curtain rod), 16 mm wide, 7 mm high and 32 or 40 cm in length. A sheet of white card 54 × 70 cm was put in front of the child and the rods were placed on it horizontally in the centre of the top half. The lower rod was visible and the top rod was placed 3 cm higher up under the cover from which it pro-jected at the left by only half a centimetre. On the lower half of the card was placed a sheet of paper for the child to draw on.

We began by asking the child to select from the four rods the ones which had exactly the same length. When he picked the two 10 cm rods we took one of these (E) and placed it in the lower position, while the other (B) was inserted in the tunnel leaving only a constant length of 5 mm visible. Then the subject was requested to show in the tunnel, by pointing with his finger, where the hidden end of B would come in relation to E for each of six positions corresponding to I.1–I.6: II.1, no stagger; II.2, quarter shift to right (2·5 cm); II.3, quarter shift to left; II.4, as II.2; II.5, three-quarter shift (7·5 cm) to right; II.6, half shift (5 cm) to right. The cover is moved, of course, with the rod for each displacement. The rod thus never projects more than 5 mm, either on the left (in II.1–II.2 and II.4–II.6) or on the right (II.3). In each of these situations the child was also ques-tioned about conservation: 'Can you tell me whether the rods are the same length, or is one of them longer than the other?'

After this we asked him to copy rod E, stressing that the drawing was to be accurate –'no longer and no shorter'. Then, 3 cm directly above rod E we placed rod B, covered by the tunnel, but its left extremity visible and in line with the corresponding end of E. The subject was asked to draw rod B with its exact length, 'as if you could see it with the tunnel taken away'. The procedure was the same for II.2–III.6, beginning each time with a copy of the fixed rod E.

After these six drawings we went on to a conservation test, using the same rods, but this time without the cover. The subject was asked if they were the same length in the following positions: (1) one directly above the other; (2) half shift (5 cm) to right, (3) half shift (5 cm) to left. If the child denied conservation, we sometimes pressed him, thus: 'But really and truly are they the same length or not?'

To start with the global results, Table 136 sets out the successes for anticipation (subjects successful both in pointing and drawing), and the successes for conservation (both in pointing and in the final test).

We would first point out that the conservation questions posed during the pointing tests naturally yield better results than the final complete questions. The former are successfully answered by 55–58 per cent of the 6- to 7-year-old subjects, whereas the latter are man-aged by only 21 per cent and 40 per cent at these ages respectively. All the subjects who were successful in the latter were also successful in the former, though the reverse is not true. It follows that there is some learning of conservation under the influence of the anticipa-tions, but also of the first of the two kinds of question: hence the lead over Table 133. It is all the more interesting, therefore, to see how frequently the conservation is negated at 5 to 7 years. If we may dwell on this aspect of the problem for a moment, we would note that

TABLE 136 *Successes (as % of the subjects) for digital and graphic antici-pations (tests II.2–II.6 entirely successful),*[22] *and for conservation*

	5 years (N=17)	6 years (19)	7 years (20)	8 years (20)
Anticipation	45	55	75	100
Conservation	29	21	40	80

particular attention was paid to those subjects whose anticipations are better than their conservation judgments, in order that due consideration could be given to any semantic confusion arising between 'further' and 'longer'. Now, this confusion does no doubt exist in the child's mind. But does non-conservation really amount to no more than a verbal misapprehension? Or is it the lack of differentiation between ordinal (more or less distant finishing points) and metrical criteria (magnitude as distance between starting and finishing points) that is the primary factor? If the latter, then the semantic apprehension in an apparently pure state would in effect be merely the verbal residuum of an anterior notional level, a residuum evidencing a not yet fully operational state. For example, it sometimes happens that the 8-year-old subjects first negate conservation and then, when asked for an explanation, succeed in recognizing it and give the right explanations; or they may introduce some such *distinguo* as the following: 'They are the same length, but one is farther than the other. – Is the one that is farther longer or not? – It's longer, but the same size!'

But the basic fact is that Table 136 does not, as did Tables 134 and 135, show a high correlation between anticipation and conservation, but rather distinct retardation of the latter. Working out the relationship of the two along the lines of Table 135 (and distinguishing, for the reactions to the conservations, between the complete successes retained exclusively as 'successes' in Table 135 and the intermediate reactions, where there is gradual approximation to the correct answer), we arrive at the results set forth in Table 137.

TABLE 137 *Relating imaginal anticipation (method II) and conservation* (As % of 76 subjects of 5 to 8 years)

	Non-conservation	Intermediate	Conservation
Unsuccessful anticipation	25	1	4
Successful anticipation	29	13	28

[22] The successes are qualitative rather than exact by measurement. All drawings or indications of *B* as projecting beyond those of *E* by 2·5% of the total length are counted correct. If *E* is drawn as 50 mm the accepted correct projection is more than 1·25 mm.

Thus 53 per cent of cases speak in favour of correlation (– – or + +), 33 per cent speak against (– + or + –), and 13 per cent are intermediate after successful as against 1 per cent after unsuccessful anticipation. This means that there is some link between the anticipations[23] and the conservations, though the former, which are slightly easier than those of Table 134, are ahead of the latter. We shall now attempt to interpret these two types of relationship.

It may seem paradoxical that the imaginal anticipations of Table 137 are successful slightly earlier than those of Table 134, in view of the fact that in the latter the starting point of the lines was given, whereas in the present case the child has to determine the degree of stagger and the original starting point for himself. But it is only when prompted by a problem or need to adapt that a *prise de conscience* will take place. Now the fact that in Table 134 the subject is provided with starting points means that he will be automatically led to centre his attention on the finishing points: hence his tendency to avoid exceeding the terminal boundary of the model. On the other hand, if the subject is, as he is here, obliged to choose his own starting point, he is induced to take stock of the general situation and consequently of the degree of projection.

But does not that make it all the odder that the present anticipations correlate less well to the conservations than those of Table 134? The answer is that in the first place the successful anticipations of Tables 136 and 137 are only qualitative (and therefore independent of the length of the projection), whereas the conservation is quantitative. In the second place – and this is the crux of the matter – it is one thing to judge two rods to be equal when one has just been displaced so as to project a certain way ahead of the other, but quite another to represent such a projection without actually perceiving it. For in the first case there is a distinct tendency to overestimate the projection (see Table 133), and in the second there is an equally distinct tendency to underestimate it! And if the lengths given in the subject's drawings of the fixed, visible rod E and the staggered rod B (under the cover) are measured, it is found that the length of B is almost always less than that of E. While the copy of E shows an average depreciation of – 17·1 to – 25·4 per cent (= copies of 7·48 to 8·29 cm), the representation of B yields averages, depending on age, of – 25·2 to – 28·4 per cent (6·77 to 7·85 cm for a 10 cm rod). Two essential facts need to be mentioned in connection with the measuring of the two projecting portions (initial d, and terminal c – see Figure 48). First, a large number of subjects do not succeed in representing projection c (by

302

reference to the bimodal curve obtained, we counted a projection as zero if it was below 2·5 per cent of E or below 0·25 cm, the actual projections being 2·5 to 7·5 cm). Second, the projection c is almost always (for eighteen averages out of twenty) lower than d. Table 138 gives the percentage of subjects by age and by test (II.2 to II.6) who do not give a projection c, and the average differences between d and c (in mm) for tests II.2–II.4 (projection of 2·5 cm) and II.2–II.6 (2·5 to 7·5 cm).

TABLE 138 *Percentage of subjects failing to draw projection c[24] and averages of the differences between initial (d) and terminal (c) projections* (In mm)

	II.2	II.3	II.4	II.5	II.6	d–c (II.2–II.4)	d–c (II.2–II.6)
5 years	35	35	30	20	25	+4·0	+6·4
6 years	26	30	20	10	10	+1·6	+2·2
7 years	5	0	10	5	5	+2·1	+2·4
8 years	0	0	0	0	0	+3·2	+2·9

We see from this that indication of the projections progresses regularly with age. But at all ages (with no progress between 6 and 8 years) the terminal projection c is appreciably shorter than the initial one d. It may be concluded, therefore, that the image tends to depreciate projection c, whereas the preoperational judgment in the conservation tests tends to overestimate both its quantitative value and its qualitative significance (see Table 133 and comments)! There is no logical contradiction here, since it means that in both cases the rods appear more equal if the degree of displacement is less. But there is an opposition of attitudes (degree of displacement minimized to conserve equality, or displacement recognized and emphasized, while conservation is waived) that is sufficient to explain why there is not a perfect correlation between the anticipation of lengths B and E and the conservation judgment. And it is striking to note that from 6 to 8 years the underestimation of the final displacement tends to increase (from +1·6 to +3·2 for II.2–II.4) at the very stage when conservation is in process of being established.

But let us remember that these details are provided by drawings relating to the lengths B and E, not by a technique designed to stress the projecting portions of the rods. This is why, in the present technique (II), the anticipations are on average successful before the

[24] Indication by pointing yields better results, but one still finds 5 per cent of subjects from 5 to 7 years who do not indicate projection c for tests II.2 and II.4 and 10 to 21 per cent for test II.3.

conservation judgments. On the other hand, when the projections *d* and *c* as such or the corresponding spaces *a* and *b* are stressed, as in methods IV and V, we find that on average conservation precedes anticipation – which poses yet another problem!

Method III. Before dealing with that, however, we should like to give some account of the results of a technique devised by S. Taponier by means of which it was possible to eliminate the tunnels. Rod *E* remains fixed in a horizontal position, while rod *B* is presented vertically. The subject is asked to draw it as it would be if it rotated on its base until it came to a horizontal position. The base is at either the left or the right extremity of *B*, and the displacements are of the same order as those in the tests 2–6 above. But as test 3 (shift to left) necessitates a slight alteration in techniques I.3 (starting point of *B* at left) and II.3 (starting point of *B* at the right-hand extremity of the tunnel, which is displaced to the left), we shall distinguish for III.3 a procedure III *A* (similar to I), and III *B* (similar to II), though the difference in results is extremely small.

Now, using twenty 5-year-old and twenty 6-year-old subjects, the results of procedures III *A* and III *B* are, curiously enough, slightly better than those of procedure I, and even of procedure II, as far as qualitative indication of the projections is concerned.

(1) At 5 years 65 per cent of the subjects succeed in all the anticipation tests using gesture or drawings (as opposed to 45 per cent in Table 4) and at 6 years 80 per cent in III *A* and 95 per cent in III *B*.

(2) On the other hand, the projections *c* remain appreciably shorter than projections *d*: a difference of + 6·4 mm between *d* and *c* at 5 years, and + 5·8 mm at 6 years.

(3) Relationship between anticipations and conservations: the lead of anticipation over conservation is at least as great as in method II (see Table 139, where what we have called intermediate cases are in effect cases that are hard to classify in terms of failure or success).

TABLE 139   *Relating imaginal anticipation (method III) and conservation* (As % of 40 subjects of 5 and 6 years)

	Non-conservation	Intermediate	Conservation
Unsuccessful anticipation	17·5	2·5	7·5
Successful anticipation	45	10	17·5

It can be seen from this that the cases of successful anticipation not followed by conservation are by far the most numerous. What is interesting in this technique, then, is that it shows that, paradoxically, it is easier to imagine a rod projecting beyond another when they do not start out parallel. The explanation is no doubt that the parallelism of the rods, which have already been seen to be equal in length, more effectively induces an image of a common boundary. But this qualitatively easier anticipation is counter-balanced by even stronger quantitative underestimation (*d-c* difference) – which again points to a link between the image and the boundary. It is, then, this underestimation by the image, in conflict with overestimation of the projection *c* in the final conservation tests (horizontal staggered rods visibly parallel), that explains why conservation appears so late compared with qualitative anticipation.

In this connection we give the distribution of subjects in respect of the difference between *d* and *c*. This will take us on to the problems arising in procedure IV. We distinguish five classes of values: (1) ≪ more than 10 mm difference on the side of *d*; (2) < from +9·9 to +5; (3) = from +4·9 to −4·9; (4) > from −5 to −9·9; (5) ≫ more than −10 mm (see Table 140).

It is quite clear from this that reactions affirming equality of length, though they increase (irregularly) with age, do not reach 50 per cent by 8 years.

TABLE 140 *Percentage of the subjects (methods II and III) according to the classes of values 1–5*
(Tests II.2–II.6 and III.2–III.6)[25]

	Zero projection (± 2·5 mm)	≪	<	=	>	≫
II:						
5 years	29	37	23	23	10	7
6 years	19	19	15	44	10	12
7 years	5	22	21	37	10	10
8 years	0	14	25	47	12	2
III:						
5 years	11	35	23	28	7	7
6 years	1	34	21	34	8	3

Method IV. We have dealt above with imaginal anticipation bearing on the staggered rods *B* and *E*, and we have seen that it is only at a late stage that the subject comes to recognize *d* and *c* and *a* and *b* as equal. It remains, therefore, to go on to consider the imagining of these elements – the projections and the corresponding spaces – as such. Now this point is of some considerable interest. If

[25] The percentages of zero projections are given separately. The other percentages relate to all the subjects who show a significant projection.

representations of the projecting portions and the blank spaces were relatively independent of representations of the rods themselves, and if it turned out that such representation were retarded to the extent that it did not form until after, and as a function of, conservation (rather than before as was the case in the qualitative anticipations described for techniques II and III) – then we should have some important evidence enabling us both to confirm that there is indeed failure to differentiate ordinal and metrical length, and to discount a purely semantic or verbal explanation of the non-conservation. Now according to this last hypothesis non-conservation of the lengths is merely the result of a semantic confusion that attributes to the word 'longer' the meaning 'be further along'. This would mean that the child would have to raise a precise representation of the lengths involved, or at least, that if he were uncertain about the absolute lengths of B and E, he would have to ascertain that c and d, or a and b were equal. If that were the case, the subject should be able to solve the questions put to him in the present technique about the projections as such, at the same time as the questions put to him in techniques II and III above, well before the conservation problems (and these, according to the hypothesis, result from a mere verbal misapprehension). But if we find the contrary to be the case, then we would have proof that non-conservation of the lengths is essentially a notional not a semantic affair, and that the failure to make a semantic distinction between 'further' and 'longer' corresponds to a failure to differentiate conceptually between ordinal and metric.

We dealt with this problem – the problem of the anticipatory image of c and d – by means of the two different methods, IV and V.

In method IV we took two rods 10 cm long (and 1 mm in diameter), one 9 cm rod, one 10 cm rod, and nine pairs of rods of various lengths ranging from 0·5 to 8 cm. One of the 10 cm rods, B, was attached to a sheet of card (in a horizontal position); one of the others was placed in a staggered position in relation to it (rod E; we used the same positions and designation as in Figure 48); and c was hidden by a cover I, or 'tunnel' (20 cm long, 2 cm wide and 0·5 cm high). The subject was required to imagine whether the hidden projecting portion c was equal or not to the visible portion d. The following questions were posed.

IV (1). Two 10 cm rods. The child was asked to select the rod that was equal in length to the fixed one (10 cm). The chosen rod was then displaced to give a length d of 2 cm. We showed the child how the tunnel worked and placed it over c. We then came to some agreement on what distance a was to be called ('hole', 'blank', 'stair', 'space', etc.), and the subject was asked to fill it in with one of the small rods (0·5 to 8 cm) equal to the projecting length d. After which, we said: 'Now choose another piece the same size ("just as big") as the hidden piece (c), and put it in the tunnel so that it is just over the top of the piece which you can't see'. And then: 'How did you pick the pieces? Both just as big, or one bigger than the other? And why?' With the 7- to 8-year-olds it is enough to inquire verbally whether the 'pieces' d and c are or are not equal.

The same questions were asked for a 7 cm displacement.

Finally, we asked the subject to estimate whether the rods themselves, B and E, were equal or not. This was to see if he had thought about it in answering the question concerning the equal length of the projections.

IV (2). This time a shorter rod of 9 cm was placed parallel to the fixed 10 cm rod. First we put the two rods exactly opposite each other so that the subjects could see they were not equal. Then we displaced the 9 cm rod by 2 cm, covering the projection c with the tunnel. We posed the same questions as before, and then repeated them for a 7 cm displacement.

IV (3). Same questions for the same 10 cm and 9 cm rods with the tunnel in position.

When the child replied correctly to questions IV.2 and IV.3 or if his answers were hard to interpret, we asked him the same questions all over again using the 10 cm and 11 cm rods with the tunnel.

Using forty-two subjects aged between 5 and 12 years, the general result was a relatively good correlation between successful responses to test IV.1 and successful responses to the conservation test. We also found that the judgments affirming conservation showed a lead over successful replies to tests IV.2 and IV.3 (see Table 141: $+A+C$ signifies successful anticipation of equal projections and successful conservation; $+A-C$ signifies successful anticipation but failure in conservation, and $\pm$ signifies successful anticipation for one out of two shifts).

TABLE 141 *Relating the successes for anticipation of equality or inequality of projections, and the successes for conservation*
(As % of the subjects)

	$+A+C$	$-A-C$	$+A-C$	$-A+C$	$\pm A-C$	$\pm A+C$
IV.1	51·2	26·9	2·4	12·1	5·0	2·4
IV.2	36·6	19·6	2·4	19·6	12·1	9·7
IV.3	28·2	33·3	0	23·0	2·6	12·9
Average	38·7	26·6	1·6	18·2	6·6	8·3

In test IV.1, 78·1 per cent of the cases favour correlation $(+ + - -)$, and only 14·5 per cent tell against it. In tests IV.2 and IV.3, however, only 58·8 per cent are for and 21·4 per cent against. But it is interesting to see that in all three tests the average of cases

307

$-A + C$ and $\pm A + C$ exceeds cases $+A - C$ and $\pm A - C$. That is to say, in the cases of non-correlation, the subjects who succeed in conservation before anticipation are three times more numerous than those who respond in the reverse order. For the values $+A - C$ and $-A + C$ alone – and they are more revealing since $\pm$ cases are ambiguous – the proportion is even larger: in 18·2 per cent of cases conservation precedes anticipation as against 1·6 per cent for the reverse order.

Our problem, therefore, is this. We have to explain why anticipation of the amounts projecting precedes conservation (Table 137), when the subject is required to imagine displacement in both directions (and why it correlates with conservation when the displacement is given and not constructed: Table 135), whereas the representation of the equality of the lengths projecting comes after. To begin with there is this: anticipation of the projections (the question concerns the rods B and E themselves and their positions, not the projections c and d or the spaces a and b as such) remains qualitative[26] in those answers counted correct in Table 137, whereas evaluation of the equivalence of the projections themselves entails their quantification. But the main point is this: the order in which the reactions occur corresponds to the logical order of construction of the notions: (1) to achieve conservation it is necessary to be able to imagine at least that if B, which is equal to E, is moved forward, then the former will project beyond the latter; (2) but in its crude form conservation requires only reversibility (i.e. if B is moved back it will again be directly opposite to E) or identity (= 'it has only been pushed along', the length being invariant), but does not yet require compensation (equal length of projecting portions), though compensation may be involved from the outset; (3) on the other hand, once conservation is attained, there is a ready frame within which compensation, if not already in play, will sooner or later register itself. From this order it follows that if the image is based on notions rather than on the mere recording of previous perceptual observation, then awareness of the equality of the projecting lengths (compensation) should either correlate with conservation or come after and not before it.

What we learn from Table 141 then, is this. In this perfectly simple situation where the child merely has to anticipate the displacement of one of two rods, as in the equally simple situation of displaced squares (Chapter Three, 1 and 2), imaginal representation is more closely connected with the notions than with any previous perceptual experience. But it should be made clear that in order to anticipate the equality of the lengths projecting in test IV.1 the subject employs

[26] That is to say, the successful response simply involves recognition of the presence of a projection ($> 2·5$ per cent of E) irrespective of its quantitative value.

methods that are representational or imaginal rather than operational in character. (Contrast tests IV.2 and IV.3, where rational procedures predominate.) The only thing is that the correct imaginal representations do not appear until the conservation level and are almost entirely missing in the subjects before this!

An analysis of the subjects' various modes of procedure shows that there are six varieties: (1) haphazard 'guessing'; (2) reliance on mere perception ('I can see'), which is most of the time illusory; (3) imagining of inaccurate laws (always equal or always unequal); (4) imagining the size of c (or b) relative to d (or a) by relating their progressive variation; (5) (operational) deduction of the equality or inequality of the projections from the equality or inequality of the rods themselves; (6) as (5) but with reference to the tunnel and its displacements.

Seventy-eight per cent of the subjects who have not attained conservation choose at random; the rest normally draw on methods 2 and 3. Of those subjects who have achieved conservation 59 per cent employ method 4 in test IV.1, 67 per cent method 5 in IV.2, and 60 per cent method 6 in IV.3 (these last two methods do not, of course, by any means preclude the presence of images). There is no doubt, therefore, that imaginal representation does indeed play an important part; but it clearly does not attain any degree of accuracy until, or after, the conservation level has been reached. One sees thus the extent to which adequation of the image to reality is determined, or at least oriented by the operations.

As for the question we posed at the beginning of this section, the answer is this. The fact that the child cannot anticipate the equality or inequality of the projecting lengths before he has reached the conservation level would clearly seem to make it impossible to attribute non-conservation of the lengths to a mere semantic misapprehension. And it proves that such non-conservation, as well as the residual semantic confusion, does in fact derive from a failure to differentiate between ordinal (±far) and metrical estimation (±long). It might be useful at this point to quote a few examples of the kind of reaction we observed during the preliminary investigations which led up to method IV. We originally began with small rulers 14, 16 and 18 cm in length. The child was asked to predict the lengths of the empty spaces a and b by choosing from $8 + 8$ cardboard strips the same width as the rulers, coloured blue and graded from 1 to 7 cm for a, coloured green and graded from 0·5 to 6 cm for b. Or else we used equal and unequal rods and asked the subject to draw the extensions d and c.

Eli (6,2), for the two 16 cm rulers, begins by carefully examining the

2 cm projections, after ascertaining that the lengths are equal. She takes 2 and 2, but says *'Perhaps there isn't the same end. –* Do you need two the same? – *No* (she measures with her finger). *Yes. –* And if I pull it more? – *If you pull a long way you need those* (5 for *b* and 3 for *a*). – And if I pull a little bit less? – *If you pull like that* (small displacement) *you need the same. –* And if I pull a lot? – *You need these two* (5 for *b* and 3 for *a*). – Why? – *Because it's very long.* – But don't you need two the same? – *No, one a bit bigger.* – Which one? – *That one* (*b*). – If I pull some more? – *Those there* (7 for *b* and 4 for *a*). – Well, have a look (the experimenter demonstrates). Is it the same? – *No, this stick* (*B*) *is bigger, because you pulled it.'* For the 18 cm and the 16 cm rods Eli sees that *b > a* and retains this difference for all the displacements. But when we go back to the two 16 cm rods, she will only accept *a = b* for the smaller displacements, and foresees *b > a* for the larger ones. She fails in the final conservation test.

Seg (5,9) starts in the same way by saying that for the shorter displacements *a = b*. But when *B* is moved farther he says: *'That one there* (*a*) *gets bigger and that one there* (*b*) *stays the same.'* Copying a 4 cm displacement from memory also yields *a > b* (3·6 and 1·7 cm), and anticipation produces the remark: *'That one* (*a*) *is bigger'* (6·7 for *a* and 4·8 for *b*). Then the rod is displaced in the opposite direction and Seg reverses his predictions. Finally *B* and *E* are moved in opposite directions: *'That makes the two ends the same.'* Conservation is denied: *'This rod* (*B*) *is longer because you pulled it. –* How do you know it's longer? – *I saw it.'*

Ber (6,1) accepts that *a = b*, for the shorter displacements, *'because the sticks are all as long* (*B = E* which implies conservation). – And if I pull some more? – *This end* (*b*) *will be longer.* – Why? – . . . – Are you sure? – *Yes.* – And are the sticks as long or not? – *Just as long* (*E* and *B*).' Here we have conservation without correct representation of the projecting lengths.

Gan (6,11) makes a correct choice for the two 16 cm rods: *'It's the same size because the two missing ends are the same . . . –* And if I pull? – *Both the same because the last two were the same. So you have to put the same. –* And if I pull a lot? – *A bit smaller* (6 for *a* and 7 for *b*). – Why? – *Because it's bigger there* (*b*).' Conservation indecisive.

Here is an example of a correct response:

Eve (7,4): *'Both the same. –* And if I pull? – *The same size.* – Why? – *Because the two sticks are the same size. –* And if I pull a lot? – *Still the same,'* etc. 16 cm and 18 cm rods: *'A bit bigger because one stick is bigger than the other.'*

These examples show clearly enough that along with non-conservation go real difficulties in evaluating the projecting lengths, even when the subject has already seen that they are equal (Eli), and even when he foresees that they will be equal after a short displacement

(Seg and Gan). They also show the way these problems can go on even after conservation is achieved (Gan), until the equality of the projections is ultimately stabilized within the frame of compensation (Eve). Finally, we may note that when the questions concern actual movements, or movements to be anticipated, the result in general is $b > a$ (Eli, Ber and Gan), whereas if the movement is imagined afterwards we find $a > b$ (Seg).

Method V and conclusions. The finding that anticipation of the equality of c and d lags behind conservation seemed to us to be important enough to call for a control using a younger set of subjects. With E. Schmid-Kitsikis we drew up the reactions of thirty-four children aged 5 to 7 years. We used a simplified procedure, similar to method IV but which involved only rods of equal length. We presented the rods first of all in line with their extremities corresponding, so that the child could see that they were equal. Then we covered the rods' right-hand extremities, and asked the subject to point with his finger to where they would be. One of the rods was then displaced 2·5 cm, then 1·5 cm and then 4 cm. For each distance the subject was required to choose the lengths of rod (from five segments 0·5, 1·5, 2·5, 4 and 5 cm long) corresponding to the visible portion d and the invisible portion c. We concluded with the usual conservation test.

The results obtained from this control are much the same as those in Table 141, if we allow for the age of the subjects. No subject is

TABLE 142   *Relating the successes for anticipations ($+A$) of the equality of the projections, and the successes for conservation ($+C$)*
(As % of the responses)

$+A+C$	$-A-C$	$+A-C$	$-A+C$	$\pm A-C$	$\pm A+C$
23·5	38·2	0	23·5	11·7	3·1

completely successful in anticipating that the projecting lengths will be equal unless he has managed the conservation; the result for the converse on the other hand is 23·5 per cent. Some subjects are half-successful without conservation ($\pm A - C$); these are the subjects who foresee equal length for the shorter but not for the longer displacements. But as it often happens that the youngest subjects choose equal lengths out of economy or perseveration without comprehending what they are doing, the $\pm A - C$ type subjects do not constitute a significant exception to the lead held by conservation.

Generally speaking then (Tables 141 and 142), correct imaginal representation of the projecting lengths (equal if $B = E$, unequal if

$B \neq E$) would seem to require the compensation framework inherent in conservation. But it is interesting to see that conservation is promoted if attention is centred on the projections (methods IV and V) or even on the exact length and position of the rods or paths (methods I–III). Taking averages for all 267 subjects questioned in methods I–V we find the following (Table 143).

TABLE 143 *Complete successes for conservation (as % of the subjects) after anticipation of the length of paths or rods (methods I–III) and of the length of projections (methods IV–V)*

	5 years (N=72)	6 years (N=78)	7 years (N=57)	8 years (N=46)	9–12 years (N=14)
Methods I–III	21	37	40	77	
Methods IV–V	5	38	70	85	100

If these results are compared with those of Table 133 one sees a distinct improvement. Now, as Vinh-Bang's results were obtained from 242 subjects, this comparison takes in more than 500 children. This would appear to preclude mere coincidence. It therefore seems clear that the effort to achieve adequate imaginal representation of the lengths promotes the transition from ordinal estimation (the source of non-conservation in the present case, where over-simple images centre attention on the terminal limits only) to metrical estimation, which lies at the source of conservation. This is particularly the case at 7 and 8 years for representation of the projections (methods IV and V). But as this latter representation proves to be possible only within a conservation framework (Tables 141 and 142), we must conclude that the image of the projecting lengths only becomes adequate when oriented by operations already structured or in process of being structured (on the brink of conservation, therefore). But the action is reciprocal, and this structuration is in turn furthered by the image.

In sum, these multiple inquiries enable us to draw at least three conclusions. First, non-conservation of lengths is an authentic non-conservation, comparable to any other, and does not derive simply from a semantic confusion, although it brings semantic confusion with it. Such confusion may, indeed, continue longer than actual non-conservation, but if so it is purely residual in character. Second, in this sphere the image is distinct from preoperational judgments, since the image tends to depreciate the length of rod B and of projection c, whereas the judgments are inclined to overestimate them. Third, imaginal representation of the projecting lengths becomes adequate only under the influence of the nascent operations. But, as we have seen, adequate imagery, or, to be more precise, the attempt to achieve adequate imagery, and the attention at least that it brings to bear on the problem of comparing c and d, in turn furthers the formation of the conservation. We have here then a prime example not only of the distinction, but also of the interaction, between the formative processes of the images and the operations.

7. Conclusion

With this investigation into the image–operation relationship we have reached the heart of the problem of the nature of anticipatory images. At the same time we have followed up the questions discussed in the conclusion of Chapter Six. To what extent does the anticipatory image depend on operations, and to what extent does it further the functioning of operations? But our original question was not quite the same; its emphasis was different. To what extent, we asked, do preoperational images help to prepare the operations? And to what extent do the operations, once they are formed, react on the image to make it anticipatory? So we have three distinct questions. It is one thing to envisage the preoperational image contributing to the formation of the operations – and this is something the results of this chapter would in any case seem to challenge. But it is quite a different matter to envisage the image, rendered anticipatory by the operations promoting their functioning – we have already seen something of this and the next chapter will show us even more. We shall therefore not discuss these two central questions immediately, but reserve them for our general conclusions. It is first necessary to complete our information by examining the images involved in geometric intuition. For the moment we shall simply recapitulate what we have learnt during the course of the present chapter about the formation of anticipatory images.

Amongst the facts that have come to light during this chapter, there are only two cases of images that could be considered anticipatory clearly appearing before the corresponding operations: namely, the anticipation of liquid levels in certain subjects who do not achieve conservation (section 1), and the purely qualitative anticipation of the projection of one of the displaced rods before the conservation of their lengths (section 5). But in neither of these cases did the child conclude from his predictions that the variables in question compensate one another. It therefore seems legitimate to consider these images as derived from the subject's past experience. For instance, he will have frequently observed that a liquid rises higher in a narrower glass than in a wider one, and that one of two equal rods, if displaced, projects beyond the other. In other words, the ability to foresee the outcome of such movements or transformations is due to reproductive, not to anticipatory, images. It is thus impossible to argue from these facts that it is permissible to speak of authentic anticipatory images formed independently of the operations.

On the other hand, there are three cases where we have in fact witnessed the formation of authentic anticipatory images: namely, the transition from transversal[27] to longitudinal anticipations in section 4, the anticipation of the equality of displacements in section 5, and the anticipation of the forms of the balls of clay in section 3. Now, in these three cases we have found that the anticipations were formed only after the formation of the corresponding operations, or at the point when they were in process of elaboration and bordering completion. It is quite clear that in cases like this imaginal anticipation, which raises no difficulties and might have emerged much earlier if the preoperational image were not so static, depends on contributory factors external to the image, and provided by the operations. This exogenous process of formation is particularly plain in the case of the longitudinal anticipation of the movement of the counters in section 4. Here the perceived apparatus invites the subject to use this type of anticipatory image. Even so, one has to wait for the operations of setting in correspondence and conservation of equivalence, before longitudinal anticipations can emerge.

We thus have a distinction between apparent anticipations preceding the formation of the operations and based on straightforward reproductive images, and authentic anticipatory images due to the intervention of operational mechanisms. This closely corresponds to the distinction we have noted in an earlier work[28] between the two types of anticipation (which we termed global and analytic) which are brought into being by the seriation operations. It is worth recalling these facts, as they usefully complement what we have already seen in this chapter.

The case in question is one in which imaginal anticipation at first sight appears to prepare for the corresponding operation: the seriation of lengths (10 small rods 10 cm to 16·5 cm long to be arranged in ascending order in a 'stair'). This is not successfully carried out by systematic operational activity (rather than by trial and error) until 7 to 8 years; but it does give rise to imaginal anticipation manifest in correct drawings executed without the model in 55 per cent of the 5-year-olds and in 73 per cent of the 6-year-old subjects. But on closer scrutiny one becomes aware of the

---

[27] These too are only based on reproduction images – indeed on immediate images – in that they rely on the structure of the apparatus.
[28] *The Early Growth of Logic in the Child.*

distinction between the image and the operation. Let us recall first of all that there are three criteria for recognizing operational activity in this context, as opposed to empirical trial-and-error construction: (a) the child selects the smallest element, then the smallest of those remaining, etc., so that he understands in advance that a member of a series E is both larger than those preceding $(E > D \ldots A)$ and smaller than those following $(E < F, G)$; (b) in this way he arrives at the transitivity $(A < B) + (B < C) = (A < C)$ that the preoperational subjects had been unable to deduce; (c) if new elements are introduced, when the initial series has been completed, the subject is able to insert them correctly without starting again. Now it is striking that the 5- to 6-year-old subjects who do a good drawing of the result to be achieved do not, when they go on actually to put the series together for themselves, succeed in arriving at the systematic method of construction we have just described. The fact is that the operation is reversible (continuation of ascending sequence $(E, F, G \ldots$ and descending sequence $E, D, C \ldots)$, whereas the drawing of the 'stair' is only one-way. And aligning the rods in ascending order of size in a free drawing is a different matter from manipulating them with respect to their given sizes.

To bring out this difference we gave the subjects a series of differently-coloured strips. They were asked to draw these either black or in the corresponding colours. Here 'analytic' anticipation (in colour) is far more difficult than 'global' anticipation (in black): 3 per cent as against 55 per cent at 5 years, 22 per cent against 73 per cent at 6 years and 80–100 per cent at 7 and 8 years. The obvious reason is that analytic anticipation presupposes the same operations as actual construction of the series, whereas global anticipation presupposes no seriation. More precisely, analytic anticipation presupposes the use of a genuine anticipatory image, whereas global anticipation is based only on a reproductive and indeed static image imitating a known 'good form' (the staircase form, which is symmetrical and regular). The 'global' image is thus not a means of preparation for the operations.

But A. Rey has envisaged another form of anticipation that, like analytic anticipation, is bound up with the seriation operations.[29] He asked the subjects to draw a square in the middle of a white sheet of paper, and then asked them to draw the smallest (or the largest) square possible on the same paper. Now from the age of 8 the children were immediately able to draw a square of 1–2·2 mm (or a square running along the edges of the paper). But the younger subjects were unable, apart from some slight oscillation in one direction or the other, to get away from the size of the original square (usually about 4×4 cm)! This ingenious experiment is extremely instructive from at least two points of view. First, it shows that the anticipatory image presupposes operational support, since it is not until operational seriation develops that the child is able in one leap to traverse the distance separating the initial square from the other extreme of the series. Second, it confirms in a striking way that preoperational images

[29] Rey, A., 'Le problème psychologique des "quantités limites" chez l'enfant', *Revue suisse psychol.*, ii (1944), 238–49.

are static in character, since the younger subjects fail to break away from the dimensions of the first square.[30]

To sum up, the facts arising from the seriation question once again show that at the preoperational level the image is not a means of preparation for the operations. On the other hand, 'analytic' anticipation and Rey's anticipation of the smallest square do in fact co-ordinate with the operational mechanisms.

[30] A. Rey has improved his test in a direction that is very interesting for our own problems: he gives the subject a horizontal line 4 cm long, and asks him to draw lines of decreasing length. Rey, A., *Études des insuffisances psychologiques*, Delachaux and Niestlé, 1947–1962, i, 48–52.

CHAPTER NINE

The Spatial Image and 'Geometrical Intuition'

We have suggested that image and operation, and, more generally speaking, the figurative and operational aspects of thought, are relatively heterogeneous. But there would appear to be an exception to this – the faculty known to mathematicians as geometrical 'intuition'. An adult subject who 'sees in space', whether he is a geometer, a draughtsman, or simply well practised, does not stop at imagining static configurations in three dimensions any more than in two. He is able to imagine movements and even the most complicated transformations thanks to a remarkable adequation of image to operation. This correspondence retains exceptional validity in spite of the well-known shortcomings of intuition (such as the difficulty experienced in visualizing curves without tangents, etc.). From the point of view of the image–operation relationship, geometrical intuition raises a whole series of problems. The two main ones are as follows.

We need to know, for one thing, how it comes about that the image can be particularly well suited to the figurative representation of spatial operations, when in the logico-arithmetical sphere its symbolism is far more sketchy. But we also need to investigate carefully whether, in view of this special correspondence, the genetic relations between images and operations are the same in the geometrical as in other spheres, or whether in the spatial context the image does not perhaps play a more important formative role in the preparation of the operations. Generally speaking, we have to try to determine (a) whether geometrical 'intuition' is primarily imaginal or whether it is essentially operational, and (b) what relationship there could be between these two possibilities.

As almost all the images studied in this book have been of a spatial nature, we might simply have gone back and analysed previous examples. But we thought it would be useful in the present context to take some problems of reasoning in the strict sense, in which some role is played by images, whether they actually determine, or are subordinate yet helpful to, the operations (this line of inquiry has been broached several times already, notably in Chapter Five, section 1, Table 73, in connection with arcs and chords).

1. *The estimation of the relative lengths of the outlines of inscribed and circumscribed figures*[1]

Take a square inscribed in a circle, as in Figure 49 I*a*. Is judging the circle's perimeter greater than the square's just a perceptual affair? One would say so. But we have seen (Table 74) that for many subjects aged 5 to 6 years the arc is equal to, and sometimes even shorter than, its chord. Now, Figure 49 I*a* consists of exactly the same arc–chord configuration repeated four times over. And although I*a* yields successes at a far earlier stage, Figure I*k* raises problems for the younger subjects that perception simply cannot solve.

Our concern, then, is with the general problem of judging the lengths of the perimeters in the various closed and half-open forms of Figure 49.[2] These problems are not only related to perceptual judgments, but also to reasoning processes as such and to the mental image. The part played by the image can be clearly seen when the subject merely has to represent the lengths in question in terms of a distance covered. It is even more in evidence when the child attempts to break the figures down (subdivision operations, but with reliance on imaginal representation), and when he tries to transform one of the lines into the other. This seemed to us to present an ideal opportunity to study the parts played by the image and the operations respectively in the elementary forms of geometrical intuition.

The subject is presented with a series of card sheets 11 × 15 cm. On these are drawn figures approximately 8 cm in diameter. The figures consist of a circumscribed element and a differently-coloured inscribed element; they are either completely closed or broken down into open or half-open (as Figure 49 I*a'*–I*k'*, as opposed to I*a*–I*k*). The experimenter says to the child: 'We have drawn these two lines, one red and the other blue (the colours are varied in order to avoid perseveration from one figure to the next). We'll call them paths. Can you tell me which path is the longer? Or do you think that they are both just as long as one another?' To ensure that the child gives his answer in terms of length, we sometimes used the following control for the younger ones. We presented them with a card on which were drawn six differently-coloured horizontal lines of five different lengths; so that the subjects would not base their judgments merely on the ordinal criterion of projecting lengths, we were careful not to align the lengths on the same vertical. We then asked the subjects: 'Which path is the longest?' 'Are any two of them the same length?' One subject was unable to answer these preliminary questions, and was eliminated from the tests. In the 5- to 6-year-old subjects we concretized the

---

[1] The experiment was carried out by M. Bovet in collaboration with H. Sinclair and L. Pecsi.

[2] We shall call those figures 'open' which are parts (half, etc.) of the corresponding closed figures.

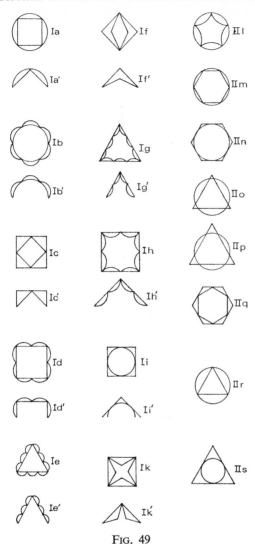

FIG. 49

notion of length by introducing two ants, one of which was said to be running along the blue path and the other along the red path. We then asked the child if one had gone a longer way than the other. The advantage of this is that the distance to be covered is stressed; but it has the disadvantage of introducing physical movement.

It is not a question here, as it was in Chapters Two–Seven and to

319

some extent Eight, of an image of a configuration, movement or transformation expressed by means of drawing, by gesture or verbally: it is rather a question of a notional or operational judgment. And what interests us primarily in these judgments, both when they are successful and when they are not, is the role of the image. In particular we are interested in the mechanism of the transition from error to success. Is this transition due to some internal evolution of the image, to some operational intervention contradicting the image, or to some reciprocal adjustment of the operations and imaginal representation?

I. In this connection let us examine the different criteria used by the subjects. These criteria may be imaginal or operational to a greater or lesser degree, and they may be accompanied by correct or incorrect responses.

(A) No justification or *invalid* justifications, such as '*I saw*', and so on. Or straightforward *descriptions* and *tautologies*, such as '*it's big*', and so on.

(B) Criteria based on *position* or *order*. These are quantifications derived from, though not included in, topological or semi-topological relations ('surrounding' and order). This will raise problems similar to those already encountered in connection with the relations between sizes and boundaries (Chapter Two, etc.). These criteria may be subdivided into three varieties.

B 1. Evaluations based on *surrounding* and *interiority*. The inside figure is judged to be smaller, even in II*l*. Mar (5,10) says of this figure: '*The red one* (the outside figure) *is longer, because it's always the middle one that's smallest.*' Ale (5,5) says of I*g*. '*The green one is longer because the red one is inside.*' And Aeg (6,11) says of the same figure: '*The green one is bigger because it goes right round.*' On the other hand, in the case of I*i*, criterion *B* 1 coincides with an accurate evaluation. Ale (5,5) says: '*The red one* (the square) *is bigger because the round is inside!*' The question then arises, of course, whether he has really arrived at the correct answer by means of his incorrect criterion, or whether he has not just brought this in as an explanation afterwards, while evaluating the figure by some other means.

Criterion *B* 1 entails two notions, one correct, the other erroneous. The first is that the surrounding figure presents a greater surface area than the other. And the second is that the perimeter is proportional to the surface. Consequently, when the smaller surface area of the inscribed figure has a greater perimeter (Figure I*h*, etc.), criterion *B* 1 results in an incorrect answer. On the other hand, in the cases where the inscribed area and perimeter are both smaller than those of the surrounding figure, the answer is correct. This suggests that even in the last two instances it is in fact this criterion that is the source of the judgment, once the illusory perimeter–area correspondence is accepted (it is immediately obvious that at 5 to 6 years this correspondence has more to do with the nature of the images than with operational reasoning).

320

This surrounding criterion *B* 1 then, leads to erroneous quantification by way of a false area–perimeter correspondence. And it should be noted that this is akin to the equally topological boundary criterion, discussed at length in Chapter Two, etc. The boundary criterion also produces erroneous quantification based on a spurious correspondence of lengths and the order of finishing points (longer = farther), and erroneous equalization based on a refusal to exceed boundaries (Chapter Five, section 1). It is not surprising, therefore, to find all the intermediaries between this criterion *B* 1 and and the next *B* 2 based on boundaries.

B 2. Evaluation according to *boundaries: order of the extremities* (projection or convergence) and *points of proximity* (local contiguity of the perimeters). Nearly all the open figures have convergent extremities. In these cases the most frequent argument is that the lengths are equal because the two lines 'touch' at the extremities (or 'come together' in a point). For example, Fran (5,7) says of Figure 1*a'*: '*It's just as big, because that one touches and so does that one.*' And Pat (5,8), for I*a'* and I*b'*, repeats over and over again: '*It's the same, they don't go past.*' Rol (6,8) says: '*It's the same. They go together.*' While Bou (6,9) says: '*It's the same: they come to the same end.*' From 7 and 8 years on this argument occurs less often, and when the subject says the figures are equal, he argues from '*the same shape*'. In the case of the closed figures, criterion *B* 2 is found together with correct answers as well as erroneous ones. As an example of the latter we quote Aeg (6,11) who said for Figure II*o*: '*The triangle is bigger because it goes past the round.*' And for II*p*: '*The triangle is bigger because it goes outside. It's bigger, even though the round goes outside too, but it doesn't go out as far as the triangle.*' (It is clear that degree of overlapping here works as a gauge for surface area.) On the other hand, for the same figures, Thi (6,11) answers correctly: '*The triangle might be bigger because it goes farther, but the round might be bigger because it goes out as well.*'

In the case of the closed figures this criterion leads to a general assumption that the figures are equal when the perimeters or boundaries are contiguous at a number of different points. Thus Figure II*l* gives rise to arguments marking the transition from non-projection to contiguity: '*it's the same because the two lines both go to the same end*', or '*because the two shapes touch one another*' (Flo 6,7). The circle inscribed in the square touching at four points (I*i*) gives rise to the same argument expressed variously by Pat (5,8): '*They touch . . . they go together . . . they don't go over.*'

It is clear that *B* 1 and *B* 2 are related. The first indirectly quantifies the length of the perimeter in terms of the two dimensional 'surroundings' providing ordinal quantification of the areas (hence the illicit transition from the ordering of areas to the ordering of perimeters). The second quantifies the length of the perimeters directly in terms of projections or non-projections, which in fact constitute one-dimensional or linear surroundings. The principle then remains the same in both cases – both topological and ordinal; and in both cases it can result in both correct and erroneous evaluations.

B 3. Evaluation based on *upper* and *lower position*. The relationship between *B* 1 and *B* 2 is corroborated by *B* 3, which consists in generalizing both of the first two criteria. In the case of the open figures it frequently happens that the subject thinks that the top line is longer, because it '*goes higher*': that is, there is projection, but projection which is halfway to surrounding, since the subject occasionally adds: '*It goes higher there; there's a space between the paths*' (Ano 6,3). In such instances the evaluation is generally correct.

A similar kind of reaction is found in the case of the closed figures. For example, Vil (6,10) says of a triangle inscribed in a circle that the circle is the larger '*because the triangle doesn't go over like the others*'. She goes on to say of the circle inscribed in the triangle that the triangle is larger '*because there are bigger spaces*'. In other words, the corners of the triangle project out of the circle and thus leave, as Ano says, '*a space between the paths*'.

This tendency to refer to the space brings us to criterion *C*.

C. Criteria based on the *general shape*, or on the *composition of the parts*. These criteria might appear to be essentially different from the foregoing. But the fact that the subject implicitly or explicitly refers to surface area ties them up fairly closely. The general principle is that a global form is compared to another and said to be 'bigger', 'fatter', etc. Now, either this is meaningless and takes us back to the tautological descriptions of criterion *A*, or it amounts to an implicit reference to the 'surrounding' (criterion *B* 1). But if we make a distinction between *C* and *B* it is not simply because they differ as verbal expressions. The reason is rather that the child starts with the general shape (criterion *C* 1) and goes on to analyse the composition of the parts. This leads him to two further sub-criteria: *C* 2 – comparison of the spaces from the point of view of number and size; and *C* 3 – comparison of the parts of the perimeters, also from the point of view of their number (they are longer because there are more 'lines' or segments, etc.) and their size (they are longer because certain segments are longer). We shall see that criterion *C* 3 constitutes a preparation for the fundamental criterion *D* based on the detours of the lines, and also and equally for the dissociation of area and perimeter.

C 1. Evaluation based on *shape* or *global area*. As we have said, the subject using *C* 1 adduces only the overall shape. Thus Fran (5,7) says of I*a*: '*The yellow one is longer because it's round: that makes it bigger.*' Again, '*It's longer because it's fatter, it's bigger*' (Nov 6,1). And '*There there's a little roof* (triangle) *and a big round*' (Ver 6,10). Or '*One makes a hump, the other a ring.*' The link between this criterion and the criterion of surrounding is confirmed by the transition from the one to the other that can be observed in some of the subjects. For example, Auc (6,3) says of the circle inscribed in a hexagon, '*It's smaller because it's inside*' (which is correct). Then, in the case of the circle circumscribed about the hexagon he says that the circle is longer '*because it's fatter*' – which in the context clearly means that the circle 'surrounds' the hexagon.[3] But, curiously

[3] Auc continues to repeat the argument 'it's fatter', which subsequently becomes 'it's bigger', until he moves on to criterion *E* based on transformations: '*If you unfolded the inside* (a star inscribed within a square) *it would get bigger.*'

enough, the transition from surrounding to global shape (understood as total surface area) is not, as it might seem to be, a step back. In point of fact criterion $C\,1$ replaces $B\,1$ and becomes general at 7 years: 23·3 per cent of the correct answers to the open figures are backed up by arguments based on shape, as against 4·2–7·2 per cent at 5 to 6 years. The reason for this progress is, as we have already said, that concentration on shape soon leads to breakdown of the constituent parts. The metrical (or hyperordinal) aspect of this, as opposed to the ordinal, constitutes a new development.

$C\,2$. Evaluation based on *free spaces* and *gaps*. The simplest mode of breaking down the figures is by reference to the empty spaces. We have seen this already in $B\,3$. But here it leads to more detailed quantification. For example, Mont (8,6) says of Figure IIp: '*The triangle is bigger because the spaces are bigger there* (points to the projecting portions) *than they are there* (points to the projecting parts of the circle).' And of Figure IIIl he says, '*The red one* (inside) *is longer because there are those spaces.*' Then for IIm he says that the circle is larger because '*here* (the empty spaces) *it's open*'. Thus the same argument is used to account for the greater length of the internal or external figure.

$C\,3$. Evaluations in terms of *number* and *size of constituent parts*. If the subject takes the general shape ($C\,1$) into account, he is soon led to break down the constituent parts in terms of their number or size. Thus he will say, '*there are four round bits*', '*there are two bars* (Ih')', or, '*there are two big lines there, and there are two little lines there*', and so on. But at first this process is inaccurate. When the subject thinks about the number of constituent parts, he often forgets their size, or vice versa. In particular, when one of the lines or 'paths' to be compared has a longer rectilinear segment than the other, its total length will often be judged greater, irrespective of the number of segments.

For example, Jar (5,6) thinks that in figure Ie' the triangle is longer because '*there are long lines, the other only has little lines*'. He answers correctly for Ic': '*The green line is longer: there are four strokes.*' But for Ih' his answer is wrong again. He thinks the triangle gives the longer line '*because there are two* (big) *strokes*'. Geo (6,11) judges the perimeter of a hexagon in which a six-point star is inscribed to be the longer, '*because it has bigger lines*'. Then he corrects himself, because in the star '*there are a lot of big bars*'. In figure Ib '*the frills look longer*'. Mor (7,5) starts off with the global shape. In Figure IIm he claims the circle is longer '*because it's round*' (and when it is split up into six he thinks the arc equals the chord). But then he gives a series of correct answers. He says the hexagon in IIn is longer '*because there are little points* (segments on either side of the angle)'. Figure Ie: '*because there are bumps*'. Figures Id and Ib: '*because there are points*'. And Figure Ii '*because there are big points*'. But this method of splitting the figures up has limits. In the case of the star inscribed in a square (Ik), the subject thinks the square's perimeter is greater '*because there are bigger sides*'.

There are two interesting points about criterion $C\,3$. First, it can be legitimately generalized once the number and the size of the constituent parts have been co-ordinated. And second, it leads imperceptibly to the next criterion, *D*, which is based on the length of detours compared with the length of the direct 'path'. Thus Jac (8,0) says that the perimeter of the hexagon in II*n* is longer than that of the circle *'because there are different parts* (i.e. angles), *and the circle is straight'*. This argument is exactly intermediate between *C* 3 (where the argument is based on sections divided off by the apices of the angles) and *D* (where the 'direct' perimeter is compared to the other). Thus Ros (8,8), who talks about 'bumps' in II*l*, goes on to say that the hexagon in II*n* is longer than the circle *'because there are ups and downs'* – deviations in the line, that is, as in criterion *D*.

D. Criterion based on detours. The most remarkable characteristic of the preceding criteria up to *C* 2 is the failure to differentiate the perimeter, which remains bound up with surface area, as if the two were proportional. In *B* 2 the emphasis is indeed on the boundaries, and thus, in a sense, on the perimeter as such. But we have seen that boundary considerations are intimately linked with considerations of surrounding. It is only in criterion *C* 3 that the perimeter begins to be differentiated. But until the number and size of the component parts are co-ordinated, such differentiation remains confused. Now co-ordination necessarily induces the subject to take into account the way the parts are organized. And this raises the question of direct and deviating 'paths'. Thus it is only in *D* that the perimeter is considered as such and completely differentiated. Criterion *D* is in fact the first of the only two valid criteria giving correct answers by objective generalization, and not by what more often than not was pure coincidence. Thus the arguments based on detour nearly always yield correct answers, with the exception of those of the 5-year-olds (and occasionally older subjects) who do not evaluate the 'straight paths' properly.

Here are some examples. Gen (5,5) says of I*e'*: '*You go round with the blue one; the other one's straight; so the blue one's longer.*' Ar (6,2) says, '*It goes up and down, the other one's straight,*' or, '*It's curved, the other one's lying down* (i.e. straight)'. Thi (6,11) thinks the inner curve of II*l* is longer, and says, '*there are more bends*'. Vel (6,0): '*It's longer, it goes round a corner,*' '*It's longer there, it makes a point,*' and for II*m*: '*it goes round and round, whereas there it goes straight ahead*'. Rob (9,8) goes wrong at first for II*m*: '*The inside one's bigger, because it has to go round corners and the other goes round in a circle.*' But when he is made to look at one portion of the figure – the arc and the chord – he corrects himself: '*No, it's the ring because it makes a detour.*' Did (9,9) says of the triangle circumscribing the circle: '*It has big corners.*' Fri (9,11) says of I*g*: '*The triangle goes straight, the other winds round.*'

E. Criteria based on transformations. The most advanced type of argument involves either mentally transforming the shape of one of the lines, so that it is identical to the other, and then comparing the lengths, or else transforming the whole configuration, so that the lines can be compared in parallel. Thus: '*If it was put straight, it would be longer*'. '*If it was round like the other it would be longer*' or '*if you put them together, it goes further*'. Generally speaking, this criterion is superior to *D*, as it involves an anticipatory transformation image and an operation. But it should be said that the only difference between the two may be a more explicit formulation introduced in *E*, and that *D* itself could well comprise implicit transformations. Compare formulations such as, '*it's round but that one's straight*', and expressions such as, '*if you put it out straight it would be longer*', or '*if you put them together* (i.e. parallel) *it goes further*'. The difference here may be purely verbal. This would explain why in the case of open figures criterion *E* predominates at 6 years, and later gives way to *D*, whereas in the case of the closed figures (where deviation is less obtrusive) *E* is uppermost at the age of 8 to 9 years.

Here are some examples: Ros (7,1) tries a transformation in I*k*, but fails to realize it: '*They are the same and the green one is bent* (the star).' Bad (7,3) first judges the square in I*h* to be longer, '*because it's square*' (criterion *C* 1), and then changes his mind: '*Because if you put it out straight* (i.e. the inner figure), *it's longer*.' He repeats this argument over and over again, and even for II*s* he says, '*If you put it out straight it would be longer*.' Stei (9,9) says for I*a*: '*If you put it in a circle, it would not go to the edge* (i.e. the other circle).' And for I*i* he says, '*If you made the circle square* (quadrature of the circle!) *it would be smaller*'. For II*l* he gives an excellent answer: '*They are equal because you can put them on top of one another*.' But he is mistaken in the case of the circle inscribed in the hexagon: '*You can push the green one* (the circle) *into the corners* (the angles of the hexagon).' Then he gives a series of correct answers, such as: '*If the triangle is made into a circle it will be bigger*', and so on. And for II*p*: '*They are equal because both transformed, they would be the same; it doesn't make any difference that the triangle sticks out*.' And for II*n*: '*If you could curve the outside one, you would see that it was bigger*.' In the case of the two hexagons (II*q*) he even goes so far as to transform them into squares to show that the outside one is the larger.

To conclude, then, the criteria used by the subjects develop from *B–C* to *D–E*. The development is two-fold: dissociation of perimeter and area, and increasing predominance of mobility (detours and transformations), the static configurations being dominated by topological and ordinal considerations.

II. We now go on from the qualitative analysis of the children's criteria to a quantitative examination of their evolution at different ages. It is not easy, however, to give any very precise quantitative results. It goes without saying that what we are interested in is not so much the successes or failures (in judging which is the longer line) as the type of criterion used, since the same criterion might produce a correct or incorrect response, depending on the figure in question. As far as the evolution of the criteria is concerned we are obliged to stick to the child's first answers, as the large number of figures involved makes more thorough interrogation impossible. Further, we initially studied a large number of open and closed figures with different subjects, but later (Tables 147–149), carried out a control experiment on the same subjects using only a few of the figures for a more systematic analysis. However, we have attempted to work out the distribution of criteria by age for all the open figures (Table 144) and for all the closed figures (Table 145). Different subjects were used, and the percentages are of the responses (not, of course, of the subjects since the responses vary according to the figures).

Criterion A, then, decreases with age. B increases from 5 to 6 years in both tables and then falls off (except that it comes in again at 9 years in Table 145 – the reason probably being the subject's inadequate mode of expression). C decreases after 7 years and D and E increase in importance with age. There is one exception to the latter in the case of the open figures where the transformation criteria E are relatively frequent at 6 years, but are replaced by D criteria later, for reasons already discussed. If we take the averages for both tables we find that static explanations ('interiority' criteria B, and 'shape' criteria C) tend to fall off with age (44 per cent at 5 to 6 years and 35 per cent at 8 to 9 years), whereas explanations based on movements (D) and transformations (E) clearly increase in importance (23 per cent at 5 to 6 years and 53 per cent at 8 to 9 years).

The latter type of argument is the only one that is correct and the only one that can be generalized, though naturally the detours and transformations on which it is based must themselves be accurate. A–C type explanations are necessarily incomplete when used on their own. For example, the interiority criterion (B) can prove nothing unless it also draws on the shape of the figure (C). Similarly, the number of the component parts proves nothing without size, and vice versa. There may be two reasons why each of these criteria produces more correct than false estimations. Either the subjects' arguments as given are incomplete and actually utilize more criteria than they express. Or else – and this is more likely – the subject achieves an accurate perceptual judgment by comparing the figures, but gives a totally unrelated explanation that expresses one aspect only of what he has actually perceived.

This difference between perceptual estimation and conceptual explanation deserves careful examination from the point of view both of imaginal representation and of geometrical intuition. If perception suffices for easy figures but not for the more complex ones, then what we need to know is this. Does the imaginal intuition necessary in the complex cases simply prolong perceptual mechanisms? Or is it more closely linked with some means of conceptualization that is in all cases distinct from actual perception? We do know, in fact, that at the preoperational level drawings of the figures do not correspond to their perceptual form.[4] For example, the child will reproduce

[4] From studying drawn copies of geometrical forms. See Piaget and Inhelder, *The Child's Conception of Space*, Chapter II.

TABLE 144 *Distribution of criteria A–E for all open figures*
(As % of the responses)[5]

	A			B			C			D			E		
	−	+	T	−	+	T	−	+	T	−	+	T	−	+	T
5 years	23	27	50	8·3	7·2	15·5	1·7	11·1	12·8	8·3	8·3	16·7	2·8	2·2	5
6 years	5·4	26·7	32	10·7	17·7	28·4	0·4	11·1	11·5	0·4	10·3	10·7	0·4	17	17·4
7 years	12	18·4	30·4	1·2	23·2	24·4	1·2	23·2	24·4	0·6	19	19·6	0	1·2	1·2
8–9 years	5·5	17·2	22·8	3·5	16·8	20·3	2	16·4	18·4	1	36·1	37·1	0	1·5	1·5

TABLE 145 *Distribution of criteria A–E for all the closed figures*
(As % of the responses)

	A			B			C			D			E		
	−	+	T	−	+	T	−	+	T	−	+	T	−	+	T
5 years	11	28·5	39·5	1	1	2	11·5	39·5	51	0	7·5	7·5	0	0	0
6 years	8·2	10·3	18·5	3	7·5	10·5	11·5	34·5	46	1·5	20	21·5	3	0·5	3·5
7 years	6·7	11·8	18·5	2·5	2·5	5	10·2	38·3	48·5	1	16·5	17·5	4·7	5·8	10·5
8 years	2·5	5·5	8	0·5	1	1·5	4	27	31	0	27	27	7	25·5	32·5
9 years	1	1	2	2·0	10·5	12·5	2·3	20·7	23	0	27·5	27·5	11·5	23·5	35

[5] Here, − signifies incorrect replies, + signifies correct replies, and T the sum of the two (out of a total of 210 responses).

perceptually distinct squares, triangles and circles uniformly as closed circular curves, since topological conceptualization still dominates over metric properties (crosses, half rings, etc., are drawn as open figures). This is a dualism similar in kind to that which we observe in the present case between conceptual explanation and perceptual estimation. And it is this problem, amongst others, that a comparison of the closed and open figures will enable us to examine.

III. Such a comparison is in fact instructive from two points of view. It not only throws light on the problem sketched above, but also, as we have already seen from Tables 144 and 145, on the relationship between the static (*A–C*) and the dynamic criteria (*D–E*). For this analysis we use the ten pairs I *a–k'* of Figure 49, in which the open figure constitutes half the corresponding closed figure. For example, a square inscribed in a circle is a closed figure, and its corresponding open figure is a right angle inscribed in a semi-circle. The results of the comparison (using different subjects)[6] are set out in Table 146.

TABLE 146 *Successes for corresponding open and closed figures*
(As % of the responses)

Figures	5 years	6 years	7 years	8–9 years
I*a*	100	100	100	89
I*a'*	60	64	50	64
I*b*	100	91	84	100
I*b'*	45	83	89	80
I*c*	89	100	78	94·5
I*c'*	45	73	89	90
I*d*	89	91	89	89
I*d'*	30	67	86	89
I*e*	100	91	56	89
I*e'*	45	83	60	81
I*f*	100	100	89	100
I*f'*	61	83	100	100
I*g*	33	40	50	83·5
I*g'*	32	67	70	91
I*h*	44	36	56	83·5
I*h'*	30	67	43	89
I*i*	89	82	100	89
I*i'*	100	100	100	82
I*k*	22	18	56	61·5
I*k'*	45	73	75	78

[6] For the open figures, eleven subjects aged 5 years, twelve aged 6 years, ten aged 7 years and eleven aged 8 to 9 years. For the closed figures, nine subjects aged 5 years, eleven aged 6 years, nine aged 7 years, and eighteen aged 8 to 9 years.

In the first six of the ten pairs the closed figure receives the better response. The next two or three pairs show no systematic difference. And the last two, or even only the last one, show superior results for the open figure. But these differences tend to decrease from 7 years.

Are we to attribute the fact that the closed figures are on the whole easier to perceptual factors? If it were a question of judging differences in area, the closed figures would obviously have the advantage, as they give far better immediate impressions of area than the open figures. But if it were a question of judging the lengths of the perimeters, then the open figures are at least equally as clear perceptually as the others. Now, the child is fully aware that the important thing is the perimeter, since the tests never concern anything other than the evaluation of the lengths of the differently coloured 'paths', 'roads' or 'lines'. If he judges these lengths in terms of area, it is not because perception leads to systematic assimilation of perimeter and surface, but because preoperational representation imagines a simple correspondence between the two – which is quite a different matter. The young subjects rely on this implicit hypothesis without questioning it. Consequently they find it easier to make up their minds in the case of the closed figures, since the surface area ('interiority', shape, etc.) to which they refer is more easily perceived. It is noteworthy that in the six pairs where the closed figures give better results, the longer perimeter corresponds to the greater area. In the two pairs where the initial results are equally low, the inverse is true. In the one case where the open figure proves the easier (the star in the square) there is also inverse relation of perimeter length to surface area, and the correct answer is given for the open figure, where the fact that the inside line has twice as many segments is more immediately perceptible than in the corresponding closed figure.

In short, the role of perception is indirect only. Imaginal representation determines the choice of criteria or indices and perception is limited to replying to the questions put to it as a result of this choice. In those cases where perception and conceptual criteria appear to go hand in hand, what we really have is a situation in which the criteria are directing perceptual exploration, rather than being derived from it.

The gradual reduction of the difference between the results for the open and closed figures is exactly what one would expect, since it is at 7 to 9 years that D–E criteria begin to supplant the inferior criteria where necessary.

IV. As this comparison of open and closed figures is of central importance, we thought it useful to submit it to the following control. In drawing up Table 146 we used two different groups of subjects for each type of figure, so that one would not influence the other. It was essential, therefore, to examine ten subjects ranging from

5 to 9 years, and to present the closed and corresponding open figures simultaneously to the same subjects, so that they could make an explicit comparison and give their reasons.

This entailed showing the child a small group of cards, from which he picked the one he judged correct (no fixed order). Each group of cards included a closed figure, and one to three open figures representing a fragment of the closed figure (a half, quarter or third) (see Figure 50).

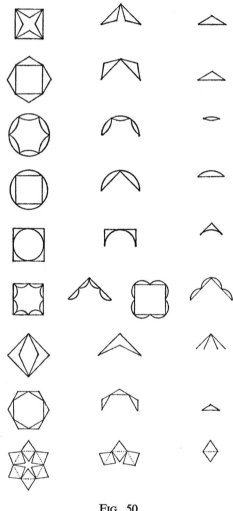

FIG. 50

330

TABLE 147 *Distribution of criteria A–E for all open figures and total of the successes*
(As % of the responses)

	A			B			C			D			E			Successes
	−	+	T	−	+	T	−	+	T	−	+	T	−	+	T	
5 years	5·2	6·4	11·6	2·3	8·2	10·5	12·3	46·4	58·7	2·2	14·7	16·9	0	1·7	1·7	67·8
6 years	0·5	2·3	2·8	5·8	18·8	24·6	6·4	29·4	35·8	1·1	11·1	12·2	2·3	28·7	31·0	90·3
7 years	1·7	1·1	2·8	0·5	12·7	13·2	5·2	26·4	31·6	1·7	8·7	10·4	7·0	35·8	42·8	84·7
8 years	0·5	0	0·5	3·5	10·5	14·0	1·7	14·1	15·8	0·5	10·5	11·0	4·7	52·9	57·6	98·0

TABLE 148 *Distribution of criteria A–E for all closed figures and total of the successes*
(As % of the responses)

	A			B			C			D			E			Successes
	−	+	T	−	+	T	−	+	T	−	+	T	−	+	T	
5 years	2	5	7	9	20	29	11	43	54	1	7	8	0	0	0	75
6 years	0	0	0	10	27	37	7	22	29	3	3	6	4	21	25	73
7 years	0	0	0	12	26	38	3	16	19	2	4	6	4	31	35	77
8 years	0	3	3	8	19	27	0	12	12	0	6	6	5	41	46	81

To facilitate comparison with Tables 144–146 we give the results obtained by means of the simultaneous presentation technique in Table 147.

Table 149 gives the global evolution of the five criteria for both open and closed figures. This table clearly confirms the decrease in

TABLE 149 *Evolution of the criteria with age for all figures and reactions combined*

	A	B	C	A–C	D	E	D–E
5 years	9·1	17·3	56·9	83·3	13·6	1·1	14·7
6 years	1·7	29·1	29·5	60·3	9·9	28·8	38·7
7 years	1·8	22·5	26·9	51·2	8·3	39·8	48·1
8 years	1·4	18·7	14·4	34·5	9·1	53·3	62·4

frequency of the inferior *A–C* type criteria and the increase with age of the 'transformations' *E*. It is interesting to see that simultaneous comparison of the open and closed figures, comprehension of which is promoted by the fact that the former result from a breakdown of the latter, leads to a substantial increase in the use of transformation criteria *E* and a correlative decrease in that of detour criteria *D*. As we have already assumed that criterion *E* is limited to making explicit what was implicit in the use of the detour criteria *D*, this general reaction to the simultaneous comparison test does not present any problems.

There is another interesting result arising from this test: the fact that the success score for the closed figures is lower (73–81 per cent) than that for the open figures (84–98 per cent, except at 5 years: 68 per cent), and the correlative fact that there is more extensive use of the inferior *B* criterion in the case of closed (27–38 per cent) than in the cases of open figures (10–24 per cent). Now, when the figures are tested separately (Table 146), the closed figures give rise to rather more successes.[7] It appears, therefore, that simultaneous comparison favours the use of type *E* criteria, as it prompts the subject to see the open figures as a breakdown of the closed figures. On the other hand, it does not prompt the subject to see the closed figures as a product of the corresponding open figures. In other words, the important thing about the closed figures is precisely that they are closed: hence the subject's natural recourse to the topological *B* criteria.

V. Our original purpose in drawing up these facts was to throw light on certain aspects of geometrical intuition and its imaginal and/or operational make-up.

The first and most obvious conclusion to be drawn is that geo-

[7] There would seem to be some discrepancy between Tables 147 and 146, but the test involved the same subjects questioned successively at the same session.

metrical 'intuition' is to begin with not adapted to its cognitive function, since in the present instance it starts out with one systematic error: namely, the belief that perimeter length is proportional to surface area. The central issue, then, is this. What are the respective roles of the image and the operation in the formation of this error and in its elimination?

With respect to this particular error, it is necessary to distinguish two phases belonging to very different levels of development. E. Lunzer and Vinh-Bang have shown that at the level of concrete operations[8] there may be pseudo-conservation of the perimeter under the influence of nascent conservation notions, when the area of a figure is retained and the form modified. Likewise, there may be pseudo-conservation of area if the perimeter is retained and the form modified. But such cases of pseudo-conservation occur relatively late and involve two essential factors: (a) inheritance of the preoperational belief in a simple area–perimeter correspondence; (b) generalization of emergent operational notions of conservation. It is, therefore, well before this pseudo-conservation level that we must distinguish the first phase – the only one of the two that really concerns us here – when, at about 4 to 5 years or earlier, belief in the area–perimeter correlation first comes into being.

Although this elementary belief belongs to the preoperational level, two different factors may be involved in its formation. These are, first, purely notional factors such as interiority in relation to boundary, which would, for example, lead the subject to conclude that if a figure A is inside a figure B and does not cross its boundaries, then both its area and its perimeter are necessarily smaller; and second, factors relating to the image itself, which might, for example, lead the subject illusively to visualize one perimeter as longer than the other or prevent him from correctly visualizing the two 'paths' stretched out as parallel lines, etc.

Now these two factors probably fulfil their respective functions in a way analogous to the kind of situation that we found in the case of one-dimensional boundaries (Chapter Two, sections 1–2, and Chapter Eight, section 5). When the younger subjects consider a line longer than another because it projects beyond the other's extremity (starting points not being considered) two attitudes come into play: (a) a general attitude of an ordinal (not yet metric) character, that obviously derives from notional activity, and (b) representational centration on finishing rather than starting points, in which the image appears to play an important part. Indeed, representational centration on the finishing point indicates primacy of the state over movement, or the primacy of what is absolute

[8] Lunzer, E., and Vinh-Bang, *Conservations spatiales*, vol. xix of *Études d'épistémologie génétique*, Paris, Presses Universitaires de France, 1965.

over what is relative (between starting and finishing points). And this primacy of the absolute state is the result of the 'cinematographic process' characteristic of the image (and not characteristic of intelligent thought, as Bergson was led to believe in consequence of his neglect of the role of operations).

Similarly in the case of the areas and perimeters one must distinguish the part played by notional interpretation and the part played by imaginal representation. The notional element is, as before, ordinal, or more generally topological: the emphasis is on the order of the figures (and of their boundaries, but in two dimensions), so that a figure surrounded by another and therefore interior to it will *ipso facto* be considered smaller where this is necessarily true of the surface area only. But just as the child in consequence of his failure to differentiate between ordinal and metrical will conceive the length of a line in terms of the order of end-points only, so he will think of two-dimensional magnitudes, whether enclosed or enclosing, not as surfaces in the metric sense, but as 'closed wholes' incorporating their boundaries as constituent parts or integral properties.[9] The direct surface–perimeter correspondence is not, therefore, due to an explicit false inference but to a representation of the surface involving an image (as in the centration on end-points). Whereas the notional surface is a system of metrical or ordinal relations, the surface represented by image is essentially a figural state. That is to say, it is imagined statically and independently of its transformations: hence the indissociability of the boundary and its content, i.e. of the perimeter and the surface as such. This is reinforced by the fact that the younger subjects imagine the geometrical figures equally as physical objects.[10]

It is no exaggeration to say that the systematic error observed at 5 to 7 years – the direct surface–perimeter correspondence – is due principally to the imaginal nature of early geometrical intuition. At the same time, however, it is bound up with the ordinal and topological aspects of the ideas characteristic of this level of development, which are liable to foster errors in imagery without being immediately responsible for them.

True, in the early stages imaginal representation entails the static criteria *B* and *C* and consequently lies behind the systematic error we are discussing. But it is also true that imaginal representation subsequently becomes capable of forming anticipatory kinetic or transformation images, which engender the superior criteria *D* and *E* and

[9] See Chapter Six, sections 1–3 where the younger subjects will not represent intersections because this violates boundaries which are part and parcel of the figures as surfaces.

[10] Cf. the results obtained by E. Vurpillot with Gottschaldt's figures for children aged 5 to 6 years who could not dissociate the lines from the object as a whole: Vurpillot, E., 'La matérialité du tracé figural chez l'enfant', in *Épistémologie de l'espace*, *Études d'épistémologie génétique*, Presses Universitaires de France, 1964, xviii.

thus enable the subject to imagine the detours and transformations leading to objective comparison of the figures. This raises an essential question – a question that is of central importance for an account of geometrical intuition, as also for a theory of images in general. Is it by virtue of some internal evolution in imagery that representations pass from a static condition to a condition of anticipatory mobility? Or is it that after acting as symbolism for the preoperational notions, the image (internalized imitation) gradually becomes adapted to imitating operations? In other words, does the image develop with the aid of external contributory factors, drawing its substance from successively 'imitated' models? It should be said right away that such external factors would not detract from the fundamental significance of the image. If the image constitutes a symbolism vital to thought, then the mere fact that it is symbolic means that, as thought progresses, it will be moulded precisely on the lines of the object to be symbolized. Now we shall see later that in geometrical intuition there is a particularly precise correspondence between the imaginal symbolizer and the operational symbolized.

But how are we to determine whether the image develops in accordance with its own internal evolution or under the influence of external operational factors? In the case of the B–C and D–E criteria, as indeed in all those cases where kinetic or transformation images have been seen to replace or complement static images, the argument one might put forward in explanation is, it is true, deductive rather than experimental. But there are instances where a fairly self-evident deduction attains a certain degree of probable agreement with experimental evidence. Now the argument is straightforward enough. Let us assume that the transition from interiority criteria B and shape criteria C, to detour criteria D and transformation criteria E is due to some internal development of the image. In order to account for this development from states to transformations we would have to adduce factors of reversible mobility, coherent coordination, and so on. But one immediately sees that these factors repeat the operational mechanisms. This being so, are we to take it that there are two totally isomorphous, autonomous but distinct evolutions, the only difference being that one concerns imageless thought and the other imaginal representation? But there is probably no thought without image (though this does not mean that thought is no more than images) and, more especially, there is no geometrical intuition without images. Further, there are probably no images without thought. Consequently the hypothesis that there are two independent, isomorphous and parallel evolutions only leads to insuperable and unprofitable complications. In simpler terms, this amounts to saying that the image evolves from the static to the kinetic or the dynamic under the influence of the operations. It does not, therefore, evolve autonomously, but in imitation of the evolution of thought which it symbolizes in internalized imitation.

Now, it is in the nature of imaginal imitation that it symbolizes thought by means of spatialized figures. Such symbolism is naturally more or less inadequate when it comes to representing operations of a non-spatial kind, such as those concerning class, relations in general or number. But in the special case of geometrical operations, whose function is precisely to describe figures in space and their transformations, the thing symbolized (spatial operations) and the imaginal symbolizer (also spatial) are homogeneous. Hence the privileged status of geometrical intuition. Its dual operational and imaginal nature constitutes a closer synthesis than in any other sphere. But geometrical intuition only achieves such a synthesis by subordinating the imaginal elements to the central operational core, and this subordination presupposes a development. This fact serves to corroborate what we have said already about the directing role of the operations in the evolution of the image.

2. Decomposition and recomposition of geometrical figures

In the preceding tests the subject was required to judge the length of the perimeter of an inscribed figure by comparison with that of the figure circumscribing it. This time we present the subject with a simple complete shape (square, circle, rhombus), and a number of assorted fragments, more numerous and varied than necessary, from which he is invited to select those that can be used to reconstruct the model. This raises a problem which certainly concerns the mental image (anticipatory transformation image by dissociation or by combined displacement and reassembly). But it also concerns geometrical intuition, since the required representation not only has a figurative role to play, but also means that a problem may be resolved into terms of correct and incorrect solutions (more particularly as we always ask for a justification of the anticipations given).

The inquiry was carried out with the assistance of E. Schmid-Kitsikis. The procedure was as follows.

The square and the circle are split up in eight different ways (Figures 51 and 52), and the rhombus in seven different ways (Figure 53). For each there is a large sheet of card on which the fragments in question (e.g. two fragments only for 2 and 4, and so on) are glued in random positions so that they are hard to recognize. There are two further sheets of card for the square, two for the circle and two for the rhombus. On these are glued fragments which cannot be assembled to make up the complete

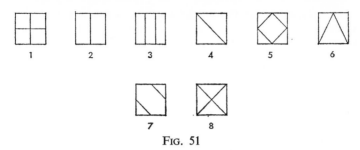

FIG. 51

figure. (Ten sheets in all for the square, ten for the circle and nine for the rhombus.)

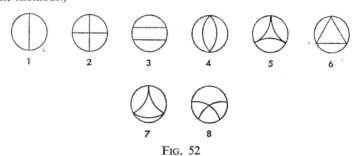

FIG. 52

The questions are in three parts. (1) For one of the three complete given figures the subject is presented with a model 3 × 5 cm and all nine or ten of the corresponding cardboard sheets. The model is visible all the time. The subject is asked which of the sheets have the fragments which could be put together to make the model in question. When he has picked one or more sheets he is pressed to pick more. Each time he is asked if he is sure he has picked the right ones, and why, and as a control the incorrect sheets are suggested.

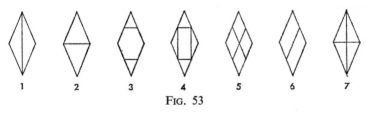

FIG. 53

(2) The subject is then presented with all the fragments (cut out of Bristol board) corresponding to each of the three figures in turn. In all this makes twenty-six elements for the square, twenty-eight for the circle, and twenty-two for the rhombus; they are divided into two groups according to whether they are easier or more difficult. The child has to find the elements he picked before, and to reassemble the model (still visible).

337

(3) Finally, we tried prompting the subject in the following ways: (*a*) for recompositions not anticipated in 1 or 2 we give the subject one or two elements and let him proceed by trial and error, (*b*) for failed recompositions in 1, 2 or 3*a* the subject is given all the necessary elements (two to five depending on the way the figure is divided) which he is then asked to assemble to make the model (still visible).

We examined 120 subjects (groups of twenty by age, from 4 to 9 years). Here are the results obtained for the square (the numerals at the top of the columns correspond to those of Figure 51).

TABLE 150   *Successes for recompositions of the square*
(As % of the subjects. In brackets, results after prompted choice)

	1		2		3		4	
4 years	88	(100)	66	(100)	61	(100)	77	(77)
5 years	90	(90)	80	(100)	65	(80)	65	(80)
6 years	66	(90)	95	(100)	85	(85)	90	(90)
7 years	90	(90)	95	(100)	76	(86)	76	(86)
8 years	80	(90)	95	(100)	90	(100)	70	(100)
9 years	95	(100)	95	(100)	80	(100)	75	(100)

	5		6		7		8	
4 years	27	(27)	15	(15)	15	(28)	0	(0)
5 years	15	(20)	5	(10)	28	(35)	0	(0)
6 years	20	(20)	0	(10)	28	(28)	9·5	(9·5)
7 years	19	(19)	19	(19)	15	(15)	14	(14)
8 years	20	(50)	35	(50)	5	(20)	5	(20)
9 years	40	(60)	45	(50)	35	(50)	20	(30)

This table shows the limitations of imaginal decomposition and recomposition, as opposed to operational composition. The easiest figures for the imaginal approach are those in which the square is split up into quadrilaterals (1, 2 and 3). If triangles are introduced the successes drop from 61–95 per cent to 0–45 per cent (models 5 to 8), unless such triangles merely break the square into two halves (model 4).[11]

If these reactions are compared with those involved in operational constructions the difference between them is perfectly plain. In the case of conservation, for instance, the child perceives the complete form (the square, for example), and when it is modified, broken up into fragments and arranged into a different figure, he may react in several ways. Either (stage 1) he denies conservation of the area, even

[11] But it should be noted that model 4 meets with a more successful response at 6 years (90 per cent) than at 7 to 9 years (70–76 per cent).

if the square is only split into two equal rectangles (as in model 1); or (3rd stage) he affirms conservation, even if the fragments are not square in form; or (2nd or intermediate stage) he affirms conservation for the minor transformations, but is uncertain about it and does not sense its logical necessity, while he negates it for the more complex modifications. The imaginal constructions of Table 150 would thus be comparable to the intermediate reactions. The essential difference, however, is this: imaginal compositions could not lead to stage 3 reactions, unless they were framed in a deductive scheme such as that of conservation. And in this case they clearly are not.

But, although in the present instance the problem is not set in terms of conservation, the reactions of Table 150 do indicate the presence of what one might call figurative, or imaginal, pseudo-conservation. We have already analysed several such examples in previous chapters of this book. The reader will recall the cases in which the children did not feel that a particular figure conserved its essential characteristics unless certain internal or external boundaries were respected (see Chapter Three, sections 1 and 2). Similarly, they felt that when a liquid was poured into a differently-shaped glass it conserved its level as well as its quantity – which also constitutes boundary effect (Chapter Eight, section 1). Again – and this is closer to the present case – the younger subjects imagine that if a surface is subdivided into increasingly small pieces, then the residual 'point' of a square will still be square, that of a triangle will be triangular, and so on.[12] Now a similar phenomenon arises in the present case. As far as the image is concerned, it seems natural to the child that a square should subdivide into quadrilaterals, but not into triangles, as triangles apparently have no link with the complete square and cannot be used to reconstruct it. No doubt recomposition requires displacements, and in particular, rotation of the presented fragments that are difficult for the subjects to imagine. The same is true for the four small squares of model 1, or the three rectangles of model 3; but their quadrilateral form makes it possible to get over the difficulty of kinetic imagination by centring on the result of the displacements and not on the movements as such, whereas in the case of the triangles anticipation of the result gives no guide to the displacement at all.

An analysis of the errors confirms these remarks. The subjects try to stick the fragments together as they are, without rotating them. Thus the child will stick together the most acute apices of the triangles in model 6, so that he gets a fan shape instead of a square. The correct method of solving the difficult models 5–8 means going beyond the

[12] See Piaget, J., and Inhelder, B., *The Child's Conception of Space*, 1956, Chapter V.

image and subordinating it sooner or later to strictly deductive or operational relation processes. The sides of the triangles will then be compared with the sides of the square (6 and 8), or the sum of the sides of the triangles with the sides of the square (7 and 5), and so on.

The evolution of the construction of the circle gives similar results: see Table 151.

TABLE 151 *Successes for recompositions of the circle*
(As % of the subjects. In brackets, results after prompted choice)

	1		2		3		4	
4 years	83	(100)	77	(77)	100	(100)	55	(61)
5 years	100	(100)	89	(89)	55	(89)	70	(70)
6 years	100	(100)	95	(100)	80	(100)	85	(100)
7 years	100	(100)	95	(100)	70	(100)	64	(100)
8 years	100	(100)	95	(100)	95	(100)	89	(100)
9 years	100	(100)	100	(100)	80	(100)	89	(100)

	5		6		7		8	
4 years	15	(15)	38	(50)	23	(23)	7	(7)
5 years	21	(21)	33	(50)	21	(21)	21	(21)
6 years	25	(43)	52	(62)	28	(43)	14	(14)
7 years	50	(67)	60	(67)	21	(43)	28	(28)
8 years	77	(77)	85	(100)	42	(62)	31	(42)
9 years	89	(100)	70	(100)	55	(75)	36	(50)

Again we find a clear division at 4 to 6 years between the models without triangles (1–4) and those split up into partially rectilinear or curvilinear triangles (5–8). But in each model at least two sections contain arcs. Consequently, when a successful response is ultimately made at 9 years, the difference between models 1–4 and 5–8 is not so great as it was in the case of the square. For model 5, which contains a curvilinear triangle and three lentiform segments, the success score rises from 15 per cent at 4 years to 89 per cent at 9 years, whereas model 7, which contains two lentiform sections and a crescent, the success score rises from 23 per cent to only 55 per cent. The most difficult model of course, is that consisting of curvilinear triangles only (8).

On the whole, then, if the fragments to be chosen contain arcs, the result is a greater difference between the ultimate (9 years) and the initial (4 years) recompositions (− 20 to + 74 per cent), whereas the differences for the square were only − 2 to + 29 per cent). The poor rate of development in the case of the square seems to show that the reactions are governed primarily by the laws of the image, whereas the curvilinear data of the circular model probably makes for greater mobility of combination once the level of concrete operations is reached (7 to 8 years). The difference is even clearer if we take into account the prompted choices: upward of 75 per cent of the 8- to 9-year-old subjects are successful for all the different figures except for models 7 and 8 at 8 years and model 8 at 9 years, whereas in the case of the square successes are poor for forms 5 and 8 at 7 and 8 years.

The results for the rhombus are interesting in that they show the part played by conceptualization in the formation of the image (Table 152).

To understand these results properly, it should be borne in mind that the child cannot successfully make a drawn copy of a rhombus until 6 to 7 years, though he can copy a square successfully at 4 years (75 per cent of subjects). Furthermore, the child's graphic image of a rhombus, as we have shown in an earlier work,[13] frequently represents his own idea of it rather than its perceptual form: a 'square with a point', that is a quadrilateral reduced to its square protype and furnished with acute angles.

TABLE 152 *Successes for recompositions of the rhombus*
(As % of the subjects. In brackets, results after prompted choice)

	1	2	3	4	5	6	7
4 years	100 (100)	84 (100)	7 (7)	0 (0)	15 (15)	15 (15)	0 (0)
5 years	85 (85)	70 (100)	15 (15)	15 (15)	7 (7)	32 (32)	0 (0)
6 years	70 (100)	100 (100)	42 (64)	42 (64)	21 (21)	50 (64)	0 (21)
7 years	92 (100)	78 (100)	28 (52)	42 (52)	50 (64)	42 (71)	15 (36)
8 years	94 (100)	94 (100)	36 (74)	47 (74)	50 (68)	47 (74)	15 (47)
9 years	100 (100)	94 (100)	77 (100)	77 (100)	61 (61)	56 (71)	22 (44)

From the reactions tabulated above one sees that the construction of the rhombus subdivided into smaller rhombuses (form 5) ranks only fifth or sixth in order of successes. Contrary to what we found for the squares and the circles, the first three highest success scores here are for those figures that combine triangles. Pseudo-conservation, which we have postulated in explanation of image mechanisms, is thus influenced more by the conceptual structuration than perception. The most difficult forms are those that keep most closely to the perceptual aspect of the rhombus, i.e. forms 5–7, subdivided diagonally and medially. The difficulties arising here are not simply due to the introduction of oblique sections (5 and 6), since the hardest form is the one divided vertically and horizontally (7). Figure 7 is simply a continuation of 1 and 2, but it requires that the subject break away from the rectangular forms which he spontaneously tends to produce when trying to arrange the four pieces.

[13] Piaget and Inhelder, *ibid.*, Chapter II.

If the choices are prompted the results naturally improve, though models 5–7 are still found difficult at 8 to 9 years.

To conclude, these apparently simple puzzle-game tests in which familiar shapes have to be reformed are far more difficult than one might have expected. There are probably two reasons why this should be so. First, the image, thrown back on its own resources, lacks kinetic mobility, and all the results so far described in the present work would seem to suggest that such mobility is only acquired under the guidance of the operational mechanisms. But for these to be brought into play the questions have to be posed within the framework of a system of logico-mathematical transformations. Such transformations, as opposed to simple modifications, or changes of physical states, are characterized by their reversibility and by the conservation of invariant properties. Now in the present case the problem is not set within such a framework of conservation. When confronted with the various fragments, the subject does not know whether they result from the division of the complete form, and so does not know whether they can be used to reconstruct it. But, when the experimenter suggests which pieces are required, the subject is indirectly provided with what amounts to a framework of conservation. This leads to a more regular evolution of success according to age, and a greater increase in success at 7 to 9 years than at 4 to 6 years (although the spontaneous successes were also better in the older children, the increase due to prompting is 9 per cent for the square and 7 per cent for the circle and rhombus at 4 to 6 years, and 11 per cent at 7 to 9 years for the square and circle, 17·5 per cent for the rhombus), this increase being particularly evident in the easier figures for the younger children, and in the more difficult ones for the older children. All this points to the conclusion that the framework of indirect conservation implicit in the prompting of responses improves the working of the images.

As far as geometrical intuition is concerned, these facts demonstrate the inadequacy of non-operational imaginal intuition. The mobility of the superior forms of this mode of intuition is due to the mutual services the images and operations render one another. This we were able to establish from the facts arising in section 1, where we saw that the detour and transformation criteria were substituted for the initial static criteria. The facts that have come up in this present section bring out all the shortcomings of the image left to its own devices. But they also show that the image improves when geometrical intuition is guided by an indirect conservation framework – when it is, in other words, well on the way to acquiring operational form.

3. *The anticipation of order in cyclic movement*

Some time ago we made a study of the way a child understands the order of bands of colour arranged longitudinally along a revolving cylinder.[14] We took up this problem again in collaboration with J. Pascual-Leone in order to study the role of imaginal anticipation.

The child was presented with a cylinder 20 cm tall and 11 cm in diameter. Half way up the lateral surface at equal intervals were attached five pictures of animals. On a second cylinder of the same dimensions were attached six differently coloured paper strips. The cylinders were placed in a cover in which there was a slit exposing one colour, or picture, at a time. To make it easier for the subject to understand, the cylinder was rolled about on the table, rather than revolved about a fixed axis. As an aid to memory the subject had before him throughout two series of cards bearing the pictures or the colours of the model.

First the subject was required to arrange the cards on the table in the order 1, 2, 3, 4, 5, 1, 2, 3, 4, 5 to correspond with the cylinder, which he was allowed to handle as he wished. He was asked to check that all the pictures were there. As a control we moved, or asked the subject to move, one or more of the cards, so that he could observe the gap; the card was then replaced.

The cylinder was then replaced in its cover and put in front of picture 3, then 1 and then 5 (variable order) with the corresponding picture showing in the slit. The child was then required to foresee the result of a rotation to the left (which we called the 'window side'), and to the right (which we called the 'door side'). For this the subject is only given cards 1, 2, 3, 4, 5. Two groups of subjects were studied. The questions were as follows:

$$\text{I} \ldots \ldots \leftarrow1; 5\rightarrow; 1\rightarrow; \leftarrow5; \leftarrow3; 3\rightarrow$$
$$\text{II} \ldots \ldots 1\rightarrow; \leftarrow5; \leftarrow1; 5\rightarrow; 3\rightarrow; \leftarrow3$$

The answers were either given orally or by means of the cards. In general the oral method proved to be easier, particularly under the age of 7. When the subject had given his answer we questioned him more generally, suggested other answers, including those offered by the other children, and asked him to pass judgment on them.

We occasionally repeated this procedure using cylinder II (colours) at positions $\leftarrow1$ and $\leftarrow4$. Adults were tested using the main technique, with additional questions after inversion of the cylinder.

We used twenty-two subjects aged 6 years, sixteen aged 7, twenty-one aged 8, fourteen aged 9, twelve aged 10, twelve aged 12 years, and twelve adults. Taking groups I and II together we worked out the percentages for those subjects who eventually answered correctly

[14] Piaget, *The Child's Conception of Movement and Speed*, 1969, Chapter II.

(after the general questioning) to all six questions: 6 per cent at 6 to 7 years, 35 per cent at 8 to 9 years, 53 per cent at 10 to 12 years, and 100 per cent in the adults. On the other hand, if only the initial answers (before detailed questioning) are included, and if the successes are split up into individual tests, the results turn out as in Table 153.

TABLE 153 *Successes for the six distinct tests*
(As % of the responses)

	6 years	7 years	8 years	9 years	10 years	12 years	Adults
← 1	90	65	75	80	70	75	92
1 →	5	50	42	60	40	67	92
← 5	10	63	42	60	60	75	92
5 →	55	50	58	78	50	50	75
← 3	55	38	33	60	40	67	92
3 →	50	44	58	50	60	67	92
Average	44	51	51	64	53	66	87

On average there is a fairly regular progression according to age (save one anomaly, at 10 years, but as the number of subjects is small, they may be taken in two-year groups to get 49 per cent at 6 to 7 years, 56 per cent at 8 to 9 years, and 60 per cent at 10 to 12 years). But if we examine the tests in detail two striking facts stand out immediately: (*a*) the appreciable difference at the lower ages between the results for the left-hand and the right-hand rotation (and it is not always the same direction that has the best response); (*b*) the occasionally bimodal distribution, as in ←1, where there is 90 per cent success at 6 years and again in the adult, with a drop in between. This latter fact indicates that the subject is using one of at least two solutions to the problem – and it might be conjectured that one is predominantly imaginal and the other predominantly operational. Let us first examine the figurative factors:

(1) In cyclic order the main cause of error is that the same elements come up whichever direction is taken: 3 comes after 5 (if . . . 5, 1, 2, 3,) just as before 5 (if 5, 4, 3 . . .). One would expect, therefore, to find that there were as many correct answers as invalid inversions of the order. And this is indeed the case up to 8 years, if we take the six questions all together. But if we examine the questions one by one, we find that this balanced distribution is not maintained. We therefore need to analyse not only the errors but also the apparently correct responses arrived at by spurious methods.

(2) There is a second cause of error, resulting from artificial factors, but of some interest in that it clearly points to perceptuo-imaginal

attitudes that are of an extremely compelling kind, since they crop up again in the adult, and are responsible for the few residual errors found at this level. When the cylinder is placed facing picture 3 and is turned to the left (i.e. rolled along the table), it gives the order 3, 4, 5, 1, 2. But in the plane the order 3, 4, 5 has to be read off by means of eye movements travelling in the opposite direction. Consequently, instead of making the necessary inversion, the subject is led to turn his imaginal anticipation in the wrong direction in vectorial correspondence with the direction of the cylinder. It is due to this factor, which was excluded in our earlier experiment,[15] that successes are delayed from 7 to 8 years to 10 years or later.

(3) This factor, however, plays only a limited role. Two things demonstrate this. First, between 6 and 12 years one finds 220 false inversions in direction → and 177 in direction ← (as against 283 apparently correct answers for the direction ←, and 240 for →, which makes 460 answers in all for both directions). Now the difference between the two directions, which is particularly marked at 6 and 7 years, reflects the primacy of the left–right direction in the succession of images for plane alignments, due to reading or writing habits. This is so strongly imagined that at 6 years question ← 1 does not give rise to vectorial convergence (the factor defined above in 2), but to 90 per cent apparently correct answers, since the younger subjects, starting with the first picture, have an unsuperable tendency to follow the rest through in the order of the row (1, 2, 3, 4, 5, instead of 1, 5, 4, 3, 2). Hence a remarkable bimodal curve.

(4) A fourth factor explains why the preceding reaction, so much in evidence in questions ←1 and 1→, is no longer found in questions ←5 and 5→. As picture 5 is next to 4, it is the fact of figural proximity that leads to the order 5, 4, 3, 2, 1. This factor coincides with factor 2 for the direction ←, producing an erroneous response (very low success score at 6 years), and is contrary to it for the direction →, which gives a medium result.

(5) Finally, we should mention some local errors, such as partial inversions (5, 2, 3, 4, 1, 4, 3, 1, 2, 5, 5, 2, 3, 4, 4, 3, 2, 5, 4, 2, 1, 3, etc.), omission of elements, difficulties in linking the extremities of the series, failure to co-ordinate the two faces of the cylinder. All these arise from factor 1 or from a combination of several of the preceding factors.

Three factors may be distinguished in the gradual subordination of perceptual data and images to operations and the eventual formation of totally correct anticipatory images.

(1) Local inversions, when passing from questions ← n to n→, of the type 'it goes to the other side, so I do the opposite'. Such inversions

[15] Piaget, *ibid.*

are correct in principle but may be applied equally to a false or correct initial response.

(2) Increasing logical coherence. This is most striking in the tests in which geometrical intuition is brought to bear on a general problem of order. The younger subjects are not in the least perturbed by the contradictions which may arise in their answers as they switch from one criterion to another. At a later second level they try to some extent to remove any contradictions, and if there is a preponderence of incorrect answers they will actually modify the correct answers out of regard for coherence. At a still later third level this coherence becomes general and thus favours the formation of accurate anticipation.

(3) But the principal operational factor is the translation of the linear order of the plane alignment into a circular order corresponding to the rotation of the cylinder. One frequently finds that the child suddenly discovers that such an arrangement is possible. Thus Des (7,7), in test 5→, takes the elements and arranges them in a vertical row and counts them out loud (using the names of the animals depicted): 5, 4, 3, 2, 1, 5, 4, 3. Other subjects make circular gestures, and so on.

In sum, this inquiry provides us with one further illustration of the essential duality of geometrical intuitions. This duality is evident from the two successive levels of reaction which in some instances are so clear-cut that they correspond to a bimodal success curve (apparent or real). At the one level the dominant factors are perceptuo-imaginal, which, either because of their inherent limitations or because of the systematic distortion they lead to, are insufficient for a solution of the problem. At the other level the image is subordinate to operations, and the resultant imaginal anticipations ultimately give rise to a more or less straightforward solution – a solution that is not to be credited solely to the image, though the image is indeed an effective auxiliary in the process of deduction.

4. Conclusion

It is doubtless in the sphere of geometrical intuition that the visual image is able to be of most service to operational functioning. The reason is self-evident: as the form, and in this instance the content also of the image, is spatial, geometrical intuition is the only field in which the imaginal form and content are homogeneous. When the image has as its 'content' (that is to say, when it tends to bear on logical or arithmetical operations), such operations may present spatio-temporal points of reference, making possible an image of their results (except in the case of purely formal operations). But these logico-arithmetical operations themselves remain transformational acts that cannot as such be represented imaginally, since any kind of spatial configuration is foreign to them. Hence the very approximate symbolism of number and class images. It is true that the image can utilize certain isomorphisms between algebraic and topological structures and thereby represent class operations by means of compartments inserted in, or taken out of, one another. But only inclusion can be symbolized in this way by isomorphism with enclosure or surrounding, and the compartments have essentially no connection with classes as such. They may be symbolized by circles (Eulerian circles), closed curves, squares, volumes, etc., whereas the spatial or geometrical image of a circle will always be different from that of a square, even if both remain no more than approximate. An image with logico-arithmetical content entails the conversion of non-spatio–temporal transformations into a necessarily spatial form. The spatial image, on the other hand, represents spatial content in forms that are likewise spatial. And spatial operations (displacements, projections, etc.) relate to transformations actually taking place in space and presenting figurative, not exclusively operative characteristics. Thus the transformations themselves are in a sense figures of space.

This state of affairs has two consequences of fundamental importance. First, the spatial image is the only image in which there is a tendency towards a real isomorphism between the symbolizing form and symbolized content. The image of a number or a class is not in itself a number or a class, but an image of numbered or classified objects, whereas the image of a square is approximately square, and the image of a straight line, while possessing breadth, can be considered as a bundle of parallel of straight lines. Second, it is only in the sphere of spatial images that transformation images are situated on the same plane as static images, and anticipatory images on the same plane as reproductive images. This accounts for why well-practised 'geometrical intuition' enables actual transformations to be 'seen in space'. Even the most complex transformations and the most remote from everyday physical experience can be imagined in this way, because the image is based on a spatialized imitation of operations that are themselves also spatial.

Within this rather special area, it was necessary to ask all over again whether the image prepares for, or at least aids the functioning of, the operations.

No doubt the preceding chapters have already given some answers to these two problems: after all, our present work has dealt with nothing else but spatial images. But earlier chapters dealt with the imaginal evocation of a particular given situation, whereas in this chapter the subjects have to solve problems by employing the image as best they can.

I. As for the first of the two questions, the results obtained present as clear a picture as ever. Although spatial transformations have a figurative aspect that can be evoked by the image, we find that as before static images are dominant over anticipatory images. No more than in the results of preceding chapters do these static images act as a means of preparing for the operations, for, their accurate aspect notwithstanding, they give rise to systematic errors deriving from the 'pseudo-conservation' characteristic of all imaginal figuration. For instance, there is a tendency to conserve a biunivocal correspondence between the length of the perimeter and the area of the surface; again, there is a tendency to consider that a global form can be reconstituted only by using elements similar in form; or again, there is a tendency to judge an arc to be equal in length to its chord; and so on and so forth.

Consequently if we compare the successive stages of development, we find two kinds of solution – an imaginal and an operational solution – to the same problems. Now the first of these types, depending on the situation, is equally as likely to produce a correct as an erroneous answer. But the correct results are misleading, since they are arrived at by unjustifiable methods (cf. the cases where one perimeter is judged longer than another because it corresponds to a larger surface area; cf. also the cases of coincidental agreement of the order of the figures on the revolving cylinder and the preferential order of the figures in plane alignment – section 3). The fact is that in these various instances the operational solution is totally unconnected with even a correct preoperational or imaginal solution: there is thus duality of interpretation and even in some circumstances a bimodal success curve (some successes being apparent only or arising from a fortuitous conjunction of imaginal laws and the objective given configuration, while the other successes are authentic).

This lack of filiation between geometrical operations and the corresponding images at the preoperational level is exemplified in a particularly striking manner by the 'rotations' which we studied in an earlier work,[16] and which are allied to those studied in Chapter Six, sections 1–3, of the present work. Their interest lies in the fact that they take us outside the framework of experiment and questioning. 'Pseudo-rotations' occur in children's drawings between the ages of 4 to 6 years: they have been excellently described by Luquet, who has termed them 'rotations', and they consist, to use his expression, of 'jumbles of viewpoints'. The question is whether the spontaneous intervention of imagery

[16] Piaget and Inhelder, *The Child's Conception of Space*, Chapter X.

in these 'rotations' does or does not enable adequate anticipatory images to be formed, so that the transformations in play in the corresponding operations can be represented visually.

In one of Luquet's examples a horse is drawn in profile pulling a cart which is drawn in plan from a viewpoint above. The wheels are also drawn in the horizontal plane, which means they are 'rotated' through 90° relative to the bottom of the cart.[17] The drawing thus involves three different jumbled and juxtaposed viewpoints. Can subjects capable of dissociating viewpoints in this fashion also anticipate by means of an image the result of unfolding cardboard cubes, cylinders and cones, so that all elements are rotated into the horizontal plane? Analysis of the reactions by age gives the following two results: (a) the ability to imagine genuine rotations appears much later than the spontaneous 'pseudo-rotations', since it requires a *co-ordination* of view-points (not merely a haphazard jumbling): it requires, in other words, an operational factor based on the action of unfolding itself; (b) the correct image of the rotations results from an internalized imitation of the unfolding action and its outcome; it does not simply prolong the perceptions, nor does it prolong the 'pseudo-rotations' of the spontaneous drawings. The latter merely translate the various possible perceptions (each being imitated separately as a reproductive image), and lack the capacity for anticipation afforded by operational co-ordination.

We observed three stages of development. During the first (up to 6 years – that is, at the ages where 'pseudo-rotations' in drawing are found) the child is not yet able to imagine a genuine rotation: he simply draws the object as it is without transformation.

During the second stage the child makes unsuccessful attempts to imagine the rotation and the drawings translate these attempts into symbolic form. For instance, the side of a cube to be rotated is shown along with a stroke indicating the direction of the rotation; or a gap may be marked symbolizing the start of the action required to unfold the side.

At the third stage (from 7 to 8 years on) the child can imagine and draw the rotation, but in stages in accordance with the order of difficulty of the objects in question: first the cylinder and the cone, then the cube, which is a little more difficult, because of its six sides, and finally the pyramid.

This example supplements those already given in this chapter and underlines the as it were bimodal character of the reactions to geometrical problems. On the one hand the subject forms spatial images without any connection with the operations, and on the other he forms anticipations which are both imaginal and operational, but which do not derive from previous preoperational images.

II. However, when the spatial images become anticipatory under the

[17] Two of the wheels are situated under the bottom of the cart as if in the same perspective as the horse; but the other two are placed above – which makes it clear that there is a 90° rotation of the four wheels irrespective of the horse's position.

influence of the operations, they start to play a supporting role as an auxiliary in deduction – a role that is particularly striking in geometrical intuition. There is no need to labour this point, but it should be made clear once again that the image–operation collaboration only begins to come into effect with the emergence of concrete operations, and that the co-operation becomes increasingly close as new spatial operations are brought into being. The natural systems of co-ordinates (horizontal and vertical) are elaborated only at about 9 to 10 years. It is thus not until this age that the child attains correct imaginal representation of the level of a liquid in a jar tilted in various directions, or of a plumb-line suspended within a frame not parallel to the line.[18] Similarly, the co-ordination of two systems of reference, such as are for instance involved in anticipatory images relating to mechanical curves, is only accomplished at the level of formal or hypothetico-deductive operations,[19] and the same is true of any system involving a combinatorial process.

In the light of these facts corroborated by the new observations contained in the present chapter it is legitimate to draw the following conclusion. It is indeed in geometrical intuition above all that imagery reaches a peak of precision, at least from a cognitive point of view (for other spheres of activity show equally striking developments, though to aesthetic ends); but this does not mean that images – even anticipatory images – are the only factors in play. Geometrical intuition is essentially operational and it is the system of operations it entails that makes it meaningful as a network of 'signifieds'. The images are the symbolic expression of, or the system of, 'signifiers' corresponding to these operations – in spite of the partial though highly developed isomorphism that is found in the spatial sphere between imaginal form and operational content. But since a symbol (in contradistinction to 'arbitrary' signs) by definition bears some resemblance to the thing symbolized, this adequation of the imaginal symbol to the operational core, however well developed it may be in geometrical intuition, in no way contradicts the essentially symbolic nature of the spatial image. And, although we have spoken of error in intuition, any such error is entirely due to the images being credited with powers they do not possess. For the role of the images as such is not to cognize, but to concretize symbolically.

[18] *The Child's Conception of Space*, Chapter XIII.
[19] See *The Child's Conception of Geometry*, 1960, Chapter X.

CHAPTER TEN

General Conclusion

One would be quite justified in considering a programme of psychological research a failure if it really said at the end what could have been assumed or deduced at the beginning. But the appearance of the unexpected in the final results might be taken as an indication of its success. We shall feel well rewarded if the reader of the facts described in this book experiences only a quarter of the surprises we had in collecting them. However, the experiments and inquiries which we thought it worthwhile including in these pages are extremely numerous and scattered. It is only appropriate at this point, therefore, that we should bring out their significance by going back to the problem first raised in Chapter One, and attempting to offer a systematic solution. At the same time we shall take stock of facts established, and, even more important, of facts remaining hypothetical or uncertain.

To begin with we give an account of what remains of our initial classification of images (section 1). The framework retained will then enable us to draw conclusions as to the laws of image evolution (section 2). In section 3 we define the general characteristics of the image, in section 4 its relation to perception and imitation, and in sections 5 and 6 its relation to preoperational notions and mental operations. Finally we turn back to discuss the symbolic nature of the image (section 7) and its epistemological significance (section 8).

1. The classification of images and the relation between reproductive and anticipatory images

A preliminary classification such as that drawn up in Chapter One may be expected to have two uses. In the first place it provides a programme of experiments, and in the second place it helps us to come to terms with the problems of structure. The first has already been exploited to the full. The second is about to be exploited as we go on now to compare the results obtained with the original hypothetical framework.

The main dichotomy of reproductive images R and anticipatory

351

images *A*, from which we started out, has in its general outline been proved correct. We have seen that it corresponds to an essential genetic sequence. Reproductive images are formed at the pre-operational level and even as soon as the appearance of the symbolic functions. Anticipatory images in the strict sense of a prior imagining of an as yet unrealized process do not develop until the level of the concrete operations.

But though this dichotomy remains and even acquires genetic significance, the content of category *R* proves to be far less rich than one might have expected. This fact is one of the most instructive results of our investigations. Once the subject is capable of reproducing by images something already perceived, it follows, if one argues *a priori*, that he can reproduce static configurations, movements, or transformations. Thus one might assume, as we did in Chapter One, the existence of static reproductive images (*RS*), kinetic reproductive images (*RK*) and reproductive images of transformation (*RT*).

Now nearly all the familiar situations utilized in order to get at the kinetic reproductive images and reproductive transformation images[1] resulted in the failure of reproductive evocation up to 7 to 8 years. (Displaced squares, Chapter Three, section 1; rotation of a rod, Chapter Three, section 3; the straightening of an arc, Chapter Five, section 1, etc.) But this does not in any way mean, as we shall see, that these broad categories of kinetic or transformational reproductive images need be eliminated, since *RK* and *RT* images are very common above a certain level, and are in fact in general use in the adult. But what led to our original classification was the question whether these images were primary or whether they derived from previous anticipatory phases (of the *AK* and *AT* type). And indeed the information gathered in Chapters Three and Four would appear to show precisely that the reproductive images of movements and transformations are formed only with the support of anticipations or re-anticipations.

On the other hand, analysis of anticipatory kinetic and transformation images (*AK* and *AT*) has shown that the relevant distinction for the problem of levels of development is not a distinction between movements and transformations, which are consistently anticipated at about the same time, but rather a distinction between anticipation of the results or products of the movement or transformation and the anticipation of the actual process of the modification[2] in its successive phases. Anticipation of the product fairly regularly precedes anticipation of the process – even if the only

---

[1] Delayed as opposed to immediate and consecutional reproductions: *RK II* and *RT II* as opposed to *RK I* images.
[2] Distinction between anticipations of the type *AKP* or *ATP* and *AKM* or *ATM*.

reason is that it is hard to seriate the stages of the modification in their temporal order of succession. Thus Tables 61 and 63 (Chapter Four, section 8) give a 73–79 per cent success score at 5 years for the change in the order of beads after rotation, whereas the anticipatory image of their trajectory comes much later.

Now, this difference between the anticipation of products or results (*AP*) and the anticipation of paths or successive modifications (*AM*) proves for one thing that there are several levels of anticipation, and that, although *AM* may require operational support, *AP* can be outlined with the aid of more elementary activity. But, above all, it shows that before it can apprehend movements or transformations as such (*AM*), the anticipatory image at first bears only on their end states. That is to say, the anticipatory image is at first only concerned with configurations, which, independently of the not yet imaginally anticipated movements or transformations, appear to be static, and which no doubt actually are static from the child's point of view. The same is true *a fortiori* for reproductive kinetic or reproductive transformation images (*RK* or *RT*). These also, as we have just pointed out, initially involved anticipation or reanticipation, and apprehend only the results or products (*RKP* or *RTP*) of transformations, before being able to reconstitute the modifications themselves (*RKM* or *RTM*). Thus a large number of images which might appear to be static, do in fact have an anticipatory dimension. But without further research, it is impossible to determine the extent of such a state of affairs.

This brings us to the question of the retarded character of reproductive kinetic or reproductive transformation images, and to the possibility that their formation is necessarily dependent on their being registered within a prior framework of anticipations. It is worth recalling in this connection that the best reproductive kinetic images obtained in our tests were direct or consecutive gestural copies of crossing, 'entraining' movements, etc. (Chapter Two, Table 14, etc.). The most important point arising from Chapter Two was that even reproductive images in a direct copy (*RSI*), and even images as static as copies of a segment of a straight line, presuppose the intervention of anticipatory execution schemes, or 'fore-images'. More generally, we learnt from Chapter Seven that deferred static reproductive images (*RSII*) are themselves improved if the models are assimilated into the subject's own action schemes. Once again this underlines the importance of the anticipatory processes.

We have found that the reproductive kinetic and reproductive transformation images (*RK* and *RT*) turn out to be far less consistent in the under 7 to 8-year-olds than we might have been led to suppose

353

before the experiments described in Chapters Three and Five. There is a single fundamental reason for this which our experiments have shown to be true generally. In order to imagine a given movement or transformation, it is necessary to reconstitute them by the identical process by which unknown movements and transformations are represented. In other words, there is in most cases no essential difference, no radical break between *RK* and *RT* reproductive images and *AK* and *AT* anticipatory images. The reason why these *R* images emerge so late is that the anticipatory images bearing on actual modifications do not come into action until the level of concrete operations. No doubt one may in certain cases find reproductive kinetic or transformation images before 7 to 8 years – for instance when a child is asked to imagine the linear path of a man going from *A* to *B*, or the expansion of a soap-bubble, or the equal division of a sheet of paper. But we still need to know what reanticipations are presupposed by these elementary reproductive images.

It would appear probable – but this is only a hypothesis which needs to be checked by further research – that the actualization of any image presupposes reconstitution comprising reanticipation or anticipation proper. There would, according to this hypothesis, be no fundamental difference between executional anticipations (= outlined or projected gestures) and authentic or straightforward anticipation. Rather there would be a continuous sequence of intermediaries leading from the image of known models rapidly reconstituted by the subject to the image of less familiar models giving rise to visible reanticipatory efforts (one thinks, for instance, of the difficulty experienced by the younger subjects in following the order of positions on the rotating rod in Chapter Three, section 3), and then leading to the image of totally unknown models requiring anticipation in the strict sense.

These reflexions suggested by our look back at the successive applications of the classification proposed in Chapter One show that while the general framework holds good, the relative frequency distributions are quite different from what we had imagined. This raises, as we should expect from any natural classification, certain general problems concerning structure and filiation.

If one were to start from the commonly held conception of the mental image as conservation or retention of past-perceived configurations and events, one would reckon on finding a relatively higher occurrence of reproductive images and a lower proportion of anticipatory images limited to extending to unfamiliar situations anything that can be supplied from the stock of familiar reproductions. As for the copy images, one would have to consider them as scarcely belonging to the domain of images at all, insofar as they are exactly and automatically cast in the form of their perceptual models. Now we in fact find that the contrary is the case. The role of reconstitution, reanticipation and anticipation is far more considerable than foreseen: almost without exception, reproductive images up to the age of 7 to 8 years are no more than static images; and direct copy images themselves entail some degree of anticipation and active structuration.

This contrast between the real distributions and the expectations raised by the proposed classification brings us back to the problems met continually during the course of this work. These we shall now endeavour to solve systematically, that is to say, genetically, by converting into terms of filiation and development the conclusions suggested by our re-examination of the original image classification. We shall see in section 2 that the evolution of the images cannot be seen merely as a system of simple and independent, self-containing filiations. We shall see rather that, precisely because of the part played by reconstitution and anticipation in the images at all levels, their development entails the continual assimilation of external factors.

But before going on to this problem it remains to draw some conclusions concerning the relations between reproductive images R and anticipatory images A. We should first point out – and we were far from starting out from such a hypothesis – that the present problem concerning that sector of the figurative functions comprised by imaginal representation is very similar to a question arising in connection with that other figurative sector, perception. Namely, the question of the relationship between field effects and perceptual activities. In the perceptual sphere there are certain organizations with essentially reproductive functions, with *Gestalt* structures, and with the appearance of being 'primary' because of their greater simplicity and permanent laws; and there are exploratory 'activities', transposition and anticipation 'activities', referral 'activities', and so on, which in principle serve to correct the former, although they also bring with them certain 'secondary' illusions. Now, analysis of the relations between these two effects led us to the assumption that such perceptual activities exist at all levels, and that the primary or field effects at all levels were merely the results or 'sedimentations' of these perceptual activities.[3]

Now, without going into a detailed comparison, it may be noted that the reproductive images, which might reasonably have been supposed to be 'primary' in character, do not in actual fact achieve any degree of accuracy within the context of kinetic and transformation reproductions (RK and RT), unless they are supported by anticipatory images (AK and AT). Even the static reproductive images (RS) presuppose executional

[3] Piaget, J., *Mechanisms of Perception*, 1969.

anticipation. In general, then, the rarity of accurate images before 7 to 8 years (particularly *RK* and *RT*), and their subsequent profusion, would seem to confirm the vital role played by imaginal anticipations.

If this is the kind of view the facts seem to lead to, at least three points are clarified. First, it explains the distribution differences between the results found below 7 to 10 years and the apparent implications of our classification; second, it brings out the active nature of the image, which suggests that its origin lies in imitation (see section 4); and third, and most important, it brings out the non-autonomous nature of the evolution of images. As far as this last point is concerned, it may indeed be the case that reproductive images depend on anticipations, but we still have to explain the progress of the anticipations themselves, and we shall now see how sooner or later such progress draws on the factors external to the images furnished by the mental operations.

2. *The evolution of images*

The development of the operations of intelligence possesses two remarkable characteristics: it proceeds by clearly defined stages, and the process is entirely autonomous. There are three necessary conditions for a system of stages. The stages must follow one another in a constant order in all subjects; each one must have a characteristic overall structure (not just one dominant characteristic); and these structures must be integrated into one another according to the order of their formation. Such an evolution is autonomous in that the structures are generated from one another under motivation from the intelligence alone (agreement with experience, internal coherence, etc.). Affective factors may speed up or slow down the formation of a structure, but they will not actually modify it *qua* structure. By 'autonomous', then, we mean not 'isolable', but 'unfolding by continuous filiation'.

The evolution of perceptions presents an entirely different picture. Certain sectors of the perceptual mechanisms scarcely change at all with age – for example, the primary or field effects (primary 'illusions' show the same qualitative structure at all ages and change only in respect of their quantitative value). In the domain of perceptual activities, which undergo greater transformations during their development, some suggestion of stages is to be observed (certain effects appearing only from a certain age), but there is no successive integration of structures comparable with that found in the development of the operations. The essential point is, however, this: the evolution of perceptions is not autonomous, in the sense that it involves mechanisms extraneous to perception itself, and that such contributory factors play a determinative role in the emergence of new effects. For instance, the appearance of perceptual co-ordinates at about 9 to 10 years in the estimation of the positions of objects in relation to one another (not just to the subject's own body) can only be satisfactorily explained if one supposes that the operations of spatial co-ordination formed at this level have some directive function and orientate referral within the perceptual activities.[4]

So returning to mental images, these are the two questions that now need to be examined: the question of the significance and indeed existence of stages, and above all the question of the mechanism of their evolution. Solutions to these problems would be able to tell us a good deal about the image's twin relationship with perception and intelligence. We shall find that the evolution of the images is of a kind intermediate between that of the perceptions and that of the intelligence.

With regard to the question of stages, note to begin with that all the tables included in this book show an evolution of results according to age. The occasional absence of development between two ages (as in the case of the straightening of angles between 6 and 8 years: Table 90, Chapter Five) does not constitute an exception to this statement if the results in question are compared with children of different ages or with adults. In most cases it should thus be possible within the partial evolutions evidenced in the tests to mark off a certain number of successive steps assimilable to stages. For example in the case of the image of a square displaced in relation to a second square (Chapter Three, Table 17, Figure 5) one sees that at 4 years A–D reactions predominate (no displacement or separation of the squares) that at 5 to 6 years $E1$–G reactions (projecting portions but squares distorted) reach a maximum, and that at 7 years 75 per cent of the subjects achieve a correct image. This gives three stages for this test. In the case of the arcs transformed into straight lines (Chapter Five, Tables 82–83) one finds that, when selecting from prepared drawings, 67 per cent of the 5-year-olds (0 per cent from 6 years on) pick out models A–D, that the reactions are intermediate at 6 to 7 years, and that at 8 to 9 years 83 per cent pick the correct model. This also gives three stages but at different ages.

However, if one tries to bring these partial stages together in order to define the general stages of the image's development, one really only finds two decisive moments and a single break of general significance. The first of these moments is the appearance of the image, which probably occurs at the same time as the formation of the symbolic function (about $1\frac{1}{2}$ to 2 years). At any rate that is when

---

[4] See *ibid.*, Chapter VII, section 4.

it occurs if we adhere to the negative criterion that sensori-motor behaviour before this level does not require the intervention of images (whereas they are indispensable in symbolic play and other representational behaviours emerging at and after this level). The second decisive moment corresponds to the only general break we can discern from the data preceding. It comes at about 7 to 8 years and points, if not to the actual emergence then at least to the rise of the anticipatory images, that is, to the kinetic and transformation images (section 1). True, within this division one could establish further divisions and sub-divisions. For example, a further break might be distinguished at the point where hyperordinal imaginal anticipations of speeds make their appearance (Chapter Four, section 10). But, as we have already seen (Table 72), such cases depend on the processes of reasoning. Hence, it is not a question of stages of the *image*, that is to say, of modifications in the structure of imagery itself, but rather of the stages of image *content*, that is to say, of the conceptual or operational 'signified' as distinct from the imaginal 'signifier'. In the case of the appearance of anticipatory images AK and AT, change affects the 'form' as well as the 'content' of the image.

In short, the two main periods of image development correspond to the preoperational (before 7 to 8 years) and the operational levels. As we have already pointed out in section 1, the images of the first period remain essentially static and consequently unable to represent even the results of movements or transformations and *a fortiori* unable to anticipate processes not yet known. But at about 7 to 8 years a capacity for imaginal anticipation makes its first appearance, enabling the subject to reconstitute kinetic or transformation processes, and even foresee other simple sequences.

Now, if this is a fair account of the evolution of the images in its broad outlines, then it would seem to be fairly self-evident that the formation of anticipatory images cannot be explained by some increase in the flexibility of reproductive images, especially the static ones. Whether the image merely prolongs perception, or whether it results from an active imitation, its function is the same – to provide a copy as faithful and accurate as possible of the perceived datum. This being so, it might be thought that the most general factor in image formation is the familiarity (or probability of occurrence) of the model, and its simplicity. Now, the kinetic models used in Chapter Three could not be considered any less familiar than, say, the static models used in Chapter Seven. And we have already, at the end of Chapter Three, stressed that the empirical frequency factor plays a very slight part in elementary images. This leaves the simplicity factor. Movements are clearly less simple to imagine than

358

static configurations, since the children fail the movement tests. But, either this argument is circular or else it means that the difficulty is relative to the subject, and that the movement is hard to grasp as long as the subject centres on states rather than on the transformations and movements linking them. In other words, the static character of the images before 7 to 8 years is due to preoperational thought which ignores transformations in favour of configurations or states, with the result that the images of this level latch on to the simplest elements available within such a context.

It is impossible, then, to account for the appearance of anticipatory images in terms of reproductive images as such. But in section 1 we put forward the view that each of the reproductive images is formed by the utilization of anticipations of execution, and that at all levels the reproductions presuppose outlined anticipations or reanticipations. Now if this is true, obviously we must consider anticipatory images proper (as AP, and above all as AM, i.e. when bearing on the modification as such and not just on its result) as deriving to varying degrees from the outlines of anticipation which are to be observed much earlier. An executional anticipation preparing a gesture for the imitation of a movement M (and thus enabling the imitation to be internalized as an image) leads sooner or later to reanticipation of such a movement, and ultimately to anticipation of other similar movements.

But that is not the whole story. Even if the outlines of anticipation observable before 7 to 8 years are enough to account for the detailed and precise anticipations AK and AT, we still have no means of explaining why they do not appear until such a late stage – and their retarded character is one of the clearest results to come out of this work. Two roads are open to us: either we adduce some internal progressive equilibration of these imaginal anticipations, or else we assume that some external contributory factor is brought in. But the equilibration process is an active reaction on the part of the subject, serving to compensate perturbations in a system. And, while not all equilibrations are operational (some are sensori-motor, perceptual, and so on), it goes without saying that where imaginal representational anticipations are concerned, the regulation of anticipation will be very close to being an operation. Now to adduce an external factor can only in the present context mean this: that after 7 to 8 years the child becomes capable of thinking in terms of transformations, thanks to the operational structures brought about by the equilibration of his intellectual processes, and that the retroactive and anticipatory mobility of the operations will, sooner or later, be reflected in the images themselves and will enrich the outlines of anticipation associated with them.

The two solutions thus amount to the same thing. In order to account for imaginal kinetic or transformational anticipation it would seem to be necessary to bring in the operations, and for the following reasons. The first is implied in what has just been said: if it is only with the formation of the operations that the subject starts to be concerned with the transformations or displacements linking static states, then it is naturally only at this point that he attempts to imagine them. The second reason is that as the operations lead to deductions and anticipations, they naturally do not remain totally abstract, but are accompanied by imaginal representations: hence the anticipatory images. The third is that any imaginal anticipation of movement or transformation presupposes that the images follow one another in a given order of succession (as we pointed out in connection with, amongst other things, the rotation of the rod, Chapter Three, section 3, IV, etc.): such order derives from operational seriation. And the fourth is that anticipatory images frequently presuppose a framework of conservation (cf. the arcs transformed into straight lines, etc.) and that only the operations can constitute such a framework.

So the evolution of the images cannot be considered autonomous, in the sense of depending only on factors relating to the image. And in the present section we have seen this to be true for anticipatory images, whose progress for several good reasons coincides with the formation of the concrete operations from 7 to 8 years on. As for the static images of the preoperational levels, it remains to examine carefully (see section 5) whether they depend on the structure of thought at those levels, whether on the contrary the thought structures depend on them, or whether, and if so how, the two interact. But before going on to that, our immediate problem is to establish whether such elementary images spring directly from a common genetic source – whether this source is in perception, or as we prefer to think, in internalised imitation – or whether at the elementary stages, contributory factors external to this main source are involved in the image's development. Now in section 1 of this chapter we saw that there may be some continuity between the anticipation of execution, at work in the direct copy images, and anticipation proper at the operational level. In Chapter Seven (see in particular the conclusion), we found some connection between the fidelity of the static reproductive image and action. And it will be recalled that the operations of intelligence also spring from action in its general co-ordinations. Now in view of these three facts, it is highly probable that external contributory factors capable of influencing the image's evolution will be found at all levels. This is one of the questions that we shall examine more closely in sections 4 and 5, but it can be seen right away that the presence of such external elements points to an imitative rather than a perceptual origin of the image, since imitation is bound up with the whole of action and intelligence.

3. *The general characteristics of the image*

The visual image is a figural evocation of objects, relations, and even classes, etc. It converts them into a concrete and simili-sensible form, though at the same time it possesses a high degree of schematization (one can have an unlimited number of perceptions of an object, but only a few images of it). Probably all researchers in this field will be in agreement on these basic characteristics. But now that we have introduced the evolution of the images, it remains, before going into it further, to see if it is not possible to isolate other general features characteristic of all levels independently of this evolution.

Before we draw attention to the common characteristics of the images between 3 to 4 and 14 to 15 years (the age limits of our inquiry), it would perhaps be useful to consider again the superior stages of imagery as found, for instance, in geometricians who can 'see' in space with a degree of mobility never achieved by non-specialists. It is a striking fact that even at these lofty heights the anticipatory kinetic or transformation image is bound by the same two fundamental limitations that are so glaringly obvious in all the cases of children's imagery described in this book (though we need to ask whether these limitations are not perhaps the obverse of certain positive qualities, peculiar to the requirements of 'figuration'). (1) If it is impossible to 'visualize' lines without breadth, points without circles, curves without tangents, etc., it is probably the case that the mathematician's image, just as the child's, differs from operational intuitions or notions in consequence of the 'pseudo-conservation' of certain concrete characteristics, which have no significance (or at least no generality) in the abstract, but which are nevertheless indispensable if the concrete is to be imitated figurally. (2) However mobile and kinetic imagery might be in geometrical intuition, it cannot *qua* imagery apprehend a continuum. If one sticks at the purely imaginal representations of the steps of the movement, Achilles never catches up with his tortoise. Right up to the level of kinetic imagery one finds a probably irreducible static residuum, in marked contrast to the operational dynamism of thought.

To return to the child again, there are two general characteristics of the image which deserve attention. They have both come up constantly during the course of this work, and derive in all probability (in proportions we have yet to establish) from the simili-sensible and schematizing properties of imaginal figuration.

(1) First, the existence of 'pseudo-conservation'. This phenomenon disappears in some cases at 7 to 8 years, in others somewhat later,

in yet other cases it is not a feature of early development at all, but is formed through secondary or derivative channels. However, it shows itself in some form at all levels, as we have just seen in connection with geometrical intuition.

Chapter Two has already familiarized us with the most common form of pseudo-conservation: namely, the prohibition against going beyond terminal boundaries, which accounts for the systematic underestimation in the direct copy image of straight lines and squares. Chapter Three showed that the same boundary taboo exists in the case of the translation of a square relative to another (section 1), and gives rise to a pseudo-conservation of the terminal boundary at the expense of conservation of the surface area. In section 2 of Chapter Three we had a similar example, this time concerning internal boundaries, or enclosure, where the subject refused to make any intersection (cf. Table 21). In section 3 we described the neglect of initial boundaries (fixed pivotal centre) in favour of the terminal boundaries. In Chapter Four, section 1, we listed a number of cases where pseudo-conservation affected the shape and the surface area of rotated squares, and in section 2 we saw that for the same reasons circumduction held the lead over rotation. Chapter Five furnished further examples of the pseudo-conservation of boundaries in the transformations of arcs and angles. In Chapter Six, however, we analysed a new and especially surprising case: the refusal to accept the surrounding or enclosure of a small circle by a square, if the square is a 'figure' whose boundary the child does not want to violate, but acceptance if the square was a hole, and therefore a 'ground' surface, which, from the perceptual point of view, does not have a proper boundary! (See Table 97.) In the same chapter, section 3, there were examples of complete superimpositions rejected for the same kind of reasons. And section 4 gave examples of the pseudo-conservation of forms and dimensions of linear figures when folded. Chapter Eight (images and operations) provided instances of pseudo-conservation in concrete anticipation (pseudo-conservation of the level of liquids, of the width of sausage-shapes, etc.). Finally, Chapter Nine added two more prime examples of pseudo-conservation to the list. The one arose in connection with biunivocal correspondence between the length of the perimeter and the surface of the figures (section 1), and the other in connection with the idea that component parts should be the same shape as the complete figure (section 2: a square cannot be made up of triangles, etc.).

Pseudo-conservation arises, then, when a subject retains certain characteristics of an object which he considers typical or exemplary, and which he clings to even at the expense of other apparently more important characteristics. Since the image is a figural not an abstract evocation, the choice of 'typical' features is no doubt to be linked with the question of figurative representation. And the question arises whether drawing difficulties are not at the heart of the matter. But for one thing, when a child refuses to represent a line by a longer one, but has no objection to representing it by a much shorter one, it appears that he is not in fact hampered by drawing problems but that he really feels himself obliged not to overstep the boundary. And for another thing, in those instances where he rejects intersection or enclosure in order to avoid violating boundaries, the child will persist in this attitude when asked to choose from ready-made drawings, and will justify his choice on figural grounds. For instance, he will argue that a circle cannot be put inside a square (though he can draw this perfectly well), because 'there's already a square there', etc.

The problem, then, is to establish whether these figural pseudo-conservations depend on perceptual, on notional factors, or on factors specific to the image. But first let us take a look at the second general characteristic of the image.

(2) Up to the level of anticipatory kinetic and anticipatory transformation images, the image is ill-equipped to grasp the dynamism of a continuum, be it a question of the continuity of movement, a change, or a decomposition process. Take the case of the transformation of arcs into straight lines. It is striking that even at the level where the subject is able to accept that the final line will be longer than the chord of the arc, he still frequently draws the arc beginning to flatten but not elongated, and then jumping abruptly and discontinuously to its final elongated state (see Figure 28, *E–G*). Not only are these models *E–G* drawn spontaneously by 30 per cent of the subjects at 7 years as against the 10 per cent who draw correct figures, and by 30 per cent as against 20 per cent at 8 to 9 years, but they are also picked out from the ready-made drawings by 40 per cent of the subjects at 7 years as against 60 per cent who do correct drawings, and still by 17 per cent as against 83 per cent at 8 to 9 years.

This discontinuity of the image, in contrast as it is to the dynamism of the operational continuum, is again no doubt due to the figurative requirements of imagery. It is impossible for a drawing to represent movement except by a series of motionless positions, clear as the symbolism of such indications may be. But the mental image itself cannot do much better. Try, for instance, imagining a cyclist's leg movement. One can visualize slight displacements as a foot goes down, round, and up again. But one thinks one has got the continuity only to realize that one has prolonged the image in thought, and that one is no longer actually 'seeing' the whole in motion.

Going back to our discussion on the nature of these two general characteristics of the image, it should be recognized that their dependence on the demands of figurative representation in itself explains nothing, since the image is a figural evocation that is both simili-sensible and schematized. The simili-sensible aspect means there must be some correspondence with perception. But let us be clear that perception is far from explaining everything. No doubt the fact that it is impossible to imagine lines without breadth and points without surface is a consequence of perception, for without breadths and surfaces nothing could be perceived at all. (Adult subjects who occasionally claim to be able to 'imagine' a line without breadth are in fact only able to 'imagine' it in thought, not in images. The fact is that, although they are able to visualize an increasingly narrow line, the only image they actually retain is precisely this narrowing process, without realizing that they leave it behind by generalizing it beyond the confines of the visual.) But the fact that one cannot imagine a curve without tangents does not have anything to do with perception, since one does not in any case perceive curves along with their tangents; nor does it have anything to do with notions, since one accepts the notion of functions without derivatives. It seems, therefore, that what we have here is indeed a peculiar characteristic of imaginal figuration as such. The inability of the image to apprehend a kinetic continuum likewise has nothing to do with perception since perception of movement can be very subtle and can even construct apparent or stroboscopic movement by means of actually motionless elements. The static character of the image and the irreducible residuum left by it at the level of kinetic and transformation images can only be due to the exigencies of figural representation. And it is interesting to find that here also there is a link between the graphic image and the strictly mental image.

We have said that these two characteristics of the image – figural pseudo-conservation and the persistence of a static element – do not derive from perception alone (in the case of the second characteristic they do not derive from it at all). Do they then derive from notional structures, not at the level of the adult image, even less at the level of specialized geometrical intuition, but at the level at which the images are formed – at the preoperational level? Before we answer yes to that question, two provisions must be made. The first concerns the fact that the image involves a certain degree of schematization, not so far advanced as that of the notions, but tending in the same direction. So before we draw any conclusions about notional influence it is necessary to give consideration to this strictly imaginal or figural schematization. Secondly, if we find that there are analogies between the images and the preoperational notions, we shall still have to determine whether the laws of the image account for this early form of thought, or whether the reverse is the case. We shall deal with this question in section 5. In the meantime we take stock of what we know about the image-

364

perception relationship, since this question governs everything that follows.

4. *Image, perception and imitation*

In contrast to the operative mechanisms, the figurative mechanisms involved in cognitive functions are only three in number: perception, imitation, image. As the image is genetically the third to appear, we have to establish whether it derives from the first or the second of the other two mechanisms ('or' is not exclusive). At the beginning of this work we summarized the genetic and psychophysiological arguments in favour of an imitational rather than a perceptual origin of images. It remains to look back and examine these arguments in the light of what we have learnt since.

It should be pointed out first of all that the facts of *content* similarities between images and perceptions – that is to say, the fact that the image is able to reproduce the content of perceptions, their shape, colour, etc., if not their 'vividness' – proves nothing either for or against the hypotheses in question. For, if the image derived from imitation, it would, in any case, imitate perceptual impressions, and would induce the partial reafference explaining the simili-sensible aspects, in exactly the same way as if it were merely a prolongation of perception as such. In other words the image may copy perception in both hypotheses. The question is whether this copying process is active and entails internalized imitation, or whether it is an automatic extension of past perceptions.

In order to reach some conclusion on this matter, it is not the content of the images we need to examine so much as their form or *structure*. Now everything we have seen so far tends to suggest that apart from one or two points of interference the structure of the images is far removed from the perceptual structures. For example, the considerable part played by boundaries in imaginal pseudo-conservation at the preoperational level has but few characteristics in common with the perceptual boundary laws (Rubin's law, etc.). And while Table 97 does show some local application of those perceptual laws, the end in view is clearly not discrimination but the non-violation of the boundaries. Similarly, the systematic under-estimations studied in Chapter Two and also attributable to the boundary taboo have nothing in common with perceptual under- or overestimations, apart from certain points of interference between the two phenomena in the case of the verticals.

In general there seems to be a systematic difference between perceptual distortions (or illusions) and the distortions of reality characteristic of the images studied in this book. Perceptual distortion results from incomplete reconstruction: while attempting to reach the object as it is, perception makes shift with a few information samples furnished by various 'centrations' and by partly chance 'encounters'. The outcome is an entirely probabilistic kind of construct that takes in only a fraction of the elements or relations to be co-ordinated. In the case of the image, on the other hand, distortion results from the exigencies of schematized figuration, and to a large extent also from the liberties taken by the subject in view of the symbolic nature of schematized figuration. In the case of the static characteristic of the image, there is a specific figurational inability to render the dynamism of a continuum, and symbolism is brought in this time in a positive way to make up for what the figural schema fails to represent. In the case of certain pseudo-conservations, however, schematic figuration could be much more exact (closer approach to boundaries without actually going over), but the symbolic character of the image permits wide approximations.

In short, the structural characteristics of the image do not favour the perceptual origin hypothesis, whereas they do as a matter of course fit in with internalized imitation. For imitation also may result in schematized figuration and may itself be used in symbolic evocation. True, there is also a perceptual schematization, but it is quite different from that of the image. If we use the term 'scheme' (*schème*) to designate a generalization instrument enabling the subject to isolate and utilize the elements common to similar successive behaviours, then there are perceptual schemes, sensori-motor schemes, operational schemes, and so on. And in this sense there also exist imaginal schemes enabling the subject to construct analogous images in comparable situations. But if we use the term 'schema' (*schéma*) to designate a simplified model intended to facilitate presentation (such as a topographical schema, etc.), then there can be no perceptual 'schemata', since the 'schema' serves only for figuration and evocation. Imaginal figuration, on the other hand, is 'schematized' precisely in the 'schema' sense, though at the same time it may entail 'schemes' (*schèmes*). Similarly, if the image is symbolic (which remains to be verified: see section 7), perception is most certainly not symbolic in the sense we have taken the term. To be sure, H. Piéron at the end of his fine book *La sensation guide de vie*[5] concludes that sensation is a symbol – but in the sense of indices or signals and not in the sense of a resemblance between symbolizer and symbolized. The author's intention is precisely to show that sensation is not a faithful copy of the stimulus.

Neither the schematism nor the symbolism of the image can be reduced to the structures of perception. So between perception and

[5] Piéron, H., *La sensation guide de vie*, Paris, Gallimard, 1945.

366

the images some other mechanisms must be in play – and these are to be found in imitation.

There are two more reasons for having doubts about the perceptual origin of images. The first concerns their mode of activity during the process of formation. As far as anticipatory images at the operational level are concerned, it goes without saying that the anticipations actuating them having nothing in common with the *Einstellungen*, or the anticipatory attitudes of perception. But in the case of static images and of direct copies, we have noted two important factors: the intervention of anticipation of execution on the one hand and, on the other, a more general link between the formation of the image and the subject's actions (see Chapter Seven). Now this is self-evident if the image does indeed derive from imitation, the accommodatory pole of action. But it is inexplicable if the image prolongs perception without more ado, that is, without supplementary activities over and above the perceptual activities.

The second reason concerns the images' mode of evolution, which, as we have seen, draws on external contributory factors springing in the first place from action as a whole, and in the second place from the operations. Now apart from the anticipatory aspect of the activities forming the image, a further problem arises in connection with the fact that its evolution is not internal and autonomous but dependent on external contributions. According to the hypothesis that the image is a prolongation of perception, the image would tend to reproduce everything that had been perceived in the past, and would then anticipate situations not previously perceived by analogy. If this were the case, the final anticipatory images would derive direct from the initial reproductive images, and the reproductive images themselves would bear just as much on familiar transformations and movements as on static configurations, since transformations and movements can also be perceived. On the other hand, if we adopt the other hypothesis that the images originate in the internalization of imitation, then both the external contributions and the order of succession that we have observed are easy to explain. Like the higher apes, the child imitates only what he can understand, or is well on the way to understanding: imitation constitutes the accommodatory pole of action in general, and of intelligent action in particular. The subject will imitate models starting with the more simple and going on to the more complex relatively to the level of his intelligence. That is to say, he will proceed from static configurations (or somatic imitations: we have not considered these in the present work since they raise the whole problem of the corporal schema, and are currently being studied elsewhere)[6] to the kinetic anticipation of movements external to his own body, which is bound up with imitation of the operations as such. In virtue of this overall process and the interactions between imitation and intelligence, the image's evolution could not be self-contained. On the contrary, it necessarily involves the utilization of external contributory factors in ever increasing numbers.

[6] Research in progress by I. Lézine and M. Stambak.

5. *The relations between images and preoperational notions*

It seems that up to 7 to 8 years – the beginning of the concrete operational level – the images are essentially static. And they are not merely static in the residual sense in which they are static at a later level: they are just not equipped to represent even the simplest physical or geometrical movements and transformations. Now pre-operational thought is equally incapable of mastering transformations, and reasons primarily on the basis of configurations. The question of the relationships and interactions between these two spheres calls for careful examination. And it is a question of some importance not only for the particular problem of the image, but also for an understanding of the child's thought and of cognitive mechanisms generally.

I. Operational thought consists of the co-ordination of states and transformations, the former being thought of either as the result, or as the starting point, of certain of the latter. On the whole, states are found to be subordinate to transformations, although they can only be understood in terms of one another. States in fact merely constitute the starting point for transformations, whereas trans-formations actually determine the properties of successive states.

This co-ordination and subordination is completely absent in pre-operational thought. This is not to say it is static in all its aspects. But if it is not, the reasons at this level are more complex. To begin with, it is true to say that preoperational thought considers states as static configurations quite independently from the transformations that may lie behind them. For instance, when a liquid is transferred from a wide glass *A* to a narrow one *B*, the 4 to 5 year old compares the initial and final configurations but neglects the transformation. Consequently, he concludes that the quantity has increased in *B*. Not that he is ignorant of transformations. He conceives them independently of external states by a process of egocentric assimila-tion to his own action. 'The liquid has been poured from *A* into *B*' – this does not signify for the child that an objective and reversible transformation has taken place, that is to say, a transfer from *A* to *B* that can be compensated or cancelled out by the reverse transfer from *B* to *A*. For him there has been a creative action, centred on the self, and whose results are incalculable, or if one prefers, not deduc-ible: witness the fact that the quantity increases or decreases as the case may be. These pseudo-transformations, assimilated to the subject's own actions in their egocentric aspect (as opposed to the general co-ordination of action, the root of logic and reversible

368

operations, from which the self is eliminated), are thus the source of finalism, animism, and other preoperational combinations. Their effect is to hinder the formation of the operations as decentred actions and transformations. The peculiar characteristic of pre-operational thought then is not that it is static in all its aspects, but that it fails to co-ordinate states and transformations. Consequently the conception of states is too static, and transformations are endowed with a spurious exaggerated dynamism, with the result that the true mobility of the reversible operations is retarded.

It is in such a context that the images we have studied are elaborated. It is important to bring out a fact already mentioned at the end of section 4 – that these images are static before 7 to 8 years precisely because we have selected them from amongst movements and transformations independent of the subject's body. If we had studied those images corresponding to the subject's own actions, to the body movement, etc., or images corresponding to the realms of finalist, animist and artificialist interpretation, we would no doubt have obtained a proliferation of pseudo-dynamic images. But these would have had no relevance to the question of the relationship between images and operational thought, which is after all our central problem. We return then to the relative static images, to the physical and geometrical spheres, within which the anticipatory images of the later level of development are formed.

II. We have seen that two big difficulties arise in the question of the relations between preoperational thought and the images. On the one hand, as the notions relating to configurations or states are more static at the preoperational than at the next level, imaginal representation plays a special part in their functioning. And on the other hand, the general characteristics of the preoperational image, and more especially the pseudo-conservations (see section 3), appear to be interpenetrated with notional schematization (in the form of conceptual or preconceptual 'schemes' not inconsistent with the formation of figurative 'schemata'). It is very difficult, therefore, to decide exactly what is contributed by the notions and the images respectively, and, more particularly, to decide exactly what are the respective roles of this hypothetical conceptual schematism and the strictly imaginal or figural schematization. And it is all the more difficult as in some respects the preoperational structures resemble perceptual structures.

The method we shall follow consists in comparing images and thoughts by reference to two particular types of situation: situations where the subject reasons with the perceived datum before him and consequently without the use of images (when for instance he observes two staggered rods of equal length and concludes that they are unequal in length because of the projecting portions) and where such reactions may be compared with reactions induced by an imaginal anticipation requirement; and situations where the subject gives a judgment either verbally or gesturally but is unable to represent the object imaginally (for example, the displacement where the subject's judgment is correct but where he cannot pick out the correct corresponding figure: Table 17). Drawing on these situations we are able to distinguish five actual relations between the image and preoperational thought, which we interpret for hypothetical instances as follows:

(A) First, there are those cases in which a characteristic x may be observed both in the thought-without-image situations (as defined above) and in imaginal representation or anticipation situations. Here we interpret the character x as due to thought and affecting the image, since x characterizes the general class (thought with or without image) and is found in the subclass (thought with image).

(B) Then there are those cases in which x may be observed both in the situations where the image is at variance with thought and in the situations where there is image – thought agreement in imaginal representation. Here the general class is the image, the subclass thought-plus-image, and we interpret x as due to the image and affecting thought.

(C) There are cases in which x is found only in the situations where the image is at variance with thought. The classes are exclusively disjunctive and we interpret x as peculiar to the image with no effect on thought.

(D) But in certain instances x may come up in three situations – discordance between images and thought, and thought with or without images (disjunction non-exclusive). Here we may say that x is common to image and thought and that there is the possibility of action and reaction from one to the other.

(E) Finally, x may appear only in the cases of image-plus-thought and not in the two others (conjunction or intersection). In this case x clearly results from a local interaction between the two spheres.

III. Having defined our method, let us go on to apply it to some individual cases of pseudo-conservation, before we draw any final conclusions about them generally and about the static nature of preoperational images.

The question of the terminal boundaries and of the neglect of starting points (cf. the pivotal centre of the rods in Table 26), has two aspects. First, there is the child's preoccupation at the preoperational level with end-point boundaries. The fact is that he is incapable of a metric estimation of the lengths based on distances as such (spontaneous measurements with choice of a unit not achieved until about 8 years). Consequently, he is reduced to ordinal estimations based on the order of succession of end-points with starting points assumed equal, though later he will (to a greater or lesser degree depending on the case) make allowance for the staggering of starting points (fairly early in the case of two towers built on different levels[7] and much less early in the case of horizontal lines). The ordinal aspect of estimation is general and is found in both thought-with-image and thought-without-image situations (type A relation): hence we may conclude that it is a product of thought, but a product of thought that can in turn affect the image. Second, we need to explain the primacy of the finishing points, which is demonstrated so strikingly in the sphere or preoperational images by the inviolability of terminal boundaries. Now, this second aspect of the problem is distinctly more complex. It does not follow directly from the ordinal aspect, for considerations of order may be just as well applied to starting as to finishing points. The primacy of the latter and neglect of the former could be accounted for by centration of thought, even when without images – centring of attention on the outcome of the movement, etc. If this were the case, then there would be overestimation of the degree of terminal stagger (between the end-points of the two moving objects or lines to be compared). But in the case of imaginal anticipation the tendency is exactly the opposite: underestimation and even suppression of the terminal stagger, that is, of the length projecting. The result of this is that the subject avoids going beyond the boundary-point of the reference element altogether, as if it were taboo. This phenomenon, so frequently encountered in the present work, is commonly to be found in situations where thought and image are at variance (for example, the displaced squares in Chapter Three, section 1), but it is also to be found in others where on the contrary there is agreement between the two (for example, the arcs in Chapter Five, section 1). Here, then, we have a type B relation: that is to say, we have a characteristic which is due to the image and affects thought. If the different aspects of these boundary phenomena were taken together as a single whole, then we would have a type D relation as an amalgamation of A and B.

A different picture is presented, however, by the reactions of refusal in the case of the small red circle surrounded by a square (Chapter Six, sections 1–2), in the case of superimpositions (Chapter Six, section 3) and more especially and more frequently in the case of intersections (Chapter Three, section 2). Such reactions appear to be peculiar to the image (type C relation), at least as far as the situations studied in this book are concerned. But before we accept that conclusion generally, and entirely rule out the possibility of a type B relation, we must first be certain that no situations exist in which these same difficulties of figurative enclosure and intersection are accompanied by tacit or explicit agreement with thought. We

[7] *The Child's Conception of Geometry*, Presses Universitaires de France, 1948.

have not added to the already too numerous investigations of this present work by undertaking particular experiments on the images of logical collections and classes. As it happens our earlier studies on classification provide us with the information we need. Besides analysing classifications carried out on request ('put the same ones together, etc.'), we analysed anticipations,[8] that is to say, projects for classification presupposing imaginal representation (the children indicate in advance what boxes or envelopes certain elements would go in without actually handling them). Both these studies have shown the close links between elementary classifications and the laws of the image with particular reference to surrounding and intersection difficulties. In connection with the surroundings or enclosures two groups of facts are worth quoting. In the first place, comprehension of the inclusion of a subclass A in a class B remains a late development, and before the level of the concrete operations is only formed in the quantified form $A < B$.[9] But before the subject is able to put objects together in small collections based on similarities, there is a stage at about 4 to 5 years when he proceeds by 'figural collections'.[10] In this procedure the objects are not in a strict sense 'enclosed' or 'surrounded' in a single class or collection (a 'parcel' or a 'pile' embracing them), but are arranged in some spatial pattern (rows or alignments, L-shapes, squares, etc.) as a result of a failure to differentiate logical from spatial extension. Nothing could show better both the initial role played by the image (distortion, in this particular case) in early classificatory thought and the difficulties of inclusion considered as the logical counterpart of spatial enclosure. (It should be made clear that the overall shape of these figural collections is not set in advance as a prior framework, or one could speak at least of spatial enclosure, but takes form progressively as a function of the elements already laid out, or to begin with, simply juxtaposed.) In connection with the intersection difficulties, we observed a distinct tendency in the younger child to prefer disjunct classes to intersection, and that intersections raised more problems than complete multiplications in the form of matrices.[11] All in all it seems quite possible that the image's characteristic rejection of figurative enclosures and intersections is reflected in thought, and to some extent enters into the difficulties encountered in thought with regard to inclusion and intersection.

There are several instances of the type E relation. There is the pseudo-conservation of the level of a liquid poured into differently shaped glasses, where anticipation is both imaginal and notional. Another example is the belief in a biunivocal correspondence

[8] Inhelder, B., and Piaget, J., *The Early Growth of Logic*, Chapter VII.
[9] *Ibid.*, Chapter IV.   [10] *Ibid.*, Chapter III.   [11] *Ibid.*, Chapter VI.

between perimeter and surface area, where the image and the notion appear to collaborate equally. And there is the idea of a necessary isomorphism between the shape of a figure and the shape of its constituent parts. We have already found in an earlier work that for young subjects the cutting up of a square or triangle into the smallest possible parts will produce square or triangular 'points'. And section 2 of Chapter Nine furnishes an example of a similar reaction – the child's difficulty in conceiving of a square as made up of triangles (cf. form 8 of Figure 51, a square divided by its diagonals, with only 14 per cent success at 7 years: Table 151). The part played by the image here is obvious. But it is a question of an image of structural analysis, not a straightforward reproductive image as in the case of the boundaries, which means that thought as well collaborates in such reactions.

In brief, pseudo-conservations as a body evidence the existence of complex relations and actual interplay between images and thought at the preoperational level. The figural schematization of the image is in several ways influenced by the conceptual schemes, while the notions themselves are in some measure cast in the mould of the images. It is no exaggeration, therefore, to consider preoperational thought, when it is centred on configurations or states as opposed to transformations, as in some degree structured by the laws of the image. But at this juncture there is a possible objection to be met. How is this interpretation to be reconciled with the contention frequently upheld by us that preoperational thought is subservient to perceptual configurations from which the operations subsequently break free? In point of fact the two assertions are complementary. And for the following reasons.

IV. It is generally true to say that preoperational thought is subordinate to perceptual configurations, if by that we mean that the subject will reason on the initial and final configurations he perceives without concerning himself with the transformations linking them. But in this sense, such subordination, in situations where the child is reasoning exclusively on the basis of perceived data, is the exact complement of what goes on when he has to anticipate part of the event by means of images. In this latter situation thought is subservient both to the initial configuration and to the image. And this is by no means inconsistent with the fact that it is subordinate to perceptions alone in the first situation.

But it is also possible to interpret this subordination to perceptual configurations in a more specific sense. Sometimes the structure of a preoperational interpretation may fairly closely resemble certain primary perceptual effects. For instance, when a subject judges that the quantity of a single whole object (say a ball of clay or a block of chocolate) is less than if it were split up, we have a reaction that recalls the Oppel–Kundt illusion of divided space. Again, an empty space between two points *A* and *B* is thought to be modified if a solid is introduced between them, because the length is not the same when evaluated in terms of the blank ('far' and 'near') as when evaluated in terms of the solid ('long' or 'short'). A reaction of this kind recalls the perceptual heterogeneity of occupied and empty space, or figure and ground, etc. But these structural analogies are in no way inconsistent with the affinities between preoperational thought and images, even though the laws of the image are distinct from those of perception. On the one hand, there may in fact be a hierarchy among affinities of different levels, and establishing this remains an open problem once such analogies are accepted as more or less general. On the other hand, the image, which actively copies the perceptual datum, may be influenced by certain perceptual laws. We have seen, for example, that lengths underestimated in drawings were overestimated when indicated between the forefingers, the difference being due to the fact that the former involves a solid line and the latter a blank space (see Chapter Two, Table 4).

Finally and above all, suppose we accept neither that the image derives from perception nor that intelligence derives from the image or from perception, and suppose instead we accept that it is a question of constructions that are both distinct and partially over-lapping: such analogies do not in any way imply filiations, which would be incompatible, but partial isomorphisms and indirect affinities springing from common sensori-motor sources.

V. It remains to examine the relationship between preoperational thought and images from the point of view of the images' static character and their resistance to the dynamism of the continuous in kinetic and transformational spheres. The analogies are obvious. Preoperational thought neglects external transformations (as opposed to personal action), while the images preserve a static residuum even in their higher anticipatory forms. But the question is this. Is this isomorphism due to the action of thought on the image, to the reverse, or to a convergence of the two? First of all let us bear in mind that the static character of preoperational thought is only temporary, and that the dynamism of the operations comes out on top at the close of this period, which is at the same time a period of preparation (with articulated intuitions, etc.). The static character of the image is more persistent since it is not entirely eliminated in subsequent anticipatory images. Far from it! More-over, it may be implicit in figuration itself, which of necessity pro-

374

ceeds 'cinematographically'. Although it is hard to see why the image should be congenitally debarred – as if by a peculiar original sin – from grasping movement in its entirety and at least in its figural continuity (as distinct from mathematical continuum).

It is true to say that preoperational thought remains partially static because the subject is ignorant of transformations and reversible operations. But there is more to it than that. And in the last analysis the reason is that lack of decentration prevents an adequate *prise de conscience* of co-ordinations. Centred as it is on personal action, preoperational thought proceeds on the basis of the results of action, and fails to go back to the general co-ordinations that would raise such actions to the rank of operations. It is through awareness of co-ordination that the operations achieve their characteristic dynamism; and at the preoperational level, it is through absence of it that the dynamic continuum fails to be apprehended.

It goes without saying that this mechanism also affects the formation of images, though in a specific manner. Since the image is an internalized imitation, it comes under the laws of imitation. Now the laws of imitation imply emphasis on the accommodatory pole of action, that is to say, that aspect of action oriented towards external reality, in contradistinction to the co-ordinating assimilation processes. In other words, if figuration is doomed to retain its static character even in its anticipatory forms, then it is because of some sort of intrinsic limitation. Its role is to imitate, not to construct or to produce; it is limited to drawing up 'schemata'; and it is incapable of creating or manipulating the 'schemes' of transformations.

We may interpret this convergence of the temporary static element in preoperational thought and the permanent static element in the image as a type D relation with partial interactions at the level under consideration. Such is the situation until modified at the next level of development. We go on in the next section to examine this modification.

6. *The relations between images and operations*

The upshot of the preceding discussion is that the laws of the image account for the existence of or at least reinforce certain aspects of preoperational thought. Reciprocally, preoperational thought explains certain characteristics of the image. But these are precisely the characteristics that constitute the obstacle in the way of the comprehension of transformations or the co-ordination of transformations with states, and that consequently retard operational mobility. So we now need to determine the extent to which the image is capable of *promoting* the functioning of operational thought, and likewise the extent to which the operations contemporaneously further the image's evolution towards some degree of mobility.

This raises three distinct and entirely independent questions; the solution of one will not prejudice the solution of either of the others. Is the intervention of the operations necessary to account for the formation of the anticipatory images? Do the preoperational images contribute to the formation of the operations? And do the images (reproductive or anticipatory) at the operational level contribute to the full functioning of the operations?

We have already suggested an answer to the first question – in particular in section 2 – and we shall not go over it again in detail. The anticipatory image does not derive simply from a spontaneous increase in the flexibility of the reproductive images or of the initial outlines of anticipation (executional anticipation, etc.). Such flexibility is in actual fact not spontaneous, and presupposes the external contribution of the operations – even if it is only because kinetic or transformational anticipations presuppose an order of succession, and because this in turn presupposes operational seriation (temporal, etc.).

I. We move on, then, to the question of the role of preoperational images in the preparation or formation of the operations. This general problem has two distinct aspects, that is to say, it can be subdivided into two separate and specific questions: the question of the use of images in the cognition of the givens of a transformation problem, more particularly in the cognition of 'states'; and the question of the images' contribution in the discovery and representation of transformations. The hypothesis according to which preoperational images further the formation of the operations is naturally concerned with the second question.

As for the first question, it is self-evident that the preoperational images, just as any other kind of images, will promote the acquisition, or at least the fixation and consolidation of data. It is obvious too that this is a very general factor involved in all cognitive progress, and consequently in the elaboration of operations. Take the case of the subjects in Chapter Eight, section 1, who were able to predict that the liquid would rise higher in the narrower glasses: in spite of this prediction they were able neither to understand the breadth–height compensation, nor to deduce conservation. Even so they had progressed further than those who gave inaccurate predictions (pseudo-conservation of the levels): they had noticed from their past experience something that had escaped the others, and if the image had not contributed to the actual discovery at least it had served to fix it in the memory, to consolidate it, and to facilitate further

376

observations. The image thus makes a positive contribution: it plays a part in improved knowledge of the liquid transfer problem, and in improved knowledge of the 'states' before and after the transformation, which, in its twin modification–conservation aspect, is the next thing to be understood.

Such is the positive role of the image at the preoperational level. But for all that it in no way serves to prepare for comprehension of the transformation as such. And this is proved by the fact that these particular subjects are no more able to comprehend compensation and conservation than the others. On the contrary, they anticipate a non-conservation, while preoperational subjects generally anticipate a pseudo-conservation of the liquid and its initial features, including level.

The situation is exactly the same in the case of the staggered rods (Chapter Eight, section 6), when none of the preoperational subjects managed to anticipate the projection of a segment of the displaced rod. Those who do manage it are the ones who have retained an image from their everyday experience. Thus the image plays a useful role in fixing and consolidating information. But, again, this does not mean that it serves to prepare for the operation as actualization and comprehension of the transformation. The subjects are unable to use their successful anticipation either to predict that the initial and terminal projecting lengths will be equal (compensation), or to discover conservation. All the same, as we said at the end of Chapter Five, it is hard to see how the image can in any case ever lead to the formation of authentic notions of conservation involving quantitative compensations understood as such, when the pseudo-conservations peculiar to the image bear only on global and qualitative characteristics without any kind of quantitative precision.

In sum, we have been unable to find in any of the results described in Chapters Three–Six and Eight–Nine any convincing indication that the operations are prepared for by the action of preoperational images. In point of fact we found that the reproductive images function in the two following ways. On the one hand they may keep close to the perceptions of which they are active copies. In this case they provide thought with nothing more than perceptual data, unless it be also an active imitation facilitating analysis and evocation of such data. This constitutes a factor in cognitive development of a general kind but of no specific relevance to the future operations. On the other hand they may modify the perceptions serving as their models and thus be prone to pseudo-conservations and distortions with a static tendency. And in this case, far from preparing for the operations, the images reinforce preoperational thought in its disposition to overrate states and to neglect transformations (cf. section 5).

II. And the situation is indeed quite different when the images become anticipatory under the influence of the operations. The image then constitutes an auxiliary that is not only useful to, but in many instances necessary for the functioning of the operations. After having structured and fashioned it in their own likeness, the operations in fact come to depend on the image. The services performed by the image are of two kinds. The first relates to the cognition of states between which are interposed the governing transformations. And the second relates to the representation of these very transformations. For though the continuity, precise detail and especially the overall implications of transformations are not susceptible of representation, yet they can be grasped and manipulated better if an outline of imaginal representation helps operational reasoning (which prolongs and goes beyond imaginal representation) get off the ground.

Chapter Six (final section in particular) offers a good example of a situation in which knowledge of states, supported by anticipatory images, is indispensable to the functioning of the operations in the deduction of transformations. In this particular case (successive foldings) the transformations are sequential, and, as in all cases of this kind, representation of the state $S(n)$ is necessary for the deduction of the transformation $T(n+1)$ and the resultant state $S(n+1)$. But in any transformation, even in a non-sequential transformation, and even if it is merely a matter of interpreting a transformation from perceptual data, rather than of deducing it by anticipation of its outcome, analysis of such data and comprehension of the transformation itself is certainly aided by imaginal anticipation. Let us take the case of the ball of clay lengthened into a sausage shape. We have seen how hard the younger subjects found it to accept that the sausage is not only longer, but at the same time thinner. But once they are able to anticipate the correlative elongation and narrowing by means of images, they will be able to understand the operational compensation all the better. True, as we recalled above, such anticipation presupposes an operational conservation framework at least in process of formation. But the fact remains – and this is all we wished to bring out – that the image, once rendered anticipatory by the operations, in turn facilitates the functioning of the operations.[12]

If we turn now to the transformations themselves, there are two facts that may be adduced to demonstrate the auxiliary function of the image at the operational level. The first fact is provided by geometrical intuition. It is possible to construct a geometry or geometries without drawing at all on imaginal intuition (that does not mean operational intuition is not drawn on – on the contrary, it is indispensable). D. Hilbert's celebrated axiomatizations are

[12] See also, for the conservation of lengths, the end of section 5, Chapter Eight.

378

entirely a matter of logic and a certain number of axioms with operational significance: no images are necessary for the demonstration. That is the first fact: it indicates the limits of the image, its lack of veridicality, and – a point to which we return in the next section – its symbolic character. But if we move from the plane of truth and demonstration to the heuristic plane, to the plane of actual functioning rather than normative structure, it becomes clear that the image is of primary importance to the geometer. The ability to 'see', rather than merely conceive the whole of the transformations of a system (a 'fundamental group', say), is clearly far more effectively conducive to discovery or invention. Now, the image is notoriously inaccurate, and no one would wish to deny it. Not only is it unable to apprehend a continuum, but it bears only upon singular figures or individuals, which may certainly serve as exemplars, but which, by virtue of the very fact that they are imaginal, remain incapable of generalization. If the image fulfils a useful function it is because it can act as a spring-board for deduction, and because, through its symbolism, it enables one to outline in rough what the operations extend and bring to conclusion.

Now the facts we have collected concerning the child's psychology, as distinct from that of the creative adult, show the same phenomenon on a smaller scale. In a large number of cases we have seen that the child can make vague, global, verbal predictions a long time before he can manage the detail (cf. the somersaulted tubes, Chapter Four, section 6), and that once he is capable of the image he will be able to arrive at a more precise deduction of the transformations themselves. In such cases, what happens is that the image becomes anticipatory under the influence of the operations and then serves them as a supporting base. But the collaboration no longer merely concerns the cognition of states and results of transformation or movement; it is comprehension of the transformation itself that is promoted by the images, however approximate and symbolic they may be. The image is not actually an element of thought, but like language, and, at least in spatial spheres, with more evident success than language, it does serve as a symbolic instrument signifying the content of cognitive significations.

7. The symbolic nature of the image

Any representational cognition (the term being taken in the broad sense of 'thought', as opposed to sensori-motor or perceptual cognition) presupposes the bringing into play of some symbolic function. It would be preferable to describe this function as 'semiotic', since it embraces arbitrary and social 'signs', motivated 'symbols' (resemblance between symbolizer and symbolized), individual 'symbols' (symbolic play, dream, etc.) and social symbols. Without this semiotic function thought could not be formulated, and consequently could not be expressed intelligibly either to others or to oneself (internal language, etc.).

Now there are two fundamental reasons why the collective sign system, or language, does not fulfil the requirements of this semiotic function, and why it needs to be complemented by a system of imaginal symbols.

The first reason is central, and though perhaps less important than the second, it is more general. It is this: the signs of language are always social. Now there are a great many forms of experience which language conveys badly. Because it is the common property of all individuals, it is necessarily too abstract. This is why, even when he is talking, an individual will concretize the words he uses by means of his own system of personal images. One of us asked an audience of psychology students, several of whom doubted the symbolic character of the image, to indicate individually how they represented the sequence of whole numbers. The variety of the replies was astounding. There were rows of vertical sticks equal or increasing in height, piled up discs, successions of points, regular stairs, stairs with landings for the tens, etc., zigzags and so on. In other words, for concepts strictly identical from one individual to the next, and strictly defined by a uniform vocabulary, there are countless corresponding personal images serving to concretize something that it might have seemed *a priori* completely pointless to express, but which nevertheless must play some functional facilitatory role. And there would be even more reason to expect this to be true for less trivial concepts or words.

The second reason why imaginal symbols as distinct from verbal signs should be necessary is this. For all its affective range, language in the cognitive sphere can only designate concepts (classes, relations, number, propositional connectives or truth functions, etc.) or individuals, and these only in terms of singular classes or relations (my father, Edward VII, etc.). Now there is a vast field which language cannot describe, unless it uses endless complicated circumlocutions. This field comprises everything perceived in the ongoing present, but also and more important everything perceived in the past in the external environment or in personal actions which it is important to retain. It might indeed be necessary or useful to communicate such experience to others, and to this end only language is available, when use is not made of graphic expression, which of course is far superior, but in any case belongs to the image category. But it is entirely indispensable to conserve a part of past experience in the memory, so that it can be drawn on as required for multiple purposes of adaptation. It is clear, therefore, that if one wishes to evoke in thought some past perception, it is necessary to supplement the verbal sign system with a system of imaginal symbols. Without some semiotic means it would be impossible to think at all. The image, then, is a symbol in that it constitutes the semiotic instrument necessary in order to evoke and think what has been perceived.

Now, these fairly self-evident arguments sometimes are, and have been in the past, opposed by associationists, according to whom the image is a simple prolongation of perception. In this view, to evoke a perception would mean simply to go on perceiving it, but with a delay and after the disappearance of the perceived object. A clear and straightforward thesis. It is based on the following two arguments: (1) the subject is not conscious of handling a symbol when he 'looks at' an internal image, and (2) this image is frequently very accurate, whereas a symbol in the usual sense of the term bears a much looser resemblance to the thing symbolized (cf. Freudian symbols). But, (1) the subject's introspection proves absolutely nothing about the problem in hand: children are not conscious of handling signs when they use words or names, since they locate them in the object named.[13] Furthermore, (2) an accurate symbol is nonetheless a symbol, if the term is understood in its general sense: namely, in the sense of a signifier 'motivated' by its resemblance to the signified, all degrees of resemblance being implied.

But since it has been contested, it would be only proper to give a thorough-going justification of the hypothesis of the image's symbolic role. Let us start with the higher forms before coming back to the origins in the child. What we said in section 6 about geometrical intuition seems to us to embody a decisive argument, especially as in this particular field the image goes far beyond the perceived, and even the perceptible, in order to pass on to anticipation of displacements and transformations. Now, geometrical intuition has two aspects, the one operational and the other imaginal. The first may be 'formalized', in the sense of axiomatized: from that point it takes on a signification of truth or demonstrability, and so constitutes a system of 'signifieds'. But, when these signifieds are not designated by 'signs', that is the signs of the mathematical language used for axiomatized demonstration, when they are manipulated 'intuitively', during spontaneous, heuristic inquiry, then these signifieds are accompanied by images. What is the images' status in this kind of situation? They have no demonstrative value: they serve only to 'represent'. Now, it cannot be the case that two systems of 'signifieds'

13 Cf. Piaget, *The Child's Conception of the World*, 1929, Chapter II, 'Nominal Realism'.

are in play at once, especially if one is demonstrative and the other has no truth value. So the images in question must be a system of signifiers, and, as they are 'motivated' and do not belong to the signs of mathematical language, they can only be 'symbols'.[14]

We turn now to the images studied in this book, which are far less precise than the geometer's (and the geometer's are not entirely precise). There are at least three reasons for concluding that they have a symbolic function.

The first is this. The degree of resemblance between the image and the object signified varies fairly widely. But if it does so, it is not just because there is some involuntary defect in accuracy, as when there is an 'error' as opposed to factual truth; but it is also because there is schematization to suit the subject: some characteristics are retained, others eliminated, and others distorted. Thus the characteristically imaginal pseudo-conservations frequently bear witness to a stylization that is, in the usual sense of the term, symbolic. Take, for example, the case where the subject reduces a displaced square to a narrow rectangle, so that it will not project beyond the other (cf. models $E1$, etc., in Figure 5). And again, when continuity is represented by a sequence of discontinuous, immobile, or only partly mobile elements (cf. strip drawings illustrating a narrative, where the procedure is similar to that constantly found in the mental image), the symbolism, however inevitable, is surely self-evident.

In the second place, whether it is a case of a more or less distorted schematization, or whether it is a case of a more or less accurate copy, the function of the image (like that of the word) is to 'designate'. The function of the concept (relation, class, etc.), on the other hand, is to interpret and comprehend, and its tendency from the start is towards legality and causal explanation or towards deductive reasoning. When the concept expresses a given geometrical figure as, say, 'a square with a side of 5 cm', it refers to all squares, defined as quadrilaterals with equal angles and sides, and to a measuring system incorporating iterable and equivalent units: in other words it is a matter of general relations which do not symbolize or 'designate' the object, but abstract the constituent characteristics, and situate them in relation to the other terms of the classes used. The words employed add nothing to this assimilatory interpretation. They merely designate the articulation of such an interpretation, and, as verbal signs, possess their own stylization and their own peculiar laws. Words, then, merely designate conceptual articulations; and if they are used to describe a given object such as a square,

[14] Needless to say, the semiotic implements which mathematicians call 'symbols' have nothing to do with images: they are 'signs' and not symbols, according to the Saussurian terminology which we have used here.

they can designate it only as a conjunction of certain conceptual relations. The image, on the other hand, designates the object itself with its particular perceptual details and its concrete figural characteristics. The image's function, then, is to designate, not to interpret. And if it appears that the image does indeed have an interpretative role in those cases where it schematizes rather than copies directly, the answer is this. Either it is simply designating an already conceptualized object, and is itself not responsible for such conceptualization (cf. in particular the image–concept interactions at the preoperational level). Or else it incorporates its own stylization, in the same way as words do. Distributed in this way, the functions of the concept, the word and the image are at once distinct and exactly complementary, whereas if the image did not play its symbolic role of 'figural signifier', it would be a useless repetition of the concept. As for the 'figural signified', it goes without saying that it is not only legitimate but indispensable to reserve a place for it. But this concrete signified is not now the image of the object, for it is the object itself.[15] Thus we arrive at the following double-entry table:

	signifieds	signifiers
figural	objects	images
general	concepts	verbal signs

One final reason for considering the image symbolic. Like language, it is polyvalent in its functions, whereas the concept is exclusively cognitive. Just as there is an affective language whose laws have been described by Charles Bally, so the image plays an essential role in symbolic play and dream. It is true that there are border-line regions where the concept appears to be charged with vital values going beyond the bounds of knowledge, and that these regions are so vast they extend from myth to metaphysics. But the question is this. Are these concepts pure concepts? Or do they not rather derive from those forms of thought, so illuminating from the psychological and sociological viewpoint, which combine images and concepts, and which one can group under the generic term of symbolic thought?[16]

8. *The epistemological significance of the image*

It is impossible to deal with the cognitive functions without being led on to consider the respective roles of the subject's activity and of the

[15] A distinction should be made between the object as such, signified by the image, and the object as a singular class, characterized (but not signified) by the concept.
[16] It might be said that the concept of 'symbolic thought' implies a link between image and thought, and that in consequence it either contradicts the symbolic character of the image, or attributes it entirely to thought. In point of fact it implies only interaction, of the same kind as is implied when we speak of 'verbalism' or verbal thought (in a pejorative sense), where the only confusion of word and thought is in the subject.

claims of the object in the progressive acquisition of knowledge. This means tackling questions of genetic epistemology.

I. The problems of the image are particularly relevant in this connection, since in classical empiricism the image was both a reflexion of the object as a prolonged perception, and the source of the concept considered as a system of composite images. The role ascribed to the image thus provided the most direct means of justifying the knowledge-as-copy hypothesis as opposed to the knowledge-as-assimilation hypothesis.

But this knowledge-as-copy ideal crops up in a realm far beyond the frontiers of empiricism. According to the empiricist view the copy is merely a tracing of perceptible physical objects. Now Platonism, which is still very much alive amongst mathematicians and logicians, also sees knowledge as a copy – but as a copy of ideal or abstract entities, not of perceptible reality. The late H. Wallon has devoted a brilliant and illuminating passage to Platonism in a work which defends theses very similar to our own concerning the image–imitation link and the role of imitation as the means of transition from the sensori-motor to the representational.[17] He shows how a *prise de conscience* of the image and the 'simulacrum' might be seen as the main inspiration of Platonism, with the *eidos* as not merely an abstract 'idea', but, far more than that, a living, figural 'form' charged with conceptual significance. To this we would add that in a mode of thought so astonishingly static as that of the Greeks the lack of reflexive awareness of the operational processes and their intrinsic dynamism would indeed lead to overestimation of the image's role, and to undifferentiation of the image and the concept.

This failure to separate, or simply adequately to differentiate image and thought comes up in a whole range of ideas and attitudes between the extremes of Platonism and empiricism. During the course of the history of ideas this has gone so far that Bergson's anti-intellectualism has been able to centre itself on an extremely subtle and penetrating analysis of the 'cinematographic process' of representation, without seeing that such an analysis is really a critique of imaginal representation, not of the intelligence. It is the image, in fact, not the dynamism of the operations, which reconstitutes the continuous, and which by virtue of its congenitally static nature falls short of movement as such. The fact that someone like Bergson, who was so concerned to include psychology in his considerations, can fall into such an over-simplification, demonstrates

[17] Wallon, H., *De l'acte à la pensée*, Flammarion, 1942, 42.

384

the possible epistemological consequences of neglecting the symbolic function of the image.

There are two questions to be considered in treating the epistemological implications of a study of the image. First, we have to establish why knowledge cannot be a straightforward copy. Second, we need to examine the idea of a copy itself, and try to establish that an exact copy could not exist without contradiction, in view of the fact that, being relative to the scale in question, it can only ever be an approximate correspondence.

II. We will start with the second problem as it governs the first. A visual image is a figural evocation of objects, etc., translated into a form that is both simili-sensible and more or less schematized. We need not dwell on that aspect of schematization which translates the subject's own activity, even if it is a matter of 'schemata' rather than 'schemes' (in the senses defined in section 4). A faithful image, then, will be a more or less accurate copy of the perceived datum. But, while no more than that is required on the psychological scale, the copy notion only has epistemological value if the copy is of the object itself, and not merely of the perception of the object. Now, what relationship is there between the imaginal copy and the object as such? The imaginal copy may be of a geometrical figure or a physical object. In the first case it is commonplace to point out that neither the mental image nor the perception reaches the object intended, since the graphic image itself remains symbolic. 'This square with a side of 5 cm' is not – even if one only wishes to get at 'this' square, and not the concepts involved in its notional description – a perfect square: its sides are not lines, the apices of its angles are not points, and so on and so forth. True, the figure conveys what one requires it to convey, but only because the deductive intelligence can understand it, and not because graphic figures, perceived or imagined, are 'copies' of the object.

The situation is different in the case of physical objects. The image may still be a copy of the perception. But the perception is not a symbol of the object as such: it provides indices or signals as to the object. A symbol simply bears a resemblance to the thing signified: the index, on the other hand, is a causal emanation of it. For instance, the colour blue, as a perceived quality, corresponds to a specific wave-length of the rays striking the retina: the blue perceived is not a symbol, but an index of the physical presence of such light-waves. Here the image copying the perception could be said to be a copy of the object as such, apprehended by perception. But a copy of what object? Unless the subject is a physicist, it is not the light-wave or its length he visualizes in his image, but the total object, the blue sky, for example. And one sees the complexity of the phenomena such an 'object' may correspond to, if one considers that the theory of the sky's blueness has only recently been introduced. This example shows eminently well what a perceived or imagined 'object' amounts to. And yet 'the blue sky' does constitute an object on a certain scale. It may be said to be 'copied' by perception, but only in the sense of a correspondence with more or less direct indices; and it may be 'copied' by the image, but only in the sense that the latter resembles perception. In both cases the copy is accurate only on the one scale. On the lower scales (light rays, etc.) and on the higher scales (astronomical distances) it is entirely inaccurate. The physicist will have at his disposal instruments with which to apprehend such scales, and microscopic or telescopic photographs which increase by n the range and precision of his perceptual field. He will thus acquire for himself new perceptions, which may be called 'copies by correspondence', and new images, which may be called 'copies by resemblance' with these perceptions. And they will indeed be accurate on the specific scale; but they will remain conspicuously inexact in terms of the other scales. And so it goes on, ten or a hundred years later. Fortunately physics has more than just perception and images at its disposal. But we shall return to this later.

To keep for the moment to the problem of copies, the implications of the foregoing commonplaces seem to be this. Let us recall, to begin with, the profound insight of the physicist Charles Eugène Guye that it is the scale that creates phenomena. Now the closer one gets to the object, the wider the gap between the terms exactitude and copy. A simple copy will only ever be faithful on the specific scale, and even then the correspondence will not be point-by-point but very approximate, while in relation to different or more distant scales accuracy will be correspondingly lower still. If representation is to be accurate (and certain physicists still require representation of all scales in spite of the doubts they have expressed about it in microphysics),[18] it must move further and further away from the 'copy' in favour of 'models', which constitute schematizations and are increasingly conceptualized.

In short, the very notion of an accurate copy of an object seems to be contradictory. For, either there is a copy, which remains global and fails to reach the object as such, unless it be on the scale where the object is not broken down into its objective components. Or there is an attempt to apprehend these components accurately: in which case one leaves copies behind in favour of schematization and the construction of models verifiable mediately only and by a combination of experiment and deduction.

[18] See the chapter on 'Concrete representation in microphysics' written by L. de Broglie for *Logique et connaissance scientifique* edited by us for the *Encyclopédie de la Pléiade*.

III. We now go on to our other problem and to a critique of the knowledge-as-copy hypothesis. This question is broader in scope and does not concern concrete representation alone. This means that psycho-genetic data as well as the epistemology of the sciences may be brought in to help solve it, whereas it would have been senseless to attempt a critique of the image-as-copy on the basis of the defects found in children's images.

The postulate common to the knowledge-as-copy and the knowledge-as-assimilation hypothesis is that the object exists. If one accepts the first view, then the perceptions and images induced by the objects are sufficient to provide knowledge of the object by means of successive approximations, and the actions necessary to separate out the factors amount to no more than removing the causes of errors, so that the object's manifestations may be made more and more direct. So there is nothing more to such cognition than the expression of these perceptual or representational manifestations, unless it be a logical language enabling them to be formulated. Classical empiricism held that images alone could make up an adequate copy of the object. Modern associationism now speaks with Hull of 'functional copies' establishing a one-to-one correspondence between external sequences and the subject's responses. And the matching epistemology will look for this correspondence between phenomena and the 'models', assuming that the subject contributes nothing more than a logico-linguistic means of expression.

In the second view, knowing the object means acting upon it in order to transform it, and discovering its properties through its transformations. The aim is always to get at the object. Cognition is not, however, based only on the object, but also on the exchange or interaction between subject and object resulting from the action and reaction of the two. As action takes effect two kinds of acquisition ensue. The first relates to the properties of the object, which have still to be interconnected, since they at first appear unorganized. The second concerns the co-ordinations of action itself, which require to be structured, for they are not preformed (as apriorism would have it – a third possible viewpoint, which we shall not, however, discuss here, as it does not really affect the image problem). Now the central hypothesis is that these two organizing processes are interdependent and complementary. Actions are co-ordinated in accordance with operational structures, which in the first place are constituted precisely as a function of the manipulation of objects. And the laws of the object are only discovered and established through the instrumentality of the operational structures, since they alone make possible the processes of relating or corresponding,

387

ordinal estimation or measurement, classification, propositional structuration, and so on. Objectivity is the result of progressive conquest, and is to be ascribed to the collaboration of experience and the logico-mathematical operations which are indispensable to the 'reading off' of experience and to representation in general, and which are not reducible to a language pure and simple but constitute the actual instrument of structuration. It is impossible, therefore, to consider knowledge as a copy of the object, since it presupposes the intervention of a general co-ordination of action, whose structures are the sole means of interpreting the objective datum.

As far as the psychological mechanisms of cognition are concerned, and especially the role of imaginal representation, the relevant difference between the two opposed viewpoints is the varying degree of stress that each puts on the figurative and the operative aspects of these mechanisms. One may indeed distinguish between those cognitive functions particularly concerned with configurations (perception, imitation, image) and those relative to their transformations (ranging from action to operations). The knowledge-as-copy type of interpretation would invoke the figurative functions: the role of perception considered as the source of physical knowledge and the role of the agents serving to express or preserve perceptual data – a function attributed to the image in classical empiricism and to language in logical empiricism. The knowledge-as-assimilation type of interpretation, on the other hand, naturally lays the emphasis on the operative functions, ranging from action to the operations proper.

Now the history of physics and its relations with mathematics – to start with the highest forms of cognitive development – would seem to show fairly clearly that perceptual verification and imaginal representation do indeed perform an essential function in the bringing together of hypothesis and fact in the construction of models. But it is also clear that this role is only a partial one, and that it needs to be complemented by mathematical deduction. The latter is far from being limited to supplying a linguistic translation of the datum. Its role is to provide structuration in the strict sense – a role that is indispensable in reading off the facts, but even more important in constructing models. Moreover, it is frequently capable not merely of retroactive deductive interpretations of already established facts, but of anticipating, sometimes years in advance facts that are not experimentally confirmed till later. Now the fact that logico-mathematical frameworks may be constructed in advance and filled in only later with experimental data (and the examples in modern physics are numerous) shows quite decisively that their function is not limited to formulation. On the contrary, the combination of deduction and experiment proves that the operational mechanisms and empirical verification are in fact interdependent.

Now this role of the operative functions in the structuration of the figurative aspects of cognition is already in evidence from the earliest beginnings of intellectual development. And the results recorded in this book confirm the fact yet again, this time within the field of the image, a field that has been so curiously abandoned by modern psychology. We have already in an earlier work attempted to show that the perceptual mechanisms depend on a variety of activities, that they may be oriented by the operations themselves, and that the evolution of these mechanisms is consequently neither autonomous nor self-contained, but subservient to a whole body of external contributory factors. The evolution of the image presents the same kind of picture, though if anything the picture is clearer, since the mechanisms in question belong to a higher level.

The essential results of our various lines of inquiry are these. First, the anticipatory image can only be formed with the help of the operations. And second, the image proves to be indispensable for a representational reconstitution of movements and transformations already known and possibly well known to the subject. It seems, therefore, that an operational framework of a logico-mathematical kind is necessary, not only, as one would expect, for notional interpretation of perceptual data, but also – and this more surprising – for the imaginal evocation of such data. True, this logico-mathematical framework is not a matter of a reflexive ability, far from it. In fact in the present instance what it amounts to is a combination of elementary spatial operations and correspondence procedures. But this does not mean they are any the less logico-mathematical and that they cannot in consequence lead to the formation of strictly deductive notions, such as conservation of length and surface, numerical equivalence, and so on. Now, as we have seen time and again, these conservations are not derived from the image, nor are they prepared by it. An arc transformed into a straight line will not conserve its length until operational conservation lays it down that a straight line resulting from the transformation of a curve will be longer than the chord. Similarly, a row of buttons moving in compartments arranged in a fan shape (see Figure 46) will not conserve their number, even though the required anticipatory image is perfectly easy, until operational conservation introduces longitudinal (individual movements of the buttons along the lanes) in addition to transversal (spreading-out of the row as a whole) anticipation. The fact of the matter is that conservation presupposes a system of quantitative compensations beyond the image's own capabilities, whereas the logico-mathematical framework, once constituted, rebounds on the image and makes objective anticipation possible.

All in all, what has been shown by our study of images, considered as the highest forms of the figurative instruments, is this. In the first place, the representation of a perceived or perceptible datum does not constitute a cognition, and it does not become a cognition until it is based on an operational comprehension of the transformations accounting for the datum. But, in the second place, we have also seen that once the functional interaction of the figurative and operative functions is assured, the image's symbolic role is by no means as negligible as the extreme reaction to classical associationism might have suggested. The image ensures finer analysis of 'states', and even aids figural anticipation of 'transformations', in spite of the irreducibly static character of such a figuration. This makes the image an indispensable auxiliary in the functioning of the very dynamism of thought – but only as long as it remains consistently subordinate to such operational dynamism, which it cannot replace, and which it can only express symbolically with degrees of distortion or fidelity varying according to circumstances.

Index

Aboudaram, M., 290
accommodation, 8, 257
actions, 11–12
  personal or free, 238–9
  and assimilation, 387–8
  and image, 229–31, 257, 360
  and perception, 211–18, 240–7
  and preoperational thought, 375
angles, transformed to straight
  lines, 178–87
Anthonioz, M., 66, 76, 80, 82,
  211n.
anticipation
  direct or graphic, 200–4, 217–19
  executional or evocational, 2
  executional, 4, 15
  anticipatory execution
    schemes, 4, 15, 18, 353–6,
    359
  global or analytic, 314–16
  kinetic; and the operations,
    152–8
  ordinal and hyperordinal,
    154–8
  imaginal, 157–8
  transversal or longitudinal, 289
anticipatory images
  apparent or authentic, 314
  kinetic or transformation, 5–6,
    334–5
  of product or process, 352–3
  transversal or longitudinal,
    276–94, 314
  formation of and operations, 228,
    313–16, 345–6, 352, 358–60,
    367, 376
  and reproductive, 2, 198, 228
    351–2, 355–6

and static, 256–7
in experiments:
  kinetic, 100–60
  and operations, 258–94,
    313–16
  spatial, 343–6
  transformations, 198–228
Antonini, M., 204n.
arcs, transformed to straight lines,
  161–78, 195, 196–7, 318, 357,
  363, 389
area, estimation of, 320, 322, 329,
  333–4, 348
Aserinsky, E., 8
assimilation, 384, 387–8
associationism, 8, 381, 387, 390

Bally, Charles, 383
beads
  levels and quantities of, 268–70
  on rotated rod, 135–45
Bergson, H., 9, 177, 227, 334, 384
Bliss, Joan, 57, 101, 231n.
Boehme, M., 152
boundaries, 54–65, 86, 98, 179, 181,
  185–7, 289, 290, 321, 324, 333–4,
  339, 362–3
  internal, 58–65
  perceptual law of, 203, 365
  preoperational concepts of, 176,
    178, 365
  starting and terminal points,
    18–20, 32–4, 163–7, 179, 197n.,
    302, 370–1
  in rotations, 66–7, 73, 76, 80,
    82–4
  of arcs, 163–7, 173, 174–5,
    195, 197

391